Brothers in Gray

The Cardwell Men Who Fought for the Confederacy

Rand Cardwell

This book series is dedicated to my son.

Corporal William T. Cardwell (1986-2020) - *Scout/Sniper, 1st Battalion, 2nd Marine Regiment, 2nd Marine Division* - *Combat Veteran of Persian Gulf, Afghanistan, and Iraq*

Contents

Brothers in Gray: The Cardwell Men Who Fought for the Confederacy

First Edition

First published: October 2025

Imprint: Published by Rand Cardwell

Editing: Bhavana Patel

Cover Design: B-RAD, LLC

Photographs and images: Sourced from family archives, Ancestry.com, FindAGrave.com, and public records. Some images edited and enhanced by the author.

ISBN: 979-8-9933293-3-8 (paperback)

Preface

This two-volume set is the culmination of over four decades of research into the Cardwell family of America. As a young man, I was always fascinated by history, which led me to begin investigating my own genealogy. Back in the 1980s, the internet didn't exist, and if you wanted to discover anything about your ancestry, it required spending long hours at local archives. I vividly recall sitting at microfilm readers, scrolling through endless reels, spending hard-earned dollars making copies, and anxiously awaiting brown envelopes—hopefully stuffed with answers—from the National Archives.

I was fortunate to receive guidance from some of the best researchers of the Cardwell surname. From my earliest correspondence, one lesson was drilled into me: **Document! Document! Document!** Thinking back on those days brings many fond memories of sharing discoveries with my mentors as we collectively attempted to piece together the story of this remarkable family.

One of those mentors was the late Helen E. Hart Peyton, author of *Some Early Pioneers of Western Kentucky*. In the late 1990s, she invited me to visit her in Charleston, South Carolina. Helen was battling cancer at the time, but we sat for hours going over her files. She gifted me several boxes of her research—material far beyond the scope of her published work—including three notebooks of correspondence dating back to the 1960s. It was a treasure trove of family histories. Some of the material contained incorrect assumptions, as we now know, but it provided a valuable foundation. Before I left, she acknowledged that her time was limited and asked me to do my best to "figure it all out." I've carried that promise with me ever since and hope she would be pleased with what has come of it.

The past two decades have brought an explosion in the availability of records online. What once took weeks to obtain from the National Archives can now be found with a few keystrokes. This digital revolution has transformed family history research in ways that earlier generations could scarcely imagine. But it has also introduced new problems. Websites like Ancestry.com provide access to millions of records, yet many users haven't learned the discipline of verifying facts or distinguishing between individuals with common names—especially when researching among the many Jameses, Johns, Thomases, and Williams. Erroneous information gets posted, then repeated by others, and the cycle continues.

This issue is compounded when early written sources, often published with good intentions, are treated as infallible. Some of these works presented assumptions as fact. I cringe when I see them cited uncritically today. My hope is that this work will stand the test of time through its careful sourcing, documentation, and dedication to accuracy.

In 2004, I launched the Cardwell Family DNA Project and served as its administrator for many years. The use of DNA in genealogy has been a game-changer, offering definitive proof in many cases. As of this writing, we have identified **four distinct genetic lines** within the Cardwell family in America. While we all share a common ancestor about 600 years ago, slight genetic mutations allow us to track specific lineages. Y-DNA, which is passed from father to son, creates a direct and reliable line for analysis.

At the end of each biography in these volumes, you will find a note identifying the individual's predicted or confirmed genetic line (e.g., *Cardwell Line I – Predicted*). A "confirmed" designation indicates that a living male descendant has tested and matches others within that line. A "predicted" designation means that the individual has been genealogically connected to a confirmed line, though no descendant has yet tested.

In the course of this research, I also encountered individuals whose paper trail did not align with their genetic profile. Through traditional documentation and DNA testing, we have identified several **Non-Paternal Events (NPEs)**—cases where a man carried the Cardwell surname but did not match any of the known genetic lines. Often, these are instances where a child was born out of wedlock and raised by a Cardwell mother, inheriting the surname but not the Y-DNA. While cataloging all of these events is beyond the scope of this series, several of the veterans included here are NPEs. They and their descendants still carry the Cardwell name, and they are rightfully part of this history.

The Cardwell Family DNA Project is hosted by FamilyTreeDNA.com, which offers detailed Y-DNA marker testing essential for identifying genetic lineage matches. Unfortunately, other commercial DNA services do not provide the specific marker data we need for inclusion in the project. I'm occasionally contacted by people who've tested with those companies, but their results cannot be compared or grouped with ours. I hope that future descendants will understand the importance of this research and choose FamilyTreeDNA when testing.

One of the most disheartening things I've come across in old correspondence is the mention of ancestor photographs—images that once existed but can no longer be found. Often, the researcher has passed away, and surviving family members have discarded their files. A painful example involves a series of letters from descendants of Anderson Huffman Cardwell, a sergeant in the 5th Missouri State Militia Cavalry (Union). In those letters, they describe a photograph of Anderson in uniform. But after the researcher's passing, the photograph and supporting documents appear to have been lost. It's a common tragedy—too often, people don't realize the historical value of what they possess until it's gone.

That's why I urge everyone with old family photographs to make digital copies and share them widely with other descendants and researchers. We cannot assume that what we have today will survive tomorrow. Every shared image is a preserved piece of our collective history.

Sadly, there are also individuals who possess heirloom photographs but refuse to share them with others. Please consider this: while you may be the fortunate caretaker of an image passed down through generations, there are dozens—perhaps hundreds—of other descendants who would treasure that same photo. Hoarding such items only deprives others of their history. If you have old family photos, **please share them**.

I fully admit to being a family history nerd. This work is the product of forty years of effort, made in the margins of life. My goal has always been to create a lasting and reliable resource for present and future researchers. If you've found value in these pages, then the effort has been worth it.

I can be reached at **cardwellhistory@yahoo.com**.

—Rand Cardwell

Introduction

A LEGACY REMEMBERED

The men documented in this volume represent a unique and significant part of American history. They fought for the Confederate cause, their lives shaped by one of the most turbulent periods in the nation's past. This book aims not to make political statements but to preserve the memory of these individuals, ensuring that their descendants and researchers have a detailed record of their service. By categorizing them by the state from which they served, we provide a structured approach that aligns with how Confederate military units were often formed—by local communities answering the call to arms.

This volume specifically focuses on members of the Cardwell family who served in the Confederate Army. Their service reflects not only their personal sacrifices but also the broader commitment of families who sent multiple members to fight in the war. By tracing the Cardwell lineage through military records, we honor their contributions and ensure that future generations can connect with their past.

Volume Two centers on Cardwell family members who served in the Union Army. In addition to their biographies, the book features an appendix that provides statistical comparisons of both Union and Confederate service, concise histories of Civil War prisoner-of-war camps, and a section titled *Battle Case Studies*. This final section offers a deeper examination of Cardwell participants in key engagements, expanding on details beyond what is covered in their individual biographies.

The Southern States at War

The Confederate States of America consisted of eleven states that seceded from the Union in 1860-1861. Each state played a distinct role in the war effort, contributing men, supplies, and strategic resources to the Confederacy. The men included in this volume served in regiments from Alabama, Arkansas, Georgia, Kentucky, Louisiana, Mississippi, Missouri, North Carolina, Tennessee, Texas, and Virginia. Some were volunteers who rushed to enlist in the early days of the conflict, while others were drafted as the war continued. Many fought in famous battles such as Shiloh, Antietam, Gettysburg, and Chickamauga, while others served in lesser-known skirmishes and defensive positions throughout the South.

While the war effort was a unified one, each state faced unique challenges. Border states like Missouri and Kentucky had divided loyalties, with many men fighting on both sides. In contrast, deep Southern states such as Alabama and Mississippi were heavily invested in the war's outcome, with entire communities emptied of their young men as they joined the Confederate ranks. Understanding these distinctions helps us appreciate the diverse experiences of the Cardwell soldiers recorded in this book.

The Importance of Military Records

Confederate military records are notoriously difficult to trace compared to their Union counterparts. The Confederate government lacked a centralized record-keeping system, and many documents were lost or destroyed in the final days of the war. As a result, the process of identifying and verifying each Cardwell soldier's service has required extensive research. This book draws upon military service records, pension applications, census data, and personal accounts to piece together their stories. Where possible, I have included photographs to provide a tangible connection to these men, helping to bring their histories to life.

While I have worked to ensure accuracy, variations in name spellings, missing documentation, and conflicting reports are inevitable. In cases where records were sparse, we have made careful inferences based on available evidence. My goal is to provide the most complete and factual representation of each Cardwell soldier's service.

The Personal Stories of War

Each name in this book represents an individual with a unique story—sons, husbands, fathers, and brothers who left their homes to fight in a war that defined their generation. Some returned home, forever changed by what they had seen and experienced. Others made the ultimate sacrifice and never returned. Their experiences varied widely, from the harrowing marches and brutal combat to long stretches of waiting in camp, dealing with disease, hunger, and the uncertainty of survival.

These biographies do more than recount military service; they provide a glimpse into personal histories. Where available, we have included details about pre-war and post-war life, family backgrounds, and occupations. Many of these men resumed civilian lives as farmers, merchants, or craftsmen, helping to rebuild a devastated South. Others faced hardships, struggling to reintegrate into society after years of conflict.

How to Navigate This Volume

This book is organized by state, with each chapter dedicated to the Cardwell men who served from that region. Within each chapter, individual biographies provide insight into the lives of these soldiers. Some chapters are longer than others due to the number of men who served from each state. The book concludes with an index that lists all Cardwell soldiers alphabetically, making it easier for descendants and researchers to locate specific individuals.

Preserving Their Memory

As time passes, the importance of preserving Civil War history only grows. The stories of these Cardwell soldiers deserve to be remembered, not only for their role in the conflict but also for the impact they had on future generations. Whether they fought in famous battles or served in lesser-known engagements, their contributions are part of the fabric of American history. It is our hope that this volume serves as a lasting tribute to their service and sacrifice.

* * *

The Confederate Soldier's Experience

Enlistment and the Call to Arms

At the start of the war, enthusiasm for enlistment ran high in the South. Young men, often no more than boys, flocked to recruitment centers, eager to prove their courage and defend their homeland. Propaganda, speeches, and local newspapers encouraged enlistment, painting the war as a noble cause. In many cases, entire towns sent their men to form companies, ensuring that neighbors and relatives fought side by side.

As the war progressed and casualties mounted, enthusiasm waned. The Confederacy introduced conscription in 1862, requiring eligible men to serve unless they met exemption criteria. This led to tensions within communities, as some wealthier individuals could pay for substitutes or avoid service altogether.

Life in the Ranks

The daily life of a Confederate soldier was grueling. Camp conditions were often unsanitary, leading to the spread of diseases like dysentery and typhoid. Food shortages were common, with soldiers subsisting on meager rations of cornmeal and salt pork. Despite hardships, soldiers formed strong bonds, relying on each other for survival and morale.

Battle and Combat Experience

Confederate soldiers fought in some of the bloodiest battles in American history. Unlike modern warfare, combat during the Civil War was brutally personal—soldiers faced enemy fire at close range, often charging directly into gunfire. Artillery barrages, bayonet charges, and cavalry attacks defined many engagements, leading to staggering casualty rates.

Survivors of these battles carried the physical and psychological scars for the rest of their lives. Many Confederate soldiers suffered amputations due to battlefield injuries, while others endured lifelong ailments from wounds that never fully healed.

.　.　.

Conclusion

The Cardwell soldiers' experience was one of hardship, sacrifice, and resilience. Each man featured in this book played a role, no matter how large or small, in shaping the course of the war. Their legacies, preserved in these pages, serve as a reminder of the personal cost of war and the endurance of the human spirit.

Cardwell Confederate Veterans
Listed by State

Alabama
The Cardwell Confederates

ALABAMA PLAYED A CENTRAL ROLE IN THE CIVIL WAR, BEING ONE OF the first states to secede from the Union in 1861. The city of Montgomery initially served as the first capital of the Confederate States before it was moved to Richmond. Alabama contributed thousands of men to the war effort, many of whom fought in major battles across the Western and Eastern Theaters. The state itself was largely spared from significant battles until late in the war when Union General James Wilson's cavalry raid devastated Alabama's industrial centers.

The Cardwell men from Alabama fought in nearly every major campaign of the war, from Virginia to the Western Theater. Their service spanned infantry, cavalry, artillery, and home defense, reflecting Alabama's full commitment to the Confederate cause.

This chapter honors the Cardwell soldiers of Alabama, ensuring their sacrifices and service remain part of the historical record of the Civil War.

* * *

Photo 1.1: *Benjamin Jones Cardwell (1844-1927) Headstone - Victoria Community Cemetery, Coffee County, Alabama.*

Benjamin Jones Cardwell (1844-1927) - *Private - Company A, 33rd Regiment, Alabama Infantry, CSA*

Benjamin Jones Cardwell was born on 05 October 1844 in Coffee County, Alabama. He was the son of Edmund Cardwell and Nancy (Sullivan) Cardwell. Benjamin is listed in the household of his parents in the 1850 Pike County, Alabama census and again in the 1860 Coffee County census, as the family moved within the region during that decade.[1,2]

On Christmas Day, 25 December 1862, at the age of 18, Benjamin enlisted as a Private in Company A of the 33rd Regiment, Alabama Infantry, CSA, at Elba in Coffee County. His older brother, John D. Cardwell, had joined the same regiment earlier in the war, enlisting in February 1862. The 33rd Alabama Infantry was composed primarily of men from south-central Alabama and was organized at Pensacola in April 1862 under the command of Colonel Samuel Adams. The unit was quickly attached to the Army of Tennessee and became engaged in some of the most grueling campaigns of the Western Theater.

The regiment first saw significant combat at the Battle of Perryville, Kentucky, in October 1862, where it endured heavy casualties during General Braxton Bragg's ill-fated Kentucky Campaign. From there, the 33rd Alabama participated in the bloody Battle of Stones River near Murfreesboro, Tennessee, at the close of 1862 and into early 1863. The regiment continued to serve with distinction in the Army of Tennessee throughout the war, fighting at Chickamauga in September 1863 and in the fierce and desperate actions around Chattanooga later that year.

In 1864, the 33rd Alabama was heavily involved in the Atlanta Campaign, engaging Union forces in a series of battles as Confederate troops attempted to halt General William T. Sherman's advance toward Atlanta. The regiment participated in actions at Resaca, New Hope Church, and Kennesaw Mountain, and later helped defend Atlanta itself. After the fall of the city, the 33rd joined the Confederate resistance in the Carolinas Campaign, participating in rear-guard actions during the retreat through Georgia and South Carolina. The regiment ultimately surrendered with General Joseph E. Johnston's forces in North Carolina in April 1865.

Although Benjamin's individual muster rolls are limited, existing records suggest that he remained with the regiment through most, if not all, of these engagements. He survived the war and returned to civilian life in Alabama, bearing the memory of a conflict that had devastated much of the Southern countryside.

Benjamin married Nancy A.E. Matheny on 27 January 1866.[3] The location of their marriage is not recorded, but they established a home in Coffee County, Alabama. Together they had the following children: Effie A. Cardwell (1868–), Zacharias Cardwell (1871–1928), Fox Cardwell (1875–1947), Wallace Lewis Cardwell (1877–1904), Louis L. Cardwell (1881–1958), Cos C. Cardwell (1885–1956), and Elmo A. Cardwell (1887–1974).

Benjamin is listed in the 1900, 1910, and 1920 census records for Coffee County, Alabama, where he spent the remainder of his life.[4,5,6] He died on 07 November 1927 in Coffee County at the age of 83. He is buried at Victoria Community Cemetery, Coffee County, Alabama.[7]

Benjamin's long life after the war and his steady presence in Coffee County serve as a testament to the endurance of those who lived through the upheaval of the Civil War and returned home to rebuild their lives. His military service in one of the most battle-hardened regiments of the Western Theater reflects the deep commitment many Alabama men had to their Confederate cause. Cardwell Line I - Predicted. Photo Credit[8]

* * *

Photo 1.2: *Benjamin M. Cardwell Headstone - Bay Springs Baptist Church Cemetery, Shelby County, Alabama.*

Benjamin M. Cardwell (1820-1910) - 2nd Sergeant - *Company K, 24th Regiment, Alabama Infantry, CSA & Company I, 44th Regiment, Mississippi Infantry, CSA* - **Wounded in Action**

Benjamin M. Cardwell was born on 22 November 1820 in Henry County, Georgia. He was the assumed son of John Franklin Cardwell and Phoebe (Gosdin) Cardwell. Before the war, Benjamin married Sarah Ann Manilla Brigman on 02 March 1851 in Montgomery County, Alabama.[9] Together they had the following children: Allis J. Cardwell (1853–1890), Lula E.K. Cardwell (1865–1878), Mary Cardwell (1868–1900), and Benjamin Roy Cardwell (1880–1966). Benjamin is recorded in the 1860 Shelby County, Alabama census, later residing in Baker County by 1870, and returning to Shelby County by the 1900 and 1910 census years.[10,11,12,13]

With prior military experience from his service in the War with Mexico, Benjamin entered Confederate service on 13 August 1861 at Talladega County, Alabama, mustering in as a 2nd Sergeant with Company K of the 24th Regiment, Alabama Infantry, CSA. His veteran status from the earlier conflict likely influenced his immediate assignment as a non-commissioned officer. He held the rank of 2nd Corporal with Company K of the Alabama Militia Infantry during the Mexican-American War. The 24th Alabama Infantry was organized during the summer of 1861 and included men from several central Alabama counties. The regiment quickly became part of the Confederate Army of Tennessee and was involved in many of the most significant campaigns in the Western Theater.

The regiment's early movements took them into Kentucky as part of Confederate efforts to secure the state for the South. It was during this early phase of the war that Benjamin's brother, Reuben Cardwell, also serving in the Confederacy, died of disease in Columbus, Hickman County, Kentucky. The 24th saw its first major combat at the Battle of Shiloh on 06 April 1862 in Hardin County, Tennessee. During this chaotic and bloody engagement, Benjamin was Wounded in Action, though the exact nature of his wounds is not recorded. The regiment suffered heavy losses, and Shiloh became one of the costliest battles in the war up to that point.

Following Shiloh, the 24th Alabama Infantry continued a long and arduous service record, participating in many of the Western Theater's decisive engagements. The unit fought at Murfreesboro (Stones River) in late 1862, and later at Chickamauga, where the Army of Tennessee achieved one of its rare tactical victories. They were heavily engaged in the Atlanta Campaign throughout the summer of 1864, battling Union forces at Resaca, New Hope Church, and Peachtree Creek as Confederate forces attempted to hold the city. The 24th then participated in the ill-fated Franklin–Nashville Campaign, where Confederate forces suffered catastrophic losses. In the final months of the war, the regiment fought at the Battle of Bentonville in North Carolina, one of the last significant engagements in the East before General Johnston's surrender in April 1865.

Despite this active service, soldiers in Company K of the 24th Alabama were only paid for four months during nearly four years of continuous duty. Of the original seventy-six men who enlisted in the company, only seven returned home in good health, a stark reflection of the brutal toll exacted by combat, disease, and hardship.

Benjamin's Civil War service is recorded under variations of his name, including "B. Cardwell" and "Ben Cardwell." He was granted a Confederate pension in 1908 while living in Shelby County, Alabama. This record, along with his early rank and battle injury, confirm his sustained service and sacrifice during the war.

Benjamin M. Cardwell died on 16 August 1910 in Shelby County, Alabama. He is buried at Bay Springs Baptist Church Cemetery in Shelby County.[14] His long life, despite the hardships of war, is a testament to his endurance. Several of his brothers also served the Confederacy and are recorded in this volume, including Reuben Cardwell, Henry C. Cardwell, John M. Cardwell, and James M. Cardwell—each contributing to the deep legacy of the Cardwell family in the war. Cardwell Line II - Confirmed. Photo Credit[15]

* * *

Henry C. Cardwell (1846-1933) - *Private - Company H, 1st Regiment, Alabama Reserves (62nd Regiment, Alabama Infantry), CSA* - **Prisoner of War**

Henry C. Cardwell was born on 08 January 1846 in Talladega County, Alabama. He was the youngest son of John Franklin Cardwell and Phoebe (Gosdin) Cardwell, and one of five brothers from the family to serve in the Confederate cause. He appears in the 1850 census of Talladega County in his father's household and again in the 1860 Shelby County census, confirming the family's relocation during that decade.[16,17]

Henry enlisted as a Private in the 1st Regiment of Alabama Reserves, CSA, on 30 January 1864 at Selma, Dallas County, Alabama. At the time of enlistment, he was still residing in Shelby County. The Alabama Reserves were formed during the later stages of the war, composed primarily of young men and older soldiers who had not yet seen front-line combat. These regiments were tasked with defending key supply routes, cities, and fortifications within the state.

Shortly after its formation, the 1st Alabama Reserves was reorganized and became part of the 62nd Alabama Infantry Regiment, CSA. The 62nd served in the Department of Alabama, Mississippi, and East Louisiana, primarily in defensive operations across southern Alabama and the Gulf Coast. The regiment was stationed in and around Mobile, one of the last major Confederate ports, where they worked to reinforce forts, entrenchments, and inland defensive lines.

During the Mobile Campaign of 1865, Union forces launched a coordinated assault to seize the city and its defenses. Although the 62nd Alabama Infantry was not among the primary front-line units at the Battle of Spanish Fort (27 March–08 April 1865) and Battle of Fort Blakely (09 April 1865), its presence within the Mobile garrison meant the men were engaged in support roles, logistical tasks, and back-line defense as the Confederate position collapsed. The Department of Alabama officially surrendered on 04 May 1865 at Citronelle, Mobile County. Henry Cardwell was paroled a week later, on 11 May 1865, at Meridian, Lauderdale County, Mississippi—a standard location for the processing of Confederate paroles in the region.

He married Martha A. "Mollie" Willoughby on 04 June 1868 in Chambers County, Alabama.[18] The couple had four children: Annie Cardwell

(1870–1946), Mary Florence Cardwell (1879–1949), Ralph L. Cardwell (1880–1947), and Will Benjamin "Ben" Cardwell (1886–). Henry appears in the 1870 census of Bibb County and in subsequent census records for 1880, 1900, and 1920 in Shelby County.[19,20,21,22]

In the final years of his life, he was residing in Coosa County, appearing in the 1930 census there.[23] He died on 23 March 1933 at Talladega Springs, Talladega County, Alabama, at the age of 87. He was laid to rest at Blue Springs Cemetery, Coosa County, Alabama.[24]

Henry C. Cardwell lived a long life after the war and remained in Alabama through its Reconstruction and postwar development. His Confederate service, though brief and during the waning days of the war, represents the final chapter of Southern enlistment—young men called upon to defend a cause already crumbling. His name is joined in this chapter by his four older brothers—Reuben, Benjamin, John M., and James M. Cardwell—all of whom also served in the war. Cardwell Line II - Predicted.

* * *

Henry Charles Cardwell (1834-) - *Sergeant - Company E (Gage's), 2nd Battalion, Alabama Light Artillery, CSA* - **Prisoner of War**

Henry Charles Cardwell was born about 1834 in Virginia, according to census records. Exhaustive research into potential parents have failed to find a possible match. What brought Henry from the agricultural heart of Virginia to the bustling Gulf port of Mobile, Alabama remains uncertain—whether trade, craft, or curiosity—but by 1861 he had relocated there, working as a carpenter when war broke out.

On 10 October 1861, Henry enlisted as a Private in Company E, 2nd Battalion of Alabama Light Artillery, CSA, at Mobile, Mobile County, Alabama. His enlistment records describe him as 28 years of age, 5 feet 7 inches tall, with blue eyes, light hair, and a light complexion, and list his birthplace as Hanover County, Virginia.

Known also as Gage's Battery, this unit was organized specifically for the defense of Mobile. Initially stationed at Fort Gaines, the battery helped guard the entrance to Mobile Bay. In early 1862, the unit was ordered to Corinth, Mississippi, to support Confederate forces massing for what would become the Battle of Shiloh. There, on 06–07 April 1862, under Brigadier General

James R. Chalmers, Gage's Battery faced intense fighting and suffered considerable losses.

Henry, who held the rank of Corporal at the time, was singled out for his valor at Shiloh. A Mobile newspaper article praised his actions, stating: *"Corporal Cardwell behaved gallantly throughout – and I have heard officers praising him highly. He is on the fourth piece. True grit, every inch of him."*[25] His bravery and reliability under fire did not go unnoticed. Just two months later, on 19 June 1862, Henry was promoted to Ordnance Sergeant by order of the Confederate Secretary of War in Richmond—a significant appointment reflecting trust in his discipline and technical skill.

Following Shiloh, Gage's Battery was reorganized and returned to Mobile, where it would spend the remainder of the war. The company was assigned to various key defensive positions including Fort Morgan, Fort Gaines, Spanish River Battery, Battery McIntosh, Battery B, and Battery Gladden. These locations were crucial to the Confederate effort to guard the port of Mobile and the Mobile Bay coastline against Union naval incursions. The battery remained in Mobile until 12 April 1865, when the city was evacuated. The formal surrender of the unit came on 04 May 1865, along with the rest of the Department of Alabama, Mississippi, and East Louisiana. Henry was paroled on 18 May 1865 in Columbus, Mississippi.

After the war, Henry returned to civilian life in Mobile. He married Amanda A. Carson on 26 November 1866 at Mobile, Mobile County, Alabama.[26] Together, they had three known children: Henry E. "Harry" Cardwell (b. 1867), John C. Cardwell (b. 1875), and Katherine "Kate" Cardwell (1878–1957). The family appears in both the 1870 and 1880 Mobile County census records, where Henry is again listed as a carpenter by trade.[27,28]

Despite his early prominence and military distinction, no further verified records of Henry Charles Cardwell have been located beyond the 1880 census. His date of death and place of burial remain unknown. It is possible he died before 1900, as he does not appear in subsequent census records or local directories.

Henry Charles Cardwell's wartime service reflects the important contributions of Mobile's defensive units—garrisoned in harsh coastal conditions, stationed far from the war's major land battles, but nonetheless vital in holding one of the last open ports of the Confederacy. His rise to Ordnance Sergeant and recognition at Shiloh serve as a testament to his character and commitment to his adopted state and its defense. <u>Cardwell Ancestry - Undetermined.</u>

* * *

Photo 1.3: *Henry Clay Cardwell (1843-1910) Headstone - Cresson Cemetery, Cresson, Johnson County, Texas.*

Henry Clay Cardwell (1843-1910) - *Private - Company B, 8th Regiment, Alabama Cavalry, CSA & Company G, 18th Regiment, Alabama Infantry, CSA -* **Prisoner of War**

Henry Clay Cardwell was born on 14 February 1843 in Tuscaloosa County, Alabama, the son of James Dudley Cardwell and Elizabeth Emeline (Foster) Cardwell. He appears in the 1850 Tuscaloosa County census in the home of his parents. After the death of his father in 1851, Henry is listed again in the 1860 census in Northport, Tuscaloosa County, Alabama, living with his widowed mother and siblings.[29,30]

Though definitive records are lacking, it is a logical and supported assumption that Henry was the man who served first in Company G of the 18th Alabama Infantry, CSA, a unit formed largely in Jefferson County, which borders Tuscaloosa County. Known locally as "Yancey's Guards" or

"Yancey's Rangers," the company was part of a regiment organized in late 1861 and saw early action in the Mobile Bay area. The 18th Alabama Infantry was assigned to the defenses of Pensacola, and later moved into Mississippi and Tennessee, where it saw action at Shiloh, Corinth, and Murfreesboro. It endured heavy combat throughout Bragg's Kentucky Campaign and fought in the Chickamauga and Atlanta campaigns. While Henry's name does not appear in the surviving muster rolls from the early years of the regiment, the absence of other viable candidates in that region lends weight to this attribution. It is likely that he either enlisted early or filled a conscripted role before transferring later in the war.

Henry is definitively linked to Company B of the 8th Alabama Cavalry, CSA, through Parole records dated 14 May 1865 at Gainesville, Sumter County, Alabama, following his capture at Citronelle on 04 May 1865. These late-war documents list Henry's residence as "North Port, Alabama," matching his listing in the 1860 Tuscaloosa County census, which helps distinguish him from other Confederate soldiers with the same name. This detail anchors the identification of the veteran and confirms that Henry Clay Cardwell, son of James Dudley Cardwell, was the man who served in this unit.

The 8th Alabama Cavalry was a fast-moving Confederate unit raised in 1864 from veterans and new conscripts. It participated in numerous skirmishes and reconnaissance missions, often targeting Union supply lines and raiding behind enemy positions. Operating primarily across northern Alabama and southern Tennessee, the 8th engaged in guerrilla-style tactics, delaying Union advances and keeping Federal troops occupied in defense. The regiment took part in delaying actions against Sherman's March to the Sea and contributed to the defense of Alabama in the waning days of the war. The unit ultimately surrendered with the Department of Alabama, Mississippi, and East Louisiana, marking the end of Confederate resistance in the region.

Henry Clay Cardwell's postwar life is sparsely documented. He does not appear in the 1870 or 1880 census records, which suggests he may have relocated or lived with extended family during that time. However, by 1900, he is found in the Chickasaw Nation, Indian Territory, living in the home of R.A. and Mattie Thompson, where he is noted as an "Uncle."[31] In 1910, just months before his death, he appears again in the Hood County, Texas census, residing with Ferdinand and Alvaretta Slocum, listed this time as "Uncle-In-Law."[32]

Henry died on 25 April 1910 in Hood County, Texas, and was laid to rest in Cresson Cemetery, located in nearby Johnson County.[33] Although his early service remains partially speculative, his late-war cavalry record, confirmed identity, and final years in Texas reflect a Confederate soldier's life shaped by shifting assignments, family bonds, and the long journey from Alabama battlefields to the postwar frontier. Cardwell Line III - Predicted. Photo Credit[34]

* * *

James M. Cardwell (1840-) - *Private - Company G, 18th Regiment, Alabama Infantry, CSA* - **Wounded in Action**

James M. Cardwell was born about 1840 in Heard County, Georgia, the son of Simon Cardwell II and Elizabeth (Combs) Cardwell. His father died around 1847, and James is listed in the 1850 Jefferson County, Alabama census, residing in the household of his widowed mother along with his siblings.[35]

On 29 July 1861, at the age of 22, James enlisted as a Private in Company G, 18th Regiment of Alabama Infantry, CSA, at Jonesboro, Jefferson County, Alabama. His enlistment records describe him as 5 feet 10 inches tall, with black eyes and dark hair. Company G was raised in Jefferson County and was known locally as one of the early volunteer companies responding to the Confederate call to arms.

The 18th Alabama Infantry was organized in the summer of 1861 and initially served in the defenses around Mobile, Alabama. In March 1862, the regiment was ordered to Corinth, Mississippi, where it was brigaded under General John K. Jackson of Georgia, along with the 17th and 19th Alabama Infantry Regiments. The unit soon faced its first major engagement at the Battle of Shiloh, fought on 06–07 April 1862, in Hardin County, Tennessee.

On the first day of the battle, the 18th Alabama was heavily engaged. Out of approximately 420 men, the regiment suffered 125 killed and wounded, a testament to the brutal and chaotic nature of the fight. The 18th played a significant role in the capture of Union General Benjamin Prentiss's division, and afterward was assigned to escort the captured Federal brigade to the Confederate rear. Because of this duty, the regiment did not participate in the fighting on the second day of the battle.

During the action at Shiloh, James M. Cardwell was wounded, suffering a slight gunshot wound to the chest, as recorded in the Register of Wounded. Though not a disabling injury on the battlefield, it is likely that the wound, combined with the effects of disease or other health issues common to military encampments of the time, contributed to his discharge.

James was formally discharged for disability on 05 July 1862, only a few months after Shiloh. His official discharge noted the effects of his wound and other contributing health concerns. Following his release, no further military or civilian records have been located for him. Despite extensive research in Confederate service records, pension files, and postwar census data, there is no definitive evidence of his life after 1862.

Given the limited nature of Civil War medical care and the high mortality rate from disease and infection—even among those with relatively minor wounds—it is possible that James M. Cardwell succumbed to illness or complications not long after his discharge. However, this remains speculative, as no death record, burial site, or additional documentation has yet been identified.

James M. Cardwell's brief but documented service with the 18th Alabama Infantry places him at one of the most pivotal early battles of the war. His experience at Shiloh reflects the sacrifice made by thousands of Alabama soldiers during the conflict, many of whom returned home wounded, broken, or not at all. Though his ultimate fate remains unknown, his contribution to the Confederate cause—however short-lived—represents the story of countless volunteers whose names appear only briefly in the annals of history. Cardwell Line II - Predicted.

* * *

Photo 1.4: *James Mathew Cardwell (1838-1904) Headstone. Bass Cemetery, Irondale, Jefferson County, Alabama.*

James Mathew Cardwell (1838-1904) - *Private - Company G, 18th Regiment, Alabama Infantry, CSA & Company A, 46th Regiment, Alabama Infantry, CSA* - **Prisoner of War**

James Mathew Cardwell was born on 06 May 1838 in Heard County, Georgia, the son of William Cardwell and Sarah (McCluskey) Cardwell. By 1850, the family had relocated to Talladega County, Alabama, where James is listed in the household of his parents.[36] He married Sandal Missouri Downs on 20 December 1859 in Coosa County, Alabama, and the couple is found in the 1860 census in that same county.[37,38]

James and Sandal had a large family, with the following known children: William Josiah Cardwell (1860–1930), J.M. Cardwell (1863–), Alex I. Cardwell (1867–1943), Anna Elizabeth Cardwell (1869–1934), Amanda Malissa Cardwell (1872–1956), Ella E. Cardwell (1872–1935), Luadar Cardwell (1874–), Marketty Cardwell (1878–), and Joseph Newton Cardwell (1882–1956). Over the years, the Cardwell family was listed in the 1870 Coosa County, 1880 Marion County, and 1900 Jefferson County, Alabama census records, reflecting a pattern of migration across the central and northern parts of the state.[39,40,41]

James enlisted as a Sergeant with Company A, 46th Regiment, Alabama Infantry, CSA, on 5 April 1862 at Fort McRae, Florida. His enlistment came during a period of intense recruitment as Confederate forces prepared for large-scale engagements in the Western Theater of the war. The 46th Alabama Infantry was composed primarily of men from central and eastern Alabama, and it quickly became active in the Confederate defense of the Mississippi River Valley.

The 46th Alabama Infantry served with distinction in some of the most strategically critical engagements of the war. After organizing, the regiment was deployed to Mississippi, where it was stationed at Vicksburg, a vital stronghold on the Mississippi River. The Siege of Vicksburg, which lasted from May 18 to July 4, 1863, was one of the pivotal battles of the war. Union General Ulysses S. Grant's prolonged encirclement of the city ultimately forced Confederate General John C. Pemberton to surrender.

James was captured along with his older brother, Joseph M. Cardwell, on 4 July 1863, the day of the Confederate surrender at Vicksburg. On 10 July 1863, both were paroled under the terms of the surrender agreement. This parole meant they were released on the condition that they would not take up arms again until formally exchanged for Union prisoners. The terms of this parole and its impact on their subsequent service are further discussed in the biography of Joseph M. Cardwell in this chapter.

It is unclear whether James Mathew Cardwell resumed active service after his parole. His Civil War records refer to him as both "J.M. Cardwell" and "James M. Cardwell." There is some suggestion that he may have been attached to the Camp of Instruction in Talladega County, Alabama, where conscripts and returning soldiers were reorganized and trained. One record exists for a "J.M. Cardwell" with no clear date, which may indicate service in that capacity following his release from Vicksburg.

Though James's military career was disrupted by captivity and limited by the scarcity of records, his participation in the 46th Alabama Infantry places him in the heart of one of the Confederacy's most critical defensive campaigns. The loss of Vicksburg divided the Confederacy and opened the Mississippi River to Union control—a blow from which the Southern war effort never fully recovered.

James Mathew Cardwell died on 29 March 1904 in Jefferson County, Alabama. He is buried at Bass Cemetery, located in Irondale, a community just east of Birmingham in Jefferson County.[42] His life, like that of many veterans of the war, was shaped by both the conflict and the challenges of Reconstruction in post-war Alabama. Cardwell Line II - Predicted. Photo Credit[43]

* * *

Photo 1.5: *James Robert Cardwell (1838-1885) Headstone - Long Creek Cemetery, Shuford, Panola County, Alabama.*

James Robert Cardwell (1838-1885) - Sergeant - *Company F, 2nd Battalion, Alabama Light Artillery, CSA -* **Prisoner of War**

James Robert Cardwell was born on 14 February 1838 in Tuscaloosa County, Alabama, the son of James Dudley Cardwell and Elizabeth Emeline (Foster) Cardwell. He appears in the household of his parents in the 1850 Tuscaloosa County census, and again in the 1860 Northport, Tuscaloosa County census, residing with his widowed mother following the death of his father in 1851.[44,45]

James enlisted as a Private with Company F of the 2nd Battalion, Alabama Light Artillery, CSA, on 29 November 1861 in Tuscaloosa County, Alabama. This company, recruited primarily from Fayette, Pickens, and Tuscaloosa counties, originally mustered 125 men and reported for active duty at Mobile. From there, the unit played an important role in Confederate artillery operations across several key theaters in the western campaigns.

Initially stationed at Fort Gaines, the battery was later sent to Tupelo, Mississippi, after the Battle of Shiloh, replacing Gage's Battery. It was there the unit was outfitted with six new artillery pieces and sent into action in northern Mississippi and Kentucky. The battery saw combat at Farmington, and then in the Kentucky Campaign, engaging Union forces at Perryville in October 1862. It was during this campaign that James was left behind sick at Harrisburg, Kentucky, and subsequently captured by Union troops.

Following his release or exchange, James returned to the battery and remained with it through the war. In June 1863, he was promoted to Sergeant, likely due to his experience and reliability in the field. The battery participated in the Battle of Chickamauga, where it suffered losses and had one of its guns captured. After that, it was active during the Dalton to Atlanta Campaign, suffering casualties at Resaca, Kennesaw Mountain, and the Battle of Atlanta, where the unit maintained a continual presence as Confederate forces attempted to defend the rail hub of the city.

In late 1864, the battery marched north with the Confederate Army during Hood's Tennessee Campaign, culminating in the Battle of Nashville. There, the unit was overwhelmed, lost all of its guns, and suffered severe casualties, including six killed and twenty-two captured. Following the failed campaign, the remnants of the battery retreated back into Alabama and were later stationed at Spanish Fort, defending Mobile Bay. Under constant fire for nearly two weeks, they sustained additional losses before withdrawing.

James was among those captured at the surrender of the Department of Alabama, Mississippi, and East Louisiana on 4 May 1865 at Citronelle, Alabama, and he was paroled five days later. His long service with Company F, despite illness and capture, reflected the endurance and hardship experienced by Confederate artillerymen during the war's western campaigns.[46]

Post-war records confirm James's presence in Panola County, Mississippi, where he married Martha Ruth Harris around 1867, based on the birth year of their first child. Together, they had the following children: James Wallace Cardwell (1868–1924), Jessie Mae Cardwell (1870–1954), Lillian Cardwell (1873–1953), John Foster Cardwell (1875–1944), Effie Cardwell (1878–1955), and C.P. Cardwell (1883–). The family appears in the 1870 and 1880 Panola County, Mississippi census.[47,48]

James Robert Cardwell died on 13 February 1885 in Panola County, Mississippi, and is buried at Long Creek Cemetery in Shuford, located in the same county.[49] His headstone incorrectly lists his birth year as 1828, but census records confirm his actual year of birth was 1838.

James's military history was verified through careful documentation, notably his own mention of Tuscaloosa County as his place of residence in Confederate records. His service in Company F, which was organized in Tuscaloosa and separate from the Mobile-based companies of the 2nd Battalion, confirms his identity as the son of James Dudley and Elizabeth Cardwell. His younger brother, Henry Clay Cardwell (1843–1910), also served in the Confederate Army and is recorded in this chapter. Another brother, John Foster Cardwell, served in a Mississippi unit and is documented in the corresponding state chapter. <u>Cardwell Line III - Confirmed</u>. Photo Credit[50]

* * *

John D. Cardwell (1843-1867<70) - *Private - Company A, 33rd Regiment, Alabama Infantry, CSA*

John D. Cardwell was born about 1843 in Coffee County, Alabama, the son of Edmund Cardwell and Nancy (Sullivan) Cardwell. He is recorded in the home of his parents in both the 1850 Pike County and 1860 Coffee County, Alabama census records.[51,52] The family had settled in southeast Alabama during a period of significant population movement from Georgia and the Carolinas into the fertile lands of the Wiregrass region.

John enlisted as a Private in Company C of the 33rd Regiment of Alabama Infantry, CSA, on 27 February 1862 at Elba, Coffee County, Alabama. His brother, Benjamin Jones Cardwell, joined the same regiment later that year. The 33rd Alabama Infantry was composed largely of men from Coffee and surrounding counties and quickly became a battle-hardened unit in the Army of Tennessee.

The regiment saw its first major action at the Battle of Perryville, Kentucky in October 1862, part of the Confederate Heartland Offensive. In that engagement, the 33rd endured intense fighting on the right flank of General Braxton Bragg's line. Following Perryville, the regiment fought at Stones River near Murfreesboro, Tennessee, in one of the war's bloodiest battles, where it again sustained severe casualties.

Throughout 1863, the 33rd took part in the Tullahoma Campaign, Chickamauga, and the Chattanooga Campaign, engaging in both large-scale battles and grueling marches. At Chickamauga, the regiment was part of the Confederate breakthrough that inflicted one of the worst defeats on Union forces in the Western Theater. However, the tide turned during the Battles for Chattanooga, especially Missionary Ridge, where the Confederates were pushed back into Georgia.

In 1864, the 33rd was heavily involved in the Atlanta Campaign, enduring almost continuous combat through a series of engagements from Resaca to Jonesboro, fighting alongside General Patrick Cleburne's Division, known for its discipline and tenacity. On 21 May 1864, during the early stages of this campaign, John D. Cardwell was admitted to Ocmulgee Hospital in Macon, Georgia, suffering from Typhoid Fever, a common and often deadly illness among Civil War soldiers due to poor camp sanitation. He was granted a furlough on 07 June 1864, likely to recover at home or in a convalescent camp. No additional military records for him have been located, and it is unclear whether he returned to his regiment.

John reappears briefly after the war in the Voter Registration List of Coffee County, Alabama, dated 17 June 1867. This roll was part of the Reconstruction-era effort to re-establish civil government in the former Confederate states and to document eligible voters under new federal requirements. His presence on this list confirms that he survived the war and was residing in Coffee County at that time.

No further census or probate records have been found for John after 1867. He does not appear in the 1870 federal census, and there is no known death record or burial site. It is assumed that he died sometime between 1867 and 1870, likely in Coffee County, Alabama, though the exact circumstances and location of his death remain unknown.

John D. Cardwell's wartime service alongside his brother Benjamin reflects the deep local commitment of men from southeast Alabama who joined the Confederate cause. Like many young soldiers of his generation, his life was shaped—and likely shortened—by war and disease. Cardwell Line I - Predicted.

* * *

John James Cardwell (1834-1863) - *Private - Company D, 48th Regiment, Alabama Infantry, CSA -* **Killed in Action**

John James Cardwell was born about 1834, likely in Marshall County, Alabama, to Thomas Cardwell and Mary D. (Long) Cardwell. He is recorded in the household of his parents in both the 1850 and 1860 Marshall County census records. By 1860, his father had passed away, and John was living with his widowed mother and siblings in Marshall County.[53,54] Although his Civil War service records identify him only as James Cardwell, the 1860 census clarifies his full name as John James, a common naming practice in the Cardwell family where many men were known by their middle name.

John James married Nancy Parks on 11 October 1860 in Marshall County, Alabama.[55] No additional documentation has been found for Nancy after their marriage, and it is unknown whether the couple had any children.

John James and his younger brother, Reuben Cardwell, enlisted together on 7 April 1862 as Privates in Company D of the 48th Regiment, Alabama Infantry, CSA. Their enlistment took place at Warrenton, a small town in Marshall County. The 48th Alabama was formed during the spring of 1862 and quickly became an active component of the Army of Northern Virginia. Company D, like the rest of the regiment, was composed primarily of volunteers from northeastern Alabama.

The 48th Alabama Infantry participated in many of the war's most significant campaigns. It was heavily engaged at Second Manassas, fought with distinction during the Maryland Campaign at Antietam, and endured fierce combat in the Battle of Fredericksburg in December 1862. The regiment was later involved in the Chancellorsville Campaign in May 1863, prior to marching northward into Pennsylvania that summer.

John James Cardwell was Killed in Action (KIA) during the Battle of Gettysburg on 02 July 1863, the second and bloodiest day of the three-day engagement. The 48th Alabama Infantry was part of Law's Brigade, under Hood's Division, within Longstreet's Corps. On the afternoon of July 2nd, Law's Brigade attacked the Union left flank in an assault on Little Round Top, one of the battle's most iconic and fiercely contested locations. During the charge through Devil's Den and toward the rocky slopes of Little Round Top, the regiment came under devastating artillery and musket fire.

According to the official after-action report by Colonel James L. Sheffield, the 48th Alabama brought 275 men into the fight that day. By the end of the engagement, the regiment had sustained 102 casualties—killed, wounded, or missing.[56] Among those killed was Private John James Cardwell. His younger brother, Reuben Cardwell, was shot in the thigh and subsequently captured by Union forces (see Reuben's biography in this chapter for additional details).

Due to the chaotic nature of the battle and the overwhelming number of casualties on both sides, it is likely that John James Cardwell was buried in a mass grave on the battlefield.[57] His exact burial location is unknown, as was the fate of many Confederate dead at Gettysburg. The Gettysburg Dead from Alabama were often not recovered or reinterred, and most remain in unmarked collective burial sites within the battlefield park.

Private John James Cardwell's military service and ultimate sacrifice at Gettysburg reflect the harrowing experiences of thousands of Alabama soldiers who fought in the Eastern Theater of the war. Though his life was cut short at the age of roughly 29, his story stands as a poignant reminder of the personal cost of the war for families throughout the South—particularly in Marshall County, Alabama, which contributed many young men to the Confederate cause. Cardwell Line II - Predicted.

* * *

John M. Cardwell (1823-1863) - *Private - Captain Falkner's Company, Alabama Cavalry (Chambers'), CSA; 8th Regiment, Alabama Cavalry, CSA & Suttles' Company, Coosa Guards, CSA* - **Died in Service**

John M. Cardwell was born about 1824 in Georgia, the son of John Franklin Cardwell and Phoebe (Gosdin) Cardwell. He married Nancy Peacock on 26 September 1844 in Chambers County, Alabama.[58] The couple had the following children: Epsy Alice Cardwell (1845–1937), Elizabeth Cardwell (1846–), Benjamin Lumpkin Cardwell (1847–1931), William Washington Cardwell (1849–1929), John Franklin Cardwell (1851–1940), and Margaret E. Cardwell (1854–1921). The family appears in the 1850 Chambers County, Alabama census.[59] Nancy passed away around 1857, and John remarried Lucinda Dickson on 24 December 1858, also in Chambers County.[60] They had two children together: Furby Cordelia "Delia" Cardwell (1860–) and Lucinda "Lucy" Cardwell (1865–1922). John and his family are recorded in the 1860 census of Chambers County.[61] Note: His son, Benjamin Lumpkin Cardwell, served in the 10th Confederate Cavalry and is recorded in the Miscellaneous Chapter.

With the onset of the Civil War, John enlisted as a Private in Captain Jefferson Manly Falkner's Independent Cavalry Company on 03 August 1861, at age 38. This unit would later become Company B of the 8th Confederate Cavalry. That unit appears to have been consolidated to the 8th Confederate Cavalry. His muster roll noted the value of his horse at $275 and his equipment at $20, a substantial investment at the time, reflecting the personal burden many cavalrymen bore to outfit themselves for service. Note: There

26

was a "J. Cardwell" that enlisted on 25 June 1861 with Company B of the 2nd Regiment Mississippi and Alabama Cavalry, CSA, at Chambers County, Alabama, that is likely this John.

Falkner's Cavalry, later absorbed into the 8th Confederate Cavalry, operated primarily in the Western Theater, with service spanning Alabama, Mississippi, and Tennessee. The regiment took part in several raids, skirmishes, and picket duties, helping to screen Confederate movements and harass Union supply lines. This type of service was physically taxing and required long periods away from home.

According to family tradition passed down by descendants and confirmed at a 1993 Cardwell family reunion, John made a long and difficult journey back home in 1863 to visit his family in Chambers County. His daughter Cordelia had been a baby when he left for war, and his second daughter, Lucinda, had not yet been born. Tragically, on the night of his return, John is said to have suffered a fatal heart attack in his sleep. He was only 40 years old.[62]

However, military documentation suggests a slightly different ending. A Confederate service record exists for a John M. Cardwell, listed as a Guard at the Coosa River Bridge, who died in November 1863 at a local hospital. This record may refer to the same individual. Though it contradicts the family account, it aligns more closely with the timeline of known military records. Lucinda's birth date, recorded as 3 March 1865 on later documents, may have been misreported or symbolic. Census records from 1870 list her as eight years old, suggesting she was likely born earlier than reported.

After John's death, Lucinda Cardwell is listed in the 1870 census as a widow, living in Chambers County with her young children. Despite the loss of her husband, she remained in the area and continued to raise their family.[63]

The location of John M. Cardwell's grave remains unknown, though it is likely in Chambers County, Alabama. His legacy lives on through his descendants, many of whom contributed valuable genealogical insight into his life and service.

John was one of several brothers who served the Confederate cause. His siblings include Benjamin M. Cardwell, Reuben Cardwell (1833–1861), and James M. Cardwell (1823–), all of whom are also recorded in this chapter. Cardwell Line II - Predicted.

* * *

Joseph M. Cardwell (1835-1870) - 2nd Sergeant - *Company A, 46th Regiment, Alabama Infantry, CSA* - **Prisoner of War**

Joseph M. Cardwell was born about 1835 in Georgia, the son of William Cardwell and Sarah (McCluskey) Cardwell. He is listed in the home of his parents in the 1850 Talladega County, Alabama census.[64]

By 1858, Joseph had married Roxanne Hall, and the couple was residing near his widowed mother in Coosa County, Alabama, as recorded in the 1860 census.[65,66] Roxanne passed away around 1867, and Joseph later remarried her younger sister, Cornelia C. Hall, on 01 December 1868 in Elmore County, Alabama. They had one son: Joseph Beauregard Cardwell (1869–1931).

On 28 February 1862, Joseph enlisted as a 2nd Sergeant in Company A, 46th Regiment of Alabama Infantry, CSA, at Montgomery County, Alabama. While some military documents list him as a Private or Corporal, his initial appointment as 2nd Sergeant suggests he may have had prior experience or was a respected figure in the local community.

The 46th Alabama Infantry was formed in the spring of 1862 and initially served in East Tennessee, performing garrison and guard duties. In the fall of 1862, it was ordered west and joined General John C. Breckinridge's Division. The regiment soon became part of General Stephen D. Lee's command and played a central role in the Vicksburg Campaign of 1863, one of the most significant military operations in the Western Theater of the Civil War.

During the Siege of Vicksburg, Union forces under General Ulysses S. Grant laid prolonged siege to the Confederate stronghold from May 18 to July 4, 1863. On 4 July 1863, Joseph, along with his younger brother James Matthew Cardwell, was captured when the Confederate forces surrendered the city. Vicksburg's fall gave the Union complete control of the Mississippi River and split the Confederacy in two.

Joseph was held briefly before being paroled on 10 July 1863, under the standard conditions applied to captured Confederate soldiers. These conditions included a solemn pledge:

"I will not take up arms again against the United States, nor serve in any military, police, or constabulary forces in any Fort, Garrison or field work, held by the Confederate States of America, against the United States of America... until duly exchanged by proper authorities."

Joseph's prisoner records describe him as 6 feet 1 inch tall, with brown hair, gray eyes, and a fair complexion—a striking physical profile, above average in height for the time.

There is no documentation indicating whether Joseph rejoined the Confederate military after his parole. Like many paroled soldiers, it is possible he returned home without resuming active service. His postwar life remains largely undocumented. However, his widow's remarriage to James A. Collier on 03 September 1871 in Coosa County, Alabama, suggests that Joseph had died by that date. No probate or burial record has yet been located, but it is assumed that he died around 1870, likely in Coosa County or the surrounding region.

Joseph's wartime service, alongside his brother, in one of the Confederacy's most hard-fought and symbolically important campaigns, marks his place among the many Alabama soldiers who endured the hardships of long sieges, sickness, and uncertain futures. Though his life ended quietly, the records of his enlistment, capture, and parole offer a valuable glimpse into the sacrifices of rural Southern men during the Civil War. Cardwell Line II - Predicted.

* * *

Reuben Cardwell (1833-1861) - *Private - Company K, 24th Regiment, Alabama Infantry, CSA & Company I, 44th Regiment, Mississippi Infantry, CSA* - **Died of Disease**

Reuben Cardwell was born on 13 November 1833 in Group County, Georgia, to John Franklin Cardwell and Phoebe (Gosdin) Cardwell. He was one of several brothers from the Cardwell family who served in the Confederate military during the Civil War. Reuben's older brother, Benjamin M. Cardwell, a veteran of the Mexican-American War, also served in the same unit.

On 13 August 1861, Reuben enlisted as a Private in Company K of the 24th Regiment of Alabama Infantry, CSA, mustering into service in Talladega County, Alabama. Company K was locally known as the "Talladega Southerns" and consisted largely of men from central Alabama. Many of its members came from farming families and small towns, answering the call to defend their state as the war began.

The 24th Alabama Infantry Regiment was organized in the summer of 1861, shortly after the outbreak of the Civil War. Initially, it was assigned to the Army of Central Kentucky, where it joined other Alabama regiments in the early Confederate efforts to secure the western border of the Confederacy. In the fall of 1861, the regiment was ordered northward to reinforce positions in Kentucky, a key border state that was divided in its loyalties and of great strategic importance.

The regiment's deployment took it to Columbus, Hickman County, Kentucky, a fortified position on the Mississippi River. There, Confederate forces under General Leonidas Polk sought to control river traffic and create a defensive line to block Union advances into Tennessee. The encampment at Columbus, while militarily significant, was also plagued with unsanitary conditions and rampant disease—common problems in the early months of the war when military logistics and medical services were still underdeveloped.

It was in Columbus, Kentucky, that Reuben Cardwell died of disease on 05 November 1861. Though he never saw combat, Reuben's death reflects the grim reality faced by thousands of soldiers during the war: disease killed more men than bullets, particularly in the early years when vaccinations, clean water, and proper hygiene were often unavailable. Reuben's service and sacrifice came at a time when the Confederate army was just beginning to organize its forces for a protracted conflict.

His father later received compensation for Reuben's service, with payment issued on 30 July 1863 for the wages and supplies owed at the time of his death. The location of Reuben's grave is unknown, though it is likely he was buried in or near one of the Confederate cemeteries established near the military post at Columbus.

Reuben's story is one of quiet duty and early sacrifice. While his life was cut short before he had the opportunity to experience the full weight of the war, his service is remembered alongside that of his brothers. His older brother Benjamin M. Cardwell continued to serve throughout the war in the same regiment, while his siblings James M. Cardwell and John Cardwell (1823–1865) also served the Confederate cause. Their stories, preserved in this volume, represent the deeply intertwined family and regional commitments that characterized the Civil War experience in Alabama and across the South. <u>Cardwell Line II - Confirmed</u>.

* * *

Reuben Cardwell (1840-1865) - *Private - Company D, 48th Regiment,*

Alabama Infantry, CSA - **Wounded in Action - Prisoner of War - Killed in Action**

Reuben Cardwell was born about 1840, likely in Marshall County, Alabama, to Thomas Cardwell and Mary D. (Long) Cardwell. He is listed in his parents' household in the 1850 and 1860 Marshall County, Alabama census records, though by the latter year his father had passed away, leaving his mother a widow.[67,68] Reuben and his older brother, John James Cardwell, both entered Confederate service during the second year of the war.

On 07 April 1862, the two brothers enlisted as Privates in Company D, 48th Regiment, Alabama Infantry, CSA, at Warrenton, a small community in Marshall County. Known locally as one of the "Warrenton Units," Company D was comprised of young men from the surrounding county and formed part of what would become a battle-hardened regiment in the Army of Northern Virginia.

The 48th Alabama Infantry was officially organized in May 1862 and quickly saw significant action. The regiment fought in the Second Battle of Manassas (August 1862), where it was engaged in heavy combat during General Robert E. Lee's aggressive northern campaign. It also participated in the Maryland Campaign, seeing action at Sharpsburg (Antietam), and later joined the Battle of Fredericksburg in December 1862. By mid-1863, the 48th was part of General James Longstreet's Corps and was ordered north once again during the Gettysburg Campaign.

At the Battle of Gettysburg, the 48th Alabama was engaged on 02 July 1863, the second and most intense day of fighting. During fierce attacks on the Union left flank at Devil's Den and Little Round Top, the regiment sustained heavy losses. In his official report, Colonel James L. Sheffield recorded that *"in this battle the regiment had 275 men engaged. There were 102 killed, wounded, and missing."* Reuben was among the wounded, receiving a gunshot wound to the thigh, while his brother John James Cardwell was killed in action during the same engagement.[69]

Following the battle, Reuben was captured by Union forces and transported north to DeCamp General Hospital on Davids Island, located in New York Harbor. The hospital was a major receiving center for Confederate wounded following the battle. He was eventually paroled, though the exact date is not recorded in the surviving documents.

Reuben later made his way south and was admitted to the Episcopal Church Hospital in Williamsburg, Virginia, on 15 September 1863, with lingering complications from his gunshot wound, listed in his records as "V.S. in thigh and hip" (vulnus sclopetarium, a Latin term for gunshot wound). He was furloughed from the hospital on 24 September 1863, likely to continue recovery at home.

Despite his extended convalescence and time away from the front, it appears that Reuben eventually returned to Marshall County, Alabama. According to a postwar account by Jonathan Gross, a fellow veteran of Company D who compiled a roster from memory: *"James Cardwell, killed at Gettysburg, 1863; Reubin Cardwell, wounded at Gettysburg, deserted and was killed near Red Hill."* While the term "deserted" appears in Gross's account, it may reflect postwar misunderstandings or a mischaracterization of Reuben's absence due to long-term injury.[70]

Reuben Cardwell died on 15 January 1865, near Red Hill in Marshall County, Alabama, during one of the final Union raids through northern Alabama. Union cavalry forces under Brigadier General Hylon B. Lyon were operating in the area at the time, targeting Confederate supply depots and engaging irregular Confederate resistance. Reuben may have been caught up in one of these skirmishes, either while defending the area or simply as a bystander, still recovering from his previous wounds.

The location of Reuben Cardwell's grave is unknown, though it is likely in Marshall County, not far from where he fell. His sacrifice, along with that of his brother John, reflects the devastating toll the war took on Southern families and communities, particularly in Alabama, where entire families were drawn into the conflict. <u>Cardwell Line II - Confirmed.</u>

* * *

Simon Cardwell (1839 - <1900) - *Private - Captain Sheldon's Company, Gid Nelson Alabama Light Artillery, CSA -* **Prisoner of War**

Simon Cardwell was born about 1839 in Georgia, the son of John Franklin Cardwell and Martha "Patsy" (Ford) Cardwell. He is found in the 1850 Talladega County, Alabama census and again in the 1860 Shelby County, Alabama census, residing in the home of his father. The Cardwell family had moved to Alabama from Georgia during the mid-19th century, settling in the central part of the state prior to the outbreak of the Civil War.[71,72] Simon married Mary Francis Helton on 26 December 1860 in Shelby County, Alabama.[73] The couple began building a family in the shadow of rising national conflict, and their first children were born just a few years after Alabama seceded from the Union.

On 02 April 1862, Simon enlisted as a Private at Shelby Springs, Shelby County, Alabama, joining Captain Sheldon's Company, known more formally as Gid Nelson's Alabama Light Artillery. This independent artillery unit was part of the Department of Alabama, Mississippi, and East Louisiana, and later served under the Department of North Carolina during the war. The battery was a mobile field artillery unit that served in a support role throughout the conflict, assigned to protect key railways, coastal fortifications, and logistical routes, often under demanding conditions.

By early 1864, Simon's service had taken him to the Atlantic coast, where he was detached at Cedar Point, Onslow County, North Carolina, from 01 January to 29 February 1864. Cedar Point was a strategic coastal location, and Confederate artillery units in the region were tasked with defending vulnerable points along the Atlantic seaboard from Union amphibious incursions and inland raids.

Although detailed battle records for Gid Nelson's Alabama Light Artillery are limited, similar independent batteries in the region were involved in a variety of defensive operations throughout the Carolinas Campaign, including actions in eastern North Carolina, and later in Mississippi as Union forces moved inland.

Simon remained with the battery until the surrender of all Confederate forces under Lieutenant General Richard Taylor on 04 May 1865, a general surrender of the Department of Alabama, Mississippi, and East Louisiana. He was formally paroled five days later, on 09 May 1865, at Meridian, Lauderdale County, Mississippi, along with thousands of other Confederate soldiers seeking to return to civilian life.

Though the Civil War records list this soldier only as "S. Cardwell," the association of birth year, place of enlistment, and presence in Shelby County confirms that this was Simon Cardwell, son of John Franklin Cardwell.

After the war, Simon and Mary raised a large family. Their children included: Della E. Cardwell (1866–1950), Viola Cardwell (1867–1891), Leonelle "Lee" Cardwell (1870–1933), Octavia Cardwell (1871–1931), Arthur L. Cardwell (1871–1961), Joseph Gallion Cardwell (1873–1941), John Malcolm Cardwell (1873–1957), and Annie L. Cardwell (1875–1910). The family appears in the 1880 Perry County, Alabama census, residing in central Alabama during the Reconstruction years.[74]

By the 1900 Montgomery County census, Mary Francis Cardwell is listed as a widow, indicating that Simon had died sometime between 1880 and 1900.[75] The exact date of Simon's death and the location of his grave remain unknown, though he is presumed to have died in Alabama.

Simon Cardwell's service in a mobile artillery unit highlights a lesser-known aspect of Confederate military operations—defensive artillery detachments assigned to protect infrastructure and key geographic locations, often far from the more famous battlefields. His story stands as one among the many quiet sacrifices made by Confederate soldiers who served faithfully in support roles throughout the South's interior and coastal defenses. <u>Cardwell Line II - Predicted</u>.

* * *

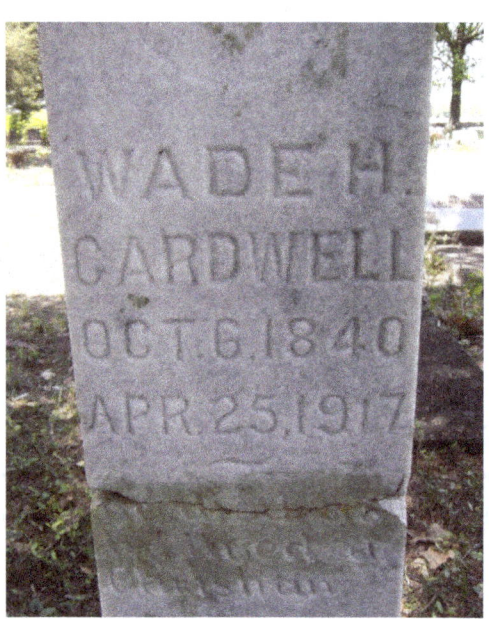

Photo 1.6: Wade Hampton Cardwell (1840-1917) Headstone - Crary Memorial Cemetery, Century, Escambia County, Florida.

Wade Hampton Cardwell (1840-1917) - *Corporal - Company D, 12th Regiment, Alabama Infantry, CSA -* **Prisoner of War**

Wade Hampton Cardwell was born on 06 October 1840 in Pike County, Alabama, the son of Nathaniel Cardwell and Elizabeth "Betsy" Ann (Barnett) Cardwell. He is listed in the household of his parents in the 1850 Pike

County, Alabama census, and ten years later, he appears with his widowed mother and siblings in the 1860 Coffee County, Alabama census.[76,77]

On 12 August 1861, Wade enlisted as a Private in Company D of the 12th Regiment of Alabama Infantry, Confederate States Army. The regiment, organized in July 1861, was part of the Army of Northern Virginia and quickly became a seasoned and battle-hardened unit in some of the most intense fighting in the Eastern Theater of the Civil War. It served under a series of well-known Confederate generals, including Robert E. Rodes and Robert E. Lee.

The 12th Alabama Infantry saw its first major action at First Manassas (Bull Run) and then moved into campaigns in Virginia and Maryland, participating in key engagements such as the Peninsula Campaign, Second Manassas, and Antietam. At Antietam in September 1862, the regiment endured heavy fighting along the infamous Sunken Road. In 1863, they took part in the Battle of Gettysburg, suffering significant losses during the Confederate assault on Cemetery Ridge.

Throughout 1864, the regiment continued to fight in major engagements such as the Wilderness, Spotsylvania, and Cold Harbor, holding the line in Lee's defensive campaigns against Union General Ulysses S. Grant. The 12th was among the units pushed back during the final siege of Petersburg, eventually falling back to Appomattox Court House.

By the war's end, Wade had been promoted to the rank of Corporal. He was present at the final surrender and was taken as a Prisoner of War on 09 April 1865 at Appomattox Court House, Virginia—the site of General Robert E. Lee's formal surrender to Union forces under General Grant. His presence there marks him as one of the last remaining members of a once-formidable Confederate regiment.

Following the war, Wade returned to the Deep South and married Frances Melvina Duck on 12 July 1868 in Escambia County, Florida.[78] Together they raised a large family, including: Edmund Riley Cardwell (1869–1952), Robert J. Cardwell (1870–1930), John Cardwell (1872–), Nathaniel Timothy Cardwell (1873–1958), Meliva Cardwell (1876–), Caldony Cardwell (1878–), Mattie Cardwell (1880–), Lettie Lee Cardwell (1883–), James Lundy Cardwell (1884–1939), and Daniel Alpheus Cardwell (1887–1946). The family remained in Escambia County, Florida, where Wade is listed in the 1870, 1900, and 1910 U.S. Census records.[79,80,81] He lived out the remainder of his life in quiet civilian life, having survived some of the fiercest battles of the war.

Wade Hampton Cardwell died on 26 April 1917 in Escambia County and was laid to rest at Crary Memorial Cemetery in Century, Escambia County, Florida.[82]

His younger brother, William McKenzie Cardwell, also served in the 12th Alabama Infantry, enlisting in Company K. William was Killed in Action on 31 May 1862 during the Battle of Seven Pines, Virginia. His biography is also included in this volume, serving as a poignant reminder of the Cardwell family's deep commitment and sacrifice during the conflict. Cardwell Line I - Predicted. Photo Credit[83]

* * *

William Cardwell (1840-) - *Private - Company A, 23rd Regiment, Alabama Infantry, CSA*

William Cardwell was born about 1840 in Chambers County, Alabama to James Cardwell and Melissa (Bohannan) Cardwell. He is listed in their home in the 1850 Chambers County, Alabama and the 1860 Tallapoosa County, Alabama census records.[84,85]

The Civil War records of William are scare and the few available do not provide a lot of details. The following is a brief account of the unit that he served. It is unknown how long he served with the 23rd or if he survived the war. The few records that exists have him listed as "W. Cardwell".

The 23rd Alabama Infantry Regiment was organized in Montgomery on November 19, 1861, with recruits from Baldwin, Choctaw, Clarke, Conecuh, Lowndes, Macon, Marengo, Monroe, and Wilcox counties. It was sent to Mobile and remained there until February 1862. During that time, 82 men died from disease. The regiment then moved to East Tennessee and participated in the Kentucky campaign.

After returning to Tennessee, the 23rd was placed in a brigade with the 20th, 23rd, 30th, 31st, and 46th Alabama Regiments. In December 1862, the unit was sent to Vicksburg and fought at Chickasaw Bayou. It suffered heavy losses at Port Gibson, where its brigade commander was killed. The regiment fought at Baker's Creek, losing many men as prisoners, and again the next day at Big Black Bridge. Left behind by oversight, the 23rd held off the entire Union army for 12 hours before retreating into Vicksburg, where it endured the siege with relatively few casualties. After the surrender, the men were paroled, exchanged, and rejoined the Army of Tennessee just after Chickamauga.

The 23rd fought at Missionary Ridge with light losses and spent the winter at Dalton, Georgia. During the Atlanta Campaign, it suffered heavy casualties at Resaca and continued fighting through Atlanta and Jonesboro, where it was severely reduced. The regiment fought at Columbia and Nashville, and lost many men in battle and capture. It covered the retreat into the Carolinas, fighting at Branchville and Bentonville before being consolidated with the 31st and 46th Alabama Infantry Regiments.

The 23rd Alabama Infantry originally had 1,200 men on its rolls but by Rocky Face Ridge, only 435 muskets remained, and at Salisbury, North Carolina, just 76 surrendered on April 9, 1865.

No other records of William Cardwell have been located after an exhaustive search. It is assumed that he did not survive the conflict, but the date of his death and location are unknown. Cardwell Line II - Predicted.

* * *

Photo 1.7: *William J. Wesley Cardwell (1844-1919) and wife Headstone - Nixon Chapel Cemetery, Nixon Chapel, Marshall County, Alabama.*

William J. Wesley Cardwell (1844-1919) - *Private - Company H, 4th Regiment, Alabama Cavalry, CSA-* **Unconfirmed**

William J. Wesley Cardwell was born on 20 November 1844 in Marshall County, Alabama, the son of Thomas Cardwell and Mary D. (Long) Cardwell. He is listed in the household of his parents in the 1850 Marshall County census, and a decade later appears with his widowed mother and siblings in the 1860 census, also in Marshall County.[86,87]

After the war, William claimed that he served in the Confederate States

Army, stating in a pension application that he had enlisted in 1863 as a Private in Company H of the 4th Alabama Cavalry, CSA, at Guntersville, Marshall County, Alabama. However, his application was denied, and an official statement from the War Department read: *"The name W.J. Cardwell has not been found on such rolls as are on file in this office of Company H of any 4th Alabama Cavalry organization, C.S.A., and no record has been found of the service, capture or parole of a man of this name as a member of any such organization."*[88]

Despite his claim, no Civil War records have been found confirming William's service in the 4th Alabama Cavalry or any other Confederate unit. Two witnesses were listed on his pension application: J.H. Carter and T.J. Patterson. Research suggests that a H.J. Carter did serve in the 4th Alabama Cavalry, which could support William's claim to some degree, but no service records have been found for T.J. Patterson.

The 4th Alabama Cavalry, organized in 1862 under Colonel Alfred A. Russell, operated in North Alabama, Tennessee, and Mississippi. It participated in Bragg's Kentucky Campaign, skirmished during Streight's Raid, and fought in Wheeler's operations against Union General Sherman's advance through Georgia. The regiment was often used to delay Union movements, disrupt supply lines, and scout enemy positions. Many Alabama cavalry records were incomplete or lost, particularly for smaller detachments or men serving in auxiliary roles. Given that possibility, William's service cannot be confirmed or entirely dismissed, and he is included here with that caveat.

After the war, William returned to civilian life in Marshall County. He married Isabelle H. Hays on 09 August 1874.[89] They had two sons: William Martin Cardwell (1873–1964) and James Henry Cardwell (1877–1962). The family is listed in the 1880 Marshall County census.[90]

Following Isabelle's death in 1884, William remarried on 6 February 1889 to Martha Ann "Jenny" Turner in Blount County, Alabama.[91] They had two additional children: Monroe H. Cardwell (1899–) and George Washington Cardwell (1903–1967).

William J. Wesley Cardwell passed away on 30 April 1919 in Marshall County, Alabama. He is buried at Nixon Chapel Cemetery, located in the Nixon Chapel community of Marshall County.[92]

Though his military service remains unverified, the presence of his pension application and sworn testimony from local acquaintances suggests he may have participated in the conflict in some capacity, perhaps in an irregular or detached role that was not officially recorded or later lost to history. <u>Cardwell Line II - Confirmed</u>. Photo Credit[93]

* * *

William McKenzie Cardwell (1833 -1862) - *Private - Company D, 12th Regiment, Alabama Infantry, CSA* - **Killed in Action**

William McKenzie Cardwell was born on 30 November 1833 in Pike County, Alabama, to Nathaniel Cardwell and Elizabeth "Betsy" Ann (Barnett) Cardwell. He appears in the 1850 Pike County census living with his family.[94] Around 1855, William married Mary "Polly" Anderson, likely in Pike County, though no official marriage record has been located. They had four children before the outbreak of war: John Thomas Cardwell (1856–1927), Richard Benjamin Cardwell (1857–1942), William Nathanial Cardwell (1859–1939), and Laura Elizabeth Cardwell (1861–1957). By 1860, the family had moved to Coffee County, Alabama, where they appear in that year's census.[95]

With the rising tide of war, William enlisted as a Private in Company D of the 12th Regiment, Alabama Infantry, CSA on 12 August 1861 at Coffee County. He was joined in service by his younger brother, Wade Hampton Cardwell, who is also recorded in this chapter.

The 12th Alabama Infantry was organized in July 1861 and became a part of the Army of Northern Virginia, under the command of General Robert E. Lee. The regiment quickly gained a reputation for its toughness and reliability, participating in many of the Civil War's most intense battles. After training at Norfolk, Virginia, the 12th saw action during the Peninsula Campaign, part of the Union's first large-scale offensive against Richmond. The regiment was engaged in the Battle of Seven Pines (Fair Oaks) on 31 May 1862, one of the bloodiest early battles in the Eastern Theater. In that engagement, Confederate forces attempted to exploit a divided Union army near Richmond, resulting in fierce fighting and high casualties on both sides.

It was during this battle—the Battle of Seven Pines, in Henrico County, Virginia—that William McKenzie Cardwell was killed in action. The clash marked the beginning of a series of brutal battles that would define the war in the East. The 12th Alabama, like many Confederate regiments, fought with determination but suffered deeply in lives lost.

Although William's exact burial site has not been identified, he is believed to be interred in a mass grave at Seven Pines National Cemetery, along with many of his fellow soldiers who perished in the battle.[96] The cemetery, established in the aftermath of the war, honors those who fell during the early Virginia campaigns.

William's widow, Mary "Polly" Anderson Cardwell, was left to raise their four children alone. William's brother, Wade Hampton Cardwell, survived the war and is documented elsewhere in this volume.

William McKenzie Cardwell's sacrifice at Seven Pines places him among the thousands who gave their lives during the Confederacy's earliest major attempts to repel Union forces from Virginia. His service with the 12th Alabama Infantry highlights the deep commitment of Alabama's soldiers to their cause and the heavy toll the war exacted on families throughout the South. Cardwell Line I - Predicted.

* * *

Photo 1.8: *William Morris "Grub" Cardwell (1847-1926) - Coosa County, Alabama - circa 1887*

Photo 1.9: *William Morris Cardwell (1847-1926) Headstone -*
Providence Methodist Church Cemetery, Elmore County, Alabama

William Morris Cardwell (1847-1926) - *Private - Company A, 46th Regiment, Alabama Infantry, CSA*

William Morris Cardwell was born on 03 January 1847 in Coosa County, Alabama, the son of William Cardwell and Sarah (McCluskey) Cardwell. He was known by the family nickname "Grub." William appears in the 1850 Talladega County census in his parents' household, and following the death of his father in 1854, he is listed in the 1860 Coosa County census with his widowed mother and siblings.[97,98]

William was the younger brother of Joseph M. "Joe" Cardwell and James Mathew Cardwell, both of whom served in Company A of the 46th Alabama Infantry, CSA. Following in their footsteps, William enlisted as a Private in the same unit on 04 January 1864, at Traveler's Rest, Coosa County, Alabama. He had just turned seventeen years old.

The 46th Alabama Infantry Regiment, organized in May 1862, was composed primarily of men from Coosa, Tallapoosa, and other central Alabama counties. The regiment was first stationed in Mobile, where it trained and performed defensive duties before being sent to the Western Theater. It saw heavy action at the Battle of Port Gibson, the Battle of Champion Hill, and was ultimately involved in the Siege of Vicksburg, Mississippi. The regiment surrendered there on 4 July 1863, and the men were paroled shortly after. Many of the survivors, reorganized after the parole period, returned to duty and continued fighting in subsequent campaigns in Mississippi and Georgia. By the time William enlisted in early 1864, the regiment had resumed operations and would later be involved in Hood's Tennessee Campaign and the defense of Mobile.

Though William joined late in the war, his enlistment into a battle-hardened unit like the 46th Alabama would have placed him in a harsh military environment, likely facing marches, skirmishes, and continued exposure to disease and hardship. Surviving records under the names "W. Cardwell" and "Wm. Cardwell" confirm his presence in Company A, although detailed documentation of his service after enlistment is limited. His inclusion in the unit alongside both of his older brothers provides compelling evidence of familial and regional continuity in service.

After the war, William returned to Coosa County and married Mary Adeline Watt on 09 January 1870.[99] The couple settled in the region and raised a large family. Their children were: Eliza Joe Cardwell (1870–1895), Sarah Caroline "Carrie" Cardwell (1872–1932), Mary Ida Cardwell (1874–1962), Oscar Thomas Cardwell (1874–1940), Willie Cardwell (1875–1875), Jane Cardwell (1878–), James Foster Cardwell (1879–1959), Evie Effie Cardwell (1881–1950), Robert Charles Cardwell (1884–1968), John Oliver Cardwell (1886–1975), Alford Clinton Cardwell (1889–1891), and Sadie Lee Cardwell (1892–1972).

William and his family are documented in the 1870, 1880, 1900, 1910, and 1920 U.S. census records, all within Coosa County, Alabama.[100,101,102,103,104] In 1928, his widow, Mary A. (Watt) Cardwell, applied for a Confederate pension, further confirming his service with the 46th Alabama.

William Morris "Grub" Cardwell died on 30 August 1926 in Rockford, Coosa County, Alabama. He is buried at Providence Methodist Church Cemetery, located in Elmore County, Alabama, not far from the communities where he had spent his life.[105] His service, alongside his two brothers, stands as a testament to the familial bonds and regional loyalties that characterized much of the Confederate military enlistment in Alabama. <u>Cardwell Line II - Predicted</u>. Photo Credits[106,107]

* * *

Note: Three brothers—**Lee Roy P. Cardwell**, **Thomas D. Cardwell**, and **William Y. Cardwell**—appear on the rolls of Forrest's Regiment of Alabama Cavalry, CSA, though they were residents of McNairy County, Tennessee. Each of the brothers also served in various regiments within

General Nathan Bedford Forrest's Cavalry Corps, and their service is documented in the Tennessee Confederate Veterans chapter of this work.

Another individual, **Samuel Cardwell**, is not included in this chapter. Despite extensive research, only limited and inconsistent records have been found for him. The evidence strongly suggests that his surname was likely misrecorded, and that the individual in question was not a member of the Cardwell family.

Benjamin Lumpkin Cardwell, son of John M. Cardwell (whose biography appears in the Alabama chapter), served as a Private in the 10th Confederate Cavalry. This regiment was a consolidated unit formed from elements of Alabama and Georgia commands and operated under the authority of the Confederate central government, rather than any individual state. As such, Benjamin's biography is included in the *Miscellaneous* chapter of this volume, which covers Confederate service not directly affiliated with a specific state's military organization.

Arkansas
The Cardwell Confederates

ARKANSAS, A KEY CONFEDERATE STATE IN THE TRANS-MISSISSIPPI Theater, seceded from the Union in May 1861 and became a battleground for control of the western frontier. With its vast forests, rivers, and mountainous terrain, the state was critical for both Confederate supply routes and Union invasion efforts. The war in Arkansas was marked by guerrilla warfare, cavalry raids, and pitched battles, with major engagements occurring at Pea Ridge, Prairie Grove, Helena, and Jenkins' Ferry. Arkansas provided thousands of troops to the Confederate cause, many of whom served in infantry, cavalry, and irregular units that fought across the region.

The Cardwell soldiers of Arkansas served in a variety of infantry and cavalry regiments, participating in battles and campaigns across the western frontier of the Civil War. Their service in the Trans-Mississippi Theater highlights the endurance and resilience of Confederate troops in the region, who faced constant hardships from Union advances, limited resources, and the chaotic nature of the war west of the Mississippi River.

This chapter honors the Cardwell Confederate soldiers of Arkansas, ensuring their service and sacrifices are remembered as part of Civil War history.

* * *

Photo 2.1: *Aaron Day Cardwell (1844-1935) - Texas - circa 1920*

Photo 2.2: *Aaron Day Cardwell (1844-1935) Headstone - Willow Springs Cemetery, Palo Pinto County, Texas.*

Aaron Day Cardwell (1844—1935) - *Private - Company I, 37th Regiment, Arkansas Infantry, CSA -* **Wounded in Action**

Aaron D. Cardwell was born on 11 April 1844 in McNairy County, Tennessee. He was the son of Hiram Clark Cardwell and Sarah (Saunders) Cardwell. He appears in the household of his parents in the 1850 McNairy County, Tennessee census.[1] During the 1850s, the family relocated to Arkansas and settled in Columbia County. By 1860, Aaron was living with his father and stepmother in Columbia County, Arkansas.[2]

On 20 May 1862, Aaron enlisted as a Private in Company I, 37th Arkansas Infantry (CSA), at Sulphur Springs, Benton County, Arkansas. His older brother, William Thomas Dobson Cardwell, enlisted alongside him on the same day. Aaron saw active service in the western theater and was Wounded in Action (WIA) during the Battle of Prairie Grove on 07 December 1862 in Washington County, Arkansas. His service record notes that he was left behind at Cane Hill to recover and rejoined his unit on 01 April 1863. According to family tradition, Aaron was initially presumed dead and left on the battlefield before being rescued. He sustained a significant thigh wound during the engagement.

The Battle of Prairie Grove was a hard-fought and bloody affair. Union forces suffered 1,251 casualties, including 175 dead, while Confederate casualties were estimated at 1,317, with 164 to 204 killed. The Confederate army, consisting largely of conscripts, suffered from poor morale and a significant number of desertions. Many of their dead were left on the battlefield, hastily covered and guarded against scavengers—a grim image that underscores the intensity of the battle Aaron endured.

Following his recovery, Aaron was granted furlough from 15 March to 21 August 1863. Due to the severity of his injuries, he was assigned to hospital duty and served as a nurse from 31 December 1863 to 29 February 1864 at Camden, Ouachita County, Arkansas. No further military records have been found regarding his service, and it is unknown when or how he was officially discharged.

Aaron married Susan A. Wallace on 16 January 1862 in Hempstead County, Arkansas.[3] They had three children: Mary Emma Cardwell (1867–1946), Dora P. Cardwell (1874–1936), and Corda "Cordie" Cardwell (1877–). The family is listed in the 1880 census of Cass County, Texas.[4] After Susan's death in 1881, Aaron remarried Emma Moore on 21 November 1882 in Cass County. They had three children together: Melvin Loftin Cardwell (1886–1955), Blanche Sloan Cardwell (1888–1976), and Phillip Moore Cardwell Sr. (1890–1969). Emma died in 1891.

Later that same year, on 04 March 1891, Aaron married a third time—to Mary Elizabeth (Scott) Prestridge—in Ellis County, Texas. They had one daughter, Hattie Burelson Cardwell (1891–1977). During this time, Aaron served as a Baptist minister in several churches throughout Ellis County. In July 1899, he applied for a Confederate veteran's pension while residing in Hunt County, Texas. He appears in the 1900 census there, and by 1910 was living in Parker County. In 1911, he was still active in the ministry, preaching at Fairview Baptist Church in Hunt County. By 1920, he was living with his son Melvin in Parker County and listed as a widower.[5,6,7]

Aaron D. Cardwell died on 21 April 1935 at the home of his daughter, Mrs. A.L. Hubbard, in Mineral Wells, Palo Pinto County, Texas. He is buried at Willow Springs Cemetery in Palo Pinto County. He was the brother of William Thomas Dobson Cardwell and Abmural Franklin Cardwell, both of whom also served the Confederacy. William served in the same unit as Aaron, and both men are featured in this volume.[8,9] Cardwell Line I - Confirmed. Photo Credits[10,11]

* * *

Photo 2.3: *Admural Franklin Cardwell - Childress County, Texas - circa 1920*

Photo 2.4: *Admural Franklin Cardwell (1848-1922) Headstone - Tell Baptist Cemetery, Tell, Childress County, Texas.*

Admural Franklin Cardwell (1848-1922) - Private - *Company G, Kilgore's Regiment, Arkansas Cavalry, CSA*

Admural Franklin Cardwell was born on 24 April 1848 in McNairy County, Tennessee. He was the son of Hiram Clark Cardwell and Sarah (Sanders) Cardwell. Admural appears in his parents' household in the 1850 McNairy County, Tennessee census and again in 1860 after the family had relocated to Columbia County, Arkansas.[12,13] His father and two older brothers, Aaron Day Cardwell and William Thomas Dobson Cardwell, all served in the Confederate Army during the Civil War and are recorded elsewhere in this volume.

Although no official Confederate service record has been located for Admural, he applied for a Confederate pension in Childress County, Texas, on 3 February 1922. That application was ultimately rejected on 16 February 1922 due to a lack of verifiable documentation. However, both family tradition and supporting affidavits, including one from his brother Albert Pryor Cardwell, attest to his Confederate service.

According to Admural's pension application, he enlisted as a Private in Company G of Kilgore's Regiment of Arkansas Cavalry on 15 March 1864 at the age of sixteen. While underage enlistments were not uncommon—especially in the later stages of the war—many such records are incomplete or missing. Admural also claimed he was later transferred to an unidentified infantry unit. This is plausible, as Kilgore's Regiment, like many late-war Arkansas cavalry commands, was reportedly dismounted and reassigned to infantry service.

Admural stated that he received an honorable discharge at Marshall, Texas, on 15 May 1865. At that time, Marshall served as the headquarters of the Confederate Trans-Mississippi Department and was a major site of surrender and disbandment for numerous Confederate units operating west of the Mississippi River. This detail adds credibility to his claim, particularly in light of the poor recordkeeping that plagued these provisional Arkansas formations.

While his precise unit cannot be confirmed, it is worth noting that several commands, including Shelby's Brigade, the 22nd and 35th Arkansas Infantry, and various unassigned Arkansas infantry units, were present in or near Marshall at war's end. Any of these could have absorbed dismounted cavalrymen such as Admural Cardwell.

Following the war, Admural returned to Arkansas and married Eliza Francis Warmack on 12 December 1866.[14] Together, they had nine children: Sarah Pandora "Dora" Cardwell (1868–1929), Annis Luellen Cardwell (1870–1949), Leonard Monroe Cardwell (1873–1934), Aaron Lawrence "Lorenzo" Cardwell (1875–1961), Albert Perry Cardwell (1878–1964), Emma Leona Cardwell (1880–1960), William Thomas Cardwell (1883–), Alonzo Hiram "Lonnie" Cardwell (1889–1971), and Effie Elvira Cardwell (1893–1961).

Admural appears in the 1870 Ouachita County, Arkansas; 1880 Nevada County, Arkansas; 1900 Hunt County, Texas; and 1910 Motley County, Texas census records. He later moved to Childress County, Texas, where he spent his final years.[15,16,17,18]

Admural Franklin Cardwell died on 17 June 1922 in Tell, Childress County, Texas. He is buried at Tell Baptist Cemetery in Tell, Childress County.[19] While his military service remains partially unverified by traditional records, the combination of sworn testimony, family history, and circumstantial evidence strongly support his inclusion among the Confederate veterans of the Cardwell family. Cardwell Line I - Confirmed. Photo Credits[20,21]

* * *

Daniel Cardwell (1826-1862) - *Private - Company G, 14th Regiment, Arkansas Infantry, CSA* - **Died of Disease**

Daniel Cardwell was born about 1826 in Carroll County, Tennessee, the son of Richard Cardwell and Christine (Cook) Cardwell. By 1840, the Cardwell family had relocated to Greene County, Arkansas, where they appear in the census. Daniel is listed in his parents' household again in the 1850 Greene County census.[22,23]

He married Annis Howard around 1853, based on the birth of their eldest child. Together, they had at least three children: Sarah Ann Cardwell (b.1854), Thomas H. Cardwell (1856–1870), and George A. Cardwell (b.1860). The family was living in Carroll County, Arkansas by 1860 and are recorded in the census for that year.[24]

Daniel enlisted as a Private in Company G of the 14th Regiment, Arkansas Infantry, CSA, on 12 July 1861 at Yellville in Marion County,

Arkansas. The 14th Arkansas Infantry was formed during the early months of the war and participated in the Battle of Pea Ridge in Benton County, Arkansas, in March 1862. This significant battle was a defeat for the Confederacy, leading to a Confederate withdrawal from much of northern Arkansas.

After Pea Ridge, the 14th Arkansas was ordered east of the Mississippi River to join Confederate forces assembling at Corinth, Mississippi. However, the regiment had already been severely reduced by combat losses and disease and was in a state of disorganization by the time it reached the area.

It was during this period, while encamped in northern Mississippi, that Daniel Cardwell became gravely ill. He was admitted to a Confederate hospital in Quitman County, Mississippi, where he died of disease on 30 October 1862. Illness was the leading cause of death among Civil War soldiers, and outbreaks of typhoid, dysentery, and malaria were especially common in the sweltering and unsanitary conditions of Confederate camps and hospitals.

The location of Daniel's burial is unknown, though it was likely near the hospital in Quitman County. No known marker survives. His service and sacrifice reflect the hardships endured by thousands of Confederate soldiers in the Western Theater—many of whom never saw major battle but still paid the ultimate price.

Daniel's brother, John A. Cardwell, also served in the Confederate Army and died during the war. His biography appears elsewhere in this volume. Cardwell Line I - Predicted.

* * *

Hiram Clark Cardwell (1820-1866) - *Private - Company E, 1st Regiment, Arkansas Cavalry (Crawford's), CSA*

Hiram Clark Cardwell was born on 18 September 1820 at Lone Mountain, Claiborne County, Tennessee. He was the son of William Cardwell and Celia (Harper) Cardwell. Sometime between 1830 and 1840, the family moved west to McNairy County, Tennessee. Hiram is recorded there in the 1840 and 1850 census records with his wife and growing family.[25,26]

He married Sarah Sanders on 07 June 1839 in McNairy County, Tennessee.[27] Together they had six children: Pandora "Dora" Ann Cardwell (1840–1908), William Thomas Dobson Cardwell (1842–1863), Aaron Day

Cardwell (1844–1935), Elizabeth Selon Cardwell (1846–1850), Admiral Franklin "Addie" Cardwell (1848–1922), and Albert Pryor Cardwell (1851–1942). Sarah died in 1852, and the following year, Hiram relocated with his children to Columbia County, Arkansas. On 03 March 1853, he married Matilda Robinson in Columbia County. They had six more children: Mary Jane Cardwell (1854–1854), Sarah Jenetta Cardwell (1856–1942), Martha P. Jane Cardwell (1858–), Robert Hiram Cardwell (1860–1923), John Henry Cardwell (1862–1935), and William Clark Cardwell (1865–1949). The family appears in the 1860 Columbia County, Arkansas census.[28]

The Civil War struck close to Hiram's home and family. His eldest son, William Thomas Dobson Cardwell, enlisted in the 37th Regiment of Arkansas Infantry, CSA and was captured at the Battle of Helena on 04 July 1863. He later died of smallpox while imprisoned at Alton POW Camp in Illinois. Another son, Aaron Day Cardwell, also served in the same unit and was wounded at the Battle of Prairie Grove on 07 December 1862. The loss and suffering of his sons may have inspired Hiram, despite being 43 years old, to join the Confederate war effort.

Hiram Clark Cardwell enlisted as a Private in Company E of the 1st Arkansas Cavalry (Crawford's), CSA on 15 December 1863. Though service records for Hiram are limited, the unit history provides insight into his likely wartime experience. The 1st Arkansas Cavalry was part of the Trans-Mississippi Department and engaged in various actions throughout Arkansas and surrounding states. The regiment participated in the Red River Campaign and Price's Missouri Raid in the fall of 1864. It operated in the Arkansas River Valley, often conducting raids and interdicting Union supply routes between Little Rock and Fort Smith. In January 1865, the unit participated in Confederate attacks on the Union garrison at Dardanelle, Arkansas. The 1st Arkansas Cavalry officially surrendered on 26 May 1865 at Fort Smith, Arkansas.

Following the war, Hiram returned to his home near Smackover in Columbia County, Arkansas. He died not long after, on 20 March 1866, at the age of 45. The cause of his death is unknown. Though the precise location of his grave has not been identified, it is believed he was buried in Columbia County, Arkansas.

Hiram Clark Cardwell's life and military service reflect the sacrifices and complex choices faced by Southern families during the Civil War. Three of his sons served the Confederacy, and two were wounded, with one dying in Union captivity. His legacy lives on through their stories, each recorded in this chapter.[29] Cardwell Line I - Confirmed.

* * *

James M. Cardwell (1823-1869) - *Private - Company F & G, 2nd Regiment, Arkansas Cavalry, CSA*

James M. Cardwell was born around 1823 in Oglethorpe County, Georgia. He was the son of John Franklin Cardwell and Phoebe (Gosdin) Cardwell. By the 1850 census, James had moved west to Richland Township in Jefferson County, Arkansas, where he was recorded as a single man working as an overseer.[30]

He married Easter M. Scythe on 17 December 1850 in Jefferson County, Arkansas.[31] She appears to have died prior to 1856, likely in Jefferson County. James remarried on 02 September 1856 to Sarah E. Freeman in Hot Springs, Jefferson County, Arkansas. Together they had one son, J.T. Cardwell, born in 1858. The family appears in the 1860 census of Jefferson County.[32]

With the outbreak of the Civil War, James was conscripted into Confederate service on 01 March 1862 at Pine Bluff, Jefferson County, Arkansas. He was enrolled as a Private in Company F of the 2nd Regiment of Arkansas Cavalry, CSA. At the time of his enlistment, James was 40 years old. According to his Confederate service record, he was 6 feet tall, with a dark complexion, black eyes, and dark hair. His occupation was listed as farmer, and his place of birth was noted as Oglethorpe County, Georgia.

James was discharged from conscription on 31 October 1862 by order of Lieutenant General John C. Pemberton, under the terms of the Conscript Act, which allowed certain men exemptions from further service. Despite his discharge, records indicate that James remained with the 2nd Arkansas Cavalry until at least 28 April 1863, suggesting he may have returned to serve voluntarily or in a limited capacity.

The 2nd Arkansas Cavalry was an active Confederate unit that engaged in mounted operations throughout Missouri, Arkansas, and Indian Territory (present-day Oklahoma). Known for its mobility and guerrilla-style tactics, the regiment participated in raids, ambushes, and small-unit engagements that disrupted Union supply lines and reconnaissance routes. While James's specific participation in these actions is not documented, his service period aligns with many of the unit's early operations.

One of the regiment's most prominent campaigns occurred later in the war during Price's Missouri Expedition in the fall of 1864, a failed Confederate effort to retake Missouri. The 2nd Arkansas Cavalry participated in several engagements during this campaign, including the battles of Pilot Knob, Boonville, and Westport. There is no record of James taking part in these later battles, and it is unclear if he remained active in the regiment beyond mid-1863.

James M. Cardwell died by 26 January 1869, as he is referenced in the probate records of Jefferson County, Arkansas on that date.[33] The exact cause of his death and the location of his burial are unknown. His short but active military service, along with his early settlement in Arkansas, marks him as one of the many Southern men who contributed to the Confederate cause while balancing family responsibilities and the hardships of frontier life. Cardwell Line II - Predicted.

* * *

John A. Cardwell (1834-1862) - *Private - Company G, 1st Regiment, Arkansas Volunteers, CSA & Coleman's Missouri Cavalry Regiment, CSA -* **Died in Service**

John A. Cardwell was born around 1834 in Carroll County, Tennessee, the son of Richard Cardwell and Christine (Cook) Cardwell. The family relocated to Greene County, Arkansas shortly after John's birth and is recorded there in the 1850 census.[34]

John married Sarah L. "Sallie" Morse on 05 August 1860 in Lawrence County, Arkansas.[35] The 1860 census, taken prior to his marriage, lists John in Greene County, Arkansas, residing in what appears to be the household of his sister. John and Sarah had one known child, John A. Cardwell Jr., born in 1862.[36]

On 08 November 1861, John enlisted as a Private in Company G of the 1st Regiment of Arkansas Volunteers, CSA, at Pocahontas in Randolph County. This early war unit was raised as a short-term volunteer force, serving for 30 days during the initial mobilization of Confederate forces in Arkansas. These early volunteers helped establish Confederate control in the region, with many later transferring into permanent regiments.

John's service would later be associated with Coleman's Missouri Cavalry Regiment, CSA—a unit organized in 1862 by Colonel William O. Coleman, who recruited former members of the Missouri State Guard, particularly in southeast Missouri and northeast Arkansas. Coleman's Regiment operated in the rugged Ozarks region and included soldiers from both states. Many of these men, including John, were from counties near the Missouri-Arkansas border. While official military records are limited, his name appears in conjunction with this unit in Lawrence County sources.

As Confederate soldiers went off to war, their families often faced extreme hardship. On 01 December 1862, Governor Harris Flanagin signed legislation authorizing state support for indigent families of Confederate soldiers. On 27 February 1863, John's widow, Sarah Cardwell (age 21), and young son, John Jr. (age 1½), were listed among those in need of support in Piney Fork Township, Lawrence County, Arkansas. The record lists John A. Cardwell as deceased and notes his affiliation with Coleman's Regiment.

John A. Cardwell died on 10 May 1862 at White County, Arkansas, according to records found under Miscellaneous Confederate Service Records. It is not known whether he was Killed in Action or died of disease—both common causes of death among Confederate soldiers—but his service was confirmed by both military and civil documentation. The location of his grave is unknown.[37]

Research into the history of Coleman's Missouri Cavalry notes that it drew heavily from the same pool of men who would later be associated with the 4th Missouri Cavalry, and many soldiers from northeast Arkansas enlisted in its ranks. While the regiment later evolved into what became the 46th Arkansas Cavalry, John had died before that formal designation.

John's older brother, Daniel Cardwell, also served in the Confederacy and is recorded in this volume. The loss of both brothers reflects the deep sacrifice made by the Cardwell family during the Civil War. Cardwell Line I - Predicted.

* * *

Thomas Addison Cardwell (1844-1863) - *Private - Company E, 1st Battalion (Stirman's), Arkansas Cavalry, CSA* - **Prisoner of War - Died in Service**

Thomas Addison Cardwell was born around 1844 in Washington

County, Arkansas. He was the son of William Harper Cardwell and Delaney (Gregg) Cardwell. He is listed in their household in both the 1850 and 1860 Washington County census records.[38,39]

At the age of 17, Thomas enlisted as a Private in Company E of the 1st Battalion Arkansas Cavalry (Stirman's), CSA, on 10 November 1861 in Fayetteville, Washington County, Arkansas. Stirman's Battalion was formed in the northwest part of the state and was stationed at Fayetteville through the winter of 1861–1862. In late February 1862, Union forces advanced into the area, forcing Confederate units, including Stirman's Battalion, to withdraw.

Thomas saw combat at the Battle of Pea Ridge in Benton County, Arkansas, on 07–08 March 1862, a key early engagement in the Trans-Mississippi Theater. Despite fighting with determination, Confederate forces were ultimately forced to retreat. After Pea Ridge, Stirman's Battalion was ordered across the Mississippi River to support operations in the Western Theater. There, the unit was dismounted and reorganized as Stirman's Sharpshooters— a specialized unit tasked with skirmishing and precision fire.

Thomas and his unit fought in the Battle of Corinth, Mississippi, in October 1862, where Confederate forces unsuccessfully attempted to recapture the strategic railroad hub. By mid-1863, Stirman's command was stationed at Vicksburg, Mississippi, a critical Confederate stronghold on the Mississippi River.

During the Siege of Vicksburg, Union forces encircled the city and subjected it to constant bombardment and starvation conditions. Thomas was captured when the city surrendered on 04 July 1863. He was paroled four days later, on 08 July 1863, after signing a pledge not to take up arms again against the United States. This was a common practice following mass surrenders, as the Union sought to reduce the burden of housing prisoners while discouraging Confederate re-enlistment.

Though his military records end with his parole, additional historical materials offer valuable insight into Thomas's experience. A collection of personal letters he wrote to his father during the war is preserved at the University of Arkansas in Fayetteville. These letters, dating from 1862 to 1863, were sent from various locations in Arkansas and Mississippi and offer firsthand accounts of his military life, thoughts on the conflict, and the hardships endured by Confederate soldiers prior to the fall of Vicksburg.[40]

Thomas Addison Cardwell died later that same month, in July 1863, in Van Buren, Crawford County, Arkansas. The cause of death is unknown but may have been the result of illness, wounds sustained during the siege, or complications from the conditions endured during his service. He was approximately 19 years old at the time of his death. Thomas is recorded on a list of men from his unit that were killed in action, died of disease, or were mortally wounded, but no detail is given.

He is buried at Stearns Cemetery in Fayetteville, Washington County, Arkansas.[41] His brief life and service are remembered through his correspondence and the sacrifice he made during one of the war's most pivotal campaigns. <u>Cardwell Line III - Predicted</u>.

* * *

Photo 2.5: *William John Cardwell (1842-1882) Headstone - Combs Cemetery, Fayetteville, Washington County, Arkansas.*

William John Cardwell (1842-1882) - *Private - Company K, 34th Arkansas Infantry (Brook's), CSA*

William John Cardwell, who appears to have gone by his middle name, was born around 1842 in Bedford County, Tennessee. He was the son of John B. Cardwell and Elizabeth (Taylor) Cardwell. By 1850, his family had relocated to Washington County, Arkansas, where William is listed in the census.

A decade later, he is recorded in the 1860 Benton County, Arkansas census, still residing with his parents.[42,43]

William enlisted as a Private in Company K of the 34th Arkansas Infantry (also known as Brooks' Regiment), CSA, on 17 June 1863 in Fayetteville, Washington County, Arkansas. His service records confirm that he was present with the unit from the time of his enlistment through at least 1864. No further Civil War records have been located for him, and the exact date of his discharge is unknown.

The 34th Arkansas Infantry was engaged in several key operations in the Trans-Mississippi Theater. Prior to William's enlistment, the regiment had already fought at the Battle of Pea Ridge in March 1862 in Benton County, Arkansas. After his enlistment, the unit participated in the Battle of Helena on 04 July 1863—a Confederate assault intended to relieve pressure on Vicksburg, though it ended in a costly defeat. The 34th also fought at the Battle of Jenkins' Ferry on 30 April 1864, a muddy and brutal engagement near the Saline River in central Arkansas.

Toward the end of the war, the 34th Arkansas Infantry was stationed at Marshall, Harrison County, Texas, where it remained until the spring of 1865. Upon hearing of General Robert E. Lee's surrender at Appomattox, the regiment was directed to report to Shreveport, Louisiana, for formal surrender. Instead, the men chose to return to Arkansas and officially surrendered at Fort Smith on 9 June 1865.

Although William John Cardwell's service records do not specifically place him in each of these battles, it is reasonable to assume that he participated in the regiment's movements and actions during his time with the 34th. The enlistment location and his continued presence on the rolls support this conclusion.

After the war, William returned to Washington County, Arkansas. He married a woman named Martha E. (surname unknown) before the 1870 census, in which they are listed together in that county. The couple is also recorded in the 1880 census for the same location. It appears that they did not have children.[44,45]

It is a logical and well-supported assumption that the "John Cardwell" who served in the 34th Arkansas Infantry is in fact William John Cardwell, son of John B. and Elizabeth Cardwell. This is based on geographic evidence, age, and the lack of any other "John Cardwell" of military age in the Fayetteville area during the period. Census records indicate that he was referred to as John, his middle name, rather than his first name, which made it more confusing to determine his proper lineage. Additionally, his cousin Thomas Addison Cardwell, who also lived in Washington County, served in the Confederacy and is profiled elsewhere in this volume.

William John Cardwell died on 18 November 1882 in Washington County, Arkansas. He is buried at Combs Cemetery in Fayetteville, Washington County, Arkansas.[46] <u>Cardwell Line III - Predicted</u>. Photo Credit[47]

* * *

Photo 2.6: *Alton POW Camp Confederate Cemetery Memorial. Alton, Madison County, Illinois.*

Photo 2.7: *William Thomas Dodson Cardwell (1842-1863) Memorial. Alton POW Camp Confederate Memorial. Alton, Madison County, Illinois.*

William Thomas Dobson Cardwell (1842-1863) - *Private - Company I, 37th Regiment, Arkansas Infantry, CSA* - Prisoner of War - Died in Captivity

William Thomas Dobson Cardwell was born on 99 June 1842 in McNairy County, Tennessee. He was the son of Hiram Clark Cardwell and Sarah (Saunders) Cardwell. Known to family and community as "Dobson," he is listed in the home of his parents in the 1850 McNairy County census. Sometime during the 1850s, the Cardwell family moved west to Columbia County, Arkansas. By 1860, Dobson is recorded living in the home of his father and stepmother in the Columbia County census.[48,49]

Dobson married Melinda Smith on 14 October 1860 in Hempstead County, Arkansas.[50] The marriage appears to have been brief, and there is no record of any children born to the couple.

On 20 May 1862, Dobson enlisted as a Private in Company I of the 37th Regiment, Arkansas Infantry, CSA, at Sulfur Springs in Benton County, Arkansas. His brother, Aaron Day Cardwell, enlisted alongside him on the same day. Dobson was 20 years old at the time and had traveled approximately 140 miles to the enlistment site—a significant journey that underscored his commitment to the Confederate cause.

His early service was marred by illness. On 30 June 1862, he was recorded as absent from duty while at a hospital in Little Rock, Pulaski County, Arkansas. Despite this setback, Dobson returned to active service and remained with the 37th Arkansas Infantry through the following year.

Dobson was captured during the Battle of Helena on 04 July 1863 in Phillips County, Arkansas. The Confederate attack on Helena was intended to relieve pressure on Vicksburg by diverting Union forces but ended in failure, with heavy casualties and numerous prisoners taken. Dobson was among those captured during the fierce fighting.

Following his capture, he was transferred to the Union Prisoner of War Camp at Alton, Madison County, Illinois, arriving there on 20 August 1863. The conditions at Alton were notoriously harsh, and the camp was plagued by outbreaks of disease—particularly smallpox. Tragically, Dobson contracted the disease and died on 30 August 1863, just ten days after his arrival.

Dobson was buried on Smallpox Island, a quarantine site located across the Mississippi River from the main Alton facility. His name is memorialized at the Confederate Cemetery in Alton, where a monument honors the more than 1,500 Confederate soldiers who died while imprisoned at the Alton POW Camp.[51]

William Thomas Dobson Cardwell was one of three sons of Hiram Clark Cardwell who served in the Confederacy. His brother Aaron survived the war, though wounded, while another brother, Admural Franklin Cardwell, also claimed service and is recorded in this volume. Dobson's brief but honorable service and ultimate sacrifice exemplify the hardship and tragedy endured by many Arkansas families during the Civil War. Cardwell Line I - Confirmed. Photo Credits[52,53]

Georgia
The Lone Cardwell Confederate

GEORGIA SECEDED FROM THE UNION ON JANUARY 19, 1861, BECOMING the fifth state to join the Confederacy. As one of the South's most populous and industrially developed states, it played a crucial role in supplying men, material, and strategic depth to the Confederate cause. Georgia's railroads, foundries, and fertile farmland made it a logistical artery for the Southern war effort, and by war's end, it had provided more than 120,000 troops to the Confederacy. Georgia's soldiers served across every major theater—from the Appalachian foothills to the trenches of Petersburg—and the state itself would become a battleground, most famously during General William T. Sherman's 1864 Atlanta Campaign and subsequent March to the Sea.

Georgia's military contribution to the Confederacy was vast, but only one known Cardwell man served in a Georgia-raised unit: Ansel F. Cardwell of Harris County. His story stands as both a personal narrative and a lens through which to view the wartime experience of many Georgia families. Enlisting in Company D of the 3rd Regiment, Georgia Cavalry, Ansel's service reflects the broader arc of citizen-soldiers from the state—men who were farmers, tradesmen, and fathers long before they became soldiers.

Though his is the only name among the Georgia Cardwells in Confederate service, Ansel F. Cardwell's story preserves a vital thread of the state's Civil War tapestry. His commitment, resilience, and postwar challenges offer a singular but meaningful example of how the conflict shaped not only soldiers but the generations that followed. The chapter that follows presents his biography in full, preserving his place in both Georgia's and the Cardwell family's shared history.

* * *

Ansel F. Cardwell (1821-1905) - *Private - Company D, 3rd Regiment, Georgia Cavalry, CSA*

Ansel F. Cardwell was born on 09 January 1821 in Harris County, Georgia. While his mother's name remains unknown, he is believed to be the son of Simon Cardwell, based on proximity to known relatives and early census records. In the 1840 census of Chambers County, Alabama, Ansel is found residing near his presumed brother, James Cardwell, further suggesting a familial link.[1]

On 16 January 1841, Ansel married Minerva J. Peacock in Chambers County, Alabama.[2] Their union produced a large family of twelve children: Frances E. California Cardwell (1841–1888), Matilda Ann "Tilda" Cardwell (1842–1923), Mary Louise Cardwell (1845–1917), Amanda B. Cardwell (1845–1924), Richard H. Cardwell (1849–1877), William R. Cardwell (1851–1883), James Alfred Cardwell (1852–1952), Magdalene Saphronia "Maggie" Cardwell (1856–1932), Minerva Jane Cardwell (1859–1944), Edward Erastus "Eddie" Cardwell (1861–1933), Sarah P. "Sallie" Cardwell (1862–1932), and Ada M. Cardwell (1864–1898).

The family made their home in Harris County, Georgia, where Ansel is listed in the 1860, 1870, 1880, and 1900 federal census records.[3,4,5,6]

During the Civil War, Ansel served in the Confederate Army, though few official service records survive to document the full scope of his military career. More information is preserved through his Confederate Pension application, filed in Harris County, Georgia, on 22 January 1896. According to that application, Ansel enlisted around April or May of 1862 in Whitesville, Harris County, Georgia, as a Private in Company D of the 3rd Regiment, Georgia Cavalry, CSA. He served as a substitute for another man, a common wartime practice in which one individual enlisted in place of another, often in exchange for payment.

Ansel reported that he served approximately ten months before he was "detailed"—not discharged—from regular field duty. It is important to note the distinction: a *discharge* means a soldier is formally released from military service, often due to the end of enlistment, disability, or other official cause. In contrast, a *detail* refers to a temporary reassignment from a soldier's primary unit to perform a specific duty, such as working in logistics, agriculture, manufacturing, or local defense. In Ansel's case, the detail likely removed him from active cavalry operations while still maintaining his enlistment status within the Confederate military structure.

The 3rd Georgia Cavalry was a regiment raised in 1862 that served in the Department of East Tennessee and Western Georgia. It participated in several skirmishes and campaigns aimed at resisting Union incursions across Georgia and Alabama. The regiment was involved in protecting supply routes, guarding flanks of larger Confederate columns, and conducting operations against Union cavalry raids throughout the region.

Ansel's exact role during this period is unclear due to his reassignment, but fellow soldier N.P. Weldon testified in Ansel's pension application that the two served together in the same unit, confirming Ansel's claim. Weldon's affidavit adds credibility to the service timeline, even if the specifics of Ansel's detail remain undocumented.

Following the war, Ansel returned to Harris County and resumed life as a farmer. Unfortunately, his later years were marked by significant physical hardship. Around 1889 or 1890, he suffered a severe spinal injury after being thrown from a buggy, rendering him largely unable to work. His pension application from 1896 describes his dire financial situation: he owned no property, had no income, and depended on the support of his grown children and charitable neighbors.

Despite his hardships, Ansel Cardwell remained a highly respected figure in his community. His obituary noted that he was "one of the oldest and best-known citizens of Harris County." He raised twelve children, all of whom were married at his home, and at the time of his death, he had 59 grandchildren and 30 great-grandchildren—an enduring testament to his role as a family patriarch.

Ansel F. Cardwell died on 22 November 1905 in Harris County, Georgia.[7] Though the precise location of his grave remains unknown, his memory lives on in the many descendants and local citizens who held him in high regard. His legacy is one of perseverance, family devotion, and service in both war and peace. Cardwell Line II - Predicted.

Kentucky
The Cardwell Confederates

ALTHOUGH OFFICIALLY NEUTRAL AT THE OUTSET OF THE CIVIL WAR, Kentucky became one of the most contested states in the Western Theater. While the Union maintained control of most of the state, many Kentuckians chose to fight for the Confederacy, particularly in the southern and central regions. Kentucky provided several notable cavalry and infantry regiments to the Confederate Army, with many of its soldiers participating in raids, skirmishes, and full-scale battles across Tennessee, Kentucky, and beyond.

Confederate raiders and cavalry units played a critical role in Kentucky's war effort, frequently disrupting Union supply lines, launching raids into occupied territory, and conducting guerrilla operations. Many of these cavalrymen served under famous Confederate leaders such as John Hunt Morgan and Nathan Bedford Forrest.

The Cardwell men from Kentucky served in some of the most mobile and aggressive units in the Confederate Army. Their involvement in cavalry raids, mounted infantry operations, and unconventional warfare reflected Kentucky's divided and tumultuous role in the Civil War.

This chapter honors the Cardwell soldiers of Kentucky, preserving their legacy as part of the state's complex Civil War history.

* * *

Charles T. Cardwell (1843–1865) **-** *Corporal – Company D, 4th Regiment, Kentucky Mounted Infantry, CSA* - **Wounded in Action - Prisoner of War**

Charles T. Cardwell was born around 1843 in Hopkins County, Kentucky, the son of John Cardwell and Mary Ann (Caranhan) Cardwell. He is listed with his family in both the 1850 and 1860 census records of Hopkins County, where he spent his early years.[1,2]

Charles enlisted as a Private in Company D of the 4th Regiment of Kentucky Mounted Infantry, CSA, on 14 September 1861 at Camp Burnett, located in Montgomery County, Tennessee. The 4th Kentucky Mounted Infantry, also referred to as part of the famed Orphan Brigade, served with distinction in the Army of Tennessee and was heavily involved in many of the major battles in the Western Theater.

In March 1863, Charles was admitted to a Confederate hospital in Tunnel Hill, Catoosa County, Georgia, for an unspecified illness or injury. However, he returned to his unit by late April 1863. He was later Wounded in Action (WIA) on 26 November 1863, during the fighting that followed the Battle of Chickamauga. While the main battle had occurred in September 1863, heavy fighting continued in the Chattanooga campaign as Union forces pressed the Confederates back into Georgia. It was during these engagements, particularly around Missionary Ridge and Tunnel Hill, that Charles sustained his wounds.

The 4th Kentucky Mounted Infantry continued to serve under General Joseph E. Johnston and later General John Bell Hood. By 06 May 1865, the remnants of the regiment surrendered to Union forces in Washington, Wilkes County, Georgia, in one of the final Confederate capitulations in the Western Theater.

Charles was taken as a Prisoner of War (POW) and on 21 May 1865, he swore the Oath of Allegiance to the United States government at Washington, Georgia. His POW record describes him as a resident of Hopkins County, Kentucky, with fair complexion, dark hair, blue eyes, and standing 5 feet 4 inches tall.

Following the war's conclusion, Charles apparently returned to Hopkins County, Kentucky, but his life was tragically cut short. He died prior to 10 November 1865, as he is listed as deceased in Hopkins County probate records on that date.[3] The exact cause of death is unknown, but it may have been related to lingering effects of his wounds or illness contracted during the war. The location of his grave is unknown.

His brother, George Stuart Cardwell, also served in the Confederacy and is documented elsewhere in this chapter. The service of both brothers reflects the commitment and sacrifice of many Kentucky families during the Civil War, especially those in border states with divided loyalties. Cardwell Line I - Predicted.

* * *

George H. Cardwell (1828–>1910) – *Private – Company A, 13th Regiment, Kentucky Cavalry, CSA* - **Prisoner of War**

George H. Cardwell was born around 1828 in Hopkins County, Kentucky, the son of James Rice Cardwell and Nancy (Egbert) Cardwell. He married Angeline W. Stone on 26 February 1848 in Hopkins County, and the couple is listed in the 1850 and 1860 Hopkins County, Kentucky census records.[4,5]

George enlisted as a Private in Company A, 13th Regiment, Kentucky Cavalry, CSA during the Civil War. Unfortunately, the Confederate service records for many Kentucky units are sparse, and his military history is pieced together from multiple sources, including the Confederate Compiled Military Service Records (CMSR) and the Kentucky Confederate Veteran Rolls compiled across 136 rolls of microfilm.[6] These records suggest that he may also have served briefly in the 10th Kentucky Cavalry, CSA, though his confirmed record is primarily with the 13th.

The 13th Kentucky Cavalry, often referred to as Caudill's Army, was involved in partisan operations across Kentucky and neighboring states. The unit specialized in guerrilla warfare, raiding, and disruption of Union supply lines. One of the regiment's more notable actions was at the Battle of Marion in December 1864, where they temporarily stalled Union forces in south-western Virginia. While there is no direct record linking George to this engagement, the timing of his capture shortly afterward suggests he may have participated in the campaign.

George was captured on 15 January 1865 in Marshall County, Alabama, a location not commonly associated with operations of the 13th Kentucky Cavalry. The circumstances of his presence there remain unclear, and it may indicate either a detachment with other Confederate forces or a withdrawal from eastern Kentucky after the Marion engagement.

Following his capture, George was transported to Louisville, Kentucky, arriving on 20 January 1865, and then forwarded to Camp Chase, a Union POW camp in Columbus, Ohio, on 25 January 1865. Prison records describe George as a resident of Hopkins County, 5 feet 9 inches tall, with dark hair and brown eyes. He was released on 25 March 1865, just weeks before the end of the war.

After the conflict, George returned to civilian life with his wife Angeline. Together, they had the following children: James A. Cardwell (1851–1891), John Cardwell (1855–), Amanda E. Cardwell (1858–1946), Mildred A. Cardwell (1859–1956), Georgiana Cardwell (1865–), Josephine "Josie" Cardwell (1869–1956), and Grace Belle Cardwell (1876–1943).

The family appears in the 1870 and 1880 census records of Hopkins County, Kentucky.[7,8] By 1900, George and Angeline were living in Christian County, Kentucky, in the home of their youngest daughter, Josie (Cardwell) Spencer.[9] In the 1910 census, they are listed again with Josie and her husband, this time in Montgomery County, Tennessee.

That 1910 record is the last known documentation of George H. Cardwell.[10] The date and place of his death and the location of his grave remain unknown. Despite the incomplete nature of his war record, George's capture and imprisonment reflect the hardships endured by Kentucky soldiers during a divided and brutal conflict. Cardwell Line I - Predicted.

* * *

Photo 4.1: *George Stuart Cardwell (1845-1929) Headstone - Cave Hill Cemetery, Louisville, Jefferson County, Kentucky.*

George Stuart Cardwell (1845–1929) – *Private – Company A, 10th Regiment, Kentucky Cavalry (Johnson's), CSA -* **Wounded in Action**

George Stuart Cardwell was born on 22 September 1845 in Hopkins County, Kentucky, the son of John Cardwell and Mary Ann (Caranhan) Cardwell. He appears in the household of his parents in both the 1850 and 1860 Hopkins County, Kentucky census records.[11,12]

Although his exact enlistment date and location remain unknown, George served as a Private with Company A of the 10th Regiment, Kentucky Cavalry, CSA. Known also as Johnson's Regiment or the 10th Kentucky Partisan Rangers, the unit operated primarily in Kentucky, Indiana, and Tennessee, conducting raids, ambushes, and guerrilla-style warfare behind Union lines. The regiment was led by the daring and unconventional Colonel Adam Rankin "Stovepipe" Johnson, whose nickname stemmed from a legendary early raid in which he deceived Union troops with stovepipes posed as cannon.

The 10th Kentucky Cavalry is best remembered for participating in General John Hunt Morgan's Great Raid in the summer of 1863, a bold incursion into Indiana and Ohio. On 19 July 1863, many of Morgan's raiders were captured at Pomeroy, Ohio, but Johnson and about 300 men escaped, crossing back into Confederate territory. Although George's name does not appear on the list of those captured, it is believed he was among the group that returned safely south.

According to his surviving Confederate records, George was Wounded in

Action (WIA) on 21 August 1864 during the Skirmish at Grubb's Cross Roads, located in Caldwell County, Kentucky. This encounter involved a surprise Confederate attack against a Union detachment camped near the crossroads. During the clash, General Adam Johnson was severely wounded, shot through the right eye by accidental friendly fire, leaving him permanently blinded. Following the incident, the unit retreated across the Cumberland and Tennessee Rivers into Paris, Tennessee to reorganize. George's wound was likely sustained during this chaotic engagement, but the extent of his injuries is not detailed in the records.

After the war, George returned to civilian life. He married Annie M. Hill on 24 February 1869 in Webster County, Kentucky.[13] The couple had one known child: Minnie Cardwell (1880–1953). George and his family are listed in the 1880 Webster County, Kentucky census, and later in 1910 and 1920 census records for Louisville, Jefferson County, Kentucky.[14,15,16]

George Stuart Cardwell died on 09 December 1929 in Louisville, Jefferson County, Kentucky, at the age of 84. He is buried at Cave Hill Cemetery, one of the most historic cemeteries in Kentucky, located in Louisville.[17] His brother, Charles T. Cardwell, also served in the Confederate Army and is documented in this volume. George's service with one of the most notable cavalry units in Kentucky's Confederate history, alongside the legendary "Stovepipe" Johnson, places him among the bold and resilient partisans who waged an unconventional war in defense of their cause. Cardwell Line I - Predicted. Photo Credit[18]

* * *

Photo 4.2: *James Jesse Cardwell (1840-1892) Headstone - Grove Hill Cemetery, Shelbyville, Shelby County, Kentucky.*

James Jesse Cardwell (1840–1892) - *Corporal – Company C, 8th Regiment, Kentucky Cavalry, CSA* - **Wounded in Action - Prisoner of War**

James Jesse Cardwell was born on 18 September 1840 in Shelby County, Kentucky, the son of George N. Cardwell and Elizabeth (Threlkeld) Cardwell. He appears in their household in the 1850 and 1860 Shelby County, Kentucky census records.[19,20] James enlisted alongside his younger brother, Thomas Logan Cardwell, as a Private in Company C, 8th Regiment, Kentucky Cavalry, CSA, on 10 September 1862 in their native Shelby County.

The 8th Kentucky Cavalry, organized in 1862, became part of General John Hunt Morgan's famed cavalry command. In the summer of 1863, Morgan launched a daring raid through Kentucky, Indiana, and Ohio with over 2,500 cavalrymen. The raid aimed to disrupt Union supply lines and communication while drawing attention and troops away from key Union operations at Gettysburg and Vicksburg.

James and his brother likely took part in the Battle of Corydon, fought on 09 July 1863 in Harrison County, Indiana, where Morgan's cavalry briefly overwhelmed local militia. The raid continued deep into Union territory, but Morgan's force was relentlessly pursued and eventually scattered or captured.

James was captured on 20 July 1863 at Wheeling, Ohio, just east of the panhandle of West Virginia. His brother Thomas managed to evade capture for a few more days before being taken at the Battle of Salineville on 26 July 1863 in Columbiana County, Ohio.

Following his capture, James was transferred to Fort McHenry in Maryland on 08 October 1863, and shortly thereafter to Point Lookout POW Camp, arriving there on 01 November 1863. Point Lookout, located on the Chesapeake Bay, was one of the largest Union prison camps, known for its harsh conditions and overcrowding. One of his records indicates that James had been wounded prior to being sent to Baltimore on 07 October 1863, though the details of his injury are not recorded.

James remained imprisoned until 10 February 1865, when he was paroled from Point Lookout. There are no additional Confederate service records for him after that date, and it is unknown whether he returned to active service before the end of the war.

After the conflict, James relocated westward. He married Margaret "Maggie" (LNU) prior to the 1870 census, and the couple settled in St. Joseph, Buchanan County, Missouri, where they are recorded in the census for that year. They appear to have had no children. By 1880, James and Margaret had moved to Nemaha County, Kansas, where they are listed in that decade's census, residing in the town of Wetmore.[21,22]

James Jesse Cardwell died on 08 October 1892 in Wetmore, Nemaha County, Kansas. His remains were transported back to his native Kentucky and interred with his family at Grove Hill Cemetery, Shelbyville, Shelby County, Kentucky.[23] His brother Thomas Logan Cardwell, also a Confederate veteran of Morgan's Cavalry, is documented elsewhere in this volume. James's service, especially during one of the most daring cavalry raids of the Civil War, speaks to his courage and endurance under extreme conditions of hardship, imprisonment, and battlefield danger. Cardwell Line I - Predicted. Photo Credit[24]

* * *

James Madison Cardwell (1841–1864) – *Sergeant – Company E, 1st Regiment, Morgan's Cavalry, CSA & 2nd Regiment, Kentucky Cavalry (Duke's), CSA* - **Killed in Action**

James Madison Cardwell was born on 03 December 1841 in Mercer County, Kentucky, the son of John Wesley Cardwell and Sophia Bledsoe

(Taylor) Cardwell. He is listed in their household in the 1850 and 1860 Mercer County census records.[25,26]

James's first recorded involvement in the Civil War came in the spring of 1862. Evidence shows that he was captured by Union forces at Harrodsburg, Mercer County, Kentucky, and transferred to Camp Chase Prison in Ohio on 24 May 1862. His prison record notes that he was twenty years old but lists him only as a "citizen," with no military rank provided. This detail is significant: members of Morgan's Cavalry were known to conduct reconnaissance and covert operations while dressed in civilian attire, a risky practice that, if discovered, could lead to swift execution as a spy. Although not yet officially enlisted in Morgan's Cavalry at the time of his capture, James was likely assisting Morgan's men in securing horses, supplies, or intelligence, and appears to have successfully concealed any connection to Confederate military operations when questioned by Union authorities.

He was released from Camp Chase on 18 June 1862 by order of Union General Jeremiah T. Boyle. The reason for his release is unstated, and notably, there is no record of him having taken the Oath of Allegiance, which was a common condition for Confederate prisoners being paroled. His survival under such circumstances suggests he had a convincing cover story and was fortunate to avoid a far graver fate.

Following his release, James officially enlisted, along with his younger brother, Thomas Mumford Cardwell, as Privates in Company E of the 1st Regiment of Morgan's Cavalry, Confederate States Army, on 01 October 1862 at Lexington, Kentucky. The 1st Kentucky Cavalry, under the famed General John Hunt Morgan, was later redesignated as the 2nd Kentucky Cavalry, CSA. James's brother, Thomas, was discharged on 30 December 1862 due to disability, and he did not return to active service. James, however, remained in the ranks.

James Madison Cardwell's service with Morgan's Cavalry was defined by daring raids and dangerous missions. He participated in General Morgan's audacious 1863 raid through Indiana and Ohio, designed to divert Union forces from Tennessee and to damage Northern morale. While many of Morgan's men, including Morgan himself, were captured during the raid, there is no record of James being among the prisoners. He successfully evaded capture and made his way back to Confederate lines. A report dated August 31, 1863, noted that a portion of Morgan's division managed to evade capture by escaping through what was then "West" Virginia, eventually making their way on foot to Georgia. This group, led by Captain J. D. Kirkpatrick of Company C, 9th Tennessee Cavalry, was subsequently reassigned to serve under General Nathan Bedford Forrest.[27]

After Morgan's escape from Union imprisonment in November 1863, the 2nd Kentucky Cavalry was transferred to the command of General Nathan Bedford Forrest, one of the Confederacy's most aggressive and resourceful cavalry leaders. Under Forrest, the regiment fought in numerous battles, including the pivotal Battle of Chickamauga in September 1863. There, the 2nd Kentucky Cavalry is credited with firing both the first and last shots of the engagement—a rare Confederate victory in the Western Theater, though one that came at a staggering cost in lives.

Although the exact date of his promotion is unknown, James eventually rose to the rank of Sergeant, a testament to his reliability and leadership under the severe demands of wartime cavalry service.

James's final battle came during the Battle of Bull's Gap, fought from 11 to 14 November 1864 across Hamblen and Greene Counties, Tennessee. This battle was part of a broader Confederate effort to disrupt Union control of East Tennessee, a region vital for its railroads and strong Unionist sympathies. By this time, the Confederate cavalry, including the 2nd Kentucky, was operating under extreme hardship, with dwindling supplies and the recent loss of General Morgan, who had been killed in Greeneville, Tennessee, just weeks earlier.

On 13 November 1864, during the fighting at Bull's Gap, Sergeant James Madison Cardwell was Killed in Action. The exact circumstances surrounding his death are unknown, and no burial record has been located. It is likely that he was interred near the battlefield, possibly in an unmarked grave, as was common for soldiers who fell in the rugged, chaotic fighting in East Tennessee.

James was part of a large contingent of Cardwell family members who served with Morgan's Cavalry. In addition to James and his brother Thomas, relatives James Jesse Cardwell, Thomas Logan Cardwell, John Ray Cardwell, and George H. Cardwell also served with Morgan or associated Confederate cavalry commands in Kentucky. Other Cardwell men from Tennessee likewise served under General Morgan, and their biographies are included in the Tennessee Confederate Veterans chapter of this series. Collectively, they reflect the deep familial, regional, and personal bonds that defined much of

Confederate service, particularly within Kentucky's embattled borders. <u>Cardwell Line I - Predicted</u>.

* * *

Photo 4.3: *John Ray Cardwell (1834-1904) Headstone - Browder's Hutch Cemetery, Hopkins County, Kentucky.*

John Ray Cardwell (1834–1904) - *Private – Company H, 6th Regiment, Kentucky Mounted Infantry, CSA -* **Prisoner of War**

John Ray Cardwell was born on 24 August 1834 in Hopkins County, Kentucky. He was the son of James Rice Cardwell and Nancy (Egbert) Cardwell. He appears in their household in the 1850 Hopkins County census.[28]

On 18 January 1857, John married Virginia E. Baugh in Hopkins County.[29] The couple had at least two known children: Mary B. Cardwell (1857–1896) and Daniel John "Jack" Cardwell (1860–). John and his family are recorded in the 1870, 1880, and 1900 census records for Hopkins County, Kentucky.[30,31,32]

John enlisted as a Private in Company H, 6th Regiment of Kentucky Mounted Infantry, CSA, on 16 July 1861 at Camp Boone, Montgomery County, Tennessee. Although his Civil War records are sparse, they confirm his capture during the conflict and subsequent imprisonment as a Confederate Prisoner of War (POW).

According to surviving documents, John was captured on 19 July 1863 at Buffington Island, a key event during General John Hunt Morgan's cavalry raid into Indiana and Ohio. This massive Confederate incursion was designed to disrupt Union operations and draw forces away from major campaigns further south. John's capture places him among the many men who attempted to follow Morgan across the Ohio River during the chaotic retreat. At the Battle of Buffington Island, which took place in Meigs County, Ohio, and Jackson County, West Virginia, Union forces overwhelmed Morgan's force as they tried to cross the river. More than half of Morgan's 1,900-man cavalry was captured. Although General Morgan and roughly 700 men escaped that day, they were later overtaken and captured at Salineville.

John was one of the many Confederate soldiers taken prisoner at Buffington Island. He was initially sent to Camp Douglas, near Chicago, Illinois—a Union POW facility notorious for its harsh conditions and high mortality rate. Roughly 17 percent of the men held at Camp Douglas died during confinement, with over 4,000 buried in a mass grave at Oak Woods Cemetery. Fortunately, John did not remain there long. He was transferred to Camp Morton, located in Indianapolis, Indiana. His name no longer appears in surviving records following that point, and no further Civil War documentation has been located for him.

It is a logical and well-supported assumption that John Ray Cardwell is the "John R. Cardwell" found in the compiled Confederate service records of the 4th Kentucky Cavalry. Several men named John Cardwell appear in the Kentucky Confederate files, often with no middle initial or inconsistent data. However, the personal information, enlistment location, and timing align most closely with John Ray Cardwell, son of James Rice and Nancy (Egbert) Cardwell.

John returned to civilian life after the war and remained in Hopkins County for the remainder of his days. He died on 23 April 1904 in Madisonville, Hopkins County, Kentucky. He is buried at Browder's Church Cemetery in the same county.[33] His older brother, George H. Cardwell, also served in the Confederate military, and his biography is included elsewhere in this chapter. Cardwell Line I - Predicted. Photo Credit[34]

* * *

Photo 4.4: *John Thomas Cardwell (1845-1913) Headstone - Cedar Grove Cemetery, Cedar Grove, Bullitt County, Kentucky.*

John Thomas Cardwell (1845–1913) - *Private – Company E, 4th Regiment, Kentucky Mounted Infantry, CSA*

John Thomas Cardwell was born on 22 February 1845 in Franklin County, Kentucky. He was the son of William Cardwell and Caroline Matilda (McQueen) Cardwell. He appears in the household of his parents in the 1850 and 1860 census records of Franklin County.[35,36]

John enlisted as a Private with Company E of the 4th Regiment, Kentucky Mounted Infantry, CSA, on 07 October 1861 at Bowling Green,

Warren County, Kentucky. He is listed as Present on the company rolls until October 1864, though no additional service records have been located.

The 4th Kentucky Mounted Infantry was an adaptable regiment that functioned in both cavalry and infantry roles, depending on the needs of the Confederate command. The regiment participated in General Braxton Bragg's 1862 Kentucky Campaign and fought at the Battle of Perryville. It later took part in numerous operations in Tennessee and Georgia, where it played a supporting role in delaying Union advances and covering Confederate withdrawals. Although John's service records are limited, it is reasonable to assume he was involved in some of these engagements, given the documented activities of his regiment and the length of his service.

It should be noted that while this soldier is listed as "John T. Cardwell" in the Kentucky Civil War records, no other Cardwell men with that name or age from Kentucky are known to have served. Although John enlisted in Warren County—a fair distance from his home in Franklin County—such travel to enlistment sites was not uncommon during the war, particularly in border states like Kentucky. The circumstantial evidence strongly supports that this John T. Cardwell is the son of William and Caroline Matilda Cardwell.

After the war, John returned to civilian life. He is listed as a single farm laborer in the 1870 Franklin County census, living in the household of Letteria Jett.[37] Around 1874, he married Ellen Kirk. They had the following children: Mattie P. Cardwell (1877–), Lettie J. Cardwell (1879–1947), Lula B. Cardwell (1882–), William Lindsay Cardwell (1885–1947), Ester Leonora Cardwell (1888–), and Elgar Cardwell (1891–). The family is recorded in the 1880 census for Franklin County and later in the 1900 and 1910 census records for Louisville, Jefferson County, Kentucky.[38,39,40]

John died on 20 March 1913 in Bullitt County, Kentucky. He was buried at Cedar Grove Cemetery in Cedar Grove, Bullitt County.[41] Interestingly, he is the only Cardwell buried in that cemetery and is not known to be connected to the larger Cardwell family of the area. However, his Kentucky death certificate confirms his parentage as William Cardwell and Caroline Matilda (McQueen) Cardwell, affirming his identity and familial ties. Cardwell Line IV - Predicted. Photo Credit[42]

* * *

Photo 4.5: *PVT Thomas Logan Cardwell (1843-1920) - Camp Douglas, Illinois - 1863*

Photo 4.6: *Thomas Logan Cardwell (1843-1920) - Grove Hill Cemetery, Shelbyville, Shelby County, Kentucky*

Thomas Logan Cardwell (1843–1920) - *Private – Company C, 8th Regiment, Kentucky Cavalry, CSA & Company C, 2nd Regiment, Kentucky Cavalry (Duke's), CSA* - **Prisoner of War**

Thomas Logan Cardwell was born on 22 January 1843 in Shelby County, Kentucky. He was the son of George N. Cardwell and Elizabeth (Threlkeld) Cardwell. He appears in the home of his parents in the 1850 and 1860 Shelby County census records.[43,44]

On 10 September 1862, Thomas enlisted as a Private in Company C of the 8th Regiment, Kentucky Cavalry, CSA, alongside his older brother, James

Jesse Cardwell. Their unit was part of the famed Confederate General John Hunt Morgan's Cavalry, and both brothers participated in Morgan's 1863 Raid through Kentucky, Indiana, and Ohio. This campaign, conducted during June and July 1863, aimed to divert Union troops by creating panic in the North. The raid coincided with the Union victories at Gettysburg and Vicksburg and was intended to relieve pressure on Confederate forces in the South.

Additional research has revealed that Thomas Logan Cardwell was transferred to Company C of the 2nd Regiment Kentucky Cavalry (Duke's) prior to or during Morgan's Raid in the summer of 1863. His service records are incorrectly indexed under the initials "F.L. Cardwell," a clerical error that likely confused later researchers. Despite the misrecorded initial, the details of these records—specifically his date and location of capture, as well as his subsequent imprisonment at Camp Chase and later Camp Douglas—align perfectly with the known facts of Thomas L. Cardwell's military service.

Extensive research into Confederate service rolls and census records has failed to locate any Cardwell man bearing the initials "F.L." during the Civil War period, further reinforcing that the records in question pertain to Thomas Logan Cardwell. This evidence, though circumstantial, provides strong support for properly attributing the service history to him.

Thomas likely fought in the Battle of Corydon on 09 July 1863 in Harrison County, Indiana, one of the few Civil War engagements fought on Indiana soil. Morgan's cavalry, numbering around 2,500 men, was relentlessly pursued by Union forces through Indiana and Ohio. On 26 July 1863, Thomas was captured at the Battle of Salineville in Columbiana County, Ohio. His brother, James, had been taken prisoner six days earlier near Wheeling, Ohio.

Following his capture, Thomas was sent to Camp Douglas in Chicago, Illinois—a Union POW camp notorious for its overcrowding and harsh conditions, on 22 August 1863. On 10 February 1865, he was transferred to Point Lookout, Maryland, another major Union prison facility. He was released as part of a prisoner exchange and paroled on 24 February 1865.

Later that same year, on 26 April 1865, Thomas was captured a second time near Knoxville, Tennessee, likely while attempting to rejoin his command or return home through contested territory. He was transferred to a Federal holding facility in Chattanooga on 06 May and then taken to Nashville, Tennessee, where he took the Oath of Allegiance to the United States on 11 May 1865. His POW release documents describe him as a resident of

Shelby County, Kentucky, standing six feet tall, with a dark complexion, dark hair, and hazel eyes.

After the war, Thomas returned to civilian life in Kentucky. Around 1873, he married Sultana Saunders, based on the birth year of their first child. They had the following children: George Duke Cardwell (1874–1955), Wade Hampton Cardwell (1875–1952), Lillie Cardwell (1886–1888), Laura Thomas Cardwell (1886–1976), and Lutie Vera Cardwell (1890–1975). The family is listed in the 1870, 1880, and 1900 Shelby County census records. By 1910, they had relocated to Jefferson County, where they appear again in the 1920 census.[45,46,47,48,49]

Thomas Logan Cardwell died on 22 January 1920 in Jefferson County, Kentucky. He is buried at Grove Hill Cemetery in Shelbyville, Shelby County, Kentucky.[50] His older brother, James Jesse Cardwell, who also served in Morgan's command, is likewise buried there. Both brothers were part of the broader network of Cardwell men who rode with Morgan during the war, many of whom are included in this volume. Cardwell Line I - Predicted. Photo Credits[51,52]

* * *

Photo 4.7: *Thomas Mumford Cardwell (1846-1915) Headstone - Spring Hill Cemetery, Harrodsburg, Mercer County, Kentucky.*

Thomas Mumford Cardwell (1846-1915) - Private - *Company E, 1st Regiment, Morgan's Cavalry, CSA & 2nd Regiment, Kentucky Cavalry (Duke's), CSA*

Thomas Mumford Cardwell was born on 22 March 1846 in Mercer County, Kentucky. He was the son of John Wesley Cardwell and Sophia Bledsoe (Taylor) Cardwell. He appears in the home of his parents in the 1850 and 1860 Mercer County, Kentucky census records.[53,54] He was one of two brothers who served the Confederacy, enlisting alongside his older brother, James Madison Cardwell.

On 01 October 1862, at the age of 16, Thomas enlisted as a Private in Company E of the 1st Regiment, Morgan's Cavalry, CSA, at Lexington, Kentucky. The 1st Morgan's Cavalry would later become the 2nd Regiment of Kentucky Cavalry, and most wartime records reflect this later designation. The regiment operated under the command of General John Hunt Morgan and was known for its daring raids behind Union lines throughout Kentucky, Tennessee, and into Indiana and Ohio.

However, Thomas's service was short-lived. He was discharged for disability on 30 December 1862, only three months after his enlistment. The nature of his disability was not specified in the available records, and no further military service has been documented for him. Due to his early discharge, he did not participate in the 1863 Morgan's Raid or other notable engagements of the unit. His brother James, who remained with the regiment, was later killed in action in 1864 and is recorded separately in this volume.

Thomas returned to civilian life and married Nannie J. Waggoner on 22 September 1864 in Mercer County, Kentucky.[55] The couple does not appear to have had any children. Thomas is listed in the 1870, 1880, 1900, and 1910 census records for Mercer County.[56,57,58,59] By 1900, he was noted as divorced, and on 24 October 1901, he married Katherine "Kittie" Hanna. She is listed with him in the 1910 Mercer County census.[60]

Later in life, Thomas became active in public service. According to his obituary, *"As a mere boy he enlisted in the Confederate army and served in General Morgan's command, and the Lost Cause was always near to his heart."* He went on to hold several public offices, including Postmaster of Harrodsburg, Police Judge for multiple terms, United States Indian Agent at White Rocks, Utah, and Assistant State Fire Marshal under Governor Wilson's administration. These roles highlight the continued civic engagement of many former Confederate veterans in postwar Kentucky society.[61]

Thomas Mumford Cardwell died on 26 August 1915 in Mercer County, Kentucky. He is buried at Spring Hill Cemetery in Harrodsburg, Mercer County, Kentucky.[62] His brother, James Madison Cardwell, who also served in Morgan's Cavalry and was killed in action in 1864, is likewise included in this chapter. Cardwell Line I - Predicted. Photo Credit[63]

Louisiana
The Cardwell Confederates

Louisiana was a crucial Confederate state due to its control of the Mississippi River and the port of New Orleans, one of the largest commercial hubs in the South. The Union's capture of New Orleans in 1862 was a major blow to the Confederacy, forcing Louisiana's remaining forces to retreat into the interior and continue the fight in the Western Theater. Louisiana troops played vital roles in major battles such as Shiloh, Vicksburg, and the Red River Campaign. The Cardwell men from Louisiana served in multiple units that contributed to key battles and defensive efforts across the state and beyond.

The Cardwell men from Louisiana served in critical roles across the Confederate war effort, from manning artillery batteries along the Mississippi River to engaging in the bloody campaigns of Virginia. Their service contributed to the broader struggle to defend the Confederacy, even as Louisiana itself fell under Union control early in the war.

This chapter honors the Cardwell soldiers of Louisiana, ensuring their service and sacrifices remain part of the historical record of the Civil War.

* * *

Henry Charles Cardwell (1834–) - *Ordnance Sergeant – 30th Regiment, Louisiana Infantry (Sumter Regiment), CSA*

Henry Charles Cardwell is recorded in Confederate military documents as serving as an Ordnance Sergeant with the 30th Regiment of Louisiana Infantry, commonly known as the Sumter Regiment. However, there is only a single Civil War record placing him in this unit, and the documentation lacks additional service details.

There are no known pre- or post-war Louisiana census listings for a Henry C. Cardwell, which raises questions about his connection to the state. A likely explanation comes from a matching individual found among Alabama Confederate veterans: Henry Charles Cardwell, born about 1834 in Charlotte County, Virginia, who served as an Ordnance Sergeant in the 2nd Battalion of Alabama Light Artillery, CSA.

This Alabama-based Henry Charles Cardwell's rank and military specialty—Ordnance Sergeant—strongly align with the Louisiana record, suggesting they are the same man. The two units—the 30th Louisiana Infantry and the 2nd Alabama Light Artillery—were both engaged at the Battle of Spanish Fort, Alabama, in March and April of 1865, during the closing months of the war. While no definitive documentation exists showing joint operations or transfers between these units, the overlapping service locations and the uncommon rank add weight to the identification.

Given the absence of other plausible candidates named Henry C. Cardwell in Louisiana records, and the presence of a confirmed Henry Charles Cardwell with matching rank and timeline in Alabama service, it is reasonable to conclude that the Louisiana reference is a clerical duplication or misattribution of the Alabama veteran.

His full biography is included under the Alabama Cardwell Confederate Veterans section of this volume.

* * *

John H. Cardwell (1834–) - *Private – Company B, 13th Regiment, Louisiana Partisan Rangers, CSA*

John H. Cardwell was born about 1834 in Charlotte County, Virginia, the son of Francis Flippin Cardwell and Edna "Edney" J. (Haskins) Cardwell. His early life was spent in rural Virginia, and he appears in the 1850 census of Charlotte County, living in the household of his mother along with his siblings.[1] His father, Francis, had traveled west during the Gold Rush era but eventually returned to Virginia, a spirit of adventure that may have also influenced John.

At some point before the Civil War, John moved to Louisiana, possibly seeking opportunity as a skilled tradesman. By 1860, he was living in Concordia Parish, listed in the census as a Machinist and Engineer, indicating technical expertise and training uncommon among rural residents of the time. His move south and occupation suggest he was part of the growing pre-war industrial and mechanical workforce along the Mississippi River.[2]

When war broke out, John joined the Confederate cause. The only surviving military record shows that he enlisted as a Private on 04 October 1862 in Company B of the 13th Regiment, Louisiana Partisan Rangers, CSA, at Providence, located in East Carroll Parish, Louisiana. This unit, also referred to as the 13th Louisiana Cavalry Battalion, was a mounted force raised primarily for regional defense, reconnaissance, and guerrilla-style warfare.

The 13th Louisiana Partisan Rangers were active in northeast Louisiana, a vital area along the Mississippi River. Their operations were generally small in scale—ambushes, raids, and skirmishes aimed at disrupting Union supply lines and movements. These partisan units often worked in tandem with local militias and regular Confederate cavalry, performing critical delaying actions and maintaining Confederate presence in contested territory.

By the winter of 1863–1864, due to manpower shortages and organizational challenges, the battalion was consolidated into Pargoud's 3rd Louisiana Cavalry Regiment. This larger force continued to operate in northern Louisiana and parts of Mississippi, occasionally clashing with Union patrols and cavalry during the later stages of the Red River Campaign and other efforts to disrupt Federal advances.

Unfortunately, no further Civil War records have been found for John H. Cardwell in either the 13th Louisiana Partisan Rangers or the 3rd Louisiana Cavalry. The absence of additional muster rolls, casualty lists, or parole records suggests that John may have been killed in action, died of illness, or otherwise disappeared from formal recordkeeping—an all-too-common fate in the chaotic conditions of irregular Confederate cavalry service in the Deep South.

No postwar records or census entries have been located for John, and the year and place of his death remain unknown. It is possible that he did not survive the war, or if he did, that he lived quietly and passed away without leaving further public trace.

Despite the limited documentation, John H. Cardwell's Confederate service is recorded here in recognition of his enlistment, family connections, and commitment to the Southern cause. His name stands among those of his brothers and cousins from Virginia and Alabama who served with distinction during the Civil War. <u>Cardwell Line I - Predicted.</u>

* * *

James Stanton Cardwell (1844–1862) - *Private – Company A, 9th Regiment, Louisiana Infantry, CSA* - **Mortally Wounded in Action**

James Stanton Cardwell was born about 1844 in McNairy County, Tennessee, the son of James Cardwell and Lucy L. Kendrick. In the 1850 census of McNairy County, he appears listed under his middle name in the household of his parents.[3] Sometime before the Civil War, his father and uncle, Pryor Lewis Cardwell, moved from Tennessee to Claiborne Parish, Louisiana, though James' father does not appear in the 1860 census. His uncle Pryor is listed in that year's Claiborne Parish census and is also recorded in this volume as a Confederate veteran.

James enlisted as a Private in Company A, 9th Regiment, Louisiana Infantry, CSA, on 07 July 1861, at Homer, Claiborne Parish, Louisiana. He was 18 years old, single, and listed his occupation as farmer and his residence as Homer.

The 9th Louisiana Infantry was a hard-fighting unit that became part of the famed Army of Northern Virginia under General Robert E. Lee. It took part in several of the war's most grueling engagements in the Eastern Theater. Known for its fierce determination and discipline, the regiment suffered heavy losses throughout the conflict. James's Civil War records place him in active service during three critical early battles: the Battle of Winchester (25 May 1862), the Battle of Port Republic (09 June 1862), and the Battle of Malvern Hill (01 July 1862). It was during the latter engagement—part of the Seven Days Battles near Richmond, Virginia—that James was Wounded in Action (WIA).

Following his injury at Malvern Hill, James was transported to a Confederate hospital in Richmond, Virginia. Records confirm that he died from the wounds sustained in battle, although the exact date of his death is not recorded. It is believed that he passed away sometime in July 1862, likely within days or weeks of his injury.

The location of his grave is unknown, though it is probable that he was buried in or near Richmond, possibly in one of the mass graves associated with the city's wartime hospitals. His death was one of thousands suffered during the Seven Days Battles, a costly but pivotal campaign that marked the end of Union General George B. McClellan's Peninsula Campaign.

James Stanton Cardwell's brief service and untimely death are a somber reflection of the high price paid by so many young soldiers during the war. His sacrifice, though largely undocumented beyond enlistment and his wound, remains remembered in this historical record. Cardwell Line I - Predicted.

* * *

Photo 5.1: *Pryor Lewis Cardwell (1831-1903) Headstone - Elizabeth Cemetery, Denton County, Texas.*

Pryor Lewis Cardwell (1831–1903) **-** *Private – Company E, 1st Louisiana Heavy Artillery, CSA* - **Wounded in Action - Prisoner of War**

Pryor Lewis Cardwell was born on 31 January 1831 in Tennessee, the son of William Cardwell and Celia (Harper) Cardwell. He is recorded in their household in the 1850 census of McNairy County, Tennessee.[4]

Around 1855, Pryor married Martha A. Thompson, though a record of their marriage has not been located. They had the following children: William Nathaniel T. Cardwell (1856–1925), Mary "Mattie" Cardwell (1861–), Pryor Lewis Cardwell Jr. (1864–1906), George Edwin Cardwell (1865–1938), Abe Leroy Cardwell (1868–), Charles Cooper Cardwell (1871–1950), and Robert W. Cardwell (1874–1911).

The family is found in Claiborne Parish, Louisiana in the 1860 census, prior to the war. After the war, they relocated to Texas and appear in Grayson County (1870) and Denton County in both the 1880 and 1900 census records.[5,6,7,8]

Pryor enlisted as a Private with Company E of the 1st Louisiana Heavy Artillery, CSA, on 2 August 1862, in Claiborne Parish, Louisiana. The 1st Louisiana Heavy Artillery played a crucial role in the defense of Confederate positions along the Mississippi River, especially in New Orleans and Vicksburg. The regiment was responsible for manning large artillery guns that protected river crossings and supply routes from Union naval incursions.

When New Orleans fell to Union forces in April 1862, Confederate forces, including many artillery units like Pryor's, were either captured, scattered, or reassigned. Pryor's records suggest that he was transferred to Vicksburg, Mississippi, where Confederate resistance stiffened in defense of the last major Confederate stronghold on the Mississippi River.

Pryor was captured on 04 July 1863, when Vicksburg surrendered to General Ulysses S. Grant after a prolonged siege. He was paroled and took the Oath of Allegiance to the United States on 08 July 1863 at Vicksburg. His records afterward note him as "absent without leave – went to Louisiana after capture of Vicksburg." This absence may have been temporary or related to his reassignment.

Though not definitively confirmed, there is a possibility that Pryor continued to serve after his parole, possibly with his brothers in one of General Nathan Bedford Forrest's Cavalry units. One military hospital record from Mississippi lists a "P. Cardwell" as Wounded in Action (WIA) at the Battle of Tupelo on 13 July 1864, where Forrest's forces clashed with Union troops in a failed attempt to disrupt Sherman's supply lines. Due to the common name and sparse details, this match is tentative but plausible.

After the war, Pryor returned to civilian life, eventually settling in Denton County, Texas. He lived out his remaining years with his family and continued to be known as a veteran of the Confederacy.

Pryor Lewis Cardwell died on 25 June 1903 in Denton County, Texas. He is buried at Elizabeth Cemetery, in Roanoke, Denton County, Texas.[9] His service in defense of the South, both in artillery and possibly later in cavalry, is remembered through his descendants and this historical record. <u>Cardwell Line I - Predicted</u>. Photo Credit[10]

Mississippi
The Cardwell Confederates

Mᴉssɪssɪᴘᴘɪ ᴡᴀs ᴀᴛ ᴛʜᴇ ʜᴇᴀʀᴛ ᴏғ ᴛʜᴇ Cᴏɴғᴇᴅᴇʀᴀᴄʏ ᴀɴᴅ sᴀᴡ sᴏᴍᴇ ᴏғ the most intense fighting of the Civil War. The state was crucial due to its location along the Mississippi River, a strategic artery for supplies and troop movements. The fall of Vicksburg in 1863 was a turning point in the war, splitting the Confederacy in two and securing Union control of the river. Mississippi's soldiers played a vital role in defending their home state and fighting in campaigns across the Western Theater.

The Cardwell men from Mississippi fought in some of the war's most pivotal battles, serving in regiments that defended the Confederacy's heartland. Their service took them from the trenches of Vicksburg to the bloody fields of Gettysburg and the final desperate battles in the Western Theater. Many endured hardships beyond the battlefield, facing starvation, disease, and long marches before the Confederacy's ultimate defeat.

This chapter honors the Cardwell soldiers of Mississippi, ensuring that their contributions and sacrifices are remembered as part of the Cardwell Family history.

* * *

Benjamin M. Cardwell (1820-1910) - *2nd Sergeant - Company K, 24th Regiment, Alabama Infantry, CSA & Company I, 44th Regiment, Mississippi Infantry, CSA -* **Wounded in Action**

See his full biography in the Alabama Cardwell Confederate Veterans section of this volume.

* * *

George W. Cardwell (1837–1876) - *Private – Company A, 11th Regiment, Mississippi Infantry, CSA*

George W. Cardwell was born around 1837 in Smith County, Tennessee. He is believed to be the son of Vernoll Loyd Cardwell and Frances (Cardwell) Cardwell, though this connection remains uncertain. There is a possibility that George may instead have been the son of James Henry Cardwell and Clarissa (Graves) Cardwell of Cardwell Line I, whose son disappears from records after the 1850 Washington County, Virginia census. A definitive answer likely rests in future participation of living descendants in the Cardwell Family DNA Project.

George married Naomi L. Strawhorn on 27 October 1858 in Lafayette County, Mississippi.[1] Together they had the following children: Joseph Henry "Joe" Cardwell (1860–1941), Thomas Milton Cardwell (1863–1890), William A. Cardwell (1866–1884), Linda H. Cardwell (1868–1948), Margaret "Maggie" Cardwell (1871–), George Dudley Cardwell (1873–1927), and Stonewall Jackson Cardwell (1877–1928). The family is recorded in the 1860 and 1870 census records for Lafayette County, Mississippi.[2,3]

George enlisted as a Private in Company A of the 11th Regiment, Mississippi Infantry, Confederate States Army, on 26 April 1861 at Oxford, Lafayette County, Mississippi. According to his enlistment records, he was 22 years old, which would place his birth year closer to 1838 or 1839. The 11th Mississippi Infantry was a prominent Confederate unit, serving with distinction in many of the war's major engagements, including the First Battle of Manassas, Antietam, Gettysburg, and the Wilderness Campaign. However, George's service was brief.

He was reported on the rolls of the Sick and Wounded at Winchester, Virginia, during June 1861. His records indicate he was suffering from exostosis, a painful, benign bony tumor, most commonly found on the great toe. Such a condition would have severely limited his ability to march or perform infantry duties. He was subsequently transferred to Lynchburg, Virginia, where he was formally discharged for disability on 21 June 1861. His discharge papers list him as 21 years old, 5 feet 8 inches tall, with a fair complexion, blue eyes, light hair, and "Mechanic" listed as his occupation. Interestingly, this record gives his birthplace as Oxford, Mississippi, differing from earlier census listings that point to Tennessee.

George returned home to Mississippi following his discharge. He is recorded with his family in the 1870 Lafayette County census, working as a carpenter. George died in 1876 in Oxford, Lafayette County, Mississippi. The location of his burial has not been determined, but his death is confirmed by the obituary of his son, Joseph Henry Cardwell.

George W. Cardwell's early discharge, combined with his physical condition and absence from the battlefield, illustrate the personal toll that even brief military service could take during the war. His legacy continued through his children, including a son named in honor of Confederate General Thomas "Stonewall" Jackson, reflecting the family's Confederate allegiance. Cardwell Line III - Predicted.

Photo 6.1: *John Foster Cardwell (1829-1900) Headstone - Benela Cemetery, Derma, Calhoun County, Mississippi.*

John Foster Cardwell (1829–1900) - *Private – Company I, 33rd Regiment, Mississippi Infantry, CSA* - **Prisoner of War**

John Foster Cardwell was born on 21 February 1829 in Tuscaloosa County, Alabama. He was the son of James Dudley Cardwell and Elizabeth Emeline (Foster) Cardwell. He appears in the household of his parents in the 1850 Tuscaloosa County census.[4]

John married Georgia Ann McLester on 05 January 1853 in Tuscaloosa County, Alabama.[5] Their marriage produced the following children: Betty

Foster Cardwell (1853–1929), Charles Samuel Cardwell (1855–1915), Sarah Amelia Cardwell (1858–1920), Amanda Jane Cardwell (1860–1938), and Martha "Mattie" Cardwell (1862–). By 1860, the family had moved to Mississippi and is listed in the census for Panola County. John later appears in the 1870, 1880, and 1900 census records for Calhoun County, Mississippi.[6,7,8,9]

During the Civil War, John enlisted as a Private in Company I of the 33rd Regiment, Mississippi Infantry, Confederate States Army, on 03 May 1862 in Eureka, Panola County, Mississippi. The 33rd Mississippi Infantry was organized in the spring of 1862 and served throughout the Western Theater. The regiment fought at the Battle of Iuka and the Battle of Corinth in 1862 and later participated in the Vicksburg Campaign. It also saw action at Missionary Ridge and took part in the Atlanta Campaign. By late 1864, many of its men were exhausted or assigned to support roles due to attrition. ohn is recorded as having served as a wagon master from 01 October to 31 October 1862, a vital logistical position responsible for overseeing the transportation of supplies and equipment—an essential function amid the demands of active campaigning.

On 31 March 1864, John was appointed Regimental Sutler, a civilian position operating under military authorization. A sutler was responsible for providing goods such as food, clothing, writing paper, tobacco, and other necessities not issued by the army. These items were sold to the troops and the position was one of trust, often filled by a soldier known to the men. John's appointment to this position suggests he was regarded as reliable and steady under pressure.

John was captured by Union forces on 03 April 1865 in his home county of Tuscaloosa, Alabama, just days before General Robert E. Lee's surrender at Appomattox. He was held briefly as a prisoner of war before being paroled on 19 May 1865, according to official Confederate records.

Following the war, John returned to Mississippi and eventually became a Reverend, dedicating his later years to religious service and community leadership. He spent the rest of his life in Calhoun County and is recorded in the 1900 census shortly before his death.

John Foster Cardwell died on 02 October 1900 in Calhoun County, Mississippi. He is buried at Benela Cemetery in Derma, Calhoun County.[10] His brothers, Henry Clay Cardwell (1843–1910) and James Robert Cardwell, also served in the Confederate Army and are recorded in this series under the Alabama Confederate veterans. <u>Cardwell Line III - Predicted</u>. Photo Credit[11]

* * *

Reuben Cardwell (1833-1861) - *Company K, 24th Regiment, Alabama Infantry, CSA & Company I, 44th Regiment, Mississippi Infantry, CSA -* **Died in Service - Disease.**

See his full biography in the Alabama Cardwell Confederate Veterans section of this volume.

* * *

Note: Two individuals—Samuel Cardwell and William J. Cardwell—are frequently listed in various indexes for Confederate veterans from Mississippi. However, thorough research has confirmed that in both instances, the surname was misread. The correct spelling in each case is Caldwell, not Cardwell. These entries reflect common transcription or interpretation errors found in historical records, particularly those compiled from handwritten documents.

Missouri
The Lone Confederate Cardwell

MISSOURI WAS ONE OF THE MOST DIVIDED STATES DURING THE CIVIL War, with strong allegiances on both sides. Officially remaining in the Union, Missouri also had a Confederate government-in-exile and contributed thousands of soldiers to both the Union and Confederate armies. The state saw intense guerrilla warfare, skirmishes, and battles as both sides fought for control of its strategic position along the Mississippi River and vital western trade routes. The conflict in Missouri was often brutal, with irregular forces engaging in ambushes, raids, and retaliatory violence against civilians.

While the Cardwell family in Missouri overwhelmingly supported the Union, with 16 men enlisting in Union regiments, one family member, Jasper Cardwell, chose to fight for the Confederacy.

Jasper Cardwell and Freeman's Regiment, Missouri Cavalry

Jasper Cardwell served in Freeman's Regiment, Missouri Cavalry, CSA, a Confederate cavalry unit that operated primarily in Missouri and Arkansas. This regiment was part of Brigadier General Joseph O. Shelby's famed Iron Brigade, known for its daring raids and aggressive guerrilla-style warfare.

Freeman's Regiment engaged in hit-and-run tactics, disrupting Union supply lines, attacking outposts, and participating in small skirmishes across Missouri and northern Arkansas. The regiment took part in Price's Missouri Expedition in 1864, a desperate Confederate attempt to reclaim Missouri for the South. Though ultimately unsuccessful, the campaign saw Freeman's men fighting in engagements such as the Battle of Pilot Knob and the Battle of Westport.

As the war turned against the Confederacy, Freeman's Regiment continued to engage in smaller raids before disbanding in 1865. Many of its men, including Jasper Cardwell, returned home still deeply divided by wartime loyalties.

Jasper Cardwell's service in Freeman's Regiment set him apart as the lone Confederate among the Cardwell men of Missouri. While most of his relatives supported the Union cause, Jasper's decision to fight for the South reflected the deep divisions that tore Missouri apart during the war. It should be noted that Jasper was a resident of northern Arkansas and that served in a Missouri unit.

This chapter honors the unique position of Jasper Cardwell, recognizing his service in a state where families often found themselves on opposite sides of the conflict. His story serves as a reminder of the complex and personal nature of Missouri's Civil War experience.

* * *

Photo 7.1: *Jasper Newton Cardwell (1847-1929) Headstone - Mount Pleasant Cemetery, Seattle, King County, Washington*

Jasper Newton Cardwell (1847-1929) - *Private - Company D, Freeman's Regiment, Missouri Mounted Cavalry, CSA -* **Prisoner of War**

Jasper Newton Cardwell was born on 07 August 1847 in Piney Fork, Lawrence County, Arkansas, the son of Jonathan Duran "John" Cardwell and Harriet C. (Shaver) Cardwell. He appears in the 1850 census in his parents' household in Piney Fork, located in the Ozark foothills of northeastern Arkansas.[1]

During the final phase of the Civil War, Jasper enlisted as a Private in Company D of Freeman's Regiment, Missouri Cavalry, CSA. Although few service records survive to document his enlistment or campaign activity, Jasper is included on the official list of men who surrendered with Brigadier General M. Jeff Thompson's command on 11 May 1865 to Major General G.M. Dodge of the Union Army. According to that record, Jasper had enlisted at Evening Shade, Arkansas, a small town in Sharp County that served as a regional muster point for Confederate units. He was 18 years old at the time of surrender, with a fair complexion, blue eyes, light hair, and standing 5 feet 9 inches tall. He reported Tennessee as his birthplace. Jasper was officially paroled at Jacksonport, Arkansas, on 05 June 1865.

Freeman's Regiment, part of Thompson's irregular cavalry brigade, operated largely in the Trans-Mississippi Theater and participated in guerrilla-style warfare throughout Missouri and northern Arkansas. This command was composed of loosely organized companies tasked with ambushing Union supply lines, gathering intelligence, and defending rural communities from occupation. By 1865, many of these cavalry units were worn down by years of hard campaigning, limited supplies, and an increasingly untenable strategic position. General Thompson's formal surrender marked one of the last Confederate capitulations west of the Mississippi.

After the war, Jasper returned to civilian life in Arkansas. He worked as a farmer in Carroll County, where he lived in the household of his widowed father, as recorded in the 1870 census.[2] On 20 February 1871, Jasper married Elizabeth Jane Gimlin in Carroll County.[3] Their marriage would span more than five decades and produce eight children: Charles Wesley Cardwell (1872–1956), William Clay Cardwell (1877–1912), Frank Cardwell (1877–1936), Myrtle Nancy Cardwell (1879–1952), Hugh Hillard Cardwell (1880–1960), Mary D. Cardwell (1888–1967), Duke Cardwell (1890–1891), and Martha Beulah Cardwell (1893–1992).

By 1880, Jasper and his family had relocated to Boone County, Arkansas.[4] His post-war life was marked by public service and business success. On 22 February 1894, he was listed on a grand jury in Green Forest, Carroll County. According to his obituary, Jasper became a prominent merchant in Carrollton, a regional hub in Carroll County before the arrival of the railroad. With the construction of the Missouri and North Arkansas Railway, commercial activity shifted from Carrollton to the newly founded town of Alpena Pass (later known simply as Alpena), and Jasper moved with it.

Around the turn of the century, Jasper left Arkansas for Washington State, settling in Garfield County. He appears in the 1900, 1910, and 1920 census records for that region, continuing to live an active life in the Pacific Northwest for nearly three decades.[5,6,7]

Jasper Newton Cardwell died in September 1929 in Seattle, King County, Washington. He was buried at Mount Pleasant Cemetery in Seattle.[8] From Confederate cavalryman to frontier merchant and westward migrant, his life spanned eras of great upheaval and transformation in American history. Cardwell Line III - Predicted. Photo Credit[9]

North Carolina
The Cardwell Confederates

NORTH CAROLINA PLAYED A SIGNIFICANT ROLE IN THE CONFEDERATE war effort, providing more troops to the Southern cause than any other state. While the state saw relatively few large battles, it was crucial for supply lines, coastal defenses, and troop movements between Virginia and the Deep South. North Carolina's soldiers fought in nearly every major campaign of the war, enduring some of the hardest battles and some of the highest casualty rates of any Confederate state.

By the war's end, North Carolina was among the last holdouts of the Confederacy, with some of its troops participating in General Joseph E. Johnston's surrender at Bennett Place in April 1865, effectively ending the Civil War in the eastern theater. Many North Carolina soldiers endured the long marches and brutal conditions of the Overland Campaign, the defense of Richmond and Petersburg, and the final battles of the war in the Carolinas. The Cardwell men from North Carolina served in several regiments that played critical roles in the Confederate war effort.

The Cardwell men from North Carolina served in some of the most well-known and hard-fought regiments of the Confederate Army. Their experiences took them from the battlefields of Virginia to the trenches of Petersburg and the surrender at Appomattox. Many endured the war's hardest conditions, fighting to the bitter end before returning home to a state devastated by conflict.

This chapter honors the Cardwell soldiers of North Carolina, ensuring that their contributions and sacrifices remain a lasting part of Civil War history.

* * *

Daniel Franklin "Frank" Cardwell (1819–1900/1910) - *Private – Company A, 5th Regiment, North Carolina Senior Reserves, CSA*

Daniel Franklin Cardwell, known throughout his life as "Frank," was born on 17 October 1819 in Wilkes County, North Carolina. He was the son of Asa P. Cardwell and Mary "Polly" LNU. In the 1840s, the family relocated briefly to Georgia, and by 1850, Frank, his wife, and children were recorded in Gilmer County, Georgia.[1]

On 14 September 1843, he married Margaret Church in Wilkes County, North Carolina.[2] Frank and Margaret had seven children: John Henry Cardwell (1844–1886), James Harrison Cardwell (1846–1918), Peter A. Cardwell (1849–1880), William Cardwell (1852–1870), Hiram H. Cardwell (1857–1870), Margaret A. Cardwell (1860–1923), and Myra Eveline Cardwell (1860–1923). Their eldest son, John Henry Cardwell, served with the 53rd Regiment of North Carolina Infantry, CSA, and is also profiled in this volume.[3]

Frank returned to North Carolina with his family, and they appear in the 1860 census of Wilkes County. As the Civil War continued into its later years, Confederate authorities expanded conscription to include older men. On 07 July 1864, Frank was conscripted into service at age 44 or 45. He enlisted as a Private in Company A, 5th Regiment of North Carolina Senior Reserves at Wilkesboro, Wilkes County.

The 5th North Carolina Senior Reserves was composed largely of men aged between 45 and 50, many of whom were beyond the age for standard military service. This unit was tasked with defensive duties within the state, including guarding railways, bridges, supply depots, and other logistical infrastructure critical to the Confederate war effort. Though these men were not often placed in direct combat, their work was essential to supporting the movements and operations of front-line units by ensuring that supply chains remained intact.

Frank's Confederate military records describe him as being 5 feet 10 inches tall, with a dark complexion, dark hair, and dark eyes. He was recorded as a farmer by trade. Unfortunately, his service was short-lived; he was listed as Absent Without Leave (AWOL) in January 1865, just months before the war's end. No explanation is included in the surviving records.

After the war, Frank returned to civilian life in Wilkes County. He is listed in the 1870, 1880, and 1900 U.S. Census records as a resident of the county.[4,5,6] No additional documentation has been located after 1900, suggesting that he likely passed away sometime before the 1910 census. Although no gravestone survives, family tradition holds that he and his wife are buried in unmarked graves at Mt. Pleasant Baptist Church Cemetery in Ferguson, Wilkes County, North Carolina.[7]

Frank Cardwell's service, though limited by age and the late stage of the war, reflects the increasing desperation of the Confederate government in its final years and the vital roles played by men of all ages in sustaining the war effort at home. Cardwell Line I - Confirmed.

* * *

Photo 8.1: *Hiram Henry Cardwell (1827-1900) Headstone - Hartman Cemetery, Hartman, Stokes County, North Carolina.*

Hiram Henry Cardwell (1827–1900) - *Private – Company K, 22nd Regiment, North Carolina Infantry, CSA*

Hiram Henry Cardwell was born in 1827 in Rockingham County, North Carolina, the son of Gabriel Cardwell and Cynthia (Humphrey) Cardwell. By 1850, he was living in the household of John K. Joyce in Rockingham County.[8] Family tradition holds that he was affectionately known by the nickname "Goone."

On 20 March 1851, Hiram married Sarah Elizabeth Stewart in Rockingham County.[9] The couple went on to have a large family: Cindy "Sidney" Cardwell (1853–1905), John Richard "Dick" Cardwell (1855–1912), Laura

Jane Cardwell (1856–1935), Lodusky Cardwell (1859–), Sarah Leanna Cardwell (1861–1901), Mary Etta "Mollie" Cardwell (1869–1941), Cora Frances Cardwell (1871–1938), Nancy Lou Cardwell (1872–1940), Mossie Eveline Cardwell (1875–1937), Hettie B. Cardwell (1878–1945), and Joseph "Joe" David Cardwell (1880–1938). Hiram and his family appear in both the 1870 and 1880 census records for Rockingham County.[10,11]

During the Civil War, Hiram was conscripted into Confederate service. On 18 March 1863, at the age of 43, he was mustered in as a Private with Company K of the 22nd Regiment, North Carolina Infantry, CSA. His relatively advanced age for military service reflects the Confederacy's increasing reliance on older men during the later stages of the war. The 22nd North Carolina Infantry had already earned a reputation for its service in the Army of Northern Virginia. Prior to Hiram's conscription, the regiment had seen fierce action in major campaigns such as the Seven Days Battles, Second Manassas, Sharpsburg (Antietam), Fredericksburg, and Chancellorsville.

By the time Hiram joined the ranks, the regiment was engaged in the ongoing operations of 1863–1864, including the Overland Campaign under General Robert E. Lee. On 03 June 1864, Hiram was admitted to the General Hospital in Petersburg, Virginia, with a diagnosis of "debilities," indicating physical weakness or chronic illness. He was transferred to the Confederate Hospital in Raleigh, North Carolina, on 05 June 1864. After this point, the official record becomes unclear. Hiram was noted as "Absent Without Leave" from the Raleigh hospital, though no specific date is listed.

A Confederate War Department document from 09 May 1865, issued by the Bureau of Conscription, reported that Hiram was residing in Stokes County, North Carolina. The order stated that if he was found to be absent from duty without proper authority, he was to be arrested. However, there is no record that Hiram was ever taken into custody or punished. Given that the war effectively ended within weeks of that report, it is likely that no action was taken.

Hiram Henry Cardwell died on 18 May 1900 in Snow Creek, Stokes County, North Carolina. He was buried at Hartman Cemetery in Hartman, Stokes County.[12] His life after the war appears to have been quiet, centered around his large family and rural life. His limited military service, like that of many late-war conscripts, reflects the desperation of the Confederacy in its final years and the burden that fell upon older citizens as the younger population was depleted by years of war. <u>Cardwell Line I NPE - Predicted</u>. Photo Credit[13]

* * *

James L. Cardwell (1844–1862) - *Private – Company F, 37th Regiment, North Carolina Infantry, CSA* - **Killed in Action**

James L. Cardwell was born about 1844 in Wilkes County, North Carolina. He was the eldest son of Nathan Parker Cardwell and Martha H. (Dockery) Cardwell. His father, Nathan, later served in the 5th Regiment of North Carolina Senior Reserves and is also profiled in this chapter. James appears in both the 1850 and 1860 census records for Wilkes County in the home of his parents.[14,15] Notably, the family is recorded twice in the 1850 census—once under the incorrect surname "Carter," and again as "Cardwell," although the enumerator mistakenly recorded Nathan's middle name, Parker, as "Phebe."[16]

James enlisted as a Private with Company F of the 37th Regiment, North Carolina Infantry, CSA, on 11 January 1862. At the time of enlistment, he was only 17 years old, standing 5 feet 7¼ inches tall, born in Wilkes County, and working as a farmer. His enlistment came at a point when the Confederacy was still actively building its early war regiments, and James most likely volunteered rather than being conscripted. The 37th North Carolina Infantry was initially raised as the 3rd Regiment of North Carolina Volunteers, but would later be redesignated as the 13th North Carolina Infantry on 24 November 1862.

During his short military service, James took part in some of the earliest and most intense fighting of the Eastern Theater. The regiment first saw action at the Battle of New Bern on 14 March 1862, a failed Confederate attempt to defend the town from Union forces in Craven County. The regiment was subsequently involved in the Siege of Yorktown and at Lee's Mill, from 05 April to 04 May 1862, where Confederate forces resisted Union advances during General George B. McClellan's Peninsula Campaign.

James was Killed in Action on 27 May 1862 during the Battle of Hanover Court House, Virginia. The engagement occurred during a heavy rainstorm as approximately 4,000 Confederate soldiers clashed with nearly 12,000 Union troops. The 37th North Carolina Infantry, fighting alongside the 18th North Carolina Infantry, launched a bold assault near the New Bridge and Hanover

Court House intersection. Initially, the Confederate attack pushed back the Union line, but the arrival of Union reinforcements overwhelmed the Confederates, who were forced into a retreat. It was likely during this charge or the subsequent withdrawal that James received the fatal wounds. Records indicate he sustained injuries to his lungs and thigh before succumbing to his wounds.

Following his death, James's father, Nathan Parker Cardwell, filed for and received a settlement from the Confederate government on 20 February 1865 —an official acknowledgment of his son's service and sacrifice. There are no further surviving records related to James.

James L. Cardwell's remains were never recovered and he is presumed to have been buried in a mass grave near the battlefield at Hanover Court House, Virginia. His young age, brief yet courageous service, and ultimate sacrifice are reminders of the toll the war exacted on families across the South. Cardwell Line I - Predicted.

* * *

Photo 8.2: *Joel Richard Cardwell (1843-1867) Headstone - Madison Presbyterian Church Cemetery, Madison, Rockingham County, North Carolina.*

Joel Richard Cardwell (1843–1867) - *2nd Lieutenant – Company H, 13th Regiment, North Carolina Infantry, CSA*

Joel Richard Cardwell was born in 1843 in Rockingham County, North Carolina. He was the son of James Legrand Cardwell and Sallie Fields (Martin) Cardwell. He appears in the household of his parents in the 1850 and 1860 Rockingham County census records.[17],[18] Both Joel and his brother, William Alexander Cardwell, served the Confederacy during the Civil War, though only Joel achieved the rank of officer.

Joel enlisted as a Private in Company H of the 13th Regiment, North Carolina Infantry, CSA, on 03 May 1861 at the age of 18. His enlistment took place in Rockingham County, North Carolina. He was immediately promoted to the rank of Corporal and quickly advanced within the company. On 05 November 1861, he was promoted to 1st Sergeant, and just two months later, on 10 January 1862, he was commissioned as a 2nd Lieutenant —a rank he held through the remainder of the war.

After mustering and initial training in North Carolina, the 13th North Carolina Infantry was ordered to Richmond, Virginia, where it became part of Longstreet's Division in the Army of Northern Virginia. The regiment was among the first to engage Union forces early in the conflict and was involved in nearly every major campaign in the Eastern Theater. It distinguished itself at the Second Battle of Manassas, Fredericksburg, and in the brutal fighting of the Wilderness Campaign. One of the most notable actions involving the 13th was its role during the Gettysburg Campaign, particularly at Pickett's Charge on 3 July 1863. The regiment sustained severe losses in this infamous assault, which ended in a disastrous repulse for the Confederacy. Despite the staggering attrition among officers and enlisted men, Joel Richard Cardwell endured through the entire campaign and continued to serve with distinction.

After the surrender and conclusion of hostilities, Joel returned to Rockingham County. On 20 July 1865, he married Nannie A. Webster in his home county.[19] Their marriage was tragically brief. Joel passed away just two years later, in 1867, at the age of 24. The cause of his early death remains unknown, though the lingering effects of wartime service or injury may have contributed. His widow later remarried to Henry W. Barrow.

Joel Richard Cardwell is buried at Madison Presbyterian Church Cemetery in Madison, Rockingham County, North Carolina.[20] Though his life was short, his rapid rise to officer rank and continued presence through some of the war's fiercest battles reflect his leadership and resilience under the harshest of conditions. <u>Cardwell Line I - Predicted</u>. Photo Credit[21]

* * *

John Henry Cardwell (1844–1886) - *Private – Company K, 53rd Regiment, North Carolina Infantry, CSA - Transferred to Confederate States Navy – April 1864.*

John Henry Cardwell was born on 24 July 1844 in Wilkes County, North Carolina. He was the eldest son of Daniel Franklin Cardwell and Margaret (Church) Cardwell. During the 1840s, the family temporarily relocated to Gilmer County, Georgia, and John appears with them in the 1850 Gilmer County census.[22] By 1860, they had returned to North Carolina and are listed again in Wilkes County, though a transcription error records them under his father's middle name.[23]

At the age of 18, John was conscripted into service on 03 November 1862 as a Private in Company K of the 53rd Regiment, North Carolina Infantry, CSA. His enlistment records confirm his age, residence in Wilkes County, and occupation as a farmer. The 53rd North Carolina Infantry was mustered into service in the fall of 1862 and became part of the Army of Northern Virginia.

John likely saw action in several of the war's major engagements. The 53rd fought at the Battle of Gettysburg, where it suffered significant casualties —losing 36% of the 322 men engaged. The regiment also fought in the Overland Campaign, including The Wilderness, Spotsylvania, and Cold Harbor. It later participated in Early's Shenandoah Valley Campaigns and the final Appomattox Campaign. John remained on the rolls until April 1864, when he was transferred to the Confederate States Navy. No further military records have been located after his transfer.

After the war, John returned to Wilkes County and married Cynthia S. McGee on 05 January 1866.[24] They had the following children: Nancy L. Cardwell (1867–), Margaret A. Cardwell (1870–), Zora C. Cardwell (1872–), Bethany E. Cardwell (1873–), Franklin Miles "Frank" Cardwell (1874–1952), Martha Matilda Cardwell (1878–), William Green Cardwell (1880–1964), and John Osco Cardwell (1882–1935). The family appears in both the 1870 and 1880 Wilkes County, North Carolina census records.[25,26]

In 1886, John's life came to a violent and mysterious end. According to a

New York Times article published on 31 July 1886, John Cardwell was scheduled to be executed by hanging for a crime committed in 1882. Before the execution could take place, a masked group—described as 200 armed and mounted men—stormed the jail in Wilkesboro in the early morning hours of 30 July 1886. They forcibly removed John from his cell at gunpoint and rode off. While the identity of the raiders was never confirmed, public belief held that Cardwell was lynched and drowned in the Yadkin River. The article reports that horse tracks indicated a halt at the river's edge and a possible disposal of the body by weighing it down. Despite a $200 reward offered by Governor Scales, Cardwell was never found, and his body was never recovered. The local community largely accepted that he had been lynched.

John was considered a divisive and, by many accounts, notorious figure. He had fled the state at one point and was forcibly returned from Virginia. His alleged crime and the delay of justice created tension in the area for years. Though some suspected he had been rescued by friends, most believed that his death was the result of vigilante justice. No burial record or marked grave has been located.

John Henry Cardwell was likely killed by a mob on 30 July 1886 in Wilkes County, North Carolina. His final resting place remains unknown. Cardwell Line I - Confirmed.

Photo 8.3: *Joseph Nathaniel Cardwell (1841-1862) Headstone - Madison Presbyterian Church Cemetery, Madison, Rockingham County, North Carolina.*

Joseph Nathaniel Cardwell (1841–1862) - *Private – Company H, 13th Regiment, North Carolina Infantry, CSA -* **Died of Disease**

Joseph Nathaniel Cardwell was born about 1841 in Rockingham County, North Carolina. He was the son of Richard Perrin Cardwell and Elizabeth Martin (Dalton) Cardwell. His father died in 1846, leaving his mother a widow with several children. Joseph is listed in her household in the 1850 and 1860 census records of Rockingham County, North Carolina.[27,28] According to family tradition, Joseph was often called "Joel" by those who knew him. He was one of three sons in the Cardwell family who served in the Confederate army during the Civil War. His brothers, Pleasant Dalton Cardwell and Richard Henry Cardwell, are also recorded in this volume for their service.

Joseph enlisted as a Private in Company H of the 13th Regiment, North Carolina Infantry, CSA, on 10 May 1861 at Wentworth, Rockingham County, North Carolina. He was 20 years old at the time of his enlistment and listed his occupation as a tobacconist. The 13th North Carolina Infantry was organized in the spring of 1861 and became part of the Army of Northern Virginia under General Robert E. Lee. The regiment saw early service in the defenses of Richmond and later participated in the Peninsula Campaign.

Though the unit's first major action came at the Battle of Yorktown and in subsequent operations in the spring of 1862, Joseph's service came to an end before he saw heavy combat. He was admitted to Chimborazo Hospital in Richmond, Virginia—one of the largest military hospitals in the Confederacy—with complications from pneumonia. His records confirm that he died of the illness on 08 June 1862, just over a year after his enlistment. While his service was brief, it is likely that he fell ill during the exhausting conditions of early campaign maneuvers, a common fate for many soldiers at the time.

Though Joseph died far from home, his body was returned to Rockingham County. He was buried in the cemetery of Madison Presbyterian Church in Madison, North Carolina. His death left a mark on his family, which would continue to serve the Southern cause through his surviving brothers.

Joseph Nathaniel Cardwell died of pneumonia on 08 June 1862 while serving in the Confederate Army. He is buried at Madison Presbyterian Church Cemetery, Madison, Rockingham County, North Carolina.[29] Note: There is a possibility that Joseph may have died while being held captive as a Prisoner of War. One record for "J.N. Cardwell of Company A of the 13th Regiment of North Carolina Infantry", is recorded in the a federal prisoner financial record with no date. More research is needed to conclusively determine if it was Joseph Nathaniel Cardwell. Cardwell Line I - Predicted. Photo Credit[30]

* * *

Photo 8.4: *Nathan Parker Cardwell (1820-1892) Headstone - Mount Pleasant Baptist Church Cemetery, Wilkesboro, Wilkes County, North Carolina.*

Nathan Parker Cardwell (1821–1892) - *Private – Company A, 5th Regiment, North Carolina Senior Reserves, CSA*

Nathan Parker Cardwell was born on 6 February 1821 in Wilkes County, North Carolina. He was the son of Asa P. Cardwell and Mary "Polly" LNU. Nathan's life was deeply rooted in Wilkes County, where he married Martha H. Dockery on 07 March 1841.[31]

Together they raised a large family, having the following children: Malinda Elisha Cardwell (1843–1887), James L. Cardwell (1844–1862), Martha L. Cardwell (1846–1921), John Larkin Cardwell (1849–1888), Susannah Cardwell (1851–1900), Leander Cardwell (1855–), Pickney Marshall Cardwell (1859–1941), Cana Cardwell (1860–), and Lindsey Vance Cardwell (1863–1927). He appears in the 1850, 1860, 1870, and 1880 Wilkes County, North Carolina census records as a farmer.[32,33,34,35]

As the Civil War progressed and younger men were depleted from Confederate ranks, older men were conscripted for local and support duty. At the age of 43, Nathan was conscripted into Confederate service as a Private with Company A, 5th Regiment of North Carolina Senior Reserves, CSA, on 27 September 1864 at Wilkesboro.

The 5th North Carolina Senior Reserves was formed in mid-1864 and composed largely of older men, typically those between 45 and 50 years of age. These units were charged with essential home-front responsibilities such as guarding bridges, supply depots, and key infrastructure across the state. Though they were not generally deployed to front-line battlefields, their service was vital to the Confederacy's ability to continue the war effort by freeing younger soldiers for field operations and ensuring the safe transport of arms and goods.

Nathan's enlistment records describe him as 5 feet 9 inches tall, with a dark complexion, dark hair, and dark eyes. His occupation was listed as a farmer. He served for several months before being marked as Absent Without Leave (AWOL) as of 15 January 1865. No further military records for him have been located. His absence may have been the result of illness, hardship, or the disintegration of Confederate authority during the closing months of the war.

Nathan's son, James L. Cardwell, also served the Confederacy and was killed in action in 1862 while serving in the 37th Regiment, North Carolina Infantry. His brother, Daniel Franklin Cardwell, served alongside him in the same unit of the Senior Reserves and is also included in this volume.

Nathan Parker Cardwell died on 01 February 1892 in Wilkes County, North Carolina. He is buried at Mount Pleasant Baptist Church Cemetery in Wilkesboro, Wilkes County, North Carolina.[36] Cardwell Line I - Predicted. Photo Credit[37]

* * *

Photo 8.5: *Parker Cardwell (1825-1864) Headstone - Old City Cemetery, Lynchburg, Lynchburg City, Virginia.*

Parker Cardwell (1825–1864) - *Private – Company K, 22nd Regiment, North Carolina Infantry, CSA* - **Mortally Wounded in Action**

Parker Cardwell was born in 1825 in Rockingham County, North Carolina. He was the son of Gabriel Cardwell and Cynthia (Humphrey) Cardwell. On 31 January 1848, Parker married Elizabeth Frazier in Rockingham County.[38] Together they had the following children: James Henry Cardwell (1848–1908), Richard H. Cardwell (1850–1904), Gabriel B. Cardwell (1856–1916), Susan M. Cardwell (1857–1925), and Minnie Emma Cardwell (1864–1905). The family appears in both the 1850 and 1860 Rockingham County, North Carolina census records, with Parker working as a farmer to support his household.[39,40]

As the war progressed and the Confederacy's manpower dwindled, Parker was conscripted into Confederate service on 23 March 1863. He was assigned as a Private to Company K of the 22nd Regiment of North Carolina Infantry, CSA. This regiment had already seen heavy action in earlier campaigns and continued to be a frontline unit in the Army of Northern Virginia. Parker joined the regiment just weeks before one of its fiercest engagements.

On 5 May 1863, Parker was Wounded in Action during the Battle of Chancellorsville in Spotsylvania County, Virginia—one of the most significant and costly battles in the Eastern Theater. During the chaotic and deadly combat, the 22nd North Carolina Infantry suffered devastating losses, with 31 killed, 125 wounded, and 16 captured. The battle was a Confederate tactical victory, but it came at a heavy human cost. Parker's wounding occurred exactly one year prior to when his brother, Wyatt Cardwell, would be wounded in the nearby Battle of the Wilderness.

Parker's injuries were severe, and he was evacuated from the battlefield to Knight's Ferry Hospital in Lynchburg, Virginia. Despite lingering for more than a year under medical care, Parker succumbed to his wounds on 12 July 1864. He was 39 years old at the time of his death.

He was laid to rest at the Old City Cemetery in Lynchburg, Lynchburg City, Virginia, a site that holds the graves of many Confederate soldiers who died in the hospitals surrounding the city.[41] Parker's loss left Elizabeth a widow with five children, the youngest born in the same year he died.

Parker's service and sacrifice are part of a broader legacy of the Cardwell family during the Civil War. His brother, Hiram Henry Cardwell, also served in Company K of the 22nd North Carolina Infantry, CSA, and is included elsewhere in this volume. Their shared service in the same regiment reflects the close ties that bound many Confederate soldiers—families, communities, and counties sending their men to fight side by side. Cardwell Line I NPE - Confirmed. Photo Credit[42]

* * *

Photo 8.6: *Pleasant Dalton Cardwell (1843-1864) Memorial -
Madison Presbyterian Church Cemetery, Madison, Rockingham County,
North Carolina.*

Pleasant Dalton Cardwell (1843–1864) - *Sergeant – Company D, 45th
Regiment, North Carolina Infantry, CSA* - **Mortally Wounded in Action.**

Pleasant Dalton Cardwell was born about 1843 in Rockingham County,
North Carolina. He was the son of Richard Perrin Cardwell and Elizabeth
Martin (Dalton) Cardwell. Following the death of his father in 1846, Pleasant
was raised by his widowed mother, appearing in her household in both the
1850 and 1860 Rockingham County census records.[43,44] All three of the
Cardwell sons—Joseph Nathaniel "Joel" Cardwell, Pleasant Dalton Cardwell, and Richard Henry Cardwell—served in the Confederate Army during
the Civil War.

Pleasant volunteered for service as a Private in Company D of the 45th
Regiment, North Carolina Infantry, CSA, on 29 April 1862 at Camp
Magnum, near Raleigh. He proved himself capable and reliable, earning
promotion to Sergeant on 01 March 1863.

The 45th North Carolina Infantry was organized in April 1862 and was
quickly sent to Virginia to join the Army of Northern Virginia. The regiment's first major action came at the Battle of Malvern Hill on 01 July 1862, a
fierce engagement outside Richmond. Shortly afterward, the unit was reas-

signed to operations in the Kinston and New Bern region of North Carolina. By the spring of 1863, the regiment returned north and participated in the Gettysburg Campaign. At Gettysburg, the 45th suffered heavily—losing 228 men out of the 570 engaged in the fighting.

Pleasant continued to serve with the 45th as it moved through a series of hard-fought battles, including the Wilderness and Spotsylvania Court House. These battles were grueling engagements that wore down both armies through sustained combat in difficult terrain. The regiment was then involved in the Battle of Cold Harbor, fought from 31 May to 12 June 1864 near Mechanicsville, Hanover County, Virginia.

On the first day of that battle—31 May 1864—Union cavalry managed to flank Confederate forces and capture the critical crossroads at Old Cold Harbor. Confederate troops, including Pleasant's regiment, launched repeated counterattacks to reclaim the position. It was during this phase of the battle that Pleasant was Wounded in Action (WIA). His wound was recorded as a "V.S. of hip," a term commonly used at the time to denote a "Vulnus Sclopetarium"—Latin for a gunshot wound.[45]

Pleasant was transported to Moore Hospital Number 24 in Richmond, Virginia, where many of the wounded from Cold Harbor were treated. Despite the best efforts of medical staff, Pleasant died of his wounds on 06 June 1864, just six days after the injury. His burial location is unknown, though it is presumed he was interred in one of the mass graves near the hospital. A memorial stone honoring his memory stands at Madison Presbyterian Church Cemetery in Madison, Rockingham County, North Carolina.[46] Pleasant's cousin, Thomas Cardwell, also served in the 45th North Carolina Infantry, though in Company K. Like Pleasant, he did not survive the war. Their shared service and sacrifice reflect the profound cost of the conflict on North Carolina families and communities. Cardwell Line I - Predicted.[47]

* * *

Photo 8.7: *Thomas Cardwell (1831-1863) - circa 1862 - Rockingham County, North Carolina*

Photo 8.8: *Thomas Cardwell (1831-1863) - Vernon Cemetery, Ayersville, Rockingham County, North Carolina*

Thomas Cardwell (1831–1863) - *Private – Company K, 45th Regiment, North Carolina Infantry, CSA* - **Died in Service**

Thomas Cardwell was born on 07 April 1831 in Rockingham County, North Carolina. He was the son of Gabriel Cardwell and Cynthia (Humphrey) Cardwell. He was one of five brothers who served in the Confederate Army during the Civil War: Wyatt Cardwell, Parker Cardwell, Hiram Henry Cardwell, Thomas Cardwell, and Walker C. Cardwell. Thomas appears in the 1850 Stokes County, North Carolina census living in the home of his parents.[48]

On 05 January 1859, he married Leatha C. Martin in Rockingham County, North Carolina.[49] Together, they had two daughters: Mary Ann Cardwell (1859–1910) and Martha Jane Cardwell (1861–1939). By the time of the 1860 census, Thomas and his young family were residing in Rockingham County.[50]

As the war progressed and manpower needs increased, Thomas was conscripted into Confederate service at the age of 32. He was enrolled as a Private in Company K of the 45th Regiment, North Carolina Infantry, CSA, on 01 September 1862. Company K, often referred to as the "North State Boys," was composed primarily of men from Guilford, Forsyth, Davidson, and Rockingham Counties.

The 45th North Carolina Infantry had already seen significant combat before Thomas joined. After early campaigns in eastern North Carolina and Virginia, the regiment took part in the Gettysburg Campaign in July 1863. At the Battle of Gettysburg, fought from 01 to 03 July 1863, the 45th was heavily engaged and suffered staggering losses—40 percent of the men engaged became casualties. Although Thomas's records do not confirm his presence in that specific battle, it is highly probable he was there, given the timing of his service and subsequent hospitalization.

On 28 July 1863, Thomas was admitted to a Confederate hospital in Lynchburg, Virginia. Unfortunately, the surviving records do not indicate whether he was wounded in battle or suffering from illness, which was a common affliction among soldiers during that campaign. There is some confusion in the documentation—one record states he died at Winder Hospital in Richmond on 01 August 1863, while another lists his death as occurring in Lynchburg in September. Due to the inconsistencies and the location where he was buried, the later date is generally accepted by researchers.

Thomas Cardwell died on 01 September 1863 at the Confederate hospital in Lynchburg, Virginia. He was thirty-two years old. He is buried at Vernon Cemetery in Ayersville, Rockingham County, North Carolina.[51] His sacrifice was one of several made by the Cardwell family, whose members served in multiple regiments throughout the war. Cardwell Line I NPE - Predicted. Photo Credits[52,53]

* * *

Photo 8.9: *Walker C. "Dock" Cardwell (1833-1905) Headstone, Cardwell Family Cemetery, Ayersville, Rockingham County, North Carolina.*

Walker C. "Dock" Cardwell (1835–1905) - *Private – Company L, 21st Regiment, North Carolina Infantry, CSA & Private - Company M, 2nd Regiment, New York Cavalry, USA*

Walker C. Cardwell, known by the nickname "Dock," was born in March 1835 in Rockingham County, North Carolina. He was the son of Gabriel Cardwell and Cynthia (Humphrey) Cardwell. He appears in the household of his parents in both the 1840 Rockingham County and 1850 Stokes County, North Carolina census records.[54,55] By 1860, Walker was likely residing in Polk County, Tennessee.[56]

During the Civil War, Walker became one of only three Cardwell men known to have served on both sides of the conflict. He initially enlisted as a Private in Company L, 21st Regiment, North Carolina Infantry, Confederate States Army, on 03 June 1861 in Wentworth, Rockingham County. The 21st North Carolina Infantry was organized in June 1861 and was part of the Army of Northern Virginia. It saw action in many of the major battles of the Eastern Theater, including First Manassas, Antietam, Fredericksburg, and

Chancellorsville. The regiment participated in Stonewall Jackson's Valley Campaign and suffered heavily at Gettysburg. Walker's brothers—Wyatt Cardwell, Parker Cardwell (KIA at the Battle of Chancellorsville), Hiram Henry Cardwell, and Thomas Cardwell (died of disease in 1863)—all served in the Confederate Army, some in the same or associated regiments.

Walker's Confederate service ended when he "deserted to the enemy" on 01 June 1863, according to his Confederate records. The exact circumstances or motivations for his desertion are unknown, though desertions among soldiers were not uncommon due to the hardships of war, disillusionment, or shifting political sentiments.

More than a year later, Walker enlisted in the Union Army on 30 August 1864 as a Private in Company M, 2nd Regiment, New York Cavalry. This unit was also known as the "Harris Light Cavalry." The 2nd New York Cavalry participated in numerous cavalry raids and skirmishes during the later stages of the war, especially in the Shenandoah Valley under General Philip Sheridan. Walker served with this regiment until he was discharged on 05 June 1865 at Alexandria, Virginia, shortly after the conclusion of the war. The reason for Walker making this decision is not known.

After returning home to Rockingham County, Walker resumed civilian life. On 13 September 1866, he married Nancy "Nannie" Fair in Rockingham County.[57] Together, they raised a large family that included: William Jackson "Will" Cardwell (1868–1942), George Thomas Cardwell (1868–1945), Mary Magdeline Cardwell (1871–1931), Lou Settie Cardwell (1872–1965), Ella Fountaine Cardwell (1877–1931), Virginia "Jennie" Cardwell (1880–1962), James Andrew Cardwell (1882–1957), and Jesse W. Cardwell (1885–1918). He appears in the 1870, 1880, and 1900 Rockingham County, North Carolina census records.[58,59,60]

Walker died on 14 February 1905 in Rockingham County. He is buried at the Cardwell Family Cemetery in Ayersville, Rockingham County, North Carolina.[61] His complex military history—serving both the Confederacy and the Union—makes him a particularly notable figure among the many Cardwells who fought in the war. He is also featured in *Brothers in Blue*, the first volume in this series. Cardwell Line I NPE - Predicted. Photo Credit[62]

* * *

William Alexander Cardwell (1845–bef. 1880) - *Private – Company D, 45th Regiment, North Carolina Infantry, CSA.*

William Alexander Cardwell was born in 1845 in Rockingham County, North Carolina. He was the son of James Legrand Cardwell and Sallie Fields (Martin) Cardwell. He appears in the home of his parents in both the 1850 and 1860 Rockingham County census records.[63,64] Two sons from this family served in the Confederate Army: Joel Richard Cardwell, who attained the rank of 2nd Lieutenant, and William Alexander Cardwell, who served as a Private.

William enlisted as a Private in Company D, 45th Regiment of North Carolina Infantry, CSA, on 11 March 1862. His enlistment was recorded as a Substitute, a common practice early in the war where men could enlist in place of others who had been drafted. At the time of his enlistment, William was just 17 years old, listed as a student, and measured 5 feet 6 inches in height. Company D of the 45th was locally known as the "Madison Greys," composed largely of men from Rockingham County.

The 45th North Carolina Infantry was organized in the spring of 1862 and immediately saw action. The regiment took part in the Seven Days Battles around Richmond, Virginia from 25 June to 01 July 1862. Not long after, William was furloughed due to illness and was away from the regiment from October 1862 through April 1863.

William returned to duty in May 1863 and remained active in the field through February 1864. During that time, he participated in one of the regiment's most significant and costly engagements—the Battle of Gettysburg (01–03 July 1863). The 45th North Carolina Infantry suffered a staggering 40 percent casualty rate during the campaign. Despite these losses, William and his two kinsmen—Pleasant Dalton Cardwell and Thomas Cardwell, who also served in the 45th—survived the battle. However, Thomas died later that year in a hospital in Lynchburg, Virginia.

In the latter part of 1864, William's health declined again. From September to November, he was listed as "sick in hospital," although no specific diagnosis was noted. On 01 February 1865, he was admitted to Jackson Hospital in Richmond, Virginia. His medical report stated that due to "unfitness for field service," he was assigned to hospital duty while also receiving treatment. He was diagnosed with "coxalgia," an outdated medical term for chronic pain or disease affecting the hip joint. On 25 March 1865, just weeks before the war's end, William was returned to duty. No additional Civil War records for him have been located.

Following the war, William appears once more in the 1870 Rockingham County census, residing in the household of his parents.[65] However, no records of him have been found after that date. He is not listed in the 1880 census or later documentation. Based on this absence, it is assumed that William Alexander Cardwell died sometime between 1870 and 1880. The exact date of his death and the location of his burial remain unknown. His service with the 45th North Carolina Infantry—especially at Gettysburg—places him among the many young soldiers who endured the hardships of war at a formative age. Cardwell Line I - Predicted.

* * *

Photo 8.10: *Wyatt Cardwell (1824-1894) Headstone - Wyatt Cardwell Cemetery, Sandy Ridge, Stokes County, North Carolina.*

Wyatt Cardwell (1824–1894) - *Private – Company K, 22nd Regiment, North Carolina Infantry, CSA -* **Wounded in Action**

Wyatt Cardwell was born in 1824 in Rockingham County, North Carolina. He was the eldest child of Gabriel Cardwell and Cynthia

119

Brothers in Gray

(Humphrey) Cardwell. By 1850, he was listed in the household of his parents in neighboring Stokes County, North Carolina.[66]

On 16 May 1851, Wyatt married Ann Eliza Amos in Stokes County.[67] The couple had at least seven children: Harriett F. Cardwell (1854–1924), Julian Frances Cardwell (1857–1894), John Frank Cardwell (1858–1912), James Monroe Cardwell (1861–1910), Thomas M. Cardwell (1863–1903), Calvin S. Cardwell (1866–), and Walter G. Cardwell (1869–1899). Wyatt and his family are enumerated in the 1860 census for Stokes County.[68]

Wyatt was likely conscripted into Confederate service late in the war, enlisting as a Private with Company K of the 22nd Regiment, North Carolina Infantry, CSA, on 06 February 1864 in Stokes County. The 22nd North Carolina Infantry had already seen extensive action by that point, including campaigns in the Army of Northern Virginia under General Robert E. Lee. The regiment had participated in battles at Seven Pines, Second Manassas, Fredericksburg, Chancellorsville, and Gettysburg. Given the date of Wyatt's enlistment, it appears that he was drafted as part of the Confederate government's effort to replenish its increasingly depleted forces.

Soon after his enlistment, Wyatt was listed as sick with rubeola (measles) on 18 April 1864. Despite this setback, he returned to duty in time to take part in the Battle of the Wilderness, fought from 05 to 07 May 1864 in the dense woods of Orange County, Virginia. This engagement marked the beginning of Union General Ulysses S. Grant's Overland Campaign against Lee's army. It was characterized by brutal, close-quarters fighting, difficult terrain, and high casualties—nearly 29,000 in total.

Wyatt was among the 21 men wounded in the 22nd North Carolina Infantry during the opening day of the battle on 05 May. He was transported to Wayside Hospital in Richmond, Virginia, on 09 May 1864. His service records do not clearly indicate if he was discharged from the hospital or returned to active duty. He was later listed as "Absent Without Leave," a designation that was not uncommon for wounded or sick soldiers recovering outside official army hospitals near the war's end.

A year later, on 09 May 1865, the Confederate War Department's Bureau of Conscription issued a notice indicating that Wyatt was residing in Stokes County, North Carolina. The order stated that if he was found absent without proper authority, he was to be arrested. However, no further military action or consequence appears to have resulted, and there is no record of his apprehension.

120

Following the war, Wyatt resumed civilian life with his family in Stokes County. He is recorded in the 1870 and 1880 census records, working as a farmer and raising his children. He lived out the remainder of his life in the county.[69,70]

Wyatt Cardwell died in 1894 in Stokes County, North Carolina. He is buried at Wyatt Cardwell Cemetery in Sandy Ridge, Stokes County—a small family burial ground that now preserves his legacy.[71] Wyatt was one of five brothers who served in the Confederacy: Hiram Henry Cardwell, Parker Cardwell, Thomas Cardwell, and Walker C. Cardwell. His service in the final and grueling year of the war placed him among the many older men called into battle as the Confederacy struggled to defend its collapsing front lines. Cardwell Line I NPE - Predicted. Photo Credit[72]

Tennessee
The Cardwell Confederates

TENNESSEE WAS ONE OF THE MOST HOTLY CONTESTED STATES DURING the Civil War, serving as a battleground for major campaigns and witnessing over 1,400 engagements—more than any other state except Virginia. As the last state to secede from the Union in June 1861, Tennessee was deeply divided, with strong Unionist support in the eastern region and significant Confederate loyalty in the central and western parts of the state. This division often meant that Tennesseans found themselves fighting against neighbors, friends, and even family members.

With key transportation routes, rich agricultural land, and vital manufacturing centers, Tennessee was crucial to both the Union and the Confederacy. The state saw some of the war's most significant battles, including Shiloh, Stones River, Chickamauga, and Franklin. The fall of key cities like Nashville and Chattanooga dealt heavy blows to the Confederate war effort, but Tennessee soldiers continued fighting fiercely until the war's end.

The 29 Cardwell men who fought for the Confederacy in Tennessee served in various regiments, enduring some of the war's fiercest campaigns. Many of them enlisted early, joining regiments such as the 24th Tennessee Infantry, the 9th Tennessee Cavalry (Ward's), and the 26th Tennessee Infantry (3rd East Tennessee Volunteers). These units played critical roles in defending Confederate strongholds and resisting Union advances throughout the state and beyond.

These men endured the full spectrum of war—long marches, disease-ridden camps, and devastating battlefield losses. Some were captured and sent to Northern prison camps, while others fought until the very end, witnessing the collapse of the Confederacy in 1865.

For the Cardwell men who survived, the war did not end with surrender. Many returned to a Tennessee transformed by conflict, its cities and farmlands ravaged by years of war. Some rebuilt their lives as farmers, laborers, or tradesmen, while others left the South entirely in search of new opportunities. Their service and sacrifices remain a part of Tennessee's Civil War legacy, a testament to the divided loyalties and complex experiences of those who fought in the war.

This chapter tells the stories of the 29 Cardwell men who served in the Confederate ranks from Tennessee, honoring their commitment, hardships, and the lasting impact of their service in one of the Civil War's most pivotal states.

* * *

Photo 9.1: *Confederate Mound Memorial - Camp Douglas POW Dead - Oak Woods Cemetery, Chicago, Cook County, Illinois.*

CARDWELL A E, SGT D 3 TENN

Photo 9.2: *Achilles E. Cardwell (1842-1862) Memorial - Confederate Mound Memorial - Camp Douglas POW Dead - Oak Woods Cemetery, Chicago, Cook County, Illinois.*

Achilles E. Cardwell (1842–1862) - *Sergeant – Company D, 3rd Regiment, Tennessee Infantry (Clack's), CSA* - **Prisoner of War – Died in Captivity**

Achilles E. Cardwell was born around 1842 in Giles County, Tennessee, the son of William Sands Cardwell and Mariah Prudence (Jefferies) Cardwell. He is listed in the 1850 and 1860 U.S. Census records in Giles County, living with his parents and siblings.[1,2] The Cardwell family suffered deeply during the Civil War—Achilles and his brother John J. Cardwell both died while serving the Confederacy. Achilles went by the nickname of "Kills" according to family tradition.

Achilles enlisted as a Private in Company D, 3rd Regiment of Tennessee Infantry (Clack's), CSA, and was later promoted to 3rd Sergeant, although the exact date of his promotion is unknown. The regiment saw its first major combat at the Battle of Fort Donelson in Stewart County, Tennessee, from 11 to 16 February 1862. The fighting around the fort was fierce and disorganized, and the 3rd Tennessee suffered 73 casualties out of 750 men during the engagement. It is likely that Achilles participated in this battle.

On 16 February 1862, the Confederate garrison at Fort Donelson, including the 3rd Tennessee Infantry, surrendered to Union forces. Achilles was taken as a prisoner of war and transported to the notorious Camp Douglas in Chicago, Illinois. He appears on a Roll of Prisoners dated 01 August 1862 and was later hospitalized with fever. Sadly, Achilles died in captivity on 09 September 1862.

Although the exact location of his grave is unknown, it is believed that Achilles was interred in a mass grave at Camp Douglas. His name is memorialized on the Confederate Memorial Mound at Oak Woods Cemetery, Chicago, Cook County, Illinois, where many of the Confederate dead from Camp Douglas are honored.[3] Cardwell Line I - Predicted. Photo Credits[4,5]

* * *

Photo 9.3: *Henry Jefferson Cardwell (1823-1895) - New Union Cemetery, Rock Island, Warren County, Tennessee.*

Henry Jefferson Cardwell (1823–1895) - *Private – Company B, 35th Regiment, Tennessee Infantry, CSA*

Henry Jefferson Cardwell was born around 1823 in Lone Mountain, Claiborne County, Tennessee, the son of Francis G. Cardwell and Judah (Lebow) Cardwell. His father moved the family from Claiborne County to Warren County, Tennessee, sometime after Henry's birth, and they are recorded in the 1830 and 1840 census records for that county.[6,7]

On 15 October 1847, Henry married Louisa Jaco in Warren County.[8] Together they had a large family: Pauline A. Cardwell (1849–1860), Laura Cardwell (1851–1939), Francis "Frank" Marion Cardwell (1856–1914), America Cardwell (1857–1931), Paralee Cardwell (1859–1936), Calhoun Smartt Cardwell (1861–1937), William Jackson Cardwell (1865–1931), and Florence Cardwell (1866–1918). Henry appears in the 1850, 1860, 1870, and 1880 U.S. Census records in Warren County, consistently working as a farmer and community leader.[9,10,11,12]

At the age of 38, Henry enlisted as a Private on 06 September 1861 near McMinnville, Tennessee, joining Company B of the 35th Tennessee Infantry, CSA. The regiment was quickly pressed into action and fought at the Battle of Shiloh on 06–07 April 1862, a brutal and pivotal conflict in the Western Theater. Though there is no explicit record of Henry's involvement in the battle, his service dates strongly suggest he was present.

Just over a month later, on 24 May 1862, Henry was discharged from service. His records do not specify a reason, and there is no indication that he rejoined the Confederate army later in the war. However, a biographical account notes that he was widely referred to as "Major Jeff Cardwell," a title stemming from his earlier appointment as a militia officer by Tennessee Governor Aaron V. Brown, a role he apparently held during the war years.

Following the war, Henry became a respected community figure. In 1882, he served as a Trustee of Irving College, a position reflecting his deep commitment to education. According to local accounts, he was frequently urged to run for the Tennessee State Legislature, but declined out of humility. He remained an active supporter of education and religious institutions in Warren County.

Henry Jefferson Cardwell died on 13 July 1895 at Cardwell Mountain in Warren County. He is buried at New Union Cemetery, located at the base of the mountain near Rock Island, Tennessee.[13] <u>Cardwell Line I - Confirmed</u>. Photo Credit[14]

* * *

Photo 9.4: *James Alexander Cardwell (1826-1903) - Dixon Springs Cemetery, Dixon Springs, Smith Count, Tennessee*

James Alexander Cardwell (1826–1903) - *Private – Company E, 1st Regiment, Tennessee Mounted Infantry (Ward's), CSA* - **Wounded in Action**

James Alexander Cardwell was born on 18 December 1826 in Smith County, Tennessee, the son of John G. Cardwell and Sarah H. (Robinson) Cardwell. After his father's death in 1843, James remained in Smith County, where he is listed in the 1850 census living with his widowed mother.[15]

On 27 October 1852, James married Lucy F. Cardwell—his distant cousin—in Smith County.[16] Together, they had five children: John Jefferson Cardwell (1853–1925), Lucy Tennessee "Tennie" Cardwell (1854–1935), Lockey Virginia Cardwell (1856–1946), Cora Emma Cardwell (1864–1961), and Sallie Dixon Cardwell (1866–1938). James and Lucy appear in the 1860, 1870, 1880, and 1900 federal census records for Smith County.[17,18,19,20]

Although no formal Confederate service records have been located, James provided details of his military service in his Confederate pension application, filed on 12 August 1891 in Smith County, Tennessee. He stated that he enlisted as a Private in Company E of the 1st Regiment of Tennessee Mounted Infantry (Ward's), under the command of Colonel W.W. Ward and General John Hunt Morgan, in February 1862.

The 1st Tennessee Mounted Infantry, often referred to as Ward's Regiment, operated under General Morgan's Cavalry Division. This unit saw a range of scouting, raiding, and skirmish duties in support of Confederate efforts in Tennessee and Kentucky. James served as a scout, a role requiring initiative, knowledge of the terrain, and close interaction with the command structure. According to testimony from a fellow soldier, W.L. Kemp, who served in a nearby unit, James was frequently scouting for multiple companies, indicating he was well-trusted by his superiors.

On 10 May 1863, James was severely wounded during the Battle of Greasy Creek in Kentucky—a relatively small but intense engagement that occurred as General Morgan's forces clashed with Union troops in the region. James recalled in his application that a shell exploded near him, and shrapnel tore into his right thigh and hip, leaving lasting damage: *"I have no strength in it [the right leg] to hold out to walk. Can only walk by the aid of a stick, can not plow, or do any labor that requires walking, my disability is permanent."*

Due to the severity of his wounds, James was honorably discharged from further service. His statements describe how he remained near the site of the battle for several days and used crutches for months following the injury. His disability left him permanently unable to work or farm effectively after the war.

Supporting documents included affidavits from his physician and fellow soldiers, all attesting to the credibility of his claims and the severity of his injuries. His widow, Lucy Cardwell, later applied for and was granted a Confederate widow's pension. Although an initial clerical error misidentified his regiment, the application was ultimately accepted following clarification.

James Alexander Cardwell died on 20 December 1903 in Smith County, Tennessee. He is buried at Dixon Springs Cemetery in Dixon Springs, Smith County. His life and service, though largely undocumented in official Confederate records, were preserved through eyewitness testimony and his own detailed account of his time in Morgan's command. His sacrifice at Greasy Creek underscores the significant toll that smaller, less-documented engagements had on local Confederate forces and their families. Cardwell Line III - Predicted. Photo Credit[21]

* * *

Photo 9.5: *James P. Cardwell - Warren County, Tennessee - circa 1885*

Photo 9.6: *James P. Cardwell (1845-1920) Headstone - Shellsford Cemetery, McMinnville, Warren County, Tennessee*

James P. Cardwell (1845–1920) - *Private – Company H, 11th Regiment, Tennessee Cavalry (Holman's), CSA -* **Prisoner of War**

James P. Cardwell was born on 09 May 1845 in Warren County, Tennessee, the son of John Cardwell and Sarah (Kell) Cardwell. He appears in his parents' household in both the 1850 and 1860 U.S. Census records for Warren County.[22,23]

During the final year of the Civil War, James enlisted as a Private in Company H of the 11th Tennessee Cavalry (Holman's) on 08 September 1864. The unit, raised during a period of dwindling Confederate manpower, was part of a series of hastily formed cavalry regiments tasked with defensive operations in the Western Theater. Their duties included patrolling for Union raiders, guarding supply lines, and occasionally skirmishing with advancing Federal troops. The 11th Tennessee Cavalry, often operating under limited resources, remained in service until the end of the war.

James served alongside his cousin, Thomas W. Cardwell, who enlisted in the same company shortly after him. Thomas's biography also appears in this chapter. Much of what is known about James's service comes from his Confederate pension application, filed on 29 April 1909 in Warren County. Although no official service records have been located, the pension was approved, confirming his honorable service. James was present with his unit when it surrendered on 09 May 1865 in Washington, Georgia, and he was paroled following the Confederate collapse.

After the war, James returned to Warren County. He married Martha Park on 11 August 1870.[24] They had one daughter, Daisy H. Cardwell (b. 1887). Martha passed away in 1899, leaving James a widower with a young child. That same year, he remarried Eliza E. Elmore on 28 February 1899 in Bedford County, Tennessee.[25] James appears in the 1870, 1880, 1900, 1910, and 1920 U.S. Census records for Warren County.[26,27,28,29,30]

James P. Cardwell died on 28 March 1920 in Warren County, Tennessee, and was laid to rest at Shellsford Cemetery in McMinnville.[31] Photo Credits[32,33]

* * *

Photo 9.7: *James R. Cardwell (1837-1911) Headstone - Cardwell Cemetery, Grainger County, Tennessee.*

James R. Cardwell (1837–1911) - *Sergeant – Company D, 26th Regiment, Tennessee Infantry, CSA* - **Wounded in Action - Prisoner of War**

James R. Cardwell was born on 23 September 1837 in Rockingham County, North Carolina, the son of Richard M. Cardwell and Sarah "Sally" Jane (Crowder) Cardwell. His father, a veteran of the War of 1812, died in January 1850. James appears in the 1850 U.S. Census living with his widowed mother and siblings in Rockingham County, and again in the 1860 census in Union County, Tennessee.[34,35] His older brother Richard was killed in action during the War with Mexico in 1847, and his younger brother, William T. Cardwell, also served alongside James during the Civil War.

James enlisted on 04 July 1861 at Knoxville, Tennessee, joining as a Private in Company D of the 26th Tennessee Infantry, CSA. At the time, he was 23 years old and had traveled 55 miles to enlist. The regiment quickly saw action and was present at the Battle of Fort Donelson in February 1862, where it suffered roughly 25% casualties before being forced to surrender. James and his brother William were captured and sent to Camp Douglas in Chicago, Illinois, a Union prisoner-of-war camp notorious for its harsh conditions. William died of pneumonia on 16 May 1862 while still a prisoner. James was exchanged at Vicksburg, Mississippi, on 05 April 1862 and rejoined his unit.

The 26th Tennessee Infantry fought in some of the fiercest battles of the war. At the Battle of Stones River (Murfreesboro) from 31 December 1862 to 02 January 1863, the regiment sustained 110 casualties. The unit endured even greater losses at the Battle of Chickamauga on 19–20 September 1863, where it lost 98 out of 229 men. During this engagement, James was wounded by grape shot in the left side beneath his ribs, as confirmed in his Confederate pension application filed on 02 May 1902. He was hospitalized for a time but ultimately returned to duty. The wound caused him lasting pain, as noted in an affidavit from his physician. Another affidavit from William N. Waller, a fellow soldier, confirmed he witnessed James being struck in battle.

The 26th Tennessee Infantry continued to serve until the Battle of Bentonville, North Carolina, one of the war's final battles. James was present when the regiment surrendered on 21 March 1865, and he took the Oath of Allegiance to the United States on 01 May 1865, later submitting a copy of this record with his pension application.

After the war, James returned to Grainger County, Tennessee, where he married Dicy Malissa Acuff on 15 November 1866.[36] He appears in the 1870, 1880, and 1900 U.S. Census records for Grainger County.[37,38,39]

James R. Cardwell passed away on 29 October 1911 and was buried in the Cardwell Cemetery, Grainger County, Tennessee.[40] Cardwell Line I - Predicted. Photo Credit[41]

* * *

James R. Cardwell (1846–) - *Private – Company K, 16th/21st Regiments, Tennessee Cavalry; Company F, 21st & 22nd Regiments, Consolidated Tennessee Cavalry, CSA* - **Prisoner of War.**

James R. Cardwell was born around 1846 in Smith County, Tennessee, the son of Daniel J. Cardwell and Addalid (Kyle) Cardwell. He appears with his family in the 1850 U.S. Census for Smith County and again in the 1860 census for Obion County, Tennessee.[42,43]

James enlisted in the Confederate Army on 10 November 1863, joining Company K of the 21st Tennessee Cavalry (Wilson's), a unit also known by its earlier designation, the 16th Tennessee Cavalry. The regiment was part of Colonel Tyree H. Bell's Brigade, serving under the renowned cavalry commander General Nathan Bedford Forrest. The 21st Tennessee Cavalry participated in numerous raids, delaying actions, and small engagements as part of Forrest's hard-hitting and mobile cavalry operations.

In February 1865, the 21st Tennessee Cavalry was consolidated with Barteau's 22nd Tennessee Cavalry to form the 21st and 22nd Consolidated Tennessee Cavalry Regiment. This reorganized unit remained active under Forrest's command through the final months of the war, continuing to engage in resistance as Confederate forces struggled to maintain control of key Southern territories.

James was present when the consolidated regiment surrendered on 04 May 1865 at Citronelle, Alabama, marking one of the last major Confederate surrenders in the Western Theater. He was recorded as a Prisoner of War, residing in Weakley County, Tennessee, and was officially paroled on 11 May 1865 at Gainesville, Alabama. No further military records have been located beyond this point.

James's fate after the war is unclear. A man listed as "J.R. Cardwell", born around 1849, appears in the 1870 census for Davidson County, Tennessee, working as a clerk in a store, but it is uncertain if this is the same individual.

The date and place of James R. Cardwell's death remain unknown, and his burial location has not been identified.[44] <u>Cardwell Line III - Confirmed</u>.

✻ ✻ ✻

James Wesley Cardwell (1839–1893) - *Private – Company E, 5th Regiment, Tennessee Infantry, CSA*

James Wesley Cardwell was born around 1839 in Simpson County, Kentucky, the son of Nelson Cardwell and Mary "Polly" (Bennett) Cardwell. Following the death of his father prior to the 1850 census, James appears living in the household of Sarah Herman in Sumner County, Tennessee—her relationship to James remains unknown.[45] His father, Nelson Cardwell, died before the 1850 census. His mother remarried in 1851 to Jeremiah Dixon, and James is recorded living with them in the 1860 census for Simpson County.[46]

James enlisted as a Private in Company E of the 5th Tennessee Infantry, CSA, on 13 June 1861 at Camp Brown in Obion County, Tennessee. While his Confederate service record is sparse, it confirms that he was discharged from Camp Brown at some point. No additional documentation of his military service has been located, suggesting that his time in uniform was likely short.

Following the war, James married Margaret L. LNU around 1866, most likely in Simpson County, though no marriage record has been found. They had one known child: Richard J. Cardwell (1867–1880). James appears with his family in the 1870 census in Simpson County, Kentucky, and later in the 1880 census in Muhlenberg County, Kentucky.[47,48]

James Wesley Cardwell passed away on 18 March 1893 in Owensboro, Muhlenberg County, Kentucky, as noted in an obituary published in the *Owensboro Messenger*. The location of his burial is unknown.

His brother, Samuel Richard Cardwell, also served in the Confederate Army and is profiled elsewhere in this chapter. <u>Cardwell Line III - Confirmed</u>.

✻ ✻ ✻

Photo 9.8: *John B. Cardwell (1839-1924) Headstone - Cardwell Cemetery, Smith County, Tennessee*

John B. Cardwell (1839-1924) - *Private - Company F, 9th Regiment, Tennessee Cavalry, CSA*

John B. Cardwell was born on 24 August 1839 in Smith County, Tennessee, the eldest son of Isaac Moody Cardwell and Serena (Richardson) Cardwell. He appears in the 1850 and 1860 U.S. Census records living with his family in Smith County.[49,50]

At the age of 23, John enlisted as a Private in Company F of the 9th Tennessee Cavalry (Ward's) on 01 September 1862 in Smith County. The regiment operated under the command of General John Hunt Morgan, participating in a series of raids and skirmishes throughout Tennessee and Kentucky. The 9th Tennessee Cavalry specialized in fast-moving cavalry operations, targeting Union supply lines and conducting hit-and-run engagements throughout the region.

According to John's Confederate pension application filed on 03 April 1911, he took part in numerous skirmishes and at least three significant engagements during his service. These included fighting at Snow's Hill and Mann's Hill, both located in DeKalb County, Tennessee, which were part of a series of local actions involving Confederate and Union cavalry in early 1863. He also participated in the Battle of Milton, also known as Vaught's Hill, which took place on 20 March 1863 in Rutherford County, Tennessee—a more formally documented engagement where Confederate cavalry under General John Hunt Morgan clashed with Union forces entrenched near the town of Milton.

John stated that he was never wounded in battle, but suffered a significant decline in health from yellow jaundice and fever, which led to his discharge and return home to Defeated, Smith County.

His application also provides a rare account of Civil War substitution. John hired a young man named Buck Smith, not yet of conscription age, to serve in his place. Affidavits from fellow Company F veterans Robert H. Yearman and W.J. Craighead confirm that *"Buck Smith made a good soldier in Cardwell's place until he was killed in battle."*

John married Alethia Jane "Letha" Kemp on 21 January 1861 in Smith County.[51] They had three children: William Thomas Cardwell (1861–1925), Annie Etta Cardwell (1863–1932), and Isaac "Ike" Newton Cardwell (1865–1945). Letha passed away in 1906, and John remarried Mary Jane Kitrell on 09 September 1908, also in Smith County. He appears in the 1870, 1880, 1900, 1910, and 1920 census records for Smith County.[52,53,54,55,56]

John B. Cardwell died on 22 January 1924 in Smith County, Tennessee, and was buried in the Cardwell Cemetery there, leaving behind a legacy both as a soldier and as a family patriarch.[57] NOTE: There are some discrepancies with John's name. Family tradition states his name was John Bransford Cardwell. Researchers have used that name in correspondence dating back to the 1970's. The discrepancy occurs in the review of the rosters for Company F, 9th Tennessee Cavalry, CSA. The roster lists him as Private Jonathan Brown Cardwell. Extensive research in Smith and surrounding counties found no individual with the name Jonathan Brown Cardwell. The closest is John B. Cardwell, eldest son of Isaac Moody Cardwell and Serena (Richardson) Cardwell. Until definitively proven, John B. Cardwell is used in this volume, since that is how it appears on census records. I lean that they are one and the same. Cardwell Line III - Predicted. Photo Credit[58]

* * *

John Henry Cardwell (1843–<1870) - *Corporal – Company D, 2nd Regiment, Tennessee Infantry, CSA*

John Henry Cardwell was born around 1843 in Tennessee, the son of Macajah D. Cardwell and Fredonia M. (Belote) Cardwell. His mother died in 1849 in Memphis, Shelby County, Tennessee, and he was subsequently raised in part by his maternal grandmother, with whom he is listed in the 1850 Shelby County census.[59] By 1860, John was living in Weakley County,

Tennessee, in the household of his father and stepmother, Polly Ann (Hicks) Cardwell, whom Macajah had married in 1846.[60]

On 14 May 1861, at the age of 19, John enlisted as a Private in Company D, 2nd Tennessee Infantry, CSA, at Hartsville, Trousdale County, Tennessee. The regiment was mustered into Confederate service in Lynchburg, Virginia, and initially assigned to General Beauregard's Brigade. During the First Battle of Manassas (July 1861), the 2nd Tennessee was tasked with defending a strategic bridge. While under heavy fire, the unit was not fully engaged in the main combat. The unit came under heavy fire, but was not actively engaged.[61]

The regiment remained in Virginia until 09 February 1862, after which it was ordered to Knoxville, Tennessee, for defensive duty in response to shifting Confederate strategy following the surrender of Fort Donelson. John's records note that he was granted a short furlough on 15 February 1862.

The 2nd Tennessee Infantry next participated in the bloody Battle of Shiloh on 06–07 April 1862 in Hardin County, Tennessee, where it was placed under Cleburne's Brigade. The regiment suffered severe losses, with more than half of its men killed, wounded, or missing. Although John's service records do not provide battle-specific remarks, he was listed as Present during this time and likely took part in the engagement.

Following Shiloh, the 2nd Tennessee took part in a number of major operations: the Siege of Corinth; the Battle of Richmond, Kentucky; the Battle of Perryville; the Battle of Stones River (Murfreesboro); the Battle of Chickamauga; the Battle of Missionary Ridge; the Battle of Ringgold Gap; and multiple battles and skirmishes throughout the Atlanta Campaign.

John appears again in the records on 20 July 1864, listed as sick with syphilis and admitted to Ocmulgee Hospital in Macon, Georgia. That document also notes that he was a resident of Sumner County, Tennessee at the time. This is the last known record for John Henry Cardwell.

His ultimate fate is unknown. Despite exhaustive searches, no postwar records for John have been found, and he does not appear in the 1870 U.S. Census. It is presumed that he died during or shortly after the war, likely due to illness. His date of death and burial location remain unconfirmed. Cardwell Line III - Predicted.

* * *

John J. Cardwell (1844–1863) - *Sergeant – Company D, 3rd Regiment, Tennessee Infantry (Clack's), CSA* - **Killed in Action**

John J. Cardwell was born around 1844 in Giles County, Tennessee, the son of William Sands Cardwell and Mariah Prudence (Jefferies) Cardwell. The family endured great loss during the Civil War, as both John and his older brother Achilles E. Cardwell died while serving in the Confederate Army. John is listed in his parents' household in the 1850 and 1860 Giles County census records.[62,63]

John enlisted as a Private in Company D, 3rd Tennessee Infantry (Clack's), CSA, on 22 May 1861 in Cheatham County, Tennessee. He was later promoted to Sergeant, though the exact date of that promotion is not recorded. The 3rd Tennessee saw its first major engagement at the Battle of Fort Donelson, fought from 11 to 16 February 1862 in Stewart County, Tennessee. During the fighting outside the fort's defenses, the regiment suffered 73 casualties out of 750 men present. It was the unit's first taste of combat, and John was likely among those engaged in the action.

Following the Confederate surrender at Fort Donelson, John and his brother Achilles were captured and transported to Camp Douglas in Chicago, Illinois, a notorious Union prisoner-of-war camp. They are both listed on the Roll of Prisoners dated 01 August 1862. While imprisoned, Achilles fell ill with fever and died on 09 September 1862.

John was exchanged along with other Confederate prisoners on 23 September 1862, and transferred to Vicksburg, Mississippi. He rejoined the reorganized 3rd Tennessee Infantry and participated in several major campaigns over the next year. The unit saw action at the Battle of Chickasaw Bayou in December 1862, the Battle of Raymond, Mississippi in May 1863—where it suffered heavy casualties—and finally at the Battle of Chickamauga, one of the bloodiest battles of the war.

John was killed in action on 19 September 1863, during the opening day of the Battle of Chickamauga in northern Georgia, according to his Confederate service records. Like many soldiers who fell in that fierce fighting, he was likely buried in a mass grave on the battlefield. <u>Cardwell Line I - Predicted</u>.

* * *

John T. Cardwell (1845–) - *Hospital Steward – 37th Regiment, Tennessee Infantry, CSA & Private – 1st Regiment, Tennessee Cavalry (Carter's), CSA*

John T. Cardwell was born around 1845 in Evergreen, Conecuh County, Alabama, the son of Perrin Henry Cardwell and Amanda Malvina (Cates) Cardwell. His father, a Doctor of Dentistry, was appointed Postmaster in Conecuh County, which likely explains the family's temporary residence there.[64] Following Amanda's death in 1850, John was raised by his maternal grandparents and is listed in their household in the 1850 and 1860 Blount County, Tennessee census records. He is recorded as a saddler by trade, an indication of early vocational training. His father remarried Mary E. Watkins on 26 July 1851 in Knoxville, Tennessee, and John also appears in their home in the 1860 Knox County census, listed in two separate households that year —both referring to the same individual.[65,66,67]

On 01 November 1861, John enlisted as a Private with Company I of the 37th Tennessee Infantry, CSA, at Knoxville. By February 1862, he had been promoted to Hospital Steward, a specialized medical role likely influenced by his father's profession. He served in that capacity for the duration of his one-year enlistment and was paid in full on 25 August 1862.

John reenlisted as a Private in Company G of the 1st Tennessee Cavalry (Carter's), CSA, on 17 September 1862 in Maryville, Blount County, Tennessee. His records note that from 01 July to 31 October 1863, he was on detached service with General Pegram's Commissary Department, a position suggesting logistical or administrative responsibilities.

John T. Cardwell's service file ends after that point, and no additional records—military or civilian—have been located for him following the Civil War. He does not appear in any postwar censuses, marriage indexes, or death records, leaving his later life and death unconfirmed.

John's placement in skilled roles such as hospital steward and departmental aide indicates that he was a highly capable and educated young man for his time. His early disappearance from historical records adds a layer of mystery to a life marked by intelligence and service. Cardwell Line I - Confirmed.

* * *

John Wesley Cardwell (1841–1894) - *Private – Company H, 6th Regiment, Tennessee Infantry, CSA*

John Wesley Cardwell was born in 1841, the son of Thomas Granderson Cardwell and Martha Washington (Acklin) Cardwell. He is recorded in the

1850 Calloway County, Kentucky census in his parents' household, and again in 1860 in Weakley County, Tennessee, still residing with his family.[68,69]

John enlisted as a Private in Company H, 6th Regiment, Tennessee Infantry, CSA, on 13 June 1861, at Union City, Weakley County, Tennessee. The 6th Tennessee Infantry was comprised largely of volunteers from western Tennessee counties and was one of the early Confederate regiments to be formed in the region. The regiment would later participate in key engagements such as the Battle of Shiloh, Perryville, and Chickamauga, but John did not remain with the unit long enough to take part in those battles.

John received a disability discharge from the service on 06 August 1861, less than two months after enlisting. His discharge indicates that a physical ailment or injury rendered him unfit for further military duty. No specific details about the nature of his disability have been found in his records.

After returning home, John married Virginia Josephine Richardson on 16 August 1865, in Rutherford County, Tennessee.[70] They had the following children: Mary Iva Cardwell (1866–1935), Edgar Cardwell (born 1870), William Clayton Cardwell (1872–1945), Jessie Y. Cardwell (1875–1922), Ada May "Addie" Cardwell (1879–1962), Florence M. Cardwell (born 1882), Blanche Virginia Cardwell (1885–1977), and Lou Steele Cardwell (1890–1931).

John is listed in the 1870 and 1880 census records for Weakley County, Tennessee, where he worked and raised his family.[71,72] He remained in the county for the rest of his life.

He passed away on 13 January 1894 in Weakley County and was buried at Cardwell Cemetery in Palmersville, Weakley County, Tennessee.[73]

His widow, Virginia Josephine Cardwell, applied for a Confederate Widow's Pension on 08 November 1907, in Weakley County, confirming his service and their marriage. Her application provides supporting evidence of John's enlistment and honorable discharge from Confederate service. Cardwell Line III - Predicted.

* * *

Photo 9.9: *Joesph Leonard Cardwell (1835-1925) - Smith County, Tennessee - circa 1875. (Photo repaired and enhanced)*

Photo 9.10: *Joseph Leonard Cardwell (1835-1925) - Wilson County, Tennessee - circa 1920.*

Photo 9.11: *Joseph Leonard Cardwell (1835-1925) Headstone. Cedar Grove Cemetery, Lebanon, Wilson County, Tennessee.*

Joseph Leonard Cardwell (1835–1925) - *2nd Lieutenant – Company H, 24th Regiment, Tennessee Infantry, CSA*

Joseph Leonard Cardwell was born on 30 September 1835 at Horseshoe Bend, Smith County, Tennessee, the son of Buckner Strum Cardwell and Mary Susan (Robinson) Cardwell. He appears in the 1850 census residing in his parents' household in Smith County.[74]

Around 1857, Joseph married Mary Carolina Timberlake, most likely in Smith County, though no formal record of the marriage has been located. The estimated year is based on census data. Together they had nine children: Buckner David Cardwell (1860–1935), Mary Virginia "Jennie" Cardwell (1861–1879), William Frank Cardwell (1863–1926), Louisa Tennessee "Lulu" Cardwell (1864–1931), Leonard Moncey "Cap" Cardwell (1867–1934), Lilly G. Cardwell (1872–1873), Martha Ward Cardwell (1874–1963), Maffie Cardwell (1876–1877), and Annie Elizabeth "Lizzie" Cardwell (1878–1968). By 1860, Joseph and his young family were living in Macon County, Tennessee.[75]

Joseph enlisted as a Private with Company H of the 24th Tennessee Infantry, CSA, on 15 July 1861, at Coffee County, Tennessee, and was elected 2nd Lieutenant on 24 March 1862. The 24th Tennessee Infantry served under General Patrick R. Cleburne's Brigade, a division known for its discipline and battlefield effectiveness. Cleburne, often called the "Stonewall of the West," led the brigade into the Battle of Shiloh on 06–07 April 1862, one of the largest and bloodiest engagements of the war. The brigade was engaged in some of the fiercest fighting of the battle, suffering more casualties than any other Confederate unit present. Though Joseph's personal file does not confirm his presence at Shiloh, the timing of his service makes his involvement very likely.

According to his records, 2nd Lieutenant Cardwell was left without a command following a reorganization of the 24th Tennessee Infantry on 02 May 1862, shortly after Shiloh. No additional Confederate service records have been located for him.

After the war, Joseph returned to Smith County, Tennessee, where he appears in the 1870, 1880, 1900, and 1910 censuses.[76,77,78,79] By 1920, he was residing in Wilson County, listed in the household of his daughter.[80]

Joseph Leonard Cardwell passed away on 15 November 1925 in Lebanon, Wilson County, Tennessee, and was buried in Cedar Grove Cemetery in the same town.[81]

Joseph's kinsmen, Silas H. Cardwell and William L. Cardwell, also served in the 24th Tennessee Infantry, and are profiled in this volume. Cardwell Line III - Predicted. Photo Credits[82,83,84]

* * *

Joseph Taylor Cardwell (1834–1915) - *Private – Company F, 1st Regiment, Tennessee Infantry, CSA & Company H, 28th Regiment, Tennessee Infantry, CSA*

Joseph Taylor Cardwell was born on 12 December 1834, the son of John B. Cardwell and Elizabeth (Taylor) Cardwell. His father was born in Bedford County, Tennessee, where Joseph's parents were married in 1832. By the mid-1840s, the family relocated to Washington County, Arkansas, and Joseph appears in their household in the 1850 census.[85] A decade later, he is recorded in the 1860 census of Hopkins County, Kentucky, living in the household of his maternal aunt, Nancy (Taylor) Galiga.[86]

Joseph enlisted as a Private with Company F, 1st Tennessee Infantry, CSA, on 09 May 1861, at Nashville, Tennessee. Company F was also known as "The Railroad Boys." His initial enlistment was for one year, but he reenlisted on 30 April 1862 at Corinth, Mississippi. His service records show that he was detached as a blacksmith, performing specialized work for both Smith's Battery and Turner's Battery, an assignment he appears to have held through February 1864. While Joseph has compiled service records in both the 1st Tennessee Infantry and 28th Tennessee Infantry, each includes identical notes regarding his detached service, suggesting this was a single individual listed under both units due to administrative overlap.

On 04 April 1863, Joseph married Theresa A. Ragsdale in Bedford County, Tennessee.[87] The couple does not appear to have had any children. After the war, Joseph resided in Bedford County (1870 census) and later in Coffee County, Tennessee, where he appears in the 1880, 1900, and 1910 censuses.[88,89,90,91]

Joseph Taylor Cardwell died on 20 April 1911 in Coffee County, as noted in his widow's Confederate pension application.[92] The location of his grave are unknown. Cardwell Line III - Predicted.

* * *

Photo 9.12: *Lee Roy P. Cardwell (1844-1917) Headstone. Bells Chapel Cemetery, Gibson County, Tennessee.*

Lee Roy P. Cardwell (1844–1917) - *Private - Company F, 17th Regiment, Tennessee Cavalry (Newsome's), CSA; Company G, 1st Regiment, Confederate Cavalry, CSA; Forrest's Regiment, Alabama Cavalry, CSA & Company F, 18th Regiment, Tennessee Cavalry (Neal's), CSA -* **Wounded in Action (Twice) - Prisoner of War**

Lee Roy P. Cardwell was born on 09 April 1844 in McNairy County, Tennessee, to William Cardwell and Celia (Harper) Cardwell. He appears in their household in the 1850 McNairy County census, and in 1860 is listed in the home of the Riley Ledbetter family, also in McNairy County.[93,94]The nature of the relationship between the families remains unclear.

According to his Confederate Pension Application, filed on 25 January 1900, Lee Roy first enlisted in the spring of 1861, claiming initial service with Company F of the 17th Tennessee Cavalry (Newsome's), CSA. However, existing records confirm that he formally enlisted as a Private on 01 June 1863, at Tuscumbia, Colbert County, Alabama, with Forrest's Regiment, Alabama Cavalry, CSA. His brother, William Y. Cardwell, enlisted alongside him (see corresponding biography).

He is also found in the records of Company G, 1st Regiment of Confederate Cavalry, which list him as having enlisted on 09 January 1862 at Henderson, likely the town in Chester County, Tennessee. His service notes indicate that he was on detached duty at Corinth, Mississippi, by order of General P.G.T. Beauregard. At the time, Confederate forces were concentrating at Corinth in anticipation of Union movements following the fall of Forts Henry and Donelson. The region became a strategic focal point leading up to the Battle of Shiloh. It is likely that he was temporarily attached to or cooperating with cavalry forces under General Nathan Bedford Forrest, who was actively operating in northern Mississippi during this period. Forrest's men were engaged in reconnaissance, screening maneuvers, and securing Confederate supply lines in the lead-up to the campaign.

Lee Roy later appeared on the rolls of the 18th Tennessee Cavalry (Neal's), CSA, a unit that operated under the command of General Nathan Bedford Forrest. His brothers, William Y. Cardwell and Thomas D. Cardwell, also served in the same regiment. While the exact date of his transfer between regiments is unclear, his service in both units demonstrates an extended involvement in Forrest's cavalry operations.

Lee Roy was wounded in action twice during the war. The first occurred at the Battle of Shiloh on 06–07 April 1862, when he sustained a gunshot wound to the foot, shattering three bones and requiring a three-month furlough to recover at home. His second and more serious wound was at the Battle of Harrisburg (Tupelo) on 15 July 1864, where he was shot in the lower back. An affidavit by W.B. Whitaker, included in his pension application, recounts that Lee Roy had been lying down when the bullet struck Cardwell in the small of the back and traveled along his spine, leaving him disabled for an extended period. These injuries reportedly troubled him for the rest of his life.

According to his statement, Lee Roy's unit surrendered at Corinth, Mississippi, and he was paroled and swore the Oath of Allegiance to the United States. No official surrender or parole documents have been located in the surviving records.

Following the war, Lee Roy married Nancy Caroline Richards on 07 January 1867 in McNairy County, Tennessee.[95] They had one child, George Henry Cardwell (1868–1910). Lee Roy appears in the 1870 McNairy County census, then relocated to Dyer County, where he is recorded in the 1880 and 1900 censuses. By 1910, he was a widower residing in Gibson County, Tennessee, with his son.[96,97,98,99]

Lee Roy P. Cardwell died in 1917 in Gibson County and was buried at Bells Chapel Cemetery, Gibson County, Tennessee.[100] Cardwell Line I - Predicted. Photo Credit[101]

* * *

Richard Livingston Cardwell (1824–1896) - *Private – Company D, 16th Battalion, Tennessee Cavalry (Neal's), CSA*

Richard Livingston Cardwell was born in 1824 in Knox County, Tennessee, the son of Thomas George Cardwell and Sarah Elizabeth (Easley) Cardwell. He married Sarah Elizabeth Liggitt on 06 January 1849, in Roane County, Tennessee.[102] Together they had six children: Austin L. Cardwell (1850–1860), Elizabeth R. Cardwell (1852–), Mary F. "Millie" Cardwell (1854–), Susan A. "Sudie" Cardwell (1857–1946), Georgia A. Cardwell (1861–1953), and Richard Henry Cardwell (1872–1945).

Richard appears in the 1850 census of Roane County, Tennessee, where his occupation is listed as working in "Apparel and Accessories Store, Except Shoes."[103] This civilian trade would later shape his Confederate service. By 1860, he was residing in Knox County, near his parents' home.[104]

He enlisted as a Private in Company D, 16th Battalion, Tennessee Cavalry (Neal's), CSA, on 20 September 1862, at Kingston, Roane County. His service records are limited, but they indicate that he was sick from the time of his enlistment through December 1862. Beginning in March 1863, he is marked as Absent Without Leave (AWOL) through June 1863. On 18 November 1863, it was noted in his records that he had been *"detailed to make clothing for the government at Kingston."* This role likely drew upon his civilian expertise in garment production.

The records suggest that Richard may have been unsuited for field service and possibly entered the army as a conscript. No further service records have been found beyond this point.

After the war, Richard returned to Roane County, where he appears in the 1870 census.[105] By 1880, he had relocated to Knox County, where he was residing with his brother.[106] Richard Livingston Cardwell died on 23 July 1896 in Knox County. The location of his burial has not been identified.[107] Cardwell Line I - Confirmed.

* * *

Photo 9.13: *Samuel Richard Cardwell (1843-1925) - Chicago, Cook County, Illinois - circa 1924*

Photo 9.14: *Samuel "Samyell" Richard Cardwell (1848-1925) Headstone. Oakland Cemetery, Trenton, Gibson County, Tennessee.*

Samuel Richard "Samyell" Cardwell (1843–1925) - *Private – Company I, 30th Regiment, Tennessee Infantry, CSA*

Samuel Richard Cardwell was born on 3 November 1843 in Simpson County, Kentucky, the son of Nelson Cardwell and Mary "Polly" (Bennett) Cardwell. His father passed away between 1840 and 1850, and Samuel appears in the 1850 census of Macon County, Tennessee, and the 1860 census of Simpson County, Kentucky, in the household of his remarried mother.[108,109] Simpson County borders Sumner County, Tennessee, where much of his military service history unfolded.

Samuel enlisted as a Private with Company I, 30th Tennessee Infantry, CSA, on 22 November 1861, at Tyree Springs, Sumner County, Tennessee. His Confederate service records contain some inconsistencies, including references to "Samyell Cardwell" and "S.R. Cardwell." Based on his birth year, regional residence, and association with William Dudley Cardwell—his nephew and fellow soldier in the same company—Samuel is reasonably confirmed as the individual behind those entries.

According to his sparse service records, Samuel was absent with leave from Fort Donelson and sent home prior to the surrender of the 30th Tennessee Infantry on 16 February 1862. As a result, he was not captured along with the rest of the regiment, which became Prisoners of War (POWs) and were sent to Union prison camps. His nephew, William Dudley Cardwell, for example, was sent to Camp Butler near Springfield, Illinois. Samuel does not appear to have rejoined his unit, and no further Confederate military records for him have been found.

Around 1862, Samuel married Sarah Elizabeth Malone, though no official marriage record has been located. Together they had at least eleven children: Mary Alice Cardwell (1863–1864), John Columbus Cardwell (1866–), Ella J. Cardwell (1867–), Fannie America Cardwell (1870–1873), Antoinette Cardwell (1872–1898), Annie Olive "Ollie" Cardwell (1873–1904), William Soloman Cardwell (1875–1930), Virgil Louis Cardwell (1876–1930), Malissa Cardwell (1879–), Hattie Cardwell (1879–), Charles Edward Cardwell (1884–1934), and one stillborn child.

Samuel and his family are found in the 1880 census of Logan County, Kentucky; the 1900 and 1910 censuses of Jefferson County, Kentucky; and the 1920 census of Cook County, Illinois.[110,111,112,113]

Samuel died on 09 January 1925 in Chicago, Cook County, Illinois.[114]

He was buried at Oakland Cemetery, Trenton, Gibson County, Tennessee.[115] Cardwell Line III - Confirmed. Photo Credits[116,117]

* * *

Photo 9.15: *Samuel Sullivan Cardwell (1841-1906), Smith County, Tennessee, circa 1900*

Photo 9.16: *Samuel Sullivan Cardwell (1841-1906) Memorial Marker. Cardwell Family Cemetery, Chestnut Mound, Smith County, Tennessee.*

Samuel Sullivan Cardwell *(1841–1906) - Private – Company H, 28th Regiment, Tennessee Infantry, CSA & Company A, 8th Regiment, Tennessee Mounted Infantry, USA*

Tennessee

Samuel Sullivan Cardwell was born on 08 December 1841 in Smith County, Tennessee, the son of Leonard H. Cardwell and Martha (Cornwell) Cardwell. He was raised in a farming family in the Upper Cumberland region and appears in his parents' household in both the 1850 and 1860 federal censuses for Smith County.[118,119] When war came, Samuel's choices would place him among a very small number of Cardwell men known to have served in both the Confederate and Union armies during the Civil War—a distinction that underscores the divided nature of Tennessee loyalties during the conflict.

On 18 December 1861, at the age of 20, Samuel enlisted as a Private in Company H of the 28th Tennessee Infantry, Confederate States Army, also known as the 2nd Tennessee Mountain Volunteers. His enlistment took place at Red Springs, Tennessee. The regiment was formed under the command of Colonel John P. Murray and drew recruits largely from Middle Tennessee, especially from Smith and surrounding counties. Initially tasked with protecting Tennessee's northern frontier, the 28th saw light action along the Kentucky-Tennessee border through early 1862.

By the spring of 1862, the 28th Tennessee was placed under General John C. Breckinridge's Brigade, part of the Army of Mississippi. The regiment moved into central Tennessee, preparing for major engagements as Confederate forces sought to reassert control in the region. However, Samuel Cardwell was discharged on 17 July 1862, according to his Confederate service records—more than five months before the regiment's significant participation in the Battle of Stones River near Murfreesboro (31 December 1862 to 02 January 1863). His discharge came during a period of transition for the Confederate army, but no explanation for his release is provided in the surviving records. Whether due to illness, injury, or hardship is unknown.

Following his brief Confederate service, Samuel returned to Smith County. On 04 April 1863, during the heart of the war, he married Marjorie Eugenia Robinson, also of Smith County.[120] The couple would go on to raise nine children, establishing a large and enduring family in the Chestnut Mound area: William Henry Cardwell (1869–1952), Mary Victoria Cardwell (1870–1960), Susan Ova Cardwell (1873–1945), Martha Charlotte Cardwell (1875–1915), Leonard Henton "Lennie" Cardwell (1879–1957), Joseph Allen "Joe" Cardwell (1881–1958), Anna Elizabeth Cardwell (1884–1959), Floy Eugenia Cardwell (1887–1985), and Fannie Bob Cardwell (1890–1982).

In a striking postscript to his earlier military service, Samuel enlisted again on 10 January 1865, this time as a Private in Company A, 8th Tennessee Mounted Infantry (U.S.), at Carthage, Tennessee. This unit, formed late in the war in a region known for its Unionist leanings, was created to help stabilize the region and suppress guerrilla activity that had flourished in Middle Tennessee after regular Confederate forces had retreated.

The 8th Tennessee Mounted Infantry (U.S.) was primarily engaged in garrison duties, scouting missions, and counter-guerrilla operations across Smith, Jackson, Putnam, and neighboring counties. By early 1865, Confederate resistance in Tennessee was largely limited to small bands of irregular fighters, and units like the 8th were instrumental in re-establishing Union authority in areas previously contested or left lawless.

Samuel is listed as present from the date of his enlistment through the end of his service, with no absences or illnesses reported. He was honorably discharged on 17 August 1865 in Nashville, Davidson County, Tennessee, having served in the final months of the war during the Union's occupation and stabilization phase.

Decades later, Samuel applied for a Federal Invalid Pension, which was approved on 03 September 1890. While the specific cause is not noted in available records, this pension suggests lasting physical hardship related to his wartime service. He appears in the 1880 and 1900 censuses for Smith County, residing in Chestnut Mound, where he worked as a farmer and raised his large family.[121,122]

Samuel died on 27 September 1906 in Smith County at the age of 64. He was buried in the Cardwell Family Cemetery, located in Chestnut Mound, where several generations of his family have been aid to rest.[123] His widow, Marjorie, survived him and later applied for a widow's pension, preserving his record as a two-service veteran of the war.

Though his service on both sides of the conflict may appear contradictory to modern readers, Samuel Sullivan Cardwell's story reflects the complex and often personal decisions made by men in a border state like Tennessee. His shift in allegiance—whatever its motive—was not uncommon among those who faced conflicting regional pressures, family dynamics, and the need to survive in a deeply fractured land. His life stands as a reminder of the blurred lines and lived realities of civil war in America. Cardwell Line III - Predicted. Photo Credits[124,125]

* * *

Silas H. Cardwell (1839–1913) - *Corporal – Company H, 24th Regiment, Tennessee Infantry, CSA*

Silas H. Cardwell was born around 1839 in Smith County, Tennessee, the son of Leonard H. Cardwell and Martha (Cornwell) Cardwell. He is listed with his parents in both the 1850 and 1860 Smith County census records.[126,127] Silas enlisted as a Private with Company H of the 24th Tennessee Infantry, Confederate States Army, on 27 June 1861 in Nashville, Tennessee. His older brother, William L. Cardwell, enlisted on the same day and is also profiled in this chapter. Silas was promoted to Corporal by January 1862, although the specific date of promotion is not recorded.

The 24th Tennessee Infantry was part of the Confederate forces engaged at the Battle of Shiloh, which took place on 06–07 April 1862 in Hardin County, Tennessee. While his records do not explicitly confirm his presence, it is likely that Silas took part in this battle. The engagement was among the bloodiest of the war, resulting in over 24,000 casualties.

Shortly after the battle, Silas was discharged for disability on 25 May 1862, while the unit was stationed near Corinth, Mississippi. There are no additional service records for him beyond this date.

Silas married Martha Victoria Robinson around 1863, based on the birth of their first child, although no official record of the marriage has been located. They had two children: William Daniel Cardwell (1864–1943) and Susan Emma Cardwell (1866–1961).

Following the war, Silas became a physician and is listed without his family in the 1870 census for Jackson County, Tennessee.[128] By the 1880 census, he is living in Smith County with his two children, as Martha had passed away.[129] In the 1910 census, he is recorded as a widower residing in Garland County, Arkansas.[130]

Dr. Silas H. Cardwell died on 01 August 1913 in Hot Springs, Garland County, Arkansas. The location of his grave is unknown.[131] Cardwell Line III - Predicted.

* * *

Thomas D. Cardwell (1833–1915) - *Private – Forrest's Regiment, Alabama Cavalry, CSA; Company A, 18th Regiment, Tennessee Cavalry*

(*Newsom's*), *CSA; Company A, 19th & 20th Consolidated Regiment, Tennessee Cavalry, CSA* - **Wounded in Action**

Thomas D. Cardwell was born in May 1833 at Lone Mountain in Claiborne County, Tennessee. He was the son of William Cardwell and Celia (Harper) Cardwell. By 1850, the family had relocated to McNairy County, Tennessee, where Thomas appears in the household census. Though his 1860 census record has not been located, he likely remained in that region.[132]

Around 1858, Thomas married Loretta "Creasy" Arnold, likely in McNairy County. No official marriage record has been found despite thorough research. They had six children: Martha Ann Cardwell (1859–1935), Andrew Jefferson Cardwell (1861–1937), Frances "Fanny" Cardwell (1862–1880), Leander Roy "Lee" Cardwell (1865–1912), George Cardwell (1869–1880), and Rebecca L. Cardwell (1872–1956). The family appears in the 1870 and 1880 McNairy County censuses and later in Dyer County, Tennessee, in the 1900 and 1910 census records.[133,134,135,136]

Thomas enlisted as a Private in Company A of Forrest's Regiment of Alabama Cavalry on 15 April 1864 at Green Hill, Tennessee, just days after the controversial Battle of Fort Pillow. This enlistment likely coincided with General Nathan Bedford Forrest's push to bolster his cavalry forces through both conscription and volunteering. Though his record does not specify which applied to Thomas, the fact that his brothers, Lee Roy and William Y. Cardwell, also served in the same regiment suggests he volunteered.

He later served with Company A of the 18th Tennessee Cavalry (Newsom's), CSA, a unit that had emerged through the reorganization of Forrest's Regiment. As the war wore on and Forrest's Cavalry Corps suffered mounting losses and internal restructuring, the 18th Tennessee Cavalry was eventually merged into the 19th & 20th Consolidated Tennessee Cavalry Regiment, in which Thomas is also recorded.

Thomas's Confederate Pension application, filed on 17 January 1900 in Dyer County, provides valuable insight into his wartime experiences. He was wounded in action at the Battle of Brice's Cross Roads—also known as the Battle of Guntown—on 10 June 1864, near Baldwyn, Mississippi. In that action, he suffered a gunshot wound to the arm and severe injuries when his horse fell on him. The impact damaged his foot and hip, and he noted in his pension that he never regained use of the wounded arm. Although he did not receive a formal disability discharge, the injuries rendered him unfit for further service.

Forrest's Cavalry Corps frequently reorganized due to high casualty rates and limited resources, complicating modern efforts to trace the service of soldiers like Thomas. Cardwell men often appeared in multiple regiments under Forrest's command due to these shifts, and analyzing enlistment dates and assignments across units was necessary to distinguish their individual paths. Thomas's records confirm this pattern, showing service in Forrest's Regiment, the 18th Tennessee Cavalry, and later the 19th & 20th Consolidated Regiment.

After the war, Thomas returned to civilian life and moved with his family to Dyer County, Tennessee. He died on 29 January 1915 at the age of 81 in Jenkinsville, Dyer County. He is buried at Mount Hope Church Cemetery in Jenkinsville.[137] His brothers Lee Roy Cardwell and William Y. Cardwell also served in Forrest's command and are documented elsewhere in this book, as is their brother Pryor Lewis Cardwell, who served in the 1st Louisiana Heavy Artillery (Regulars), CSA. Cardwell Line I - Confirmed.

* * *

Photo 9.17: *Thomas W. Cardwell (1836-1922) - probably Nolan County, Texas - circa 1920.*

Photo 9.18: *Thomas W. Cardwell (1836-1922) Memorial Marker. Roby Cemetery, Roby, Fisher County, Texas.*

Thomas W. Cardwell (1836–1922) - *Private – Coffee's Company, Douglas' Battalion, Tennessee Partisan Rangers, CSA; Company H, 11th Regiment, Tennessee Cavalry (Holman's), CSA*

Thomas W. Cardwell was born in November 1836 in Warren County, Tennessee, the son of Francis G. Cardwell and Judah (Lebow) Cardwell. His father passed away in 1845, and Thomas appears in the 1850 census in the household of his widowed mother.[138]

He married Amelia "Milly" Douglas on 6 March 1858 in Warren County. Together, they had eight children: Elza Cardwell (1859–1936), John Ramsey Cardwell (1861–1935), Victor Clark Cardwell (1863–1942), Magdalene "Maggie" Delene Cardwell (1866–1945), Robert Lee Cardwell (1868–1950), James Cardwell (1869–1880), Florence Cardwell (1875–1967), and Minnie Lee Cardwell (1879–1957). The family is recorded in the 1860 Warren County census before the onset of the Civil War.[139]

Thomas enlisted as a Private in Coffee's Company of Douglas' Battalion, Tennessee Partisan Rangers, CSA, on 15 September 1862 at McMinnville, Warren County. Partisan ranger units like Douglas' Battalion operated as irregular cavalry forces, conducting raids, disrupting Union supply lines, and gathering intelligence behind enemy lines. Douglas' Battalion would later become part of a larger cavalry reorganization under Confederate command.

On 01 October 1863, Thomas joined Company H of the 11th Regiment, Tennessee Cavalry (Holman's), CSA, which was formed through the consolidation of Holman's and Douglas' Battalions, along with other scattered cavalry companies. The 11th Tennessee Cavalry was incorporated into General Nathan Bedford Forrest's Cavalry Brigade, a highly mobile and aggressive fighting force known for lightning-fast raids and cavalry charges across the Western Theater. The regiment participated in key engagements, including the Battle of Brentwood, actions during the Chickamauga Campaign, the Atlanta Campaign, and Hood's operations in Tennessee.

Thomas's Confederate service records are limited. They show that he was absent without leave from March through June 1863, though it's unclear whether this affected his later service with the consolidated 11th Cavalry. No additional wartime documents confirm whether he remained with the unit through its final surrender to Union forces in May 1865. However, the unit itself continued to serve in Tennessee and northern Mississippi until the close of the war.

After the war, Thomas returned home to Warren County, where he appears in the 1870 and 1880 census records.[140,141] Around 1890, Thomas and most of his adult children relocated to Texas. He is recorded in the 1900 census in McLennan County and in 1910 in Nolan County, where he lived with his youngest daughter and son-in-law.[142,143]

Thomas died on 26 December 1922 in Nolan County, Texas. He is buried at Roby Cemetery, Roby, Fisher County, Texas.[144] Thomas's military service connects him to other Cardwell family members who fought for the Confederacy, including his older brother, Henry Jefferson Cardwell, and his nephew, James P. Cardwell, both of whom are documented in this chapter. Cardwell Line I - Confirmed. Photo credits[145,146]

* * *

William C. Cardwell (1834–) - *Private – Company I, 53rd Regiment, Tennessee Infantry, CSA* - **Prisoner of War**

William C. Cardwell was born around 1834 in Smith County, Tennessee, the son of Leonard Jefferson Cardwell and Lockey (Robinson) Cardwell. He appears in the household of his parents in both the 1850 and 1860 Smith County census records.[147,148]

William enlisted as a Private on 13 December 1861 in Nashville, Tennessee, joining Company I of the 53rd Regiment, Tennessee Infantry, CSA. The regiment quickly found itself in one of the earliest major engagements in the Western Theater — the Battle of Fort Donelson, which took place from 11 to 16 February 1862 in Stewart County, Tennessee. The Confederate defense ultimately failed, and the entire regiment, including William, was captured when the fort surrendered on 16 February 1862.

William was taken to Camp Morton, a Union prisoner of war camp located near Indianapolis, Indiana. His name appears on the prisoner rolls at that location as of June 1862. After several months of captivity, he was exchanged on 28 August 1862 at Vicksburg, Mississippi, in a prisoner exchange agreement between Union and Confederate authorities.

Following his release, William was granted furlough and returned home to Smith County, Tennessee. His service records indicate he remained on furlough from August to October 1862, but there are no further Confederate records available for him after that point. It is unknown whether he resumed service with the 53rd or another unit following his recovery and return.

William is listed in the 1870 Smith County, Tennessee census, but there is no indication that he ever married or had children.[149] There is no other known documents or records for William. The date and circumstances of his death remain undocumented, and his final resting place is unknown.

William C. Cardwell's brief but active service—marked by early combat, imprisonment, and release—reflects the often disjointed and perilous path of many Civil War soldiers. His story remains a part of the broader narrative of the men who fought with the 53rd Tennessee Infantry, particularly during the critical early years of the conflict. Cardwell Line III - Predicted.

* * *

Photo 9.19: *William Dudley Cardwell (1842-1926) - Reno County, Kansas - circa 1920 (Photo cropped and enhanced)*

Photo 9.20: *William Dudley Cardwell (1842-1926) Headstone. Fairview Cemetery, Elmer, Reno County, Kansas.*

William Dudley Cardwell (1842–1926) - *Private – Company I, 30th Regiment, Tennessee Infantry, CSA* - **Prisoner of War**

William Dudley Cardwell was born on 16 December 1842 in Sumner County, Tennessee, the eldest son of Dudley D. Cardwell and Elizabeth (Hinton) Cardwell. He appears in the household of his parents in the 1850 and 1860 Sumner County census records.[150,151]

William enlisted as a Private in Company I, 30th Regiment, Tennessee Infantry, CSA, on 22 November 1861 at Fort Donelson, Tennessee. His regiment was immediately involved in the defense of the fort, which became the site of a pivotal early engagement in the Western Theater. From 11 to 16 February 1862, Confederate forces at Fort Donelson faced overwhelming Union attack. When the fort surrendered on 16 February 1862, William was among the thousands of Confederate troops captured by Union forces.

He was taken as a Prisoner of War and transported to Camp Butler, near Springfield, Illinois—a Union POW camp notorious for harsh conditions and disease. During his captivity, William took the Oath of Allegiance to the United States government. Despite this, he was later exchanged and released at Vicksburg, Mississippi, on 23 September 1862. There are no further military service records indicating that he resumed Confederate service after his exchange.

Following the war, William returned to civilian life and married Julia Ann McDowell around 1867, likely in Sumner County, Tennessee, though no marriage record has been located. They had at least six children: Fannie Elizabeth Cardwell (1868–1948), Jane Cardwell (1869–1870), John Dudley "Jack" Cardwell (1871–1949), Willa Armistice Cardwell (1875–1970), Joseph "Joe" Wesley Cardwell (1877–1949), and Hattie M. Cardwell (1881–).

The 1870 census lists William and his family in Sumner County, Tennessee. By 1880, they had moved west to Miami County, Kansas, and continued their life as pioneers on the frontier. The family later settled in Coffey County, where they are recorded in the 1900 and 1910 censuses, and eventually moved to Reno County, where William appears in the 1920 census.[152,153,154,155,156]

William Dudley Cardwell passed away on 05 February 1926 in Hutchinson, Reno County, Kansas. He is buried at Fairview Cemetery in Elmer, Reno County, Kansas. His journey from Confederate soldier to Kansas settler reflects the broader path taken by many veterans who sought peace and pros-

perity in the decades following the Civil War.[157] <u>Cardwell Line III -
Predicted</u>. Photo Credits[158,159]

* * *

William G. Cardwell (1838–1862) - *Private – Company K, 6th Regiment,
Tennessee Infantry, CSA* - **Killed in Action**

William G. Cardwell was born around 1838 in Hardeman County,
Tennessee, the eldest son of Thomas T. Cardwell and Susan (Street) Cardwell. His parents had married in 1836 in Halifax County, Virginia, before
relocating to Tennessee. The family first appears in the 1840 census in
Hardeman County and later in Madison County by 1850, where they are
listed in both the 1850 and 1860 census records. William is enumerated in
the household during both census years.[160,161,162]

On 15 May 1861, William enlisted as a Private in Company K, 6th Regiment, Tennessee Infantry, CSA, at Jackson, the county seat of Madison
County. Company K, locally known as "The Danes," was raised from residents of Madison County and formed part of the original organization of the
regiment early in the war. The 6th Tennessee Infantry was assigned to
Brigadier General Patrick R. Cleburne's Brigade and quickly earned a reputation for toughness and discipline.

Early in his service, William was listed as on sick furlough as of 28 July
1861, indicating he had likely been ill during the initial months of training
and encampment. He returned to duty before the spring of 1862, when the
6th Tennessee was moved to Hardin County, preparing to face its first major
combat.

The regiment saw heavy action at the Battle of Shiloh on 06–07 April
1862, one of the bloodiest engagements in the Western Theater. During the
second day of fighting, Confederate forces attempted to regroup after early
momentum faltered. It was during this phase, on 07 April 1862, that
William G. Cardwell was Killed in Action. His exact circumstances are
unknown, but based on the timing and location, he likely died during the
chaotic Confederate counterattacks and defensive stands near Pittsburg
Landing.

Due to the high number of casualties and the conditions of the battlefield,
it is probable that William was buried in a mass grave, as was common for
many fallen soldiers at Shiloh. His name stands among the thousands who

perished in what became a turning point in the Civil War. <u>Cardwell Line III -
Predicted</u>.

* * *

Photo 9.21: *Confederate Memorial Mound - Camp Douglas POW
Dead - Oak Woods Cemetery, Chicago, Cook County, Illinois.*

Photo 9.22: *William H. Cardwell (1836-1864) - Confederate Mound
Memorial - Camp Douglas POW Dead - Oak Woods Cemetery, Chicago,
Cook County, Illinois.*

William H. Cardwell (1836-1864) - *Private — Company F, 9th Regiment,
Tennessee Cavalry (Ward's), CSA; Also associated with: 15th Regiment,
Tennessee Cavalry, CSA -* **Prisoner of War - Died in Captivity.**

William H. Cardwell was born around 1836 in Smith County,
Tennessee, the son of Daniel J. Cardwell and Addalid (Kyle) Cardwell. He
appears with his family in the 1850 U.S. Census in Smith County and again
in the 1860 census in Obion County, Tennessee.[163,164]

William initially enlisted on 23 May 1861 as a Private in Company G of the 9th Tennessee Infantry, CSA, at Jackson, Madison County, Tennessee. His record from this period indicates that he was listed as deserted on 25 November 1862, though this likely reflects a transfer rather than abandonment, as most of his remaining service records are with Company F, 9th Tennessee Cavalry (Ward's).

The 9th Tennessee Cavalry, commanded by Colonel William Ward, was attached to General John Hunt Morgan's Brigade and actively engaged in Confederate operations across Tennessee and Kentucky. One of their most significant actions was the Battle of Hartsville on 07 December 1862, where Morgan's forces executed a successful surprise attack, capturing over 1,800 Union soldiers with relatively few Confederate losses.

In June 1863, the 9th Tennessee Cavalry joined Morgan's Raid, a bold cavalry incursion into Indiana and Ohio, intended to draw Union forces away from Southern strongholds. The raid culminated in the Battle of Buffington Island on 19 July 1863, where Union troops intercepted Morgan's column. The result was disastrous for the Confederates, with hundreds killed, wounded, or captured—including William H. Cardwell, who was taken prisoner at Buffington, Ohio.

William was transferred to Camp Morton near Indianapolis, Indiana, on 23 July 1863, and later sent to the notorious Camp Douglas in Chicago, Illinois, arriving there on 17 August 1863. Conditions at Camp Douglas were notoriously harsh, with overcrowding, limited rations, and rampant disease. On 25 March 1864, a notation in William's record reflects his deteriorating spirit, reading: *"Is tired of the unholy rebellion. Wants to take the oath and become loyal."* Such declarations were not uncommon among Confederate prisoners facing dire conditions.

Tragically, William died of chronic diarrhea on 04 November 1864 while imprisoned at Camp Douglas. He was initially buried at Chicago City Cemetery, but his remains were later reinterred at Oak Woods Cemetery, Chicago, Cook County, Illinois, in the Confederate Mound.[165]

Some Confederate records also associate William with Company F, 15th Tennessee Cavalry, CSA, a unit with no official documentation. This reference likely stems from consolidation or confusion within prison rolls, as other members of the 9th Cavalry also claimed affiliation with that unit while in captivity. Cardwell Line III - Predicted. Photo Credits[166,167]

* * *

William L. Cardwell (1831–) - *Private – Company H, 24th Regiment, Tennessee Infantry, CSA -* **Prisoner of War**

William L. Cardwell was born around 1831 in Smith County, Tennessee, the eldest son of Leonard H. Cardwell and Martha (Cornwell) Cardwell. He appears in the home of his parents in both the 1850 and 1860 Smith County census records.[168,169]

On 16 April 1851, he married Susan F. Robinson in Smith County.[170] Together, they had at least five children: Martha Tennessee Cardwell (1853–1883), Eliza Virginia "Jennie" Cardwell (1853–1920), William Henton Cardwell (1857–1930), George Lemuel Cardwell (1858–1920), and Robert Brown Cardwell (1861–1925).

William enlisted as a Private in Company H of the 24th Regiment, Tennessee Infantry, CSA, on 27 June 1862, in Nashville, Tennessee. His younger brother, Silas H. Cardwell, enlisted with him the same day and is also profiled in this chapter. Although William's enlistment came after the Battle of Shiloh (April 06–07, 1862), it is possible he may have served unofficially or in a support role during that time, as some unit records mention personnel present before formal muster dates.

The 24th Tennessee Infantry, part of Cleburne's Brigade, participated in several major engagements during the war. William likely saw action at:

• Battle of Perryville (October 1862), where the regiment held the Confederate left

• Battle of Stones River (December 1862 – January 1863), where both sides suffered heavy losses

• Battle of Chickamauga (September 1863), the most significant Confederate victory in the Western Theater

• Battle of Missionary Ridge (November 1863), where the Confederate line collapsed under Union assault

• The Atlanta Campaign (Summer 1864), a prolonged and grueling series of engagements

• Battle of Franklin (November 1864), one of the bloodiest and most tragic Confederate defeats

Having survived nearly three years of continuous campaigning, William was finally captured on 10 December 1864 near Granny White Bridge during the Battle of Nashville. Following his capture, he was first held at a military prison in Louisville, Kentucky, and then transferred to the infamous Camp Douglas, a Union prisoner-of-war camp in Chicago, on 21 December 1864.

On 10 May 1865, shortly after the war's conclusion, William took the Oath of Allegiance to the United States. His parole documentation describes him as a resident of Smith County, Tennessee, with a sandy complexion, red hair, blue eyes, and standing 5 feet 7½ inches tall.

Despite his survival of numerous battles and time as a POW, no post-war records for William L. Cardwell have been located. His wife and children appear without him in the 1870 Smith County census, suggesting he may have died shortly after the war or disappeared from public records.[171]

His date of death and final resting place remain unknown. Cardwell Line III - Predicted.

* * *

William Mankin Cardwell (1843–1922) - *Private – Company F, 9th Regiment, Tennessee Cavalry, CSA*

William Mankin Cardwell was born on 08 December 1843 in Smith County, Tennessee, the son of Isaac Moody Cardwell and Serena (Richardson) Cardwell. He is recorded in the home of his parents in both the 1850 and 1860 Smith County, Tennessee census records.[172,173]

While no official Confederate service record has been located for William, his widow's Confederate Pension application, filed on 13 November 1922 in Brazoria County, Texas, offers insight into his Civil War service. She stated that William served for approximately two years in Company F of General Morgan's Cavalry and noted that he became sick and went on extended leave prior to the end of the war. Although his name does not appear in surviving rosters of the unit, the application was approved, suggesting that his service was verified through affidavits or community testimony—common practice in cases where records were lost or destroyed.

It is a logical assumption that William served in Company F, 9th Regiment, Tennessee Cavalry, CSA, the same unit in which his older brother, John B. Cardwell, served. The 9th Tennessee Cavalry was part of General John Hunt Morgan's command and was engaged in cavalry operations across Tennessee and Kentucky. Morgan's Cavalry gained fame for bold raids into Union territory, including Morgan's Raid into Indiana and Ohio in 1863. The unit also participated in numerous skirmishes and battles before Morgan's eventual capture and death in 1864. William likely saw action during this turbulent period and was eventually sidelined by illness.

Following the war, William returned to Smith County and married Melvina I. LNU on 16 January 1868, according to his widow's pension affidavit. No official marriage certificate has been located, but the date is supported by census data and family records. The couple had two known children: Von Herbert Cardwell (1868–1955), and Lillian E. Cardwell (1868–1956).

In 1870, William and his young family were living in the household of his parents in Smith County.[174] By 1880, they had moved next door to his parents and remained in the same area.[175] Around the turn of the century, William relocated to Texas, where he is listed in the 1900, 1910, and 1920 McLennan County, Texas census records.[176,177,178]

William Mankin Cardwell died on 05 November 1922 in Brazoria County, Texas, and was laid to rest in the Confederate Cemetery in Alvin, Brazoria County, Texas.[179] Though his wartime service is lightly documented, his legacy lives on through his descendants and the recognition granted by the State of Texas for his Confederate service. His brother, John B. Cardwell, who also rode with Morgan's Cavalry, is recorded elsewhere in this book. Cardwell Line III - Predicted.

Photo 9.23: *Confederate Memorial Mound - Camp Douglas POW Dead - Oak Woods Cemetery, Chicago, Cook County, Illinois.*

Photo 9.24: *William T. Cardwell (1842-1862) - Confederate Mound Memorial - Camp Douglas POW Dead - Oak Woods Cemetery, Chicago, Cook County, Illinois.*

William T. Cardwell (1841–1862) - *Private – Company D, 26th Regiment, Tennessee Infantry, CSA* - **Prisoner of War - Died in Captivity.**

William T. Cardwell was born in 1841 in Grainger County, Tennessee, the son of Richard M. Cardwell and Sarah "Sally" Jane (Crowder) Cardwell. His father passed away in January 1850 in Rockingham County, North Carolina, where William is listed living with his widowed mother and siblings in that year's census.[180] By 1860, the family had relocated to Union County, Tennessee, where William appears again in the household of his mother.[181]

At the age of 19, William enlisted as a Private in Company D of the 26th Regiment, Tennessee Infantry, CSA, on 14 August 1861, at Knoxville, Tennessee. He traveled 55 miles to enlist, a testament to his commitment to the Confederate cause. His older brother, James R. Cardwell, also enlisted in the same company and is profiled separately in this volume.

The 26th Tennessee Infantry saw early action at the Battle of Fort Donelson, fought from 11 to 16 February 1862 in Stewart County, Tennessee. It was the regiment's first major engagement and proved costly, with the unit suffering approximately 25% casualties before ultimately surrendering alongside much of the Confederate garrison. William and his brother were among those taken as prisoners of war.

Following the surrender, William was transferred to Camp Douglas, a Union POW camp located in Chicago, Illinois. Infamous for its brutal conditions, Camp Douglas quickly earned the grim nickname "Eighty Acres of Hell." Poor sanitation, overcrowding, and inadequate shelter and medical care led to rampant disease and malnutrition. More than 6,000 Confederate prisoners perished there during the war.

On 15 May 1862, William was admitted to the Camp Douglas prison hospital, suffering from pneumonia. He died the next day, on 16 May 1862, never having seen freedom again. He was likely interred in one of the mass graves established for Confederate dead at Camp Douglas, now memorialized at Oak Woods Cemetery, in Chicago, Cook County, Illinois.

His brother, James R. Cardwell, was exchanged as a POW at Vicksburg, Mississippi in April 1862, a few weeks before William's death, and returned to duty with the 26th Tennessee Infantry. James's continued service is described elsewhere in this chapter.

William T. Cardwell's sacrifice represents the tragic fate of many young Confederate soldiers who suffered not only on the battlefield but in the prison camps that followed. His date of death is well-documented, but the precise location of his burial remains unknown. Cardwell Line I - Predicted. Photo Credits[182,183]

* * *

Photo 9.25: *Alton POW Camp Confederate Cemetery Memorial. Alton, Madison County, Illinois.*

Photo 9.26: *William Y. Cardwell (1839-1863) Memorial. Alton POW Camp Confederate Memorial. Alton, Madison County, Illinois. The use of Missouri is incorrect.*

William Y. Cardwell (1839–1863) - *Private – Company F, Forrest's Regiment, Alabama Cavalry, CSA & Company F, 18th Regiment, Tennessee Cavalry (Newsome's), CSA -* **Prisoner of War - Died in Captivity**

William Y. Cardwell was born around 1839 in McNairy County, Tennessee, the son of William Cardwell and Celia (Harper) Cardwell. He is listed in their household in the 1850 McNairy County census.[184] Around 1858, William married Letha Ellen Ledbetter, likely in McNairy County. They had one known child, Margaret Cardwell (born 1859). The 1860 McNairy County census records the young family together.[185] After Letha's death, which occurred sometime after 1860, William remarried to Margaret Moore on 13 May 1863, also in McNairy County, Tennessee.[186]

William enlisted as a Private in Company F of Forrest's Regiment,

Alabama Cavalry, CSA, on 01 June 1863, at Tuscumbia, Colbert County, Alabama. His brother Lee Roy P. Cardwell enlisted alongside him, and another brother, Thomas D. Cardwell, joined later in April 1864. These men would serve in the famed cavalry commanded by General Nathan Bedford Forrest, known for bold raids, rapid movements, and aggressive tactics.

Just over four months into his service, William was captured by Union forces on 22 October 1863 at Corinth, Alcorn County, Mississippi. He was transferred to the Alton Prison in Madison County, Illinois, on 08 November 1863, arriving four days later. His Prisoner of War (POW) records show various entries under the names William, William G., William U., and William Y. Cardwell, which caused some archival confusion. Military units listed under his records include Porter's Cavalry, Moodie's Cavalry, Damerson's Cavalry, and Forrest's Cavalry—though all documentation has since been consolidated, confirming it was the same individual throughout. The multiple aliases and unit names suggest William may have intentionally obscured his affiliations during captivity.

While at Alton, William contracted smallpox and was sent to Smallpox Island, a quarantine site across the river from the prison. Conditions were notoriously poor, and the disease was rampant. Over 1,500 Confederate prisoners died at Alton during the Civil War. On 15 December 1863, William succumbed to the illness and was buried at Smallpox Island. His name is engraved on the Confederate monument erected at Alton Cemetery in Madison County, Illinois, although it incorrectly lists him as a member of Porter's Missouri Cavalry.

Ten days prior to his death, he refused to take an oath of allegiance to the United States government. The exact quote from the records states,"*Conscripted objects to exchange of desires to take the oath of allegiance.*"[187]

His widow, Margaret Moore Cardwell, applied for a Confederate Widow's Pension on 03 January 1912, affirming his true service with Forrest's Cavalry.

William's brothers, Thomas D. Cardwell and Lee Roy P. Cardwell, also served in Forrest's Cavalry Corps, and both are recorded in this volume. William and Lee Roy even enlisted on the same day, 01 June 1863. Their joint service highlights the profound familial commitment to the Confederate cause and the widespread impact of the war on the Cardwell family. Cardwell Line I - Predicted. Photo Credits[188,189]

* * *

NOTE: There are three individuals that after exhaustive research appears to be incorrectly indexed as Cardwell men. Their BIOs are not included, but are added for the sake of being through.

H.L. Cardwell - 154th Senior Regiment, Tennessee Infantry (1st Tennessee Volunteers), CSA

Leonidas Cardwell - Lynch's Company, Tennessee Light Artillery, CSA

Robert J. Cardwell - 46th Regiment, Tennessee Infantry, CSA - Service Records state him as Caldwell

Texas
The Cardwell Confederates

TEXAS, THOUGH GEOGRAPHICALLY DISTANT FROM MANY OF THE CIVIL War's major battles, played a vital role in the Confederate war effort. As one of the original states to secede, Texas contributed troops, supplies, and strategic access to trade routes through Mexico. The state was largely spared from large-scale battles, but its soldiers served in critical engagements across the Western and Trans-Mississippi Theaters. Texas cavalry units were particularly well-regarded, often utilized for reconnaissance, raids, and hit-and-run tactics against Union forces.

The Cardwell men who served in the Confederate ranks from Texas were part of a variety of regiments, each contributing in different ways to the war effort. Their service was part of Texas' broader military contributions, which saw thousands of men enlist to fight for the South.

Though the war largely spared Texas from major battles, the Cardwell men who served in its regiments faced the same hardships as soldiers elsewhere—long marches, disease, and the ever-present threat of combat. James Albert Cardwell, Robert Wilkerson Cardwell, Thomas Sterling Cardwell, and John Madison Cardwell, all brothers and sons of Anthony R. Cardwell and Mary Condray (Perryman) Cardwell of Caldwell County, Texas, served faithfully in the Confederate ranks. Whether defending the Gulf Coast or pushing back Union advances in Louisiana, these men were part of a broader effort to maintain Texas' role in the Confederacy.

This chapter tells the stories of the Cardwell brothers from Texas, honoring their service and sacrifice as part of the Confederate war effort.

* * *

Photo 10.1: *James Albert Cardwell (1827-1908) - Caldwell County, Texas - circa 1885 (Provided by Margaret Anderson)*

Photo 10.2: *James Albert Cardwell (1827-1908) Headstone - Lytton Springs Cemetery, Lytton Springs, Caldwell County, Texas*

James Albert Cardwell (1827–1908) - *Unknown Rank and Unit – Confederate Service Tradition*

James Albert Cardwell was born on 27 August 1827 in Grainger County, Tennessee. He was the son of Anthony R. Cardwell and Mary Condray (Perryman) Cardwell. By 1850, James had relocated to neighboring Jefferson County, Tennessee, where he is listed in the household of A.G. Watkins.[1]

This connection may have been familial, as he later married Margaret Reese Watkins on 19 April 1855 in Caldwell County, Texas.

James and his younger brother, Robert Wilkerson Cardwell, migrated to Texas sometime between 1850 and 1855. They settled in Caldwell County and appear as neighbors in the 1860 census.[2] James and Margaret raised three children: Margaret Louisa Cardwell (1856–1942), Lawson Aubrey Cardwell (1858–1915), and Mary Alice Cardwell (1861–1955). The family remained in Caldwell County, Texas, where James is listed in the 1870, 1880, and 1900 census records.[3,4,5]

There is no known Confederate service record for James Albert Cardwell, despite strong family tradition and community recognition of his participation in the war. His obituary noted, "He was a Confederate soldier who served with honor to himself & the South," and this sentiment was echoed by local residents who described him as a "highly esteemed" citizen. Given the reliability of similar statements in other obituaries and the social importance placed on military service among Confederate veterans, it is likely that James did indeed serve.

The absence of official records is not unusual for Confederate soldiers. Many rosters, enlistment rolls, and service documents were lost or destroyed during and after the war. In numerous cases examined throughout the research for this book, men whose service was acknowledged by pensions, affidavits, or community statements had no formal muster or enlistment records surviving. Unfortunately, no Confederate pension application has been located for James, possibly due to his choice not to apply or to missing documentation.

James Albert Cardwell died on 07 December 1908 in Caldwell County, Texas. He is buried at Lytton Springs Cemetery in Lytton Springs, Caldwell County, Texas. While the exact nature of his service remains undocumented, the legacy of his contribution to the Confederate cause endures through family memory and the testimony of his peers. His brothers—Robert Wilkerson Cardwell, Thomas Sterling Cardwell, and John Madison Cardwell—served in documented Confederate units from Texas and are also recorded in this volume. <u>Cardwell Line II - Confirmed</u>. Photo Credits[6,7]

* * *

Photo 10.3: *John Madison Cardwell (1836-1917) - Lockhart, Caldwell County, Texas - circa 1900 (photo enhanced)*

Photo 10.4: *John Madison Cardwell (1836-1917) Headstone - Lockhart Municipal Burial Park, Lockhart, Caldwell County, Texas.*

John Madison Cardwell (1836-1917) - *Private - Company B, 26th Regiment, Texas Cavalry (Debray's) (Davis' Mounted Battalion), CSA*

John Madison Cardwell was born on 18 June 1836 in Jefferson County, Tennessee. He was the son of Anthony R. Cardwell and Mary Condray (Perryman) Cardwell. He appears in the home of his parents in the 1850 Jefferson County, Tennessee census. During the 1850s, his family moved westward, settling in Caldwell County, Texas. By 1860, John is listed in their household in that county's census.[8,9]

When the Civil War began, John enlisted as a Private with Company B of the 26th Regiment, Texas Cavalry, CSA, on 28 August 1861, at Galveston, Texas. He was 25 years old at the time of enlistment. The unit, also known as Debray's Regiment or Davis' Mounted Battalion, was organized for service in the Trans-Mississippi Department. Initially formed as a cavalry regiment, the unit was later dismounted and operated primarily as mounted infantry, responding to the logistical and strategic demands of the Confederate defense of Texas and Louisiana.

Cardwell's early military service took place during the unit's garrison duties at Galveston, where Confederate forces worked to fortify the port city and resist Union naval blockades. From the time of his enlistment through June 1862, John is consistently listed as present for duty, indicating active participation in training, defensive drills, and coastal patrols.

On 28 August 1862, one year to the day after his enlistment, Cardwell was granted a 20-day furlough to recover from illness in Lockhart, Caldwell County. He rejoined his company by November 1862, as the 26th Texas Cavalry was being shifted to Louisiana to participate in field operations, primarily in defense of the Red River region. From late 1862 into early 1863, the regiment took part in minor engagements and reconnaissance operations, supporting Confederate troop movements in the Opelousas and Teche areas.

By December 1863, John had demonstrated qualities of reliability and competence, as he was assigned to special duty as a courier to Brigade Headquarters and served as a personal escort to General Xavier Debray. This trusted role required him to carry important orders and communications, often under hazardous conditions between dispersed commands.

Cardwell remained with the regiment through 1864, but records indicate that he was placed on sick leave once more and returned to Caldwell County. His medical furlough extended until at least 05 April 1865, shortly before the conclusion of hostilities in the Trans-Mississippi Theater. His extended absence from duty suggests that he suffered from a prolonged illness or physical debility incurred during earlier campaigns. No additional service records have been located beyond this point.

The 26th Texas Cavalry, while not engaged in many of the war's major battles, played an important role in Confederate operations across the western theater. The unit defended key infrastructure, protected supply routes, and fought in regional campaigns in Louisiana. Its role was vital in maintaining Confederate control over vast areas of territory despite limited manpower and resources.

After the war, John returned to civilian life in Caldwell County. He married Martha "Mattie" Withers on 28 December 1869.[10] Together they had eight children: Jesse Phillips Cardwell (1871–1956), Burma Cardwell (1874–), James Albert Cardwell (1876–1969), John Ireland Cardwell (1879–1957), Mary Allie Cardwell (1884–1944), Mattie Josie Cardwell (1885–1888), August Withers "Gus" Cardwell (1889–1961), and Walter Wilcox Cardwell (1892–1960). John appears in the 1870, 1880, 1900, and 1910 Caldwell County census records.[11,12,13,14]

He remained in the Lockhart area until his death on 22 December 1917. He is buried at Lockhart Municipal Burial Park in Lockhart, Caldwell County, Texas.[15] His life and service reflect the experiences of many soldiers in the Trans-Mississippi—marked by long distances, illness, and the shifting demands of war in the western Confederacy. Cardwell Line II - Confirmed. Photo Credits[16,17]

* * *

Photo 10.5: *Robert Wilkerson Cardwell (1829-1914) Headstone - Lytton Springs Cemetery, Lytton Springs, Caldwell County, Texas*

Robert Wilkerson Cardwell (1829-1914) - *Private - Company K, 17th Regiment, Texas Infantry (Allen's), CSA*

Robert Wilkerson Cardwell was born on 14 July 1829 in Grainger County, Tennessee. He was the son of Anthony R. Cardwell and Mary Condray (Perryman) Cardwell. Robert appears in the home of his parents in the 1850 Jefferson County, Tennessee census.[18] Sometime after 1850, he moved west with family members to Texas. While their father did not settle in Caldwell County until around 1858, Robert and his brother James Albert Cardwell are believed to have arrived earlier, likely by 1852. In the 1860 Caldwell County, Texas census, Robert is listed with his wife and living next to his brother, though both families were incorrectly indexed under the surname "Cordwell."[19] Robert is living with his wife and next to his brother, James Albert Cardwell, in the 1860 Caldwell County, Texas census.

Robert married Tompsey C. Watkins on 15 August 1855 in Caldwell County, Texas. The marriage is documented in a family Bible. Despite their long marriage, it appears that they had no children.

Robert enlisted as a Private in Company K of the 17th Texas Infantry, CSA, on 27 March 1862 at Lockhart, Caldwell County, Texas. He was 34 years old at the time, born in Tennessee, and working as a farmer. His service records describe him as standing six feet tall, with a fair complexion, blue eyes, and light-colored hair—a physical description common among frontier Texans of the period.

The 17th Texas Infantry was formed in early 1862 with companies drawn from central Texas counties, including Caldwell. Company K represented men from Lockhart and the surrounding area. The regiment became part of Walker's Texas Division, one of the most active Confederate commands operating west of the Mississippi River in the Trans-Mississippi Department. Their initial duties included training and garrison operations in Texas, followed by deployment to Arkansas and Louisiana, where they helped guard supply lines and counter Union activity along the Mississippi and Red Rivers.

Private Cardwell's time in the army, however, was short-lived. By September 1862, just six months after his enlistment, he had become seriously ill and was granted an extended furlough to recover. Illness, particularly in the Gulf region, was one of the greatest threats to Confederate soldiers. Disease often decimated units more severely than combat, and Robert's experience was no exception.

His health did not improve, and he never returned to active duty. After nearly two years on medical leave, he was formally discharged on 24 February 1864 due to "very feeble health," as noted in his disability papers. His discharge reflects a common fate for many Civil War soldiers who, though willing to fight, were sidelined by chronic illness, unsanitary camp conditions, and the exhausting environmental realities of war in the western Confederacy.

After the war, Robert resumed life in Caldwell County, Texas. He lived out his remaining years in the Lytton Springs area.

Robert Wilkerson Cardwell died on 03 February 1914 in Caldwell County, Texas. He is buried at Lytton Springs Cemetery in Lytton Springs, Caldwell County.[20] His quiet postwar life and brief military service mirror the experiences of many Southern volunteers whose battles were often not with bullets, but with the slow toll of disease. <u>Cardwell Line II - Confirmed</u>. Photo Credit[21]

* * *

Photo 10.6: *Thomas Sterling Cardwell (1833-1899) - Caldwell County, Texas - circa 1885 - (photo enchanced)*

Photo 10.7: *Thomas Sterling Cardwell (1833-1899) Headstone - Lockhart Municipal Burial Park, Lockhart, Caldwell County, Texas.*

Thomas Sterling Cardwell (1833-1899) - *Private - Company C, 3rd Regiment, Texas Infantry, CSA*

Thomas Sterling Cardwell was born on 04 August 1833 in Grainger County, Tennessee. He was the son of Anthony R. Cardwell and Mary Condray (Perryman) Cardwell. By 1850, he appears in the home of his parents in Jefferson County, Tennessee, and moved with the family to Caldwell County, Texas, during the 1850s as part of the broader westward migration of Southern families in the antebellum years[22]

Thomas married Catherine "Kate" Copenhaver on 29 December 1859 in Caldwell County, Texas.[23] Together, they had eight children: Alonzo "Lonnie" Madison Cardwell (1861–1958), William Alexander Cardwell (1862–1946), Mabry E. Cardwell (1866–1869), Robert Lee Cardwell (1869–1946), Charles M. Cardwell (1871–1955), Albert James Cardwell (1873–1953), Betty Lou Cardwell (1875–1976), and Kate "Kittie" Cardwell (1878–1968). Thomas and his family are listed in the 1860, 1870, 1880, and 1900 Caldwell

County census records, where he worked as a farmer and remained an active member of the community.[24,25,26,27]

Thomas enlisted in the Confederate Army as a Private in Company C of the 3rd Texas Infantry on 12 July 1862. He was 28 years old, 5 feet 8 inches tall, with blue eyes and light hair, and was living in Caldwell County at the time of his enlistment. The 3rd Texas Infantry, known for its service in the Trans-Mississippi Department, was made up of volunteers from Central and East Texas and played a key role in coastal defense and supply line protection in the western Confederacy.

Much of the regiment's service took place in Texas and Louisiana, where they guarded ports, rivers, and transportation routes against Union incursions. Though the regiment did not participate in major battles of the Eastern Theater, it served a vital function in maintaining Confederate control of the Gulf Coast and protecting important logistical hubs.

Thomas Cardwell's Civil War service reflects the struggles common to Confederate soldiers stationed in disease-prone areas. In May 1863, he fell ill and was admitted to the General Hospital in Houston, Texas, on 09 September 1863 with "febris remittens"—a form of remittent fever, likely malaria. After nearly three weeks of recovery, he was furloughed until 28 September 1863.

He rejoined his unit on 20 October 1863 at Sabine City, Texas—a strategic Gulf Coast port town vital to the Confederate defense of the eastern Texas border. There, Cardwell served in a logistical support role, a necessary assignment given the ongoing threat of Union naval landings and inland raids.

By April 1865, in the final weeks of the war, Cardwell was serving as a teamster, responsible for driving wagons and transporting supplies. This was a critical assignment that kept Confederate forces operational as the war dragged on. Though the 3rd Texas Infantry did not see large-scale combat, its efforts ensured the continued Confederate presence in Texas until the general surrender in May 1865.

No additional Civil War records have been located for Thomas following this period. After the war, he returned to civilian life in Caldwell County, where he resumed farming and raised a large family.

Thomas Sterling Cardwell died on 16 December 1899 in Lockhart, Caldwell County, Texas. He is buried at Lockhart Municipal Burial Park in Lockhart, Texas, near other members of the Cardwell family.[28] His service, while far from the major battlefields of the East, reflects the endurance and vital contributions of Texas Confederate soldiers in the Trans-Mississippi theater. <u>Cardwell Line II - Confirmed</u>. Photo Credits[29,30]

* * *

NOTE: There is another veteran who was incorrectly indexed as a Cardwell but was a Cadwell. The correct index should identify Samuel Cardwell as Samuel Cadwell. Another one of interest is J.A. Cartwell, but research proved him to be James A. Cartmell. I initially thought that this might be James Albert Cardwell.

Virginia
The Cardwell Confederates

VIRGINIA WAS THE EPICENTER OF THE CIVIL WAR, HOME TO THE Confederate capital of Richmond and the site of some of the most pivotal battles of the conflict. As the war's most contested state, Virginia witnessed more major battles than any other, including Manassas, Fredericksburg, Chancellorsville, and Appomattox. The state's strategic importance meant that its men, including the Cardwell soldiers, served in numerous regiments defending its soil and fighting in campaigns that defined the war.

The Cardwell men from Virginia served in a diverse range of roles, from frontline infantry and cavalry skirmishes to artillery and local defense battalions. Their contributions helped define the war in the Eastern Theater, and many fought in the most significant battles of the conflict.

This chapter honors their service, preserving their stories as part of Virginia's Civil War legacy and Cardwell family history.

* * *

Berry A. Cardwell (1842-<1900) - *Private - Company F, 1st Virginia Artillery, CSA; Company E, 32nd Regiment, Virginia Infantry, CSA & Company B, 7th Regiment, South Carolina Cavalry (Holcombe), CSA*

Berry A. Cardwell was born around 1842 in York County, Virginia, the son of William Cardwell and Eliza (Austin) Cardwell. He is listed in the home of his parents in the 1850 York County census.[1] His early service in the

Confederate Army began on 13 May 1861, when he enlisted as a Private in Company G of the 32nd Regiment of Virginia Infantry, CSA, at Williamsburg, Virginia. The 32nd Virginia Infantry was formed in May 1861 and initially served in defensive operations along the Virginia Peninsula. Composed of men primarily from the Tidewater region, the regiment participated in the early defense of the Confederate capital and engaged in garrison duties around strategic points like Yorktown and Williamsburg. Berry's record in this unit is brief, noting that he was sick for a week beginning on 28 August 1861.

Shortly thereafter, on 20 May 1861, Berry was transferred to Company F of the 1st Virginia Artillery, CSA, also at Williamsburg. The 1st Virginia Artillery, organized in 1861, was assigned to coastal defense and saw duty across southeastern Virginia. As part of the state's early artillery forces, the regiment manned fixed batteries along rivers and roads, prepared to repel Federal incursions. Berry remained sick through the end of 1861 and was subsequently discharged, likely due to ongoing health issues.

Despite his earlier medical troubles, Berry returned to Confederate service later in the war. On 12 February 1863, he enlisted at "Diascow Bridge" with Company B of the 7th Regiment, South Carolina Cavalry (Holcombe's Legion), CSA. The location recorded as "Diascow Bridge" is most likely a misspelling of Diascund Bridge in New Kent County, Virginia—a known crossing point over Diascund Creek that saw military traffic and minor skirmishes during the war. It served as a recruiting and staging area for Confederate troops moving between Richmond and the lower Peninsula.

Holcombe's Legion was a composite unit from South Carolina, initially formed with infantry, artillery, and cavalry components. Its cavalry battalion later evolved into the 7th South Carolina Cavalry. By 1863, Berry had become part of this cavalry element. The regiment spent time patrolling coastal regions in South Carolina and Georgia before being transferred to the Army of Northern Virginia in early 1864. Under General Wade Hampton's cavalry corps, the 7th South Carolina Cavalry fought in the Overland Campaign, including engagements at Spotsylvania, Trevilian Station, and Cold Harbor. It continued in action during the Siege of Petersburg and played a role during the Confederate retreat to Appomattox in April 1865.

Berry is listed as present with the 7th South Carolina Cavalry from his enlistment through at least 01 April 1864. There are no Confederate records documenting his presence at the war's end, and it remains unknown whether he surrendered at Appomattox or was discharged earlier.

After the war, Berry married Frances Drewry around 1871, though no formal record of the marriage has been located. They had two children: Samuel Archibald Cardwell (1872–1948) and Mary E. "Mamie" Cardwell (1875–1946). By the 1870 census, Berry and his family were residing in York County, Virginia.[2] Frances appears to have passed away between 1875 and 1880, and Berry later remarried Elizabeth "Bettie" Chandler around 1879. Their union produced one son: Filmore Hubbard Cardwell (1880–1939).

Berry appears one final time in the records as the administrator of the estate of Rebecca Miller on 07 April 1881 in York County, Virginia. No additional information has been found about his later life. The date and circumstances of his death remain unknown, as does the location of his burial.

Berry A. Cardwell's service in both Virginia and South Carolina units—particularly his transition from early infantry and artillery assignments to late-war cavalry service in Holcombe's Legion—speaks to the evolving needs of the Confederacy and the fluid nature of wartime enlistment patterns. His experience reflects the mobility, attrition, and adaptability of Confederate soldiers during the long course of the Civil War. Cardwell Line I - Predicted.

* * *

Photo 11.1: *Charles Wesley Cardwell - circa 1880*

Photo 11.2: *Charles Wesley Cardwell - The Last Surviving Confederate - circa 1940*

Photo 11.3: *Charles Wesley Cardwell (1848-1947) Headstone - Concord Cemetery, Concord, Appomattox County, Virginia.*

Charles Wesley Cardwell (1848-1947) - *Private - Company A, 20th Battalion, Virginia Heavy Artillery, CSA -* **Prisoner of War**

Charles Wesley Cardwell was born on 29 January 1848 in Campbell County, Virginia, the son of James Elliott Dixon Cardwell and Judith Baldwin (Moore) Cardwell. He is recorded in the home of his parents in both the 1850 and 1860 census records for Campbell County.[3,4] The Cardwell family had deep roots in central Virginia, and two sons of James and Judith served the Confederacy during the Civil War—Robert Dibrel Cardwell and Charles Wesley Cardwell.

Charles holds the distinction of being recognized as the last surviving

Confederate veteran, a status that brought him considerable attention in his later years. His service is documented in the book *A Place Called Appomattox*, which recounts his wartime experience with remarkable detail.[5] According to that source, Charles enlisted in the 20th Battalion, Virginia Heavy Artillery (Seavy's Battalion) at Drewry's Bluff near Richmond shortly after his seventeenth birthday in February 1865. At the time of his enlistment, the Confederacy was nearing collapse, and many late-war enlistees like Charles were driven by a sense of duty rather than expectation of victory.

The 20th Battalion, Virginia Heavy Artillery was assigned to the defenses of Richmond and played a support role in manning fortifications and heavy guns along the James River. As the Union army advanced in the spring of 1865, the battalion was ordered to join General Robert E. Lee's retreating Army of Northern Virginia. Their only significant engagement came during the Battle of Farmville, fought on 06 April 1865, just three days before the surrender at Appomattox.

The Battle of Farmville was part of Lee's final, desperate effort to obtain supplies and elude Union forces. The 20th Virginia Heavy Artillery, with Charles among its ranks, was cut off and surrounded by Federal troops. As recorded in *A Place Called Appomattox*, none of the Appomattox men escaped unless they fled into the woods at the first sign of battle. Charles, only a month into his military service, was taken prisoner with the remainder of his battalion.

He was sent to Point Lookout, a Union prisoner-of-war camp in Maryland known for housing thousands of Confederate soldiers. Charles was paroled and took the Oath of Allegiance to the United States on 24 June 1865. His parole records describe him as a resident of Appomattox County, 5 feet 9 inches tall, with a light complexion, light brown hair, and grey eyes. He was released the same day.

After the war, Charles returned to Virginia and married Sallie D. Rector on 16 February 1875. Together, they had six children: Mary Ellen Cardwell (1876–1895), Clarence Elliott Cardwell (1877–1947), Susan Baylis Cardwell (1880–1960), Alfred Cardwell (1882–1895), James Ernest Cardwell (1882–1960), and Charles Herbert Cardwell (1886–1961). He is listed in the Appomattox County census records for 1880, 1900, 1910, 1930, and 1940.[6,7,8,9,10]

Charles Wesley Cardwell passed away on 04 November 1947 in Stonewall, Appomattox County, Virginia, at the remarkable age of 99. He is buried at Concord Cemetery in Concord, Appomattox County.[11] At the time of his death, he was celebrated as the last surviving Confederate soldier, a title symbolizing the final living link to one of the most transformative and turbulent periods in American history. <u>Cardwell Line II - Predicted</u>. Photo Credits[12,13,14]

* * *

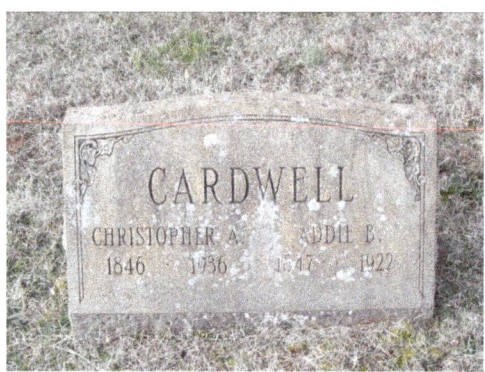

Photo 11.4: *Christopher Anthony Cardwell (1841-1926) Headstone - Concord Cemetery, Concord, Appomattox County, Virginia.*

Christopher Anthony Cardwell (1841-1926) - *Sergeant - Company I, 42nd Regiment, Virginia Infantry, CSA -* **Prisoner of War**

Christopher Anthony Cardwell was born in May 1841 in Campbell County, Virginia. He was the son of John Thomas Cardwell and Mary (Ransberger) Cardwell and is listed in their household in both the 1850 and 1860 Campbell County census records.[15,16] The Cardwell family had deep ties to the region and strong Confederate sympathies—five of John and Mary's sons served in the Southern cause: James Robert, John Alexander, Thomas Henry, Christopher Anthony, and Josephus A. Cardwell.

Christopher enlisted on 11 July 1861 at Lynchburg, Virginia, as a Private in Company I, 42nd Virginia Infantry, CSA. This company, known locally as the "Campbell Guards," was composed primarily of volunteers from Campbell County. His brother Thomas Henry Cardwell enlisted in the same unit and on the same day.

The 42nd Virginia Infantry was organized in the summer of 1861 and assigned to the Army of Northern Virginia, serving under notable Confederate generals including Stonewall Jackson, Richard Ewell, and Jubal Early.

Over the course of the war, the regiment participated in some of the most intense and pivotal battles in the Eastern Theater. These included:

• First Kernstown (March 1862) – where Stonewall Jackson suffered a tactical defeat but gained strategic advantages for the Confederacy.

• Jackson's Valley Campaign – a series of rapid maneuvers and victories that made Jackson famous.

• Seven Days Battles, Second Bull Run, and Antietam (1862) – during which the 42nd endured heavy casualties and continued to gain combat experience.

• Fredericksburg and Chancellorsville (1862–63) – where the regiment fought in key engagements as part of Jackson's corps.

• Gettysburg (July 1863) – likely participating in attacks on the Union center and right during the three-day battle.

• Cold Harbor and the Siege of Petersburg (1864–65) – long, grueling campaigns that tested the endurance of every Confederate unit.

• Appomattox Campaign (April 1865) – the final retreat and collapse of the Confederate Army of Northern Virginia.

Christopher advanced steadily through the ranks. He was promoted to 3rd Corporal on 20 September 1861, then to Corporal on 23 October 1861 at Lewisburg, and again to Sergeant on 01 September 1862. Though many of his specific battlefield actions are not recorded in surviving documents, his continual presence on muster rolls during these critical campaigns indicates he was a seasoned and reliable soldier who endured the full arc of the war's progression.

After the Confederacy's collapse, Christopher surrendered and took the Oath of Allegiance to the United States on 30 May 1865 at the Campbell County Courthouse. His name does not appear in later wartime records, and it is likely that his military service ended with the formal disbanding of the Confederate forces.

Christopher returned home to Campbell County following the war and is recorded in the 1870 census in his parents' household.[17] Around 1872, he married Adalaide "Addie" B. Quesenberry, although the exact date and place of the marriage remain undocumented. The couple had at least two children: William Hansford Cardwell (1873–1947) and Ethel L. Cardwell (born 1885). Christopher appears in the 1880 Campbell County census, and in both the 1900 and 1910 census records for Appomattox County, Virginia.[18,19,20]

He later moved to the city of Lynchburg, where he died on 26 April 1926. He is buried at Concord Cemetery in Appomattox County, although there is a possibility that a memorial also exists for him at Cardwell Cemetery in neighboring Campbell County.[21,22] It should be noted that the birth year inscribed on his headstone is incorrect, as verified by early census records and other documentation. <u>Cardwell Line II - Predicted</u>. Photo Credit[23]

* * *

Photo 11.5: *David Adams Cardwell, Jr. - circa 1910*

Photo 11.6: *David Adams Cardwell, Jr. - circa 1920 - Columbia,
Richland County, South Carolina*

Photo 11.7: *David Adams Cardwell, Jr. (1846-1921) Headstone - First
Presbyterian Churchyard, Columbia, Richland County, South Carolina*

David Adams Cardwell, Jr. (1846-1921) - *Private - McGregor's Battery,
2nd Stuart Horse Artillery, CSA* - **Prisoner of War**

David Adams Cardwell, Jr. was born on 22 February 1846 in Richmond,
Virginia, the son of David Adams Cardwell, Sr. and Rebecca Miller (Drinker)
Cardwell. By the 1850s, the family had relocated to the District of Columbia,
where David is recorded in the 1850 and 1860 Washington, D.C. census.

The Cardwell family supported the Southern cause, with both David and his brother, George Drinker Cardwell, serving in the Confederate Army.[24,25]

At the age of sixteen, David enlisted as a Private in McGregor's Battery, part of the 2nd Stuart Horse Artillery, CSA. His enlistment came shortly after the unit's return from the Gettysburg Campaign, during which the battery had provided mobile artillery support for General J.E.B. Stuart's Cavalry Corps. David joined a well-seasoned outfit that was highly regarded for its rapid deployment and precision fire—key attributes for an artillery unit attached to cavalry forces.

Through the remainder of 1863, McGregor's Battery operated across northern Virginia, frequently engaged in screening maneuvers, raids, and rear-guard actions as Union forces advanced deeper into Confederate territory. In 1864, the battery saw heavy action during the Overland Campaign, including the Battle of Yellow Tavern, where General Stuart was fatally wounded. The battery also fought at Cold Harbor and participated in the long defense of Richmond and Petersburg, lending artillery support to Confederate cavalry raids and delaying actions throughout the campaign.

As the Confederate lines broke in the spring of 1865, McGregor's Battery joined the general retreat of the Army of Northern Virginia, playing a critical role as part of the rearguard during the final days leading up to the surrender at Appomattox Court House on 09 April 1865. Despite shortages in men and materiel, the unit continued to operate with the mobility and resilience that had defined its wartime reputation.

David's official Confederate record confirms his surrender with McGregor's Battery. He took the Oath of Allegiance on 05 May 1865 and was paroled the following day. His obituary later noted that he "was under fire sixty-seven times," and fought in battles such as Seven Pines, The Wilderness, Cold Harbor, Five Forks, and Appomattox, mirroring the service record of the artillery unit he rode with.

After the war, David returned to civilian life and built a distinguished career in the railroad industry. Beginning on 09 January 1869, he worked for the Columbia and Augusta Railroad in Columbia, South Carolina, and ulti-mately became General Freight Agent for the Southern Railway. He remained in Columbia for over fifty-two years and was widely respected in both business and veteran circles.

He married Anna Cook Sinton around 1873, and they had four children: David Adams Cardwell III (1876–1935), Edward "Edwin" Sinton Cardwell

(1879–1941), Thomas Savant Cardwell (1881–1937), and Virginia Cook Cardwell (1886–1967). The family appears in the 1880, 1900, 1910, and 1920 census records of Columbia, Richland County, South Carolina.[26,27,28,29]

David became affectionately known as "General David Cardwell," a nickname born from a chance encounter. A passerby once noticed the sign above his office door—"D. Cardwell, General Freight Agent"—and saluted him as "General." Though David protested that he hadn't even been a colonel during the war, the title stuck.[30] It eventually became official, as he was appointed Colonel on the staff of Governor John Peter Richardson of South Carolina and served in several high-ranking ceremonial and veteran capacities.

He was Adjutant General and Chief of Staff of the South Carolina Division of the United Confederate Veterans and also served as Chairman of the Board of Trustees for the State Confederate Infirmary in Columbia. Additionally, David authored a history of Pelham's Battery, Stuart Horse Artillery, a detailed account of the unit's wartime service and legacy.

David Adams Cardwell, Jr., died on 19 February 1921 in Columbia, Richland County, South Carolina, just three days before his 75th birthday. He was laid to rest in the First Presbyterian Churchyard in Columbia.[31] A respected soldier, dedicated public servant, and active guardian of Confederate memory, he left behind a legacy of service both on and off the battlefield. Cardwell Line I - Predicted. Photo Credits[32,33,34]

* * *

David Adams Cardwell, Sr. (1809-1898) - Private - *Company D, 3rd Regiment, Virginia Infantry, Local Defense (Henley's) (McAnerney's), CSA*

David Adams Cardwell, Sr. was born about 1809 in Virginia, the son of Richard Lee Cardwell and Lucy Ann (Adams) Cardwell. He married Rebecca Miller Drinker around 1840, though no official marriage record has been found. Together, they had the following children: Susan Elizabeth "Betty" Cardwell (1840–1930), Lucy Cardwell (1842–), George Drinker Cardwell (1844–1883), David Adams Cardwell, Jr. (1846–1921), a stillborn son (1848–1848), Francis M. "Frank" Cardwell (1852–), and Charles Cardwell (1856–1870).

The family is documented in the 1850 and 1860 census records of Washington, D.C., and by 1870 and 1880 had relocated to Richmond, Henrico County, Virginia.[35,36,37,38] During the Civil War, despite his advanced age,

David enlisted at 54 years old as a Private in Company D, 3rd Regiment, Virginia Infantry (Local Defense) on 22 July 1863, in Richmond, Virginia.

The 3rd Virginia Local Defense Infantry was organized to provide crucial support to the Confederate capital's internal security during the latter half of the war. It was comprised largely of older men, government employees, and those otherwise exempt from regular military service. As part of the Department of Richmond, this unit's primary mission was to guard vital infrastructure such as railroads, bridges, armories, and supply depots, as well as provide auxiliary manpower during emergencies.

Company D, like the rest of the regiment, served a reserve and garrison role throughout much of its existence, but its responsibilities increased dramatically during 1864 and 1865, when General Ulysses S. Grant's forces began to threaten the city directly. During the Overland Campaign and subsequent Siege of Petersburg, local defense troops were pressed into action to bolster depleted Confederate ranks, manning defensive positions, responding to Union cavalry raids, and supporting the general defense of Richmond.

While not officially a front-line combat unit, the 3rd Virginia Infantry (Local Defense) was considered a key home guard force, especially during the Evacuation of Richmond in April 1865. At that time, the Confederate capital came under increasing pressure from the advancing Army of the Potomac. Many members of the regiment helped in the defense of outer fortifications or assisted in destroying Confederate property to prevent its capture. Though no records confirm David's specific activities during this period, his unit was undoubtedly involved in the final days of the Confederate defense of Richmond.

David's Confederate service ended sometime in 1865, though the exact date of discharge is not recorded, and there is no documentation that he was ever captured or paroled.

Following the war, David continued to reside in Richmond until at least the 1880 census. Family tradition holds that in his later years, he moved south to Columbia, Richland County, South Carolina, to live with his son, David Adams Cardwell, Jr., who had become a prominent railway executive and Confederate veteran himself.

David Adams Cardwell, Sr. passed away on 31 March 1898 in Columbia, South Carolina. Despite dying in the South, his remains were returned to Virginia and interred at Shockoe Hill Cemetery in Richmond, though his grave remains unmarked.[39] He lived to witness the full span of the war and its aftermath, and both of his sons—George Drinker Cardwell and David Adams Cardwell, Jr.—served in the Confederate ranks, continuing the family's direct contribution to the Southern war effort. Cardwell Line I - Predicted.

* * *

Francis Flippin Cardwell (1803-1891) - *Private - Company I, 44th Regiment, Virginia Infantry, CSA* - **Wounded in Action**

Francis Flippin Cardwell was born about 1803, likely in Stokes County, North Carolina, the son of William M. Cardwell and Mary (Flippin) Cardwell. He married Edna "Edney" J. Haskins on 16 December 1830 in Charlotte County, Virginia.[40] The couple had the following children: Mary F. Cardwell (1832–1874), John H. Cardwell (1834–), William Cardwell (1835–), Lucy N. Cardwell (1837–1860), Wiltshire Marion Cardwell (1837–1924), Francis C. "Frank" Cardwell (1843–), Fannie Elizabeth Cardwell (1844–1935), Edna "Edney" Cardwell (1846–1935), and Sarah "Sallie" O. Cardwell (1847–1938).

Francis is found in the 1840 census of Charlotte County, Virginia, and later in the 1880 census of Pittsylvania County, Virginia, listed in the household of his son Wiltshire Marion Cardwell. Interestingly, tradition handed down by descendants notes that Francis traveled west during the Gold Rush era, likely in search of fortune. He appears to be the "F. Cardwell" listed in the 1854 Jackson County, Oregon census, while his wife Edna remained in Virginia and is listed as head of household in the 1850 and 1860 censuses of Charlotte County.[41,42,43]

Returning to Virginia sometime after 1860, Francis enlisted at nearly 60 years of age as a Private in Company I, 44th Virginia Infantry, CSA, on 08 May 1861. Despite his advanced years, he joined a unit that would become heavily engaged in the most significant campaigns of the Eastern Theater.

The 44th Virginia Infantry was organized in the spring of 1861 and became part of the famed "Stonewall Brigade" under General Thomas J. "Stonewall" Jackson. Its early engagements included the First Battle of Kernstown, followed by participation in Jackson's celebrated Shenandoah Valley Campaign.

On 08 May 1862, during the Battle of McDowell, Francis was wounded in the leg. The engagement, also known as the Battle of Sitlington's Hill, was part of Jackson's effort to hold off advancing Union forces in Highland County, Virginia. Jackson's outnumbered troops successfully repelled the Federals, gaining momentum for subsequent victories in the valley. Although the battle itself was relatively small in scale, its strategic importance lay in derailing Union plans in western Virginia and bolstering Confederate morale.

Due to the severity of his wound, Francis was discharged for disability on 18 September 1862. No further service records have been located for him. However, some sources suggest that a "Frank Cardwell" later served with Lanier's Company of Virginia Artillery (Local Defense and Special Service), CSA, appearing briefly on the rolls in November 1863. While this cannot be definitively confirmed as Francis, it remains a reasonable possibility, particularly given the rarity of the name and age alignment.

After the war, Francis lived with his son Wiltshire in Pittsylvania County, Virginia, and worked as a carpenter, according to the 1880 census. His wife Edna appears to have died prior to this time.

Francis Flippin Cardwell died on 16 October 1891 in Pittsylvania County and was buried at Bethel Methodist Church Cemetery, Mountain Hill, Pittsylvania County, Virginia[44]. His life spanned nearly nine decades, during which he witnessed the rise of the Republic, the tragedy of civil war, and the trials of Reconstruction. His willingness to serve at an advanced age, and the sacrifice of multiple sons to the Southern cause, underscore the deep family commitment to the Confederacy. <u>Cardwell Line I - Predicted</u>.

* * *

Photo 11.8: *George Drinker Cardwell (1844-1883) Headstone - Hollywood Cemetery, Richmond, Richmond City, Virginia.*

George Drinker Cardwell (1844-1883) - *Private - Company B, 25th Battalion, Virginia Infantry (Richmond Battalion) (City Battalion), CSA & Goochland Light Artillery, CSA -* **Prisoner of War**

George Drinker Cardwell was born in 1844 in Virginia, the son of David Adams Cardwell, Sr. and Rebecca Miller (Drinker) Cardwell. By the early 1850s, the Cardwell family had relocated to the District of Columbia, where George appears in both the 1850 and 1860 Washington, D.C. census records.[45,46] Though living in the capital of the Union, the family remained loyal to their Virginian roots and ultimately cast their lot with the Confederacy. George, along with his younger brother, David Adams Cardwell, Jr., served in the Southern cause during the Civil War.

George enlisted as a Private in Company B of the 25th Battalion, Virginia Infantry—commonly referred to as the Richmond Battalion or City Battalion —on 21 January 1863 in Richmond, Virginia. The 25th Battalion was composed primarily of men from the city and its surrounding counties and was initially tasked with local defense duties. As the war progressed, the battalion was placed under the command of the Department of Richmond, which managed the Confederate capital's security against increasingly aggressive Union operations.

On 05 May 1863, George transferred to the Goochland Light Artillery, a move that placed him in one of the artillery batteries charged with manning fixed emplacements along key defensive lines. The Goochland Light Artillery was responsible for guarding strategic points along the James River, including bridges, transportation routes, and approaches to Richmond. Although not a frontline battlefield battery, the unit played an indispensable role in the layered defense system that shielded the Confederate capital from Union attacks.

During the Overland Campaign of 1864 and the extended Siege of Petersburg, the Goochland Light Artillery was deployed in the defenses south of the James River. The battery's role in these engagements often involved intense periods of bombardment and counter-battery duels, and although not mobile like field artillery, they were vital in maintaining the Confederate line's integrity.

In the chaotic final days of the war, as Confederate defenses around Richmond crumbled, the Goochland Light Artillery participated in the general retreat westward alongside the rest of the Army of Northern Virginia. On 06 April 1865, George was captured during the Battle of Sailer's Creek (often referred to as Harper's Farm in Confederate records), one of the last major confrontations before Lee's surrender. Sailer's Creek proved disastrous for the Confederates—over 7,700 men were taken prisoner, signaling the effective end of Lee's capacity to resist.

George was sent to Point Lookout, Maryland, a Union prisoner-of-war camp known for its harsh conditions and overcrowding. On 26 June 1865, he took the Oath of Allegiance to the United States. His parole record describes him as 5 feet 6¼ inches tall, with a dark complexion, black hair, blue eyes, and lists his residence as Richmond, Virginia.

After the war, George returned to civilian life in Richmond. He married Ida G. Hersman around 1869, based on the birth year of their first child. The couple had three children: George Hersman Cardwell (1870–1895), Guy Adams Cardwell (1872–1943), and Frank Churchill Cardwell (1875–1896). George and his family are listed in both the 1870 and 1880 Richmond, Henrico County, Virginia census records, living in the household of his parents, a reflection of the common postwar practice among Southern families of consolidating households for economic survival.[47,48]

George Drinker Cardwell died in 1883 in Richmond at the age of approximately 39. He was buried at Hollywood Cemetery, one of the most iconic resting places for Confederate soldiers, located in Richmond, Virginia.[49] His burial among so many of his fellow countrymen signifies his participation in one of the most transformative and tragic chapters in American history. Though his wartime role was largely in the defense of Richmond and its surrounding approaches, his service through to the very end—culminating in the retreat and his capture at Sailer's Creek—speaks to his dedication and endurance.

George's legacy, along with that of his brother David, highlights the divided loyalties and lasting sacrifices of families with Confederate ties, even those living at the political center of the Union. Their stories reflect not just military service, but the complexities of identity, place, and allegiance during the American Civil War. Cardwell Line I - Predicted. Photo Credit[50]

* * *

George W. Cardwell (1829-1902/1910) - *Private - Company G, 26th Regiment, Virginia Infantry, CSA* - **Wounded in Action**

George W. Cardwell was born on 4 September 1829 in Little Plymouth,

King and Queen County, Virginia. He was the son of George Cardwell and Mary "Polly" (Walton) Cardwell. George and Mary had at least two sons who served in the Confederate military—George W. and William R. Cardwell. Their father appears to have died before 1850, as Mary is listed as the head of household in both the 1850 and 1860 census records for King and Queen County. George is recorded in her household in 1850 and is found living next door by 1860.[51,52]

Around 1858, George married Collin Richardson, likely in King and Queen County, although a marriage record has not been located. The couple had three children: Milton Cardwell (1859–1885), George Cardwell (1861–1884), and Virginia Cardwell (1869–1929). The family appears together in the 1860 and 1870 census records.[53,54]

On 2 June 1861, George enlisted as a Private in Company G of the 26th Virginia Infantry Regiment, CSA, at Little Plymouth. His service record indicates he was 32 years old at the time of enlistment.

The 26th Virginia Infantry Regiment began its service by defending the Tidewater region of southeastern Virginia. It took part in early engagements such as Sewell's Point and later played a role in the Peninsula Campaign of 1862. Initially under the command of Brigadier General Henry A. Wise and later part of Montgomery Corse's Brigade in Pickett's Division, the regiment saw steady and grueling service throughout the war.

The 26th Virginia served in both Virginia and the Carolinas and was particularly engaged in the defense of Richmond and Petersburg. The regiment fought in major actions such as the Battle of Drewry's Bluff and Cold Harbor and played a prolonged role during the Siege of Petersburg (1864–1865), where Confederate troops endured constant hardship in trench warfare against advancing Union forces.

George was Wounded in Action on 11 February 1864 at John's Island, South Carolina, during one of the smaller engagements that foreshadowed the larger battle fought there the following year. He was hospitalized in Charleston and placed on a 60-day furlough starting on 19 March 1864. Later that year, he was admitted to Chimborazo Hospital in Richmond, suffering from a gunshot wound. His stay extended from 01 September through 19 December 1864, suggesting complications and a difficult recovery, though the precise nature of his wound is not detailed.

He returned to duty by early 1865 and is recorded as being on guard detail on 08 February 1865. No further service records have been located. It is unclear whether he was present with the regiment when the 26th Virginia Infantry surrendered alongside the rest of the Army of Northern Virginia at Appomattox Court House on 9 April 1865, but his return to active duty in the final weeks of the war indicates a strong likelihood that he remained with his unit through the end.

After the war, George returned to his home in King and Queen County. His first wife appears to have died sometime after the 1870 census, and on 24 November 1874, he married Martha E. Hilliard in King and Queen County. They had several children: Edward R. Cardwell (1875–), Harold Howell Cardwell (1877–1946), Mary E. Cardwell (1878–), Lulu Cardwell (1880–1880), and Roger Washington Cardwell (1887–1946).

George is listed in the 1880 and 1900 census records, residing in King and Queen County with his family.[55,56] On 22 July 1902, at age 73, he filed for a Confederate pension, affirming his service and injury during the war. His wife is recorded as a widow in the 1910 census in Baltimore, Maryland, indicating that George passed away sometime between 1902 and 1910.[57] His exact date of death and the location of his burial remain unknown. Cardwell Line IV - Predicted.

* * *

George Washington Cardwell (1836-1910) - Private - *Company E, 53rd Regiment, Virginia Infantry, CSA & Otey's Company, Virginia Light Artillery, Local Defense, CSA*

George Washington Cardwell was born on 19 April 1836 in Pittsylvania County, Virginia. He was the son of Thomas Cardwell and Coley (Bomar) Cardwell. The couple had at least two sons who served in the Confederate Army during the American Civil War—William Thomas Cardwell and George Washington Cardwell. George is listed in his father's household in the 1850 and 1860 census records for Pittsylvania County, working as a farm laborer in the rural tobacco-growing region of southern Virginia.[58,59]

On 20 April 1862, just one day after his twenty-sixth birthday, George enlisted as a Private in Company E of the 53rd Regiment, Virginia Infantry, CSA, at Suffolk, Virginia. The 53rd Virginia Infantry was part of the Army of Northern Virginia and saw significant combat in some of the most iconic battles of the Civil War. The regiment was organized in 1861 and was eventually assigned to Armistead's Brigade, Pickett's Division, Longstreet's Corps.

It gained renown for its role in the Battle of Gettysburg, particularly in the famous assault known as Pickett's Charge, although George had separated from the unit prior to that engagement.

According to his compiled military service record, George was reported as having deserted on 30 October 1862. The reason for his departure is not documented, but desertion was not uncommon in the early war years, especially as conditions in camp and field worsened and enlistment enthusiasm waned. Illness, family hardship, or disillusionment may have contributed to his absence.

Despite this early departure, it appears that George returned to Confederate service the following year. A single record from October 1863 lists a "G.W. Cardwell" enlisting in Otey's Company, Virginia Light Artillery, a local defense artillery unit based in Danville, Virginia. While not definitively confirmed, this man is believed to be George Washington Cardwell of Pittsylvania County, as Danville was formed from the same county in 1855 and there are no other known individuals in the area with matching initials and birth details.

Otey's Company, Virginia Light Artillery, was formed as part of the Richmond Defenses and operated under the Department of North Carolina and Southern Virginia. The company saw action around the defensive perimeter of Richmond and Petersburg and supported operations along the Weldon Railroad and other critical supply lines. Composed primarily of men unfit for field duty or drawn from local defense reserves, the company was responsible for manning fixed artillery emplacements and protecting vital infrastructure from Union cavalry raids and infantry pushes. While not involved in large-scale field campaigns, these artillerymen played an essential part in defending Confederate logistical operations in the war's final phase.

George married Ann Virginia "Jennie" Brandon in about 1863, likely during the time between his departure from the 53rd Virginia and his enlistment in the Danville-based artillery company.[60] The couple had three known children: Joseph Thomas Cardwell (1865–1933), Pattie L. Cardwell (born 1879), and Lily Mae Cardwell (born 1879). The family is recorded in the 1870, 1880, and 1900 census records of Pittsylvania County, Virginia. George worked as a farmer for most of his life, continuing to reside in the region where he was born and raised.[61,62,63]

George died on 17 February 1910 in Pittsylvania County at the age of seventy-three. While his exact burial site has not been located, it is presumed he was interred in the county where he lived and died. He is remembered as one of the many men from southern Virginia whose wartime experience reflected both the hardship and the shifting allegiances that characterized the Civil War for countless soldiers.

George's distant kinsman, Peter Saunders Cardwell, also served in the 53rd Virginia Infantry, though he was a member of Company I. Their shared presence in the same regiment illustrates the strong local connections that often shaped the composition of Confederate units, where neighbors, relatives, and friends enlisted together and shared the burdens of war side by side. Cardwell Line III - Predicted.

Photo 11.9: *George Washington Cardwell (1840-1916) Headstone - Blandford Cemetery, Petersburg, Petersburg City, Virginia.*

George Washington Cardwell (1840-1916) - *Corporal - Company F, 12th Regiment, Virginia Infantry, CSA -* **Wounded in Action**

George Washington Cardwell was born on 13 February 1840 in Petersburg, Virginia. He was the son of Henry C. Cardwell and Martha H. (Wallace) Cardwell. The family is documented in the 1860 census in Greensville

County, Virginia.[64] Henry and Martha had three sons who served the Confederacy during the Civil War: Richard H. Cardwell, John T. Cardwell, and George Washington Cardwell.

At the outbreak of the war, George enlisted as a Private in Company F of the 12th Regiment, Virginia Infantry, CSA. His enlistment took place at Hicksford, a key junction in Greensville County, where the Petersburg Railroad met southern lines. The 12th Virginia Infantry had been organized in May 1861 and drew heavily from the southeastern counties of the state, including Petersburg and surrounding areas.

The 12th Virginia Infantry quickly established a reputation as a reliable combat regiment. It fought in the Seven Days Battles during the Peninsula Campaign in 1862 and was heavily engaged at Second Manassas, Antietam, Fredericksburg, and Chancellorsville. George was promoted to Corporal on 20 February 1862, during the early months of the regiment's sustained campaigning.

By January 1863, George was detailed to provost guard duty with Anderson's Division. Provost guards were responsible for maintaining order behind the lines, supervising prisoners, and securing critical roads and crossroads. While not front-line duty, this role was vital to army cohesion during extended campaigns.

In October 1863, George returned to his company for field service. The 12th Virginia Infantry continued to serve with distinction under Mahone's Brigade in the Army of Northern Virginia. In 1864, during the grueling Siege of Petersburg, the regiment saw some of its most brutal combat. On 30 July 1864, at the Battle of the Crater—one of the most infamous and costly episodes of the siege—George was seriously wounded. Union forces had tunneled beneath Confederate lines and detonated a massive mine under Elliott's Salient. The ensuing chaos saw a brief breakthrough by Union troops, which was ultimately repelled. The 12th Virginia was heavily engaged in the effort to seal the breach.

George lost an eye in the fighting, a grievous injury that ended his front-line service. On 11 December 1864, he was formally transferred from the 12th Virginia Infantry to the Confederate Invalid Corps. This administrative unit was composed of men who were no longer fit for field duty due to wounds or chronic illness but could still serve in limited roles such as clerks, guards, or hospital aides.

Shortly before the war's end, George married Emma Ann Eggleston on 30

March 1865 in Petersburg, Virginia.[65] Emma died on 10 August 1879, leaving no known children from their union. In 1896, George remarried, taking Susan B. Dunstan as his wife. The 1900 census confirms this second marriage, and the couple is listed as living in Petersburg. George appears in the 1870 census for the Independent City of Petersburg, in 1880 in neighboring Dinwiddie County, and again in Petersburg in the 1900 and 1910 census records. No children are known from either marriage, and George likely spent his later years in the city where he had lived much of his adult life.[66,67,68,69]

George Washington Cardwell died on 05 May 1916 in Petersburg, Virginia, at the age of 76. He was buried in the historic Blandford Cemetery, a burial ground that contains the remains of thousands of Confederate veterans and is known for its memorial significance.[70] His grave lies among those of comrades who, like him, bore the hardships of war and its aftermath.

Though wounded and permanently disabled during the war, George's continued service in the Invalid Corps and his resilience after the war demonstrate the quiet determination of many Confederate veterans. His burial in Blandford is a testament to the esteem with which he was held in his community and among fellow soldiers. Cardwell Line II- Predicted. Photo Credit[71]

* * *

James Cardwell (1817-1885) - *Private - Company C, 15th Regiment, Virginia Infantry, CSA -* **Prisoner of War**

James Cardwell was born around 1817 in King William County, Virginia, the son of Elijah A. Cardwell and Mildred "Milley" (Richeson) Cardwell. By the late 1840s, he had settled in neighboring Hanover County, where he married Lucy Ann Adams Lambert around 1849. No marriage record has been located, but the couple appears consistently in census records, beginning with the 1850 enumeration. Together, they had eight children: Julia E.G. Cardwell (1850–1914), John William Cardwell (1852–1916), James H. Marcellus Cardwell (1855–), Thomas W. Cardwell (1858–1889), Mary L. "Mollie" Cardwell (1861–), Robert Lee Cardwell (1864–1932), Cetia Cardwell (1869–), and Charles Coleman Cardwell (1869–1933). The family remained in Hanover County throughout James's life and is recorded in the 1860, 1870, and 1880 census returns.[72,73,74]

With the outbreak of the Civil War, James was conscripted into the

Confederate Army. He entered service on 23 April 1861 as a Private in Company C, 15th Virginia Infantry Regiment, at Ashland in Hanover County. The 15th Virginia was one of the earliest infantry regiments raised for Confederate service, with men drawn largely from Hanover County, Richmond City, and surrounding areas. Initially tasked with defending Virginia's Peninsula and key transportation points near the Confederate capital, the regiment played a crucial role in the early strategic posture of the Army of Northern Virginia.

Between November 1861 and February 1862, James was detailed to King's Mill Wharf, a logistical hub near Williamsburg on the James River. Guarding this strategic point would have been critical for ensuring the delivery of supplies and troop movement in the Tidewater region. Duties at the wharf likely included protecting boat landings, overseeing the unloading of military goods, and contributing to the construction or maintenance of fortifications that guarded the approaches to Williamsburg and, ultimately, Richmond.

James's active service in the field is confirmed through Confederate pay records, which indicate he remained with the 15th Virginia Infantry until at least 21 July 1862. At that time, he was formally discharged, having completed the term of service required under the provisions of his conscription. According to his discharge record, James stood 5 feet 8 inches tall, had a light complexion, blue eyes, and brown hair, and worked as a carpenter—a useful trade both in civilian life and within an army that constantly required repairs to roads, bridges, and defensive works.

As the war drew toward its final year, the Confederate government expanded conscription efforts to replenish ranks depleted by years of heavy casualties and desertion. In March 1865, James was again called into service, this time ordered to report for duty with the 2nd Regiment, Virginia Infantry, Local Defense, CSA. Units such as this were composed of older men, boys, and others not normally eligible for front-line service, but who were needed for emergency defense of key cities such as Richmond, particularly during the final Union offensives of 1865.

James appears to have sought exemption from this second conscription, citing his occupation as a miller—an essential service given the food shortages across the South. While such claims sometimes led to deferment, it seems his request was ultimately denied. Shortly thereafter, he was taken as a Prisoner of War by Union forces in the final days of the conflict. His record shows he took the Oath of Allegiance to the United States on 24 April 1865 in Ashland, Hanover County, not long after General Robert E. Lee's surrender at Appomattox. At that time, the Confederacy was in its final days, and mass paroles were taking place across Virginia.

Following the war, James returned to civilian life in Hanover County. Though his profession and physical health in the postwar period are not detailed in surviving records, it is likely he returned to milling and farming to support his large family. His death occurred on 06 July 1885, and though the exact location of his burial is not documented, it was likely in a now-unmarked grave near his home in Hanover County.

James Cardwell's wartime service, which spanned the early defensive efforts on the Peninsula through the closing chaos of the Confederacy's final months, reflects the experience of thousands of older Southern men—called from their trades and families, performing essential guard and labor duties, and then drawn into renewed service as the Confederacy collapsed. His quiet persistence through conscription, exemption efforts, and final surrender underscore the endurance of civilian-soldiers in the broader narrative of the American Civil War. <u>Cardwell Line IV - Predicted</u>.

* * *

James Robert Cardwell (1829-1907) - Private - *Company G, 5th Regiment, Virginia Cavalry, CSA & Patterson's Company, Virginia Heavy Artillery (Campbell Battery), CSA* - **Prisoner of War**

James Robert Cardwell was born in February 1829 in Campbell County, Virginia, the son of John Thomas Cardwell and Mary (Ransberger) Cardwell. The Cardwell family had deep roots in the area and was among those families whose sons came of age just as the American Civil War erupted. James is listed in his parents' household in both the 1850 and 1860 Campbell County census records, part of a large farming family.[75,76] His parents would see five of their sons—James Robert, John Alexander, Thomas Henry, Christopher Anthony, and Josephus A. Cardwell—serve in the Confederate Army.

James first entered Confederate service on 05 March 1862, enlisting as a Private in Patterson's Company, Virginia Heavy Artillery (Campbell Battery), CSA, raised locally in Campbell County. Patterson's Company was one of several independent heavy artillery units organized early in the war to defend key points in the Confederate interior and around Richmond. Batteries like

Patterson's were primarily assigned to man fixed fortifications, coastal and inland defense positions, and heavy gun emplacements guarding rivers, bridges, and supply routes. While less glamorous than front-line infantry or cavalry, these units were essential to the war effort. Patterson's Company appears to have been largely tasked with defensive assignments near the James River and within the Department of Richmond.

Interestingly, James's brothers, John Alexander and Josephus A. Cardwell, enlisted in the same battery on the same day, suggesting a coordinated family decision. Unfortunately, James's specific service in Patterson's Company appears to have been short or interrupted, as there are no further detailed records of his activity in that unit. It's possible that illness, reassignment, or administrative reshuffling accounts for this gap.

On 01 April 1864, James reenlisted or transferred into a new role, joining Company G of the 5th Regiment, Virginia Cavalry, CSA, again as a Private. This marked a shift from static artillery service to the far more mobile and dangerous life of a cavalryman. The 5th Virginia Cavalry was a storied unit, part of the famed Laurel Brigade, and saw extensive service under Confederate cavalry leaders such as General J.E.B. Stuart and General Fitzhugh Lee. Organized in 1861, the 5th Virginia Cavalry had already participated in numerous engagements by the time James joined in 1864, including battles at Brandy Station, Chancellorsville, and Gettysburg.

During James's tenure with the unit, the 5th Virginia Cavalry was engaged in near-constant action during the Overland Campaign, the defense of Richmond and Petersburg, and ultimately, the Appomattox Campaign. Cavalry units like the 5th Virginia were heavily used for screening, reconnaissance, delaying actions, and raids on Union supply lines. As Union forces under General Ulysses S. Grant pressed relentlessly against the Confederate defensive lines around Petersburg in 1864 and 1865, the 5th Virginia found itself tasked with increasingly desperate operations to blunt the advance and buy time.

On 01 April 1865, James was captured at the Battle of Five Forks, a pivotal and disastrous defeat for the Confederacy southwest of Petersburg. This battle marked the collapse of Confederate lines and directly led to the evacuation of both Petersburg and Richmond. James was sent to Point Lookout, Maryland, a large Union prisoner-of-war camp situated on the Chesapeake Bay.

He remained a prisoner for over two months. On 24 June 1865, James took the Oath of Allegiance to the United States and was released the same day. His parole records describe him as having a dark complexion, dark brown hair, blue eyes, and standing 5 feet 7½ inches tall. He gave his residence as Campbell County, Virginia.

Shortly before his reenlistment in the cavalry, James married Ann "Annie" Maria Land on 24 March 1864 in Campbell County. This marriage is documented through her Confederate Widow's Pension application filed on 04 July 1911, years after James's death. Though the couple remained together until his passing, it appears they had no surviving children.

In the postwar years, James returned to Campbell County, where he resumed life as a civilian. He is recorded in the 1870, 1880, and 1900 federal census returns, residing in the Concord area. His occupations during these decades are not specifically recorded, but like many former soldiers, he likely returned to farming or trade work to support his household.[77,78,79]

James Robert Cardwell died on 20 December 1907 in Concord, Campbell County, Virginia, at the age of seventy-eight. He is buried at the Dixon Cemetery, Concord, Campbell County, Virginia. He is remembered as one of five brothers who answered Virginia's call and served in the Confederate cause. <u>Cardwell Line II - Predicted</u>.

* * *

Photo 11.10: James Upshur Cardwell (1845-1864) Headstone - Woodlawn National Cemetery, Elmira, Chemung County, New York.

James Upshur Cardwell (1845-1864) - *Private - Company G, 26th Regiment, Virginia Infantry, CSA* - **Prisoner in War - Died in Captivity**

James Upshur Cardwell was born on 14 December 1845 in King and Queen County, Virginia. He was the son of Upshur Cardwell and Elizabeth (Walton) Cardwell, and is listed in the 1850 census in his mother's household following the apparent death of his father. Raised in a rural area deeply tied to agricultural life and traditional Virginia loyalties, James came of age just as the American Civil War was reaching its most violent years.[80]

Like many young men across the South, James was conscripted into Confederate military service as the conflict dragged on and manpower needs became dire. On 07 February 1863, at the age of seventeen, Private James Cardwell was enrolled in Company G of the 26th Regiment, Virginia Infantry, CSA, at New Prospect, Virginia. This was a critical moment for the Confederate war effort in Virginia, as Union forces increased pressure on the eastern front and began probing the defenses of Richmond.

Organized in May 1861, the 26th Virginia Infantry was composed largely of men from southeastern counties such as King and Queen, King William, and Gloucester. Initially tasked with defending the Virginia coastline and guarding strategic ports and rivers, the regiment operated under Brigadier General Henry A. Wise and later became part of Brigadier General Montgomery Corse's Brigade in Pickett's Division of the Army of Northern Virginia.

During the early months of 1863, the regiment was stationed along the James River and within the Department of Richmond, reinforcing the Confederate capital's outer defenses. The soldiers spent much of their time manning earthworks, conducting fatigue duty, and preparing for what would soon become a relentless campaign by Union General Ulysses S. Grant to capture Petersburg and, ultimately, Richmond itself.

As the Overland Campaign commenced in May 1864 and transitioned into the Siege of Petersburg, the 26th Virginia Infantry took up critical positions on the defensive lines stretching around that city. Grant's forces launched a series of powerful assaults in an attempt to break the Confederate hold on the area, resulting in months of trench warfare and attrition.

It was during this time, on 15 June 1864, that Private James Cardwell was captured during the opening engagement of the Petersburg Campaign. The Union's initial assault struck Confederate positions along the Dimmock Line, and although Confederate reinforcements eventually stabilized the front, early losses were significant. James was among those taken prisoner by Union forces.

He was first sent to Point Lookout, a Union prisoner-of-war camp in Maryland notorious for overcrowded conditions and exposure to the elements. From there, he was transferred to the Elmira Prison Camp in Elmira, New York, on 27 July 1864. Known among Confederate prisoners as "Hellmira," the camp held thousands of captured soldiers in conditions that were among the worst in the North. The camp was established hastily in 1864 and suffered from inadequate shelter, poor sanitation, contaminated water, and insufficient rations, especially during the brutal winter of that year.

Within six weeks of his arrival, Private James Cardwell died at Elmira on 05 September 1864, a victim of rubella (German measles). His death came amid a wave of disease-related fatalities that plagued the camp throughout its operation. His name is one of nearly 3,000 Confederate soldiers listed among those who perished while imprisoned at Elmira.

Adding to the tragedy, James's cousin, Private Joseph B. Cardwell, also of the 26th Virginia Infantry, was captured near Petersburg and sent to the same camp. Joseph died at Elmira on 20 October 1864, succumbing to pneumonia. The two young men—born in the same county, serving in the same regiment, and perishing far from home—embody the dual suffering of battlefield trauma and the harsh realities of Civil War imprisonment.

James's remains were interred at Woodlawn National Cemetery, located adjacent to the former Elmira prison grounds, in Chemung County, New York.[81] Though buried under the uniform headstones of Union dead, his grave stands among thousands of fellow Confederates who died in captivity.

NOTE: It is a logical and well-supported assumption that the individual identified in Confederate service records as James Cardwell, born in King and Queen County, is indeed James Upshur Cardwell, son of Upshur Cardwell. Census records confirm that Upshur had a son named James who disappears from civil records after 1860, and there are no other known Cardwell men from that county who match the profile. Thus, despite the lack of explicit post-war documentation, James's identification with the soldier who died at Elmira is a highly credible conclusion. <u>Cardwell Line IV - Predicted</u>. Photo Credit[82]

* * *

Photo 11.11: *John Alexander Cardwell (1833-1883) Headstone - Dixon Cemetery, Concord, Campbell County, Virginia*

John Alexander Cardwell (1833-1883) - *Private - Patterson's Company, Virginia Heavy Artillery (Campbell Battery), CSA & Company D, 20th Battalion, Virginia Heavy Artillery, CSA*

John Alexander Cardwell was born on 13 August 1833 in Campbell County, Virginia. He was the son of John Thomas Cardwell and Mary (Ransberger) Cardwell. The Cardwell family was deeply impacted by the Civil War, with five sons serving the Confederacy: James Robert, John Alexander, Thomas Henry, Christopher Anthony, and Josephus A. Cardwell. John appears in the household of his parents in the 1850 Campbell County census.[83]

He married Bridget Ann Letitia Martin on 17 December 1855, in Campbell County, Virginia.[84] They had the following: Mary Barger Cardwell (1857-1892), Nannie C. Cardwell (1859-1873), John Alexander Cardwell, Jr. (1861-1936), Thomas Andrew Cardwell (1865-1934), Judith Ann Cardwell (1868-1944), Sarah Elizabeth Cardwell (1870-1962), and Emma Evans Cardwell (1874-1952). John is listed in the 1860, 1870, and 1880 Campbell County, Virginia census records.[85,86,87]

He enlisted as a Private on 05 March 1862 in Patterson's Company of

Virginia Heavy Artillery, also known as the Campbell Battery. His brothers James and Josephus enlisted on the same day, and all three were initially assigned to this local artillery unit raised in Campbell County. However, Patterson's Company was disbanded shortly thereafter, and the men were redistributed to other artillery formations. John and his younger brother Josephus were transferred to Company D of the 20th Battalion, Virginia Heavy Artillery, CSA.

The 20th Battalion, Virginia Heavy Artillery, served in the Department of Richmond and was responsible for defending key fortifications, batteries, and river approaches near the Confederate capital. While not engaged in constant combat like frontline infantry units, heavy artillery battalions were frequently exposed to skirmishing, shelling, and the strain of maintaining defensive positions under harsh and often unsanitary conditions.

John's transfer to the 20th Battalion became official on 05 July 1862, though his service records show that he was unwell and at home at the time of his reassignment. A muster roll dated 04 October 1862 indicates that he still had not reported for duty with the unit. His poor health proved debilitating. On 23 June 1863, he was formally discharged from Confederate service after a medical examination determined he suffered from chronic pleurisy—an inflammation of the lung lining that could be both painful and life-threatening, especially with no effective treatment in the 1860s.

John's discharge papers provide a personal description: he had a dark complexion, blue eyes, sandy hair, and stood 5 feet 11 inches in height. He was listed as a farmer, residing in Campbell County.

After leaving military service, John returned to civilian life and continued to raise his family in Concord, a community in eastern Campbell County. He appears in census records through 1880, listed as a farmer and head of household.

John Alexander Cardwell died on 23 March 1883 in Concord, Campbell County, Virginia. He is buried at Dixon Cemetery, Concord, Campbell County, Virginia.[88] His military service, though limited by illness, reflected the commitment of thousands of Confederate volunteers who were physically unable to endure the rigors of prolonged campaigning but who nonetheless answered the call to serve. <u>Cardwell Line II - Predicted</u>. Photo Credit[89]

* * *

Photo 11.12: *John Lewis Cardwell (1832-1899) Headstone - Hollywood Cemetery, Richmond, Richmond City, Virginia.*

John Lewis Cardwell (1832-1899) - *Sergeant - Company H, 9th Regiment, Virginia Cavalry, CSA; Company G, 2nd Regiment, Virginia Artillery, CSA; & Company C, 87th Regiment, Virginia Militia, CSA*

John Lewis Cardwell was born around 1821 in King William County, Virginia. He was the son of John Cardwell and Harriet (Garnett) Cardwell. In the 1850 census, John appears in a school household alongside his younger brother, William R. Cardwell, indicating the family's emphasis on education. By 1860, he was back in the home of his parents in King William County, listed as residing there at the age of nearly 40.[90,91]

He married Caroline Virginia Upshaw around 1854, probably in King William County. They had two daughters: Ida Virginia Kate Cardwell (1854-1926), and Martha Lewis "Lewtie" Cardwell (1865 -).

John's Confederate service was both varied and extensive, involving enlistment in three different military branches: militia, artillery, and cavalry. His earliest known service began on 16 December 1861, when he enlisted at the King William County Courthouse and was mustered into Captain Joseph B. Moore's Company of the 87th Regiment, Virginia Militia. This local defense force was later reorganized and redesignated as Company C. Within

211

a month, John had advanced through the non-commissioned ranks, being elected 1st Corporal and promoted to 4th Sergeant on 24 January 1862. However, his tenure with the 87th was brief; he was discharged just two weeks later, on 05 February 1862.

Determined to continue serving the Confederate cause, John reenlisted just days before his official discharge. On 31 January 1862, he enrolled at Gloucester Point in southeastern Virginia, where he was mustered into Company G of the 2nd Regiment, Virginia Light Artillery, CSA, with the rank of 2nd Sergeant. This battery served within the Department of the Peninsula and was tasked with defending the lower Chesapeake Bay and the approaches to Richmond. Gloucester Point, where the battery was initially stationed, was a fortified position used to monitor and resist Union naval movement along the York River. Though John appears regularly on unit rolls from March through May of 1862, no further records indicate whether he remained with the battery during later deployments.

With Confederate manpower severely depleted by 1864, and the war escalating in intensity, John was conscripted again on 15 February 1864. He was mustered into service at Camp Lee in Richmond and assigned to Company H of the 9th Regiment, Virginia Cavalry, CSA, on 11 March 1864. This unit, also known as "Lee's Rangers," was originally formed in King and Queen County and was composed primarily of men from Virginia's Tidewater region. The 9th Virginia Cavalry had a distinguished history, having served in nearly every major campaign of the Army of Northern Virginia. By the time John joined, the regiment was part of W.H.F. Lee's Brigade under Fitzhugh Lee's Cavalry Division.

In 1864, the 9th Virginia Cavalry was engaged in constant mounted operations during General Ulysses S. Grant's Overland Campaign. Cavalry units like the 9th were critical for conducting reconnaissance, screening infantry movements, and engaging in skirmishes and raids against Union supply lines. John was marked present for duty through August 1864—a time that included the defense of Richmond, the battles around Cold Harbor, and the early stages of the Siege of Petersburg. However, on 06 October 1864, he was listed as absent without leave (AWOL) on the final regimental roll, and no further military records indicate his return to active duty.

After the war, like many veterans of the Confederacy, John struggled with the cumulative toll of war, age, and poor health. By 1895, he was living with his daughter, Mrs. Martha L. Richardson, and without means of support. On

11 January 1895, at the age of 63, he applied for admission to the Robert E. Lee Camp Soldiers' Home in Richmond, a facility established for indigent and disabled Confederate veterans. His application was approved on 14 February 1895, and he resided there for the remainder of his life.

John Lewis Cardwell died on 17 January 1899 at the Soldiers' Home. His remains were laid to rest at Hollywood Cemetery in Richmond, a hallowed resting ground for many Confederate veterans and figures of the era.[92] Though his service record was marked by movement between units and the physical strain of three different military roles, his participation in Virginia's militia, artillery, and cavalry illustrates the varied and demanding paths taken by citizen-soldiers in defense of their home state during the Civil War. Cardwell Line IV - Predicted. Photo Credit[93]

* * *

John Randolph Cardwell (1830-<1884) - *Private - Company B, 14th Regiment, Virginia Cavalry, CSA*

John Randolph Cardwell was born around 1830 in Charlotte County, Virginia, according to his Confederate enlistment records. He was the son of Wyatt Cardwell and Martha "Patsy" (Cary) Cardwell. John came from a prominent Virginia family and pursued higher education at the University of Virginia, where he studied during the 1847–1848 academic session. By 1850, he was still residing in his parents' household in Charlotte County, as recorded in that year's census.[94]

A decade later, by 1860, John was working as a Deputy Sheriff in Charlotte County and living in the household of his paternal aunt, Mary (Cardwell) Cary, who had married Harwood Cary.[95] His occupation and household placement reflected a position of both social standing and professional responsibility. The census also notes that he possessed a personal estate valued at $5,000, indicating a degree of wealth uncommon for men of his age in rural Virginia. His brothers, Wiltshire M. Cardwell and William W. Cardwell, would also serve in the Confederate ranks, making the family deeply intertwined with the Southern cause.

John enlisted early in the war as a Private, on 15 May 1861, in Ashland, Hanover County, Virginia—months before the formal organization of the 14th Regiment, Virginia Cavalry. His early service was with Smith's Virginia Cavalry, one of the independent units raised during the initial surge of

Confederate mobilization. Smith's Cavalry would later be absorbed into what became Company B of the 14th Virginia Cavalry Regiment, which was largely composed of men from Charlotte County and accordingly referred to as the "Charlotte Cavalry."

The 14th Virginia Cavalry was formally organized in September 1862, drawing many of its troopers from provisional companies and local mounted militia. John's early enlistment meant he was present during the formative months of Confederate cavalry development in Virginia, a time when the Army of Northern Virginia was still solidifying its organization.

In the summer of 1861, Private Cardwell was stationed near Monterey in Highland County, along the western reaches of Virginia. This mountainous region—close to the border with present-day West Virginia—was of high strategic importance. Union forces had begun early incursions into western Virginia that spring, and Confederate leaders such as Generals Garnett, Loring, and Henry R. Jackson organized defenses to maintain control of the rugged Allegheny front. While Monterey itself did not witness a large-scale battle during John's known time there, it was a staging area for cavalry pickets, mountain scouting, and small-unit skirmishes with Union patrols pressing eastward from the Kanawha Valley and northern Virginia.

These early operations in the western theater were difficult and disorganized, and many units suffered from poor supply lines, bad weather, and disease. It was not uncommon for early war volunteers—especially those who enlisted before unit structures were standardized—to be reassigned, detached to local commands, or lost from the official record due to illness, injury, or even early discharge. John Randolph Cardwell's military service appears to follow this pattern. After the summer of 1861, his name disappears from known Confederate muster rolls, including those of the 14th Virginia Cavalry following its formal organization.

The 14th Virginia Cavalry itself would go on to serve in some of the most active and prestigious cavalry commands in the Confederacy. Assigned to W.H.F. Lee's Brigade in Fitzhugh Lee's Division of the Cavalry Corps, the regiment took part in General J.E.B. Stuart's cavalry campaigns, including the Battle of Brandy Station—the largest cavalry engagement of the war—along with Gettysburg, the Overland Campaign, the Siege of Petersburg, and finally the Appomattox Campaign, where the regiment surrendered in April 1865.

Though it is uncertain whether John remained affiliated with the regiment through these later campaigns, his early enlistment and presence near

Monterey in 1861 place him among the first waves of Confederate cavalrymen to defend Virginia's mountainous frontier. His disappearance from the records after 1861 remains unexplained. There are no known service, census, pension, or civilian records that conclusively identify him after the war.

It is assumed by family historians and researchers that John Randolph Cardwell may have died during the war, possibly from illness, accident, or battle-related circumstances while stationed in the difficult and remote western theater. Without a recorded date of death or known burial site, his fate remains one of the many unresolved stories of the Civil War—an early volunteer who stood for his home state and vanished from the historical record, leaving only the quiet testimony of a few surviving muster cards and the absence that followed. <u>Cardwell Line I - Predicted</u>.

* * *

John Richard Cardwell (1821-1884) - *Private - Company B, 14th Regiment, Virginia Cavalry, CSA & Jeffress' Company, Virginia Light Artillery (Nottoway Light Artillery), CSA*

John Richard Cardwell was born on 16 August 1821 in Rutledge, Grainger County, Tennessee. He was the son of Daniel Cardwell and Elizabeth (Abbott) Cardwell. Sometime in the late 1840s, John married Mary Isabella Lewark, likely in Washington County, Virginia, though no official marriage record has been located. The couple appears in the 1850 census residing in the household of Mary's parents in Abingdon, Washington County, Virginia. Their marriage is estimated based on the birth year of their eldest known child.

John and Mary raised a large family, having at least eight children: Martha L. Cardwell (1850–1896), David Winfield Cardwell (1852–1900), Joseph Wayland Cardwell (1857–1936), John H. Cardwell (1858–), William King Cardwell (1860–1871), Mary T. Cardwell (1863–1945), Laura Isabella Cardwell (1867–), and Eugene "Genie" Cardwell (1869–1945). The family is listed in the 1860, 1870, and 1880 census records for Washington County, Virginia.[96,97,98,99]

When the Civil War erupted, John answered Virginia's call for volunteers early. On 26 April 1861, he enlisted as a Private in the 14th Regiment, Virginia Cavalry, CSA. This unit was originally formed from Wise's Legion, a composite force created under former Virginia governor Henry A. Wise. The

14th Virginia Cavalry was formally organized in September 1862 but had its roots in local mounted companies formed in 1861, including early cavalry operations in western Virginia. These frontier engagements involved reconnaissance missions, raiding Union outposts, and suppressing pro-Union sentiments in what would later become West Virginia. John's service, however, was brief—he was discharged on 30 September 1861, likely due to age or health concerns. At forty years old, he was already older than most of his fellow enlistees.

Despite this early discharge, John remained committed to the Southern cause. He later reenlisted, joining Jeffress' Company of Virginia Light Artillery, more commonly known as the Nottoway Light Artillery. This unit was formed in southern Virginia and saw active service in both defensive garrison roles and as a mobile field artillery unit. The battery supported Confederate operations in Virginia and the Carolinas, contributing to the network of smaller artillery units tasked with holding rail lines, river crossings, and vital transportation corridors that kept the Confederate war machine moving.

As the war continued and manpower shortages worsened, older or infirm veterans were often reassigned to less physically demanding duties. On 09 January 1864, John was officially detailed for light guard duty in Abingdon, Virginia, based on a surgeon's evaluation citing "feebleness of body." While no longer fit for front-line service, such assignments remained vital. Men on guard duty oversaw supply depots, maintained order in rear areas, guarded rail yards, or monitored prisoner transport—logistical functions crucial to sustaining Confederate operations during the increasingly strained final phase of the war.

John's name appears on the company rolls through 01 January 1865, indicating he remained faithfully at his post well into the closing months of the conflict. By then, Confederate forces were stretched thin across every front, and men like John Richard Cardwell—who despite physical limitations continued to serve—provided essential backbone to the home front war effort.

Following the war, John returned to Abingdon in Washington County, Virginia, where he resumed civilian life. He remained there through the 1870s and into the 1880s, appearing in census records as a farmer. Although his later years were spent quietly, his wartime contributions—both as a cavalryman in the opening months of the conflict and later as a member of

Virginia's home defense network—reflected a quiet perseverance and devotion to duty.

John Richard Cardwell died on 08 February 1884 in Abingdon, Washington County, Virginia. The location of his grave is currently unknown, but his legacy survives in the wartime service he rendered and the large family he helped raise during one of the most turbulent periods in American history. Cardwell Line I - Predicted.

* * *

Photo 11.13: *John T. Cardwell (1840-1907) Headstone. Blandford Cemetery, Petersburg, Petersburg City, Virginia.*

John T. Cardwell (1840-1907) - *Private - Company I, 12th Regiment, Virginia Infantry, CSA*

John T. Cardwell was born on 22 February 1840 in Petersburg City, Virginia, the son of Henry C. Cardwell and Martha H. Wallace. He is listed in the household of his parents in the 1850 and 1860 census records for Greensville County, Virginia.[100,101] Henry and Martha raised three sons who served the Confederate cause during the Civil War: Richard H. Cardwell, George Washington Cardwell, and John T. Cardwell.

John enlisted as a Private in Company I of the 12th Regiment, Virginia Infantry, CSA, on his twenty-second birthday, 22 February 1862, in Greensville County, Virginia. The 12th Virginia Infantry had been formed in May 1861, with volunteers from Petersburg and several surrounding counties, including Greensville. Known for its tenacity and hard fighting, the regiment was attached to Mahone's Brigade and served in numerous key battles throughout the war, including the Peninsula Campaign, Second Manassas, Antietam, Chancellorsville, and Gettysburg. Company I itself was composed largely of local men, many from rural farms and small towns.

Unfortunately, John's service with the 12th Virginia was short-lived. After only about five months in the ranks, he was discharged due to a debilitating affliction of the left knee. His military service record indicates that this condition rendered him permanently lame, and he was found unfit for continued field duty. A surgeon's certificate was issued authorizing his honorable discharge.

John's discharge documentation provides a detailed physical description: he was born in Petersburg, stood 5 feet 8 inches tall, with a fair complexion, blue eyes, light hair, and had been working as a farmer prior to his enlistment. No additional records of Civil War military service have been found for John following this early discharge, suggesting he did not rejoin Confederate forces in any capacity.

Following the war, John returned to Petersburg and resumed civilian life. On 23 March 1871, he married Lucy Taylor Winfield in Petersburg, Virginia.[102] The couple does not appear to have had any children. John is found in the 1870 census for Petersburg City, and in 1880 he is listed residing in Dinwiddie County, before returning to Petersburg by the 1900 census, where he remained for the rest of his life.[103,104,105] According to his obituary, John T. Cardwell was employed by the Norfolk and Western Railroad for an impressive forty-seven years. In an era when railroads were central to commerce and transportation, such longstanding service indicates a man of steady character and reliability. He was reportedly well-respected within his community and among his colleagues.[106]

John T. Cardwell died on 19 February 1907 in Petersburg, just three days before his 67th birthday. He was laid to rest at Blandford Cemetery in Petersburg, one of Virginia's most historic Confederate burial grounds.[107] Though his active military service was cut short by disability, his early enlistment, family legacy of service, and post-war contributions as a dedicated railroad worker earned him a place of remembrance in both military and civic life. Cardwell Line II - Predicted. Photo Credit[108]

* * *

Photo 11.14: *John Wesley Cardwell (1821-1887) - Founder of J.W. Cardwell & Company Machine Shop, Richmond, Virginia - circa 1875 - Provided by Nancy Harding*

John Wesley Cardwell (1821-1887) - *Private - Company A, 1st Regiment, Virginia State Reserves (2nd Class Militia), CSA & 57th Regiment, Virginia Infantry, CSA -* **Prisoner of War**

John Wesley Cardwell was born on 25 February 1821 in Petersburg, Virginia, the son of Richard Lee Cardwell, a veteran of the War of 1812, and Lucy Ann (Adams) Cardwell. Following the early death of his father, John was raised by his widowed mother, and by the 1830s the family had relocated to Richmond, where he would spend much of his life. He is recorded in her household in the 1850 Richmond (Independent City) census.[109]

As a young man, John was apprenticed to James Parker, a Richmond machinist and manufacturer of agricultural equipment. This formative experience would shape his lifelong career. By 1849, he had entered into a partnership with a Mr. Baldwin, forming J.W. Cardwell & Company, a general machine works known for its innovation and excellence in farm machinery. The business was highly successful in antebellum Richmond, and John came to be regarded as one of the city's prominent industrialists.

He married Henrietta Jacobs Hinton on 04 June 1846 in Richmond, although the only surviving record of this union is a family Bible entry. They had the following children: William Hinton Cardwell (1847–1861), Ida Jacobs Cardwell (1849–1931), Ella Frances Cardwell (1850–), Cora Belle Cardwell (1853–1871), John Edward Cardwell (1856–1857), Richard Wyatt Cardwell (1858–1938), Gertrude Adams Cardwell (1862–1865), Lee Russell Cardwell (1864–1894), and Charles Wesley Cardwell (1866–1956). John is listed with his family in the 1860 and 1880 census records for Richmond, Henrico County, Virginia.[110,111]

With the outbreak of the Civil War, John found himself just above the age threshold for regular military service. Nonetheless, he rendered active support to the Confederate cause in several important capacities. He first enlisted as a Private in Company A of the 1st Virginia State Reserves, commonly referred to as Farinholt's Regiment, organized in August 1864. The State Reserves were composed primarily of older men and others exempt from frontline duty. Their service included guarding Union prisoners, protecting supply depots, and fortifying key infrastructure, particularly around the capital. The mention in his service record that he had been "detailed by the Secretary of War" suggests that John's mechanical expertise and status as a master machinist were likely utilized for specialized logistical or administrative duties.

According to family accounts, John was stationed for a time at Belle Isle, overseeing Union prisoners of war. Due to the critical need for agricultural support in the region, he was subsequently discharged and detailed as a public necessity to assist Cumberland and Powhatan County farmers by repairing farm machinery—a service essential to sustaining food production in the war-torn Confederacy. This aligns with Confederate policy in the later war years to allow skilled tradesmen to return to civilian duties under special exemption orders.

Despite being released from earlier military obligations, John reentered Confederate service briefly in the final weeks of the war. He is listed as a Private with the 57th Regiment, Virginia Infantry, CSA, and was surrendered near Richmond on 25 April 1865, just weeks after General Lee's surrender at Appomattox. His name appears on a Prisoner of War Roll submitted by Colonel D.M. Evans of the 20th Regiment, New York Cavalry, suggesting he had been drawn into local militia or Home Guard service during the chaotic final days of the Confederacy's collapse.

An account written by his son, Richard Wyatt Cardwell, dated 11 March 1927, offers additional insight into John's wartime service and character. He described his father as "genial, kind-hearted, a Christian gentleman," affectionately known as "Boss John" by his workers. Employees would often turn to him with personal and professional challenges, and he was known for meeting them with understanding and practical help.

Following the war, John reestablished his mechanical works, regaining prominence as a respected inventor and businessman. His company, J.W. Cardwell & Company, played a significant role in the postwar rebuilding of the South, and he remained highly esteemed in Richmond's civic and industrial circles.

John Wesley Cardwell died suddenly on 10 January 1887 in Richmond, Virginia, at the age of 65. He was buried in an unmarked grave at Shockoe Hill Cemetery, one of Richmond's most historic burial grounds.[112] Though his direct military service was limited by age and health, his contributions to the Confederate war effort and the agricultural backbone of Virginia were considerable. His legacy lived on through his children—particularly his son Richard Wyatt Cardwell, who would rise to become a respected jurist—and through the innovations and reputation of the machine company he built. Cardwell Line I - Predicted. Photo Credit[113]

* * *

Photo 11.15: *John William Cardwell (1847-1919) Headstone - Early's Chapel UMC Cemetery, Concord, Campbell County, Virginia.*

John William Cardwell (1847-1919) - *Private - Company I, 2nd Regiment, Virginia Cavalry, CSA -* **Prisoner of War**

John William Cardwell was born on 15 February 1847 in Concord, Campbell County, Virginia, the son of Thomas Dixon Cardwell and Edna Ann "Edney" (Neighbors) Cardwell. He is listed in the household of his parents in the 1850 and 1860 Campbell County census records.[114,115] Two sons of Thomas and Edna would serve the Confederate cause: Robert Richardson Cardwell and John William Cardwell.

John's Confederate service record is fragmentary, but by comparing details and matching local enlistment patterns, we can reasonably conclude that he served in Company I of the 2nd Regiment, Virginia Cavalry, CSA, alongside his older brother Robert. Robert enlisted on 10 August 1862 in

Campbell County, and it is likely that John—only fifteen at the time—enlisted around the same date or shortly thereafter. Company I, known locally as the "Campbell Rangers," was composed almost entirely of men from Campbell County and the surrounding region.

At the time of their enlistment, the 2nd Virginia Cavalry was a seasoned and well-respected regiment within General Fitzhugh Lee's Brigade, part of Major General J.E.B. Stuart's Cavalry Division in the Army of Northern Virginia. The unit had already distinguished itself in the early campaigns of the war and continued to serve at the forefront of Confederate cavalry operations through 1862 and beyond.

During the Second Manassas Campaign in August 1862, the 2nd Virginia Cavalry played a critical role in reconnaissance and screening maneuvers, disrupting Union communications and harassing supply trains. In the autumn, they participated in Stuart's audacious ride around McClellan, a daring operation that boosted Southern morale and affirmed Stuart's role as Lee's cavalry commander.

The regiment remained highly active through the Maryland Campaign, providing flank coverage and patrolling during the Battle of Antietam. In 1863, they fought at Brandy Station, the largest cavalry engagement of the war, and followed Stuart into Pennsylvania during the Gettysburg Campaign. Although Stuart's cavalry was criticized for arriving late to Gettysburg, the 2nd Virginia's involvement in deep raids and screening operations was consistent with Confederate cavalry doctrine at the time.

Throughout 1864, the regiment engaged in nearly continuous fighting during Grant's Overland Campaign and Sheridan's cavalry raids. The loss of Stuart in May 1864 dealt a blow to the Confederate cavalry, but Fitzhugh Lee's command—including the 2nd Virginia—remained committed to delaying Union advances and defending the roads into Richmond and Petersburg. By this point, the unit had been in near-constant combat for nearly three years.

John's specific actions during this period are not documented, but as a member of Company I, he would have endured long days in the saddle, skirmishes, scouting missions, and raids against vastly better-equipped Union forces. His continued presence with the unit is supported by his inclusion on a Prisoner of War roll dated 17 April 1865, following the surrender of the Army of Northern Virginia at Appomattox Court House on 09 April 1865. He was paroled shortly thereafter in Lynchburg, Virginia, a common location for paroles issued to returning cavalrymen from nearby Campbell County.

One alternate or additional record exists that may also pertain to this John William Cardwell. A "John W. Cardwell" enlisted as a Private in Booker's Regiment, Virginia Reserves (Third Reserves), on 16 April 1864. Given the scarcity of Cardwell men with that full name in the region, it is plausible that he may have briefly served in this local defense unit before returning to the cavalry. Booker's Regiment was composed of older men, boys, and those otherwise exempt from regular service, assigned to defend railroads, depots, and bridges across central Virginia during the war's final year.

Following the war, John returned to Campbell County, where he resumed civilian life and built a large family. He married Marietta Miles on 24 February 1869 in Campbell County.[116] Together, they had ten children: Edna Frances Cardwell (1870–1956), Nannie Mae Cardwell (1872–1924), Mary J. "Mollie" Cardwell (1875–), Alice Kathryn "Kate" Cardwell (1877–1963), Willie Plunket Cardwell (1879–1967), Charles Travis Cardwell (1883–1956), Etta Reva Cardwell (1884–1919), James Richardson Cardwell (1886–1942), Annie Burton Cardwell (1889–1954), and John Daniel Cardwell (1893–1986).

John William Cardwell is listed in the 1870, 1880, 1900, and 1910 Campbell County census records, consistently residing near his birthplace of Concord.[117,118,119,120] He lived to see the turn of the century and the full reconstruction of the South after the devastation of war. He died on 01 December 1919 at the age of 72 and was buried at Earlys Chapel United Methodist Church Cemetery, in Concord, Campbell County, Virginia.[121] Though his service record is limited in scope, John William Cardwell was a youthful cavalryman who likely fought through some of the most storied campaigns of the Eastern Theater. His life after the war—as a husband, father of ten, and resident of his home county—reflects the quiet perseverance of many Confederate veterans who endured war and returned to rebuild their lives in peace. Cardwell Line II - Predicted. Photo Credit[122]

* * *

Photo 11.16: *Joseph B. Cardwell (1822-1864) Headstone - Woodlawn National Cemetery, Elmira, Chemung County, New York.*

Joseph B. Cardwell (1822-1864) - *Private - Company C, 26th Regiment, Virginia Infantry, CSA -* **Prisoner of War - Died in Captivity**

Joseph B. Cardwell was born around 1823 in King and Queen County, Virginia, the son of John Cardwell and Mary "Polly" (Driscoll) Cardwell. He married Ann Elizabeth LNU around 1849, though no formal record of their marriage has been located. The couple is listed together in the 1850 census for King and Queen County. By the time of the 1860 census, Ann appears to have passed away. Joseph, a carpenter by trade, was then living near his widowed mother and several siblings, still in King and Queen County.[123,124]

Joseph was conscripted into Confederate service as a Private in Company C of the 26th Regiment, Virginia Infantry, CSA, on 07 May 1861, at New Prospect, a community in Prince Edward County. At that time, the 26th Virginia was part of the early organizational efforts of the Confederate Army, formed largely from central and southeastern Virginia volunteers. The regiment initially served in the Tidewater region, where it performed garrison duties and constructed fortifications near Norfolk and along the James River, guarding approaches to Richmond and the strategic Hampton Roads area.

During the early years of the war, the 26th Virginia was tasked with defending southeastern Virginia and training its men for extended field service. By 1862 and into 1863, it became increasingly active in field operations, especially as Union pressure grew along the eastern Confederate frontier. During this time, Joseph served in an essential non-combat capacity.

From January through August 1863, he was detailed as a Hospital Nurse for the regiment—an assignment that, while not on the front lines, was grueling and vital. Medical resources were often scarce, and Confederate hospital staff were responsible for tending to the wounded and ill with limited supplies and in difficult conditions.

In 1864, the regiment was entrenched in the Petersburg Campaign, defending the outer fortifications of the city as part of General Robert E. Lee's Army of Northern Virginia. The 26th Virginia was stationed along defensive lines southeast of Petersburg during some of the most intense trench warfare of the conflict.

On 17 June 1864, during these defensive operations, Joseph was captured by Union forces near Webb's Farm, close to the Union siege lines surrounding Petersburg. He was taken to City Point, a major Union depot and prisoner processing center on the James River, arriving there on 24 June.

From City Point, Joseph was transported to Elmira Prison Camp in Elmira, New York, arriving there on 27 July 1864. Known for its harsh climate, overcrowding, and poor sanitation, Elmira was among the most notorious Union prison camps. Conditions were particularly harsh during the fall and winter of 1864, leading to high rates of illness and death among the inmates.

Tragically, Private Joseph B. Cardwell died of pneumonia on 20 October 1864, just three months after arriving at the camp. He was one of more than 2,900 Confederate prisoners who perished at Elmira during its operation.

Joseph is buried at Woodlawn National Cemetery in Elmira, located within sight of the camp where he spent his final days.[125] His sacrifice, along with that of his cousin James Upshur Cardwell—also of the 26th Virginia and who also died at Elmira—serves as a poignant reminder of the toll the war took not only on the battlefield but in captivity. Cardwell Line IV - Predicted. Photo Credit[126]

* * *

Photo 11.17: *Josephus A. Cardwell (1843-1924) Headstone - New Concord Presbyterian Church Cemetery, Concord, Campbell County, Virginia.*

Josephus A. Cardwell (1843-1924) - *Private - Patterson's Company, Virginia Heavy Artillery (Campbell Battery), CSA & Company D, 20th Battalion, Virginia Heavy Artillery, CSA -* **Prisoner of War**

Josephus A. Cardwell was born on 04 August 1843 in Campbell County, Virginia, the son of John Thomas Cardwell and Mary (Ransberger) Cardwell. He appears in their household in the 1850 Campbell County census.[127] The Cardwell family gave deeply to the Confederate cause, with five sons—James Robert, John Alexander, Thomas Henry, Christopher Anthony, and Josephus —all serving in various units of the Southern forces.

Josephus enlisted on 05 March 1862 as a Private in Patterson's Company of Virginia Heavy Artillery, also known as the Campbell Battery. His brothers John and James also enlisted with the same battery on that date. Organized in Campbell County, this unit was formed for the defense of Confederate strongholds and transportation routes, often manning fixed artillery positions along key roads and river crossings. However, the company's structure proved temporary. On the very day Josephus enlisted, the unit was disbanded, and the men were reassigned—some to Company D of the 18th Battalion of Virginia Artillery, and others, including Josephus and John, to Company D of the 20th Battalion of Virginia Heavy Artillery, CSA.

The 20th Battalion served within the Department of Richmond and played a role in the defenses of the capital and its surrounding approaches. Throughout 1863 and into early 1864, the battalion was posted at various points along the James River and helped to guard vital Confederate infrastructure against Union incursions. These positions became more critical as Ulysses S. Grant's Overland Campaign unfolded in mid-1864, culminating in the prolonged Siege of Petersburg.

By 1865, the unit was still entrenched in the Richmond–Petersburg theater and took part in the Confederate retreat following the collapse of those cities. Josephus was captured on 05 April 1865 at the Battle of Amelia Springs, a sharp engagement during the final days of the Appomattox Campaign. This battle, fought between Union cavalry under General George Crook and retreating Confederate units, marked one of the last efforts by Southern forces to regroup before the surrender.

Following his capture, Josephus was transferred to the Union prisoner of war camp at Point Lookout, Maryland, arriving there on 13 April 1865. He was held in the camp for over two months before taking the Oath of Allegiance and being released on 24 June 1865. His prison documents describe him as six feet tall, with a light complexion, brown hair, and blue eyes—details that place him among the tallest of the Cardwell men in Confederate service.

After the war, Josephus returned to Campbell County and resumed civilian life. He married Mary Willie Evans on 09 April 1874.[128] Together they had one daughter: Ura Layton Cardwell (1875–1966). Josephus is listed in the 1870, 1880, 1900, 1910, and 1920 Campbell County census records, where he is shown to have remained in Concord for the rest of his life.[129,130,131,132,133]

Josephus A. Cardwell died on 11 August 1924 in Concord, Campbell County, Virginia. He was laid to rest at New Concord Presbyterian Church Cemetery.[134] A veteran of artillery service and the final desperate months of the war, he lived to witness the long postwar years of reconciliation and rebuilding in the South. Cardwell Line II - Predicted. Photo Credit[135]

* * *

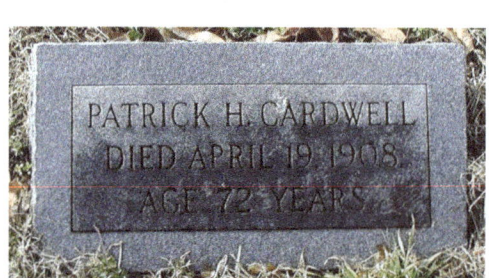

Photo 11.18: *Patrick H. Cardwell (1839-1908) Headstone. Greenlawn Memorial Park, Newport News, Newport News City, Virginia.*

Patrick Henry Cardwell (1843-1908) - *Private - Company D, 1st Virginia Artillery, CSA; Company G, 32nd Regiment, Virginia Infantry, CSA & Company E, 1st Regiment, US Veteran Volunteer Infantry, USA -* **Prisoner of War**

Patrick Henry Cardwell was born about 1839 in Virginia, the son of George W. Cardwell and Ann E. (LNU) Cardwell. He is recorded in their household in the 1850 census of James City County, Virginia. By 1860, Patrick had relocated and was living in the home of Patrick Jordan in Henrico County, Virginia, where he likely worked or boarded in preparation for adult life.[136,137]

On 20 May 1861, Patrick enlisted as a Private in Company D, 1st Regiment of Virginia Artillery, CSA, at Williamsburg, James City County. The 1st Virginia Artillery, originally composed of several batteries including the Williamsburg Artillery, served in the Army of Northern Virginia and was active in many of the early defensive campaigns along the Virginia Peninsula. The regiment was equipped with field artillery and assigned to protect strategic Confederate positions, especially around Yorktown, Gloucester Point, and other fortifications in the Tidewater region.

Patrick's service record also mentions a detachment to Company G of the 32nd Virginia Infantry, CSA. This regiment was engaged in coastal defense early in the war before seeing significant action during the Seven Days Battles and the campaigns around Richmond. However, the bulk of Patrick's time appears to have remained with the 1st Virginia Artillery, likely providing artillery support during those same operations in eastern Virginia.

Patrick was captured during the Gettysburg Campaign on 05 July 1863 at Waterloo, Pennsylvania, just after the Confederate withdrawal from the battlefield. He is recorded as being a teamster with the 1st Virginia Artillery, CSA, at the time of his capture, which was witnessed by Captain R.L. Christian. Records show he was with the unit from 01 May 1863 until his capture. He was sent to Point Lookout, Maryland, a Union prisoner of war camp that housed thousands of Confederate soldiers in difficult conditions marked by overcrowding and exposure.

In a surprising turn, Patrick took the Oath of Allegiance to the United States on 17 February 1864 while still imprisoned at Point Lookout. On that same day, he enlisted in the Union Army as a Private in Company E, 1st Regiment, United States Veteran Volunteer Infantry (U.S.V.V.I.). This unit, composed primarily of former Confederate soldiers who had pledged loyalty to the Union, served in non-combat and garrison roles, often guarding facilities, infrastructure, or fellow prisoners.

The 1st U.S.V.V.I. was part of a controversial initiative by the Union to replenish manpower by recruiting from Confederate POWs willing to change allegiance. Though not always welcomed by fellow Union troops, these men—often referred to as "Galvanized Yankees"—played an important role in rear-area security, freeing up regular units for front-line duty. Patrick served in this capacity until he was honorably discharged on 27 November 1865.

After the war, Patrick returned to Virginia and married Roselia Alice Chandler on 21 June 1866 in James City County. Together they raised a large family, including: Saint George Cardwell (1867–1940), Charles Edward Cardwell (1870–), Nellie Josephine Cardwell (1873–1962), Susan Elizabeth Cardwell (1875–1960), Mary Lucy Cardwell (1878–1954), and Franklin Henry Cardwell (1881–1954).

The Cardwell family is found in the 1870 census of York County and the 1880 census of James City County, Virginia. Patrick was listed as a farmer, and it appears he continued working until his health began to fail in later life.[138,139]

On 23 October 1900, Patrick was admitted to the National Home for Disabled Volunteer Soldiers in Hampton, Virginia. He suffered from paralysis and was described in the admission ledger as 57 years old, 5 feet 6 inches in height, with a fair complexion, gray eyes, and gray hair. His service with the Union Army, though relatively brief and non-combative, entitled him to medical and housing benefits as a veteran.

Patrick Henry Cardwell died on 18 April 1908 in Newport News, Virginia. He was buried with military honors at Greenlawn Memorial Park in Newport News City.[140] His unusual service in both the Confederate and Union armies places him among a small group of men whose wartime paths crossed the battle lines more than once. Cardwell Line I - Predicted. Photo Credit[141]

* * *

Photo 11.19: *Peter Saunders Cardwell (1820-1889) Headstone - Cardwell-McCormick Family Cemetery, Clays Mill, Halifax County, Virginia.*

Peter Saunders Cardwell (1820-1889) - Private - *Company A, 53rd Regiment, Virginia Infantry, CSA*

Peter Saunders Cardwell was born on 20 November 1820 in Halifax County, Virginia, the son of Giles M. Cardwell and Frances "Fanny" (Moore) Cardwell. After the death of his mother, Peter remained in Halifax County and was recorded in the 1850 census living with his widowed father. His occupation at the time was listed as a teacher, indicating a man of education and local standing.[142]

Peter married Melvina R. Hill on 30 November 1853, in Halifax County, Virginia.[143] Together they had a large family: Mary Rasley Cardwell (1855–1884), Giles T. Cardwell (1856–1921), Bettie A. Cardwell

(1858–), Peter A. Cardwell (1860–), Rosalia H. Cardwell (1862–1884), Rebecca Cardwell (1868–), William Cabbell Cardwell (1870–1879), Mattie Cardwell (1874–1877), and Minnie W. Cardwell (1877–1957). The family appears in the 1860, 1870, and 1880 census records for Halifax County, where Peter continued to live and raise his children.[144,145,146]

Although 41 years old at the time—well beyond the average age of Civil War volunteers—Peter nevertheless enlisted in the Confederate Army. On 21 April 1862, he mustered into service as a Private in Company A of the 53rd Regiment, Virginia Infantry, CSA, at Suffolk, Virginia. Company A was known to have been drawn largely from the southern counties of the state, including Halifax.

The 53rd Virginia Infantry Regiment had been organized just months earlier, in early 1862, and quickly became part of the famed Pickett's Division within the Army of Northern Virginia. This regiment would go on to fight in some of the most well-known engagements of the war, including the Seven Days Battles, Antietam, Fredericksburg, Gettysburg, and the Overland Campaign, culminating in the Siege of Petersburg and the final surrender at Appomattox in 1865.

However, Peter's time with the regiment was brief. Just under a month after enlisting, he was discharged on 17 May 1862 under a Confederate military directive that ordered the release of any men over the age of 35. Though he never saw active combat with the 53rd, his willingness to serve—despite being middle-aged with a large family—underscores his sense of duty and local patriotism during a time of deep regional crisis.

After his discharge, Peter returned to Halifax County, where he resumed civilian life. He is recorded in the post-war census as a farmer, continuing to raise his children and contribute to his community. Several of his children went on to live long lives, and the family maintained deep roots in Halifax County.

Peter Saunders Cardwell died on 17 April 1889 in Halifax County, Virginia. He was buried in the Cardwell-McCormick Family Cemetery in Clays Mill, a testament to his place within the longstanding heritage of that region.[147] Though his wartime service was brief, it links him to one of the Confederacy's most storied infantry regiments and reflects the commitment of older Virginians who nonetheless stepped forward to support the Southern cause. Cardwell Line III - Predicted. Photo Credit[148]

* * *

Photo 11.20: *Richard H. Cardwell (1834-1862) Headstone - Ettrick Cemetery, Chesterfield, Chesterfield County, Virginia.*

Richard H. Cardwell (1834-1862) - *Private - Company F, 16th Regiment, Virginia Infantry, CSA* - **Killed in Action**

Richard H. Cardwell was born about 1834 in Chesterfield County, Virginia, the son of Henry C. Cardwell and Martha H. (Wallace) Cardwell. He appears in the home of his parents in the 1850 Chesterfield County census.[149] Henry and Martha raised a family of patriotic Virginian sons—three of whom answered the call to serve the Confederacy: Richard H. Cardwell, John T. Cardwell, and George Washington Cardwell.

Richard married Mary Ann E. Branch sometime in the 1850s, likely in Chesterfield or nearby Petersburg, Virginia. The couple had at least one known child: Emmett Francis Cardwell (1857–1931). Richard, Mary, and young Emmett appear together in the 1860 census of Petersburg, an industrial and transportation hub. Richard is listed as a laborer, supporting his family during a time of growing political division and approaching war.[150]

With the outbreak of the Civil War, Richard enlisted as a Private in Company F of the 16th Regiment, Virginia Infantry, CSA, on 31 October 1861 at Norfolk, Virginia. At the time of his enlistment, the 16th Virginia Infantry was undergoing reorganization and preparation for active service. Formed primarily from enlistees across southeastern Virginia—including men from Norfolk, Portsmouth, and surrounding counties—the regiment was assigned to General Henry A. Wise's Brigade in the early stages of the war.

Initially stationed in the Norfolk area and later assigned to the Army of Northern Virginia, the 16th Virginia Infantry became an active component of

Confederate operations during the Peninsula Campaign in 1862. The regiment was engaged in the Seven Days Battles, a series of fierce engagements aimed at defending Richmond from the advancing Union Army under General George B. McClellan. These included the Battles of Mechanicsville, Gaines' Mill, Savage's Station, and Malvern Hill.

Private Richard Cardwell's service record indicates that he remained present with his unit throughout the early months of 1862, never being listed as absent or on sick furlough—a reflection of his reliability and physical endurance in a time of grueling military demands. His war came to a tragic end during the Battle of Malvern Hill, fought on 01 July 1862, the final and bloodiest engagement of the Seven Days Battles.

During the assault on Union positions atop Malvern Hill, Confederate forces—relying on frontal charges across open ground against well-prepared Union artillery and infantry—suffered devastating losses. The 16th Virginia Infantry was among the many Confederate units ordered into the assault, and it was during this futile and costly battle that Private Richard H. Cardwell was Killed in Action. He was one of 889 Confederate soldiers who died that day, many of them buried in haste near the battlefield.

Richard's death left behind a young widow and child. On 09 June 1863, Mary Cardwell received a settlement from the Confederate government in the amount of $43.61, representing the pay due to her husband at the time of his death. Decades later, on 09 April 1888, she applied for a Confederate widow's pension while residing in Chesterfield County. Her application reflected both the financial hardship and the enduring grief carried by families of fallen soldiers.

Richard H. Cardwell is buried at Ettrick Cemetery, in Chesterfield, Chesterfield County, Virginia.[151] Although his life was cut short early in the war, his sacrifice in one of the campaign's bloodiest battles underscores the deadly nature of Civil War combat and the commitment of men like him, who gave their lives in defense of their home state. <u>Cardwell Line II - Predicted</u>. Photo Credit[152]

* * *

Robert D. Cardwell, Co. I

Photo 11.21: *Robert Dibrel Cardwell (1846-1918) - circa 1870*

Photo 11.22: *Robert Dibrel Cardwell - circa 1915*

Photo 11.23: *Robert Dibreil Cardwell (1846-1918) Headstone - City Cemetery, Roanoke, Roanoke City, Virginia.*

Robert Dibrel Cardwell (1846-1918) - *Private - Company I, 2nd Regiment, Virginia Cavalry, CSA* - **Wounded in Action - Prisoner of War**

Robert Dibrel Cardwell was born on 12 March 1846 in Campbell County, Virginia, the son of James Elliott Dixon Cardwell and Judith Baldwin (Moore) Cardwell. He is recorded in the home of his parents in the 1850 Appomattox County and 1860 Campbell County census records.[153,154] James and Judith had two sons who served in the Confederate Army: Robert Dibrel Cardwell and Charles Wesley Cardwell, the latter becoming widely known as the last surviving Confederate veteran.

At the age of seventeen, Robert enlisted as a Private in Company I, 2nd Virginia Cavalry, CSA, on 10 August 1863. By the time of his enlistment, the 2nd Virginia Cavalry was a seasoned regiment, having participated in every major campaign of the Eastern Theater. Originally organized in 1861 and composed largely of men from central and southern Virginia, the regiment had earned a reputation for hard fighting under the command of Colonel Thomas T. Munford, and later under Brigadier General Thomas L. Rosser in Fitzhugh Lee's Cavalry Division of the Army of Northern Virginia.

The 2nd Virginia Cavalry played a crucial role in Confederate mounted operations—screening infantry movements, conducting raids on Union supply lines, and skirmishing against Union cavalry units throughout Virginia and Maryland. By 1864, the regiment was engaged in nearly continuous combat as part of General Robert E. Lee's defensive efforts during the Overland Campaign. This included the ferocious battles of The Wilderness, Spotsylvania Court House, and the North Anna River.

On 01 June 1864, during the bloody Battle of Cold Harbor, Private Cardwell was Wounded in Action (WIA). The battle, notorious for its brutal frontal assaults and staggering casualties, saw the Confederate lines hold fast under withering Union fire. Cardwell's injury, received amid one of the most decisive Confederate defensive victories of the war, temporarily removed him from active service.

After recovering, Robert returned to duty with his unit but soon suffered further hardship. On 20 September 1864, he was hospitalized due to measles, and again on 25 February 1865, for scabies, a skin condition common among soldiers enduring the unsanitary conditions of camp life. These recurring health issues underscore the physical toll exacted on cavalrymen during the later stages of the war, especially amid the grueling winter of 1864–1865.

Despite illness, Cardwell remained on the regimental rolls through the final campaigns of the war. The 2nd Virginia Cavalry continued to operate under Fitzhugh Lee's Division during the Petersburg siege, performing delaying actions and shielding Confederate supply routes. As Union forces broke through the lines in early April 1865, the regiment joined the general retreat westward toward Appomattox Court House, where Robert was present with Company I when the Army of Northern Virginia surrendered on 09 April 1865.

From the time of his enlistment in 1863 until the end of the war, Private Cardwell exemplified the endurance and sacrifice of Confederate cavalrymen, enduring both combat wounds and illness while remaining loyal to his unit until the final surrender.

Following the war, Robert returned to civilian life in Campbell County, Virginia, where he is listed in the 1870 census.[155] He married India V. Harvey on 13 May 1877 in Campbell County, Virginia.[156] The same year, the couple relocated to Roanoke, Virginia, where Robert became actively involved in the city's postwar development.

Robert and India raised five children: Anna Maude Cardwell (1878–1955), Eula R. Cardwell (1879–1966), Mattie Reva Cardwell (1880–1901), Lillian Ruth Cardwell (1882–1968), and Robert Williamson Cardwell (1887–1959). The family is listed in the 1880, 1900, and 1910 Roanoke City, Virginia census records.[157,158,159] Robert's obituary noted that he was "prominently identified with the growth and public activities of Roanoke's early days," contributing to the community in both civic and veteran affairs.

He was a proud member of the William Watts Camp of Confederate

Veterans, which played an important role in preserving the legacy and cama-raderie of former Confederate soldiers well into the twentieth century.

Robert Dibrel Cardwell died on 12 September 1918 in Lebanon, Russell County, Virginia, at the home of his daughter Eula R. (Cardwell) Burns and her husband William E. Burns. He is buried at City Cemetery, Roanoke, Roanoke City, Virginia.[160]

Robert's wartime service—marked by endurance through battle wounds, illness, and hardship—reflects the resilience and commitment of Virginia's Confederate cavalrymen. His younger brother, Charles Wesley Cardwell, also served with distinction and lived until 1947, when he passed away as the last surviving Confederate veteran. Together, their lives bookend the story of a generation shaped by war, struggle, and survival. Cardwell Line II - Predicted. Photo Credits[161,162,163]

* * *

Robert E. Cardwell (1843-1899) - *Private - Company A, 59th Regiment, Virginia Infantry, CSA & Company B, 45th Regiment, Pennsylvania Militia, USA*

Robert E. Cardwell was born on 20 June 1842 in Pennsylvania, the son of Calvert Owen Cardwell and Ann (Elliot) Cardwell. He is listed in the home of his parents in both the 1850 and 1860 Delaware County, Pennsylvania census records.[164,165] His early life was spent in the North, making his appearance in Confederate service records both unusual and intriguing. While definitive proof remains elusive, there is strong circumstantial evidence suggesting that the Robert Cardwell who served briefly in the 59th Regiment, Virginia Infantry, CSA was the same individual from Delaware County, Pennsylvania.

According to Confederate service records, "Robert Cardwell," "R.E. Cardwell," and "R.P. Cardwell" enlisted or was conscripted into Company A, 59th Virginia Infantry in June 1861 at Chaffin's Farm, a key Confederate position just east of Richmond. The 59th Virginia Infantry, originally orga-nized as a battalion of state troops in southeastern Virginia, was later mustered into Confederate service. The unit operated under the Department of Norfolk and took part in the defense of Virginia's coastline and interior rivers, including actions in North Carolina, most notably the Roanoke Island campaign in early 1862.

Robert's military record suggests that he ran afoul of military discipline. He was charged with being absent without leave and disobedience of orders, ultimately escaping from a guardhouse near Elizabeth City, North Carolina, in February 1862. The records list him as deserted, and a later note indicates his "whereabouts are unknown." No further Confederate documentation regarding his service has been located.

There is no known match for this Robert Cardwell among native Virginians or Marylanders in Confederate records—an oddity, given the detail typically available in muster rolls. The best and perhaps only fitting candidate from the region is the Robert E. Cardwell of Delaware County, Pennsylvania. If he had found himself in Virginia at the war's outset—whether visiting, studying, or working—he may have been conscripted into Confederate service during the early, chaotic months of the war when manpower was critically needed and records sometimes incomplete or hastily prepared. Given the unusual birthplace listed in the Confederate rolls—Maryland—it is possible that Cardwell, if indeed a Northern-born man, claimed a border-state origin to avoid suspicion or worse treatment during his brief conscription.

The theory continues that after deserting from the Confederate army, Robert made his way back to Pennsylvania, where he resumed civilian life until new demands arose. With the Gettysburg Campaign in full motion during the summer of 1863, Pennsylvania called up militia units to defend against the Confederate advance into the Commonwealth. Robert was conscripted as a Private in Company B, 45th Regiment, Pennsylvania Militia, USA, on 29 June 1863, at Upland, Pennsylvania.

The 45th Pennsylvania Militia was a 90-day emergency unit, activated specifically in response to General Robert E. Lee's invasion of Pennsylvania. The regiment was tasked with guarding infrastructure, defending transportation lines, and supplementing the state's defensive readiness. Although it did not see direct action at Gettysburg, its presence contributed to the broader strategic mobilization that helped protect Philadelphia and other critical areas.

While Robert's time in both the Confederate and Union military was brief, his case is a rare and complex example of the war's deep social and regional entanglements. He appears to be one of the very few Cardwell men to have served in both armies, and perhaps the only one to have done so under such uncertain and conflicting circumstances. The absence of clear documentary continuity means that this account rests largely on well-reasoned assumptions rather than confirmed facts. However, the match of name, age, and region provides strong justification for his inclusion in the record of Cardwell men of Virginia during the Civil War.

Following the war, Robert returned to life in Delaware County, Pennsylvania, where he is believed to have lived quietly for the remainder of his years. He died on 16 September 1899, and is possibly buried at Chester Rural Cemetery, Chester, Delaware County, Pennsylvania, though a grave marker has not been conclusively verified.[166]

Though his military service was short and troubled, Robert E. Cardwell's wartime story stands as a testament to the complexity of individual experience during the Civil War—a conflict where geography, circumstance, and identity often blurred the lines of allegiance. <u>Cardwell Line - Undetermined</u>.

* * *

Photo 11.24: *Robert Richardson Cardwell (1844-1922) Headstone - Bethany United Methodist Church Cemetery, Rustburg, Campbell County, Virginia.*

Robert Richardson Cardwell (1844-1922) - *Private - Company I, 2nd Regiment, Virginia Cavalry, CSA* - **Wounded in Action** - **Prisoner of War**

Robert Richardson Cardwell was born on 08 July 1844 in Concord, Campbell County, Virginia, the son of Thomas Dixon Cardwell and Edna Ann "Edney" (Neighbors) Cardwell. He appears in the home of his parents in both the 1850 and 1860 Campbell County, Virginia census records.[167,168] Thomas and Edna had two sons who served in the Confederate military: Robert Richardson Cardwell and John William Cardwell.

Although Robert's surviving Confederate service records are limited, there are several details that allow for a reliable reconstruction of his service. His brother, John William Cardwell, served in Company I of the 2nd Virginia Cavalry, and it is likely the two enlisted together or around the same time. Robert's known enlistment occurred on 10 August 1862, in Campbell County. Company I, often referred to as the "Campbell Rangers," was composed primarily of men from the county and surrounding region.

By the time Robert joined, the 2nd Virginia Cavalry Regiment had already distinguished itself as part of the Confederate Army of Northern Virginia, operating under Brigadier General Fitzhugh Lee within J.E.B. Stuart's Cavalry Division. The regiment had seen action in earlier campaigns and continued to play a vital role in the Confederate cavalry's increasingly mobile and aggressive tactics. Stuart's cavalry, including the 2nd Virginia, became known for audacious raids, screening maneuvers, and intelligence-gathering operations critical to General Robert E. Lee's strategic planning.

The regiment participated in the Second Manassas Campaign in August 1862, where they screened Confederate movements and disrupted Union logistics. Later that fall, they were part of Stuart's famed ride around McClellan, and then engaged in the Maryland Campaign, where they helped secure Confederate flanks during the Battle of Antietam. In June 1863, the 2nd Virginia fought at Brandy Station, the largest cavalry battle of the war, and advanced into Pennsylvania during the Gettysburg Campaign. While the Confederate cavalry's absence during the initial phases of Gettysburg remains controversial, the 2nd continued its operational role throughout the campaign and its retreat.

Through 1864, the regiment saw intense service during the Overland Campaign and in the prolonged defense of Richmond and Petersburg. After the death of J.E.B. Stuart in May 1864, Fitzhugh Lee assumed a larger command role, and the 2nd Virginia remained at the forefront of the Army of Northern Virginia's cavalry operations.

On 31 August 1864, Robert was Wounded in Action at Berryville, Clarke County, Virginia, just days before the Battle of Berryville began on 03 September. This engagement, though relatively small, was part of the broader Valley Campaigns of 1864, as Union General Philip Sheridan sought to neutralize Confederate forces in the Shenandoah Valley. The skirmishing around Berryville delayed Sheridan's plans and exemplified the aggressive defense Confederate cavalry continued to mount despite dwindling resources.

Following his wounding, Robert was hospitalized on 24 February 1865 in Richmond for scabies, a common ailment in the unsanitary conditions of wartime bivouacs and hospitals. He appears to have returned to active service thereafter, remaining with his unit through the final weeks of the war. Although he is not explicitly mentioned in the parole rolls, his brother John William Cardwell was paroled at Lynchburg on 17 April 1865, strongly suggesting that Robert too was present and received his parole there.

After the war, Robert returned to Campbell County and resumed civilian life. He married Sallie Kit Wright on 27 April 1871 in Concord, Campbell County, Virginia.[169] Together they had the following children: Dudley Hopkins Cardwell (1872-1949), Nellie Bridget Cardwell (1874-1889), Thomas Dixon Cardwell, Jr. (1876-1877), Annie Grace Cardwell (1878-1966), John Robert Cardwell (1882-1918), Martha Hilda Cardwell (1885-1966), Marian Gladys Cardwell (1889-1995), and Bennett Beckman Cardwell (1893-1975).

Robert is listed in the 1870, 1880, 1900, 1910, and 1920 census records for Campbell County, where he lived the remainder of his life.[170,171,172,173,174] He died on 20 December 1922 in Rustburg, Campbell County, Virginia, at the age of 78. He was buried at Bethany United Methodist Church Cemetery, also in Rustburg.[175] His widow, Sallie, later filed for a Confederate Widow's Pension, confirming his long and loyal service in the Southern cause.

Although his military records are sparse, the known facts and the movements of his unit suggest that Private Robert Richardson Cardwell saw some of the most active and grueling service in the Eastern Theater. From the rolling valleys of Virginia to the high-stakes cavalry operations of 1864–1865, his service with the 2nd Virginia Cavalry stands as a testament to the commitment and endurance of the Confederate mounted arm. Cardwell Line II - Predicted. Photo Credit[176]

* * *

Thomas Henry Cardwell (1838-1915) - *Corporal - Company I, 42nd Regiment, Virginia Infantry, CSA*

Thomas was born on 20 April 1838 in Campbell County, Virginia. He was the son of John Thomas Cardwell and Mary (Ransberger) Cardwell. He is listed in the home of his parents in the 1850 and 1860 Campbell County, Virginia census.[177,178] John Thomas and Mary had five sons that fought for the Confederacy: James Robert Cardwell, John Alexander Cardwell, Thomas Henry Cardwell, Christopher Anthony Cardwell, and Josephus A. Cardwell.

Thomas enlisted as a Private with Company I of the 42nd Regiment of Virginia Infantry, CSA, on 11 July 1861, at Lynchburg, Campbell County, Virginia. His younger brother, Christopher Anthony Cardwell, also enlisted with the same unit on that date. Company I was also known as the "Campbell Guards". He was promoted to Corporal on 23 October 1861, at Lewisburg, Greenbrier County, (West) Virginia. This unit participated in numerous major battles and smaller skirmishes throughout the conflict.

He was placed on sick furlough on 31 October 1861, according to his records. Thomas received a disability discharge for *"spinal irritation and anemia"*, on 14 July 1862. Additionally, in his disability papers, was his description. Thomas stated he was born in Campbell County, Virginia and was 24 years of age. He was 5 feet and 7 inches in height, fair complexion, blue eyes, light hair, and his occupation at time of enlistment was a farmer.

Thomas was a life-long bachelor and is listed in the 1870, 1880, 1900, and 1910 Campbell County, Virginia census records.[179,180,181,182]

Thomas died on 12 February 1915 at Lynchburg, Campbell County, Virginia. He is buried at the Dixon Cemetery, Concord, Campbell County, Virginia.[183] Cardwell Line II - Predicted.

* * *

William J. Cardwell (1821-1890) - *Private - Shoemaker's Company, Virginia Horse Artillery (Beauregard Rifles) (Lynchburg Beauregards), CSA*

William J. Cardwell was born in 1821 in Campbell County, Virginia, the son of James Dixon Cardwell and Phoebe Elvira (Cheatham) Cardwell. He married Mary J. Moore on 10 December 1844 in Campbell County.[184] The couple is listed in the 1850 Campbell County census, with William working as a farmer.[185] Together, they had the following children: Mary Ella Cardwell (1846–), Thomas N. Cardwell (1852–1885), John J. Cardwell (1853–1929), and Sarah A. Cardwell (1867–). By 1860, the family was still living in Campbell County, and William was continuing to support his household through agriculture. Later census records place him in Washington County, Virginia in 1880, suggesting a postwar relocation to southwestern Virginia.[186,187] Family tradition states that William went by the nickname of "Billy" and *"was a tall man with curly blond hair and a fine singing voice."*[188]

William enlisted as a Private in Shoemaker's Company, Virginia Horse Artillery (Beauregard Rifles), CSA, on 30 April 1862 in Lynchburg, Virginia. At the time of his enlistment, the company was transitioning from a local militia battery into a formalized horse artillery unit—uniquely mobile, fast-firing, and designed to accompany cavalry forces in the field. Unlike standard field artillery, horse artillery moved with greater speed, allowing it to keep pace with cavalry columns and respond swiftly to shifting tactical situations on the battlefield.

Shoemaker's Company, also known as the Lynchburg Beauregards, was quickly assigned to the Horse Artillery Battalion under the Cavalry Corps of the Army of Northern Virginia. The battery earned a distinguished reputation for its speed, efficiency, and deadly accuracy, and it saw action in many of the war's pivotal campaigns. Under the overall cavalry leadership of General J.E.B. Stuart, and later Wade Hampton and Fitzhugh Lee, Shoemaker's Battery participated in key battles such as Second Manassas, Antietam, Fredericksburg, Chancellorsville, and Gettysburg.

During these campaigns, Shoemaker's guns were often called upon to provide close artillery support for Confederate cavalry raids, screening operations, and rearguard actions. Their rapid-firing artillery became an indispensable element of Confederate battlefield strategy, especially in cavalry-heavy operations where agility and surprise were paramount.

By February 1864, William had been assigned to duty as a teamster, an essential logistical role responsible for driving the wagons and handling the horses that hauled artillery pieces, ammunition, and supplies. Although less glamorous than front-line fighting, teamsters faced their own hazards, often working under fire during marches, retreats, and while maneuvering artillery on muddy, narrow roads. Their work was crucial to maintaining the operational mobility of units like Shoemaker's Battery, especially during high-tempo campaigns.

As the war entered its final, grinding phase in 1864–1865, Shoemaker's Battery remained active during the Overland Campaign, where it supported the cavalry during battles at Yellow Tavern, Cold Harbor, and other clashes along the Richmond-Petersburg line. During the Siege of Petersburg, the battery continued to serve in a mobile role, often reinforcing weakened sections of the line or accompanying cavalry raids to disrupt Union communications and logistics.

In the final days of the war, Shoemaker's Company joined the retreat westward toward Appomattox, continuing to serve until General Robert E. Lee's surrender on 09 April 1865. Although William's name does not appear on the formal parole rolls from Appomattox, there is no indication in his record of desertion or detachment, suggesting he likely remained with the battery through the surrender.

After the war, William and his family relocated to Smyth County, Virginia, where he lived in Rich Valley, a rural community known for its rolling farmland. He is last documented in the 1880 census residing in nearby Washington County, Virginia, before moving slightly west to Smyth. He died there in May 1890 at the age of approximately 69.[189] The exact location of his grave is currently unknown.

William J. Cardwell's service with Shoemaker's Horse Artillery placed him at the heart of the Confederate cavalry's fast-moving and dangerous campaigns, from the wooded slopes of Maryland to the trenches outside Petersburg. As a teamster, he contributed directly to the effectiveness and mobility of one of the South's most agile artillery units—a role that, while often overlooked, was indispensable to the Confederate war effort. Cardwell Line II - Confirmed.

* * *

William R. Cardwell (1825-1900/1910) - *Private - Company G, 26th Regiment, Virginia Infantry, CSA & Company E, 5th Regiment, Virginia Cavalry, CSA* - **Prisoner of War**

William R. Cardwell was born about 1825 in Little Plymouth, King and Queen County, Virginia, the son of George Cardwell and Mary "Polly" (Walton) Cardwell. George and Mary had two sons who served in the Confederate Army during the Civil War: William R. Cardwell and his younger brother George W. Cardwell. William is listed in the 1850 and 1880 King and Queen County, Virginia census records.[190,191]

William married Eudorah Crittenden around 1876, likely in King and Queen County or a nearby locality, though no formal marriage record has been found. They had one son, L.A.L. Cardwell, born in 1877. William is also listed in the 1900 Richmond City, Virginia census, living with his family late in life.[192]

William's service in the Confederate Army spanned two different branches and multiple periods of enlistment, although his official records are limited. He initially enlisted as a Private in the 26th Virginia Infantry Regiment, though his exact enlistment date and location are not documented. The regiment was formed in May 1861 and was originally stationed along the lower James River and southeastern Virginia coastline, tasked with guarding critical water approaches to Richmond and the Hampton Roads region. It participated in early engagements at Sewell's Point, Bethel Church, and later supported actions during the Peninsula Campaign of 1862.

William's military record states that he was discharged from the 26th Virginia Infantry on 07 May 1862. The reason for discharge is not noted, but it was a time of significant reorganization within Confederate forces following the expiration of initial 12-month enlistments and the passage of the Confederate Conscription Act. Many soldiers were discharged, reassigned, or reenlisted under new terms.

Later in the war, William appears to have re-entered service—likely by conscription—on 13 September 1863, when he was mustered as a Private in Company E of the 5th Regiment, Virginia Cavalry, at Orange County Courthouse, Virginia. The 5th Virginia Cavalry was part of the Cavalry Corps of the Army of Northern Virginia, operating under generals W.H.F. Lee and Fitzhugh Lee. The regiment saw near-constant action in Virginia, particularly during the Bristoe Campaign, Mine Run, and the intense cavalry battles of 1864, including the defense of Richmond during Sheridan's Raids.

In March and April of 1864, William was listed as Absent with Leave, though the nature of his absence is not detailed. His return to the unit was short-lived. On 11 June 1864, during the Battle of Trevilian Station, William was captured by Union forces. Trevilian Station, fought in Louisa County, Virginia, was the largest all-cavalry battle of the war, where Confederate cavalry under Hampton and Fitzhugh Lee clashed with Sheridan's Union troopers in a desperate attempt to disrupt Union supply lines and protect the Virginia Central Railroad.

After his capture, William was transported to a Union prisoner of war facility, where he remained until the end of the war. He took the Oath of Allegiance to the United States and was released from custody on 20 May 1865, more than a month after General Lee's surrender at Appomattox.

In the postwar years, William returned to civilian life and eventually settled in Richmond, Virginia, where he lived with his wife and son. On 18 April 1900, he applied for a Confederate Pension from the Commonwealth of Virginia, stating his service and hardships endured during the conflict.

The date of William R. Cardwell's death is not known, and no burial record has yet been discovered. He remains one of the many Confederate veterans whose precise resting place is lost to history. Nonetheless, his service —spanning both infantry and cavalry, and including capture and imprisonment—reflects the complex and shifting experience of many Southern soldiers who served through the war's most intense campaigns. Cardwell Line IV - Predicted.

* * *

Photo 11.25: *William Thomas Cardwell (1815-1907) Headstone - Highland Burial Park - Danville, Danville City, Virginia.*

William Thomas Cardwell (1815-1907) - *Private - Company E. 5th Regiment, Virginia Cavalry, CSA -* **Prisoner of War**

William Thomas Cardwell was born on 15 October 1815 in Pittsylvania County, Virginia, the son of Thomas Cardwell and Coley (Bomar) Cardwell.

Thomas and Coley had two sons who would later serve in the Confederate Army during the Civil War: William Thomas Cardwell and George Washington Cardwell (1836–1910).

William married Wilmoth W. Towns on 20 December 1845 in Pittsylvania County, Virginia.[193] They had two daughters: Mary Cardwell (1847–) and Catherine Cardwell (1849–), and were listed together in the 1850 Halifax County, Virginia census.[194] Tragically, Wilmoth passed away in 1851, leaving William a widower with young children. He later remarried, taking Virginia Caroline Oliver as his second wife, likely around 1852—a fact confirmed by the 1900 census, although no official marriage record has been found. Together, William and Virginia had several more children: William T. Cardwell (1854–1920), Sarah W. Cardwell (1856–), Elizabeth "Bettie" Cardwell (1859–1952), Ella Cardwell (1862–1930), George Y. Cardwell (1864–1910), Thomas H. Cardwell (1868–1920), and Mattie Cardwell (1872–1965).

The family is documented in the 1860, 1870, 1880, and 1900 census records of Pittsylvania County, Virginia, where William lived most of his life.[195,196,197,198] Despite being nearly 48 years old at the time of his enlistment, William joined the Confederate Army during the later years of the war. On 13 September 1863, he enlisted as a Private in Company E, 5th Regiment of Virginia Cavalry, CSA, at Orange County, Virginia.

The 5th Virginia Cavalry had been formed in 1861, composed primarily of men from southern and central Virginia. By the time William joined in late 1863, the regiment had already established a reputation for aggressive cavalry actions, often under the leadership of Generals W.H.F. Lee and Fitzhugh Lee. Operating as part of the Army of Northern Virginia's Cavalry Corps, the 5th participated in reconnaissance, screening movements, raiding, and rear-guard engagements throughout the Eastern Theater.

In early 1864, the regiment was engaged in the Overland Campaign, contesting Union General Philip Sheridan's cavalry forces during operations near the Rapidan and Rappahannock Rivers. During this intense period of skirmishes and mobile warfare, William was reported as Absent Without Leave (AWOL) in March 1864. However, this appears to be a clerical error in the muster rolls. In reality, William had been captured by Union forces and is listed on a Federal report of prisoners of war taken in April 1864 by the 20th Regiment, New York Cavalry, USA.

Though records of his imprisonment are scarce, this capture likely resulted in his internment at a Union prison camp. Unfortunately, no additional Confederate service records have been located, leaving the details of his release or parole unknown. What remains clear is that his brief but earnest service in the Confederate cavalry—despite his age and large family—mirrors the determined participation of many older Southern men drawn into the conflict during its later and more desperate years.

After the war, William returned to civilian life in Pittsylvania County. He is listed in successive censuses, continuing his occupation as a farmer and head of a large household. In 1900, he was still living with his wife, Virginia, and several of their children.

William Thomas Cardwell died on 12 February 1907 in Pittsylvania County, Virginia, at the age of 91. He is buried at Highland Burial Park in Danville, Danville City, Virginia.[199] His long life, marked by service to his state and dedication to his family, reflects the endurance of the Southern rural class whose lives were deeply shaped by both the war and its aftermath. Cardwell Line III - Predicted. Photo Credit[200]

* * *

William W. Cardwell (1832-<1884) - *Private - Company B, 14th Regiment, Virginia Cavalry, CSA*

William W. Cardwell was born around 1832 in Charlotte County, Virginia, according to his Confederate enlistment records. He was the son of Wyatt Cardwell and Martha "Patsy" (Cary) Cardwell. Wyatt and Martha had three sons who served the Confederate cause during the Civil War: Wiltshire M. Cardwell, John Randolph Cardwell, and William W. Cardwell.

While no formal enlistment record survives for William, available documentation confirms that he served as a Private in Company B of the 14th Regiment, Virginia Cavalry, CSA. His service is likely connected with the same unit and company as his older brother, John Randolph Cardwell, who is known to have enlisted in the early months of the war, even before the official organization of the regiment in September 1862.

The 14th Virginia Cavalry was largely composed of men from central and southern Virginia, including Charlotte County, and evolved from several independent companies and earlier volunteer formations, including those from Wise's Legion. Company B, often referred to as the "Charlotte Cavalry," was formed primarily of local men from Charlotte County, and it is highly probable that William joined during the consolidation of these local units into the larger 14th Virginia Cavalry structure in 1862.

Assigned to W.H.F. Lee's Brigade, later part of Fitzhugh Lee's Cavalry Division, the 14th Virginia Cavalry saw extensive and dangerous service throughout the war. The regiment engaged in numerous pivotal actions, including:

• The Battle of Brandy Station (June 1863), the largest cavalry engagement of the war and a proving ground for Confederate and Union mounted forces.

• The Gettysburg Campaign, where the regiment was involved in screening maneuvers, intelligence gathering, and rear-guard actions throughout the campaign's long march north and back into Virginia.

• The Overland Campaign (spring 1864), where Confederate cavalry was heavily employed in shielding General Robert E. Lee's movements and countering Union cavalry raids.

• Cavalry raids, long-range scouting, and hit-and-run engagements in the Shenandoah Valley, Central Virginia, and the Petersburg Campaign, where the cavalry's mobility was critical to Confederate strategy in the face of a prolonged siege.

Despite the increasing hardship, dwindling supplies, and relentless Union pressure, the 14th Virginia Cavalry remained in action through the final stages of the war. They were among the cavalry forces that covered Lee's retreat toward Appomattox Court House, where the regiment ultimately surrendered alongside the rest of the Army of Northern Virginia on 09 April 1865.

There is no indication that William was present at the surrender, nor do any parole or muster rolls list him in the final months of the conflict. It is assumed that he may have died during the war, potentially in one of the regiment's engagements or due to illness, which claimed the lives of thousands of soldiers on both sides. No record of his death or burial has been found, and he does not appear in any known census or official documents after 1862. His service remains one of the many whose stories are partially lost to history but whose sacrifice forms part of the collective legacy of those who served.

William's inclusion in Company B of the 14th Virginia Cavalry, alongside his brother John Randolph Cardwell, points to a deeply rooted family commitment to the Confederate cause. The absence of further information about him reflects the tragic obscurity that befell so many soldiers of the Civil

War—young men whose names survive only through fragmentary enlistment rolls and scattered recollections.

William W. Cardwell's final resting place remains unknown. <u>Cardwell Line I - Predicted</u>.

Photo 11.26: *William Wiltshire Cardwell (1838-1898) Portrait - circa 1860/70*

William Wiltshire Cardwell (1838-1898) - *Private - Paris' Company, Virginia Artillery (Staunton Hill Artillery), CSA*

William Wiltshire Cardwell was born about 1838 in Prince Edward County, Virginia, the son of Thomas T. Cardwell and Nancy (Cary) Cardwell. After his mother's death prior to 1850, William is listed in the household of his widowed father in the 1850 and 1860 Charlotte County, Virginia census records.[201,202] He attended Randolph-Macon College in Charlotte County in 1857, suggesting a well-educated background and family of some standing in the region.

At the outbreak of the Civil War, William joined a unit closely tied to his community. He enlisted as a Private on 06 January 1862 in Paris' Company,

Virginia Artillery, commonly referred to as the Staunton Hill Artillery. The company had been organized in late 1861 in Charlotte County and was composed largely of local men, including his cousin, Wiltshire M. Cardwell, who enlisted on the same day. The battery initially fell under the command of Captain Charles Bruce, later succeeded by Captain Alexander D. Paris.

The Staunton Hill Artillery served primarily as a heavy artillery unit, meaning they operated large-caliber guns in fixed fortifications rather than as a mobile field battery. These heavy artillery companies were crucial to Confederate efforts in safeguarding major rail junctions, coastal cities, and strategic river crossings. Early in the war, the battery was posted in south-eastern Virginia and North Carolina, manning defensive positions along the Cape Fear River, near Wilmington—one of the South's last vital ports for blockade runners.

In the summer of 1862, Wilmington was struck by a deadly yellow fever epidemic that killed hundreds and caused mass evacuations. Private Cardwell was hospitalized on 23 August 1862, with his records noting "cholera," though it is possible this was a misidentification of yellow fever, which was the prevailing and rapidly spreading disease in the city at the time. The threat of illness was a constant reality in the Confederate camps, particularly in coastal areas like Wilmington, where sanitation was poor and medical resources limited. William survived the outbreak, but his cousin, Wiltshire M. Card-well, died of disease on 17 September 1864. Although the cause and location were not specified, it's plausible he succumbed to lingering illnesses during this same period of regional epidemic.

After his recovery, William W. Cardwell resumed his duties with the Staunton Hill Artillery. The unit continued to serve in North Carolina and southern Virginia, where it formed part of the Department of North Carolina and Southern Virginia. As Union offensives intensified in 1864, the battery was reassigned to defend the approaches to Richmond and Petersburg. Although heavy artillery units were not typically used in offensive operations, their presence in the trenches became increasingly important during the Petersburg Campaign. The Staunton Hill Artillery likely rotated through defensive positions supporting the Confederate earthworks, contributing suppressive and counter-battery fire during prolonged sieges and skirmishes.

In the final weeks of the war, as General Robert E. Lee's Army of Northern Virginia collapsed under overwhelming pressure, many artillery batteries—including the Staunton Hill Artillery—were either absorbed into infantry units or simply disbanded. While there is no clear record of William's parole or formal surrender, it is presumed he served until the cessation of hostilities in April 1865.

Following the war, William returned to civilian life. On 07 January 1868, he married Martha J. (Womack) Russell, a widow, in Caswell County, North Carolina.[203] They had one daughter, Nannie Cary Cardwell, who sadly died young in 1875. William and Martha appear in the 1870 and 1880 Caswell County census records, where he resumed life as a farmer in the Piedmont region.[204,205] He died in 1898 in Caswell County and is buried at the Hatchett-Womack Family Cemetery in West Yanceyville, Caswell County, North Carolina.[206]

Though his military record is modest, William Wiltshire Cardwell's service in the Staunton Hill Artillery reflects the endurance and hardships faced by Confederate heavy artillerymen. Stationed far from the main lines of glory, these men stood guard over vital Confederate territory, often battling disease, monotony, and exposure more than bullets—but playing a critical role in the South's defensive strategy throughout the war. Cardwell Line I - Predicted. Photo Credit[207]

* * *

Wiltshire M. Cardwell (1821-1864) - Private - *Paris' Company, Virginia Artillery (Staunton Hill Artillery), CSA*

Wiltshire M. Cardwell was born about 1821 in Charlotte County, Virginia, the son of Wyatt Cardwell and Martha "Patsy" (Cary) Cardwell. He appears in his father's household in both the 1850 and 1860 Charlotte County census records, working the land as part of a family deeply rooted in Southside Virginia.[208,209] One of three brothers who would serve the Confederacy, Wiltshire came of age in a time of sectional tension and was well into his forties when war broke out.

On 06 January 1862, at the age of about 41, Wiltshire enlisted as a Private in Paris' Company of Virginia Artillery, more commonly known as the Staunton Hill Artillery. He joined alongside his first cousin, William Wiltshire Cardwell, who enlisted the same day. The battery was raised in Charlotte County and named after the local Staunton Hill plantation, a prominent landmark in the area. The unit entered Confederate service as a heavy artillery battery, meaning it was tasked with operating large-caliber guns in fixed fortifications, rather than the more mobile field or horse artillery units that traveled with infantry or cavalry.

Initially, the Staunton Hill Artillery was assigned to protect vital infrastructure in North Carolina and southeastern Virginia, guarding key river crossings, railroads, and supply depots. The battery's early duties were largely static in nature, operating heavy guns from earthworks and defensive emplacements rather than taking part in open battle. These defensive assignments were essential in keeping coastal cities like Wilmington, North Carolina, in Confederate hands, particularly as Union naval and land forces tightened their grip on the Southern coastline.

In July and August 1862, while the unit was stationed in Wilmington, the city was struck by a deadly yellow fever epidemic—one of the worst of the war. The outbreak caused widespread panic, with thousands fleeing the city and more than 650 people perishing from the disease. Confederate soldiers stationed there were particularly vulnerable due to cramped quarters and poor sanitation.

Service records from the battery show that William Wiltshire Cardwell—Wiltshire's cousin—was hospitalized for cholera on 23 August 1862, though it is highly likely that yellow fever was the actual cause, as the two diseases were often confused in the 19th century due to similar early symptoms. Wiltshire M. Cardwell likely remained with the unit through this difficult period and may have suffered exposure to the same disease.

Wiltshire M. Cardwell died on 17 September 1864. The exact cause and place of his death are not stated in surviving military records, but given the context and timing, it is probable that he died of yellow fever or another camp disease while still serving with the Staunton Hill Artillery. His cousin William's continued presence with the battery in Wilmington suggests that Wiltshire likely died in that area as well.

Though not recorded in any known burial register, Wiltshire M. Cardwell was almost certainly interred near his place of death, most likely in or near Wilmington, North Carolina, alongside other Confederate soldiers who succumbed to illness rather than battle. His quiet service and ultimate sacrifice reflect the overlooked toll that disease and hardship took on thousands of soldiers during the Civil War—especially those stationed in static defense roles where sanitation and exposure created deadly conditions. His service in a heavy artillery battery, though not marked by famous battles, was essential to the Confederate war effort in guarding the South's vulnerable coastline and supply lines. Cardwell Line I - Predicted.

* * *

Wiltshire Marion Cardwell (1837-1924) - *Private - Company K, 18th Regiment, Virginia Infantry, CSA* - **Wounded in Action - Prisoner of War**

Wiltshire Marion Cardwell was born on 10 October 1837 in Charlotte County, Virginia, the son of Francis Flippin Cardwell and Edna "Edney" J. (Haskins) Cardwell. He appears in the home of his parents in the 1850 Charlotte County census.[210] Francis and Edna had two sons who fought for the Confederacy: John H. Cardwell and Wiltshire Marion Cardwell.

Wiltshire enlisted as a Private on 24 April 1861 in Company K of the 18th Regiment of Virginia Cavalry, CSA. At the time of enlistment, he was 19 years old, working as a carpenter, and had traveled approximately 86 miles from his home to Richmond to join the Confederate ranks. Although his compiled service record places him in the 18th Virginia Cavalry, it is likely that this refers to a provisional cavalry formation or early Confederate designation. The 18th Virginia Cavalry as it is most commonly known was not formally organized until 1863, drawing men from western Virginia (now West Virginia). Given the April 1861 enlistment and Wiltshire's association with Richmond, it is more probable that he initially served in the 18th Virginia Infantry, which was actively organizing and engaged during that time. Unit confusion in early war records is not uncommon.

Wiltshire was wounded in the First Battle of Manassas (Bull Run) on 21 July 1861—one of the first major engagements of the Civil War. In his later Confederate pension application, he claimed to have been injured while involved in the charge on Sherman's Battery during that battle. He sustained a gunshot wound to the right hip; the ball remained lodged in his body for the rest of his life, migrating inward and causing chronic pain and infection.

Surgeon Charles Brewer of the Confederate Army issued Wiltshire a disability discharge on 20 October 1861 in Richmond. The wound ultimately disqualified him from continuing in active field service, though Wiltshire claimed in later testimony that he continued to serve in a support role in the Confederate Ordnance Department.

The Confederate pension application Wiltshire filed on 31 December

1903 in Pittsylvania County offers more detail about the lingering effects of his wound. He described the musket ball's location near his hip bone and noted that it was "working into [his] bowels," resulting in a painful, chronic condition. He emphasized that the pain was especially severe during damp weather, but that it persisted constantly. His description underscores the hardships faced by soldiers who, although no longer able to fight, continued to suffer from the long-term consequences of their battlefield injuries.

Further records reveal that Wiltshire was conscripted on 18 May 1863 in Pittsylvania County, Virginia, for industrial duty at the Confederate States Arsenal in Danville. His occupation was listed as a sawyer—an essential trade that contributed to the production of wooden components, such as rifle stocks, crates, and artillery carriages. Though removed from the battlefield, his work supported the logistical backbone of the Confederate war effort. He remained at this post until the war's conclusion. On 18 May 1865, precisely two years after his conscription to Danville, he was captured and required to take the Oath of Allegiance to the United States.

Wiltshire married Elizabeth Adams Haraway on 25 March 1863 in Pittsylvania County. The couple remained in the county after the war, where Wiltshire resumed civilian life while battling the effects of his wartime wound. He is listed in the 1870, 1880, 1900, and 1910 census records of Pittsylvania County, Virginia.[211,212,213,214,215]

Wiltshire Marion Cardwell died on 22 June 1924 in Pittsylvania County. The exact location of his grave is unknown.[216] His service—though cut short by injury—reflects the early enthusiasm of Southern volunteers in 1861 and the enduring sacrifices made by those who bore the physical costs of war for the rest of their lives. Cardwell Line I - Predicted.

* * *

Wyatt Henry Cardwell (1845-1895) - *Private - Company A, 56th Regiment, Virginia Infantry, CSA* - **Wounded in Action - Prisoner of War**

Wyatt Henry Cardwell was born on 03 December 1846 in Mecklenburg County, Virginia. He was the son of Dr. John Randolph Cardwell and Lucy Ann (Henry) Cardwell. His mother was a granddaughter of the famed Virginia orator and statesman, Patrick Henry. Wyatt is recorded in the home of his parents in the 1850 Mecklenburg County census.[217] According to later newspaper accounts, he received an exceptional education and graduated from Washington University. He was said to possess a remarkable gift for memorization, often reciting lengthy poems with ease.

At just fourteen years of age, Wyatt enlisted as a Private in Company A of the 56th Virginia Infantry, CSA, on 14 October 1861, at Richmond, Virginia. This unit had formed earlier that summer and drew heavily from Southside Virginia counties. The 56th served within Mahone's Brigade and was active in many of the Eastern Theater's pivotal campaigns. Initially engaged in training and local defense, the regiment eventually joined the Army of Northern Virginia and became part of its core infantry force.

Wyatt's military service quickly brought him face to face with the harshest realities of war. He was Wounded in Action at the Second Battle of Manassas on 30 August 1862—a brutal Confederate victory where Mahone's Brigade helped drive Union forces from the field. Less than a month later, on 29 September 1862, he was captured near Warrenton, Virginia. He was later released and returned to duty, but the injury to his knee sustained at Second Manassas would have lasting consequences. Though he attempted to remain with his regiment, his wound proved severe.

Wyatt was discharged due to disability on 20 January 1863, likely because of lingering effects from his injury. Yet his desire to serve did not wane. On 17 June 1863, he wrote directly to the Confederate Secretary of War, seeking a position as a clerk—an indication of his literacy and continued willingness to contribute to the Southern cause despite his physical limitations.

Remarkably, Wyatt rejoined Company A of the 56th Virginia Infantry on 15 September 1864, this time with the rank of Sergeant. It is unclear how active his role was during this late stage of the war, but his receipt of government-issued clothing and supplies suggests some level of participation. His hospitalization in Lynchburg in January 1863 points to ongoing health struggles, and it is known that his leg was ultimately amputated after the war due to the effects of his wound.

With the fall of the Confederacy, Wyatt was among those paroled in Richmond. He took the Oath of Allegiance to the United States on 18 May 1865, formally ending his Confederate service.

In the years that followed, Wyatt's life took a tragic turn. Suffering from the physical and psychological aftershocks of war, and likely untreated post-traumatic stress, he drifted from city to city. Contemporary newspapers documented his travels through New York, Cincinnati, Louisville, and Washington. A widely reprinted article out of Memphis dubbed him "The Prince of Tramps," painting a sad portrait of a one-legged former soldier, plagued by alcoholism and hardship, regularly arrested for vagrancy and public drunkenness.[218]

Despite this decline, there were moments when Wyatt tried to reclaim his dignity. On 02 February 1881, he wrote a letter to Major John McPhail, asking for $10 to $15 to buy a suit and secure employment. He claimed to have abandoned alcohol and was seeking to get back on his feet. The letter reveals a man aware of his reputation but hopeful for redemption.

Sadly, Wyatt Henry Cardwell never fully overcame the toll of war and personal demons. He died on 27 May 1895 in Waco, McLennan County, Texas, likely from complications related to alcoholism. He was buried in Oakwood Cemetery in Waco in an unmarked grave—far from his Virginia roots and the promise of his youth.[219] Cardwell Line I - Predicted.

* * *

Note: After exhaustive research, three individuals appear to have been incorrectly indexed as Cardwell men. Their biographies are not included in this work, but they are listed here for the sake of completeness. Despite extensive investigation, no connection could be established between these individuals and any known Cardwell family members of the period:

• **John T. Cardwell** – Company A, 52nd Regiment, Virginia Militia, CSA

• **Samuel T. Cardwell** – 37th Regiment, Virginia Infantry, CSA

• **Toby Cardwell** – 14th Regiment, Virginia Cavalry, CSA

Miscellaneous
The Cardwell Confederates

Not all those who served the Confederate cause were easily categorized by state affiliation. As the war progressed and attrition took its toll on the armies of the South, new formations emerged that did not align neatly with individual state designations. Some men were consolidated into units labeled simply "Confederate" rather than associated with their home states. Others found themselves serving in vital non-combat roles that supported the Confederate military infrastructure—wagon masters, teamsters, clerks, hospital staff, and even civilian contractors such as seamstresses.

This chapter is devoted to those Cardwell individuals whose service records place them within the broader, and often overlooked, framework of the Confederate war machine. Whether they wore a uniform under the banner of the 10th Confederate Cavalry—a unit formed from the remnants of various depleted state regiments—or served the war effort from behind the lines, their contributions formed an indispensable part of the Confederate struggle to sustain its armies across four grueling years.

The majority of these men and women appear in archival collections such as the *U.S. Civil War Service Records (Confederate – Miscellaneous, 1861–1865) and U.S. Civil War Service Records (Confederate – Confederate Government (CSA), 1861–1865)*, both preserved by the National Archives. These collections document individuals who served under direct control of the Confederate government or within non-standard units whose scope extended beyond state lines.

Although these roles often lacked the martial prestige of front-line service, they were essential to the survival and movement of Confederate forces. Supply lines had to be maintained, horses and wagons managed, and ordnance and quartermaster duties performed by men who may never have fired a shot in anger—but without whom the Confederate armies could not have functioned.

This chapter honors those Cardwells whose commitment to the Confederate cause took them down less conventional paths. Whether in improvised units or in the vital web of support services, their service was no less real, and their legacy deserves equal recognition among their kin.

* * *

Benjamin Lumpkin Cardwell (1847-1931) - *Private - Company A, 10th Regiment, Confederate Cavalry, CSA* - **Prisoner of War**

Benjamin Lumpkin Cardwell was born on 27 January 1847 in Chambers County, Alabama. He was the son of John M. Cardwell and Nancy (Peacock) Cardwell. Benjamin appears in the household of his parents in the 1850 and 1860 Chambers County census records.[1,2] His father, John M. Cardwell, served in the Confederate Army and died during the conflict; his biography is included in the Alabama chapter of this volume.

Benjamin entered Confederate service as a Private on 29 January 1864 at Dalton, Georgia. Interestingly, his records also show that he was hospitalized on 19 January 1864—ten days prior to his recorded enlistment date. This discrepancy is likely due to the complex reorganization of Confederate cavalry units during this period. Benjamin served in the 10th Confederate Cavalry, a unit formed from the consolidation of the 19th Regiment of Georgia Cavalry and the 5th Battalion of Hilliard's Legion of Alabama Volunteer Cavalry. Service records for him under either of the predecessor units have not been located, but it is reasonable to assume he had been attached to one of them before their merger into the 10th Confederate Cavalry.

The 10th Confederate Cavalry operated across multiple theaters in the latter half of the war, participating in skirmishes and raids throughout Georgia, Alabama, and the Carolinas. As Union forces intensified their campaigns in the Deep South, the regiment served in a mobile capacity—engaging in delaying actions, protecting Confederate supply routes, and disrupting Federal troop movements.

Benjamin was surrendered as a Prisoner of War on 28 April 1865 at Hillsboro, North Carolina, and was paroled there on 03 May 1865. He was eighteen years old at the time of the surrender.

Following the war, Benjamin worked various jobs across Alabama. In the 1870 census, he is listed as a teamster in Shelby County.[3] By 1880, he was living in Cherokee County and working as a woodchopper—an occupation reflecting the difficult economic conditions faced by many Confederate veterans in Reconstruction-era Alabama.[4]

He eventually settled in Jefferson County, Alabama, where he appears in the 1900, 1910, and 1930 census records.[5,6,7] In the 1900 census, Benjamin is listed as a "Sanitary Pipe Moulder," a position likely tied to the growing industrial base around Birmingham at the turn of the century. He married Jennie Smith on 07 June 1897 in Jefferson County, Alabama.[8] It appears Jennie had children from a previous relationship, though they are mistakenly listed with the Cardwell surname. Together, Benjamin and Jennie had one known son: Jackson "Jack" Howell Cardwell (1900–1984).

Census records suggest that Benjamin had two other marriages during his lifetime, though no documentation of those unions has been found. He spent the later years of his life in Jefferson County, where he remained active in his work into old age. He died on 07 April 1931 in Bessemer, Jefferson County, Alabama, at the age of 84.[9] The location of his grave remains unknown. Cardwell Line II - Predicted.

* * *

Photo 12.1: *Conrad P. Cardwell (1806-1879) - Richmond, Henrico County, Virginia - Circa 1875* (Courtesy of Nancy Harding)

Conrad P. Cardwell (1806-1879) - *Private - Company G, Arsenal Battalion, CSA*

Conrad P. Cardwell was born in 1806 in Dinwiddie County, Virginia. He was the son of Richard Lee Cardwell and Lucy Ann (Adams) Cardwell. By mid-century, Conrad had relocated to Richmond, where he is listed in the home of his brother, John Wesley Cardwell, in both the 1850 and 1860 census records for Richmond, Henrico County, Virginia.[10,11] Like his brother John, Conrad worked as a machinist, likely assisting in the operations of J.W. Cardwell & Company, a prominent machinery business that specialized in agricultural implements and iron works. The firm was a respected fixture in Richmond's industrial landscape and played an important logistical role before and during the Civil War.

Conrad's involvement in the Confederate cause appears to have been in a non-combatant capacity, consistent with his age and skill set. At nearly sixty years of age by the time of the war's final year, Conrad would have been too old for field service. However, men with mechanical expertise were vital to the Confederate war effort, particularly in roles related to ordnance, munitions, and the maintenance of equipment. It is likely that Conrad worked at the Richmond Arsenal or a similar facility, applying his machining knowledge to support Confederate logistics and manufacturing.

His only surviving service-related record is an admission to the Wayside Hospital in Richmond, Virginia, dated 13 February 1865. The Wayside Hospital functioned primarily as a receiving and transit hospital for Confederate soldiers traveling to and from the front lines or convalescing from illness and minor injuries. The document lists him as a Private with Company G of the Arsenal Battalion, but it does not note the reason for admission or the length of his stay. Given his advanced age and industrial background and performed supportive duties rather than front-line combat service.

Conrad's two younger brothers, David Adams Cardwell, Sr. and John Wesley Cardwell, also served the Confederate cause. David served in the 3rd Virginia Infantry, Local Defense, and John was detailed to guard duty and machinist work with the 1st Virginia State Reserves and later associated with the 57th Virginia Infantry.

After the war, Conrad remained in Richmond. He never married and continued to live a quiet life. He died of apoplexy (likely a stroke) on 28 September 1878 in Richmond City, Virginia. His passing was recorded in the Mortality Schedule of that year, noting that he was single at the time of his death. Conrad is buried in an unmarked grave at Shockoe Hill Cemetery in Richmond, a resting place he shares with other members of the Cardwell family who contributed to the Confederate war effort in a variety of capacities.[12] Cardwell Line I - Predicted. Photo Credit[13]

* * *

Lucy Adams (Cardwell) Fisher (1842-1872) - *Seamstress - Clothing Bureau, Quartermaster Department, CSA*

Lucy Adams Cardwell was born around 1842 in Virginia, the daughter of David Adams Cardwell and Rebecca Miller (Drinker) Cardwell. She is listed with her family in the 1850 and 1860 federal census records for Washington, District of Columbia, where her father, a skilled machinist, had moved for work.[14,15] Sometime after 1860, the Cardwell family returned to their native state of Virginia, appearing in the 1860 Richmond, Henrico County census as well. During the Civil War, the Cardwells aligned themselves with the Southern cause. Lucy's father and her two brothers—George Drinker Cardwell and David Adams Cardwell Jr.—each served the Confederacy, with her brothers taking up arms and her father supporting the war effort as a machinist.

Lucy contributed to the Confederate cause through service in the Quartermaster Department's Clothing Bureau, which was responsible for producing uniforms and textiles for the Southern army. Her name appears in official Confederate records, confirming that she worked as a seamstress for the bureau. She is listed in February 1863 alongside two other women: Mary Cardwell—presumed to be her paternal aunt—and Tennie Cardwell, whose precise relationship to the family is not yet established. Their presence in the Clothing Bureau reflects the crucial, though often overlooked, contributions of women in sustaining the Confederacy's logistical and supply networks.

The work of seamstresses like Lucy was labor-intensive and essential. The Clothing Bureau in Richmond employed hundreds of women who stitched uniforms, mended garments, and worked under strict quotas to meet the demands of a war that strained the South's industrial resources. Seamstresses endured long hours in crowded facilities with limited materials, yet their work ensured that Confederate soldiers in the field were clothed and equipped.

After the war, Lucy returned to civilian life and remained in Richmond, living with her father as shown in the 1870 Henrico County census.[16] In 1871, she married Stephen McGee Fisher, a Confederate veteran who had served in Company K of the 3rd Virginia Infantry. Their union was brief; tragically, Lucy died less than a year later, on 03 January 1872, at just 30 years of age. She was laid to rest at Hollywood Cemetery in Richmond, a site that would come to hold many of the city's Confederate dead.[17]

Though her life was short, Lucy's story represents the vital, behind-the-scenes roles played by Southern women during the war. Her recorded work as a seamstress for the Quartermaster's Clothing Bureau, alongside female family members, underscores the domestic front's importance to the Confederacy's war-making capacity.

Note: Based on extensive genealogical research and analysis of census and military records, Lucy Adams Cardwell, daughter of David Adams Cardwell Sr., is the most probable individual identified in Confederate documents as the seamstress listed with the Clothing Bureau. No other women named Lucy Cardwell of appropriate age and location have been found to match as closely. Cardwell Line I - Predicted.

* * *

Photo 12.2: *Mary F. Cardwell (1828-1897) - Richmond, Virginia - circa 1870*

Mary F. Cardwell (1828-1897) - *Seamstress - Clothing Bureau, Quartermaster Department, CSA*

Mary F. Cardwell was born around 1828 in Virginia, the youngest child of Richard Lee Cardwell and Lucy Ann (Adams) Cardwell. Her early years were marked by the death of her father when she was about six years old, leaving her mother to raise a large family in the face of economic and personal hardship. Mary grew up in a household shaped by the industrious and enduring spirit of her widowed mother and older siblings, several of whom would later play roles in support of the Confederacy during the Civil War.

By 1850, Mary was living with her mother in Richmond, Henrico County, Virginia, as recorded in the federal census.[18] A decade later, in 1860, both women were residing in the household of Mary's brother, John Wesley Cardwell, a successful machinist and founder of the J.W. Cardwell & Company machine works in Richmond.[19] At this time, Mary remained unmarried and helped maintain the household.

When the Civil War broke out, Mary contributed to the Confederate war effort not on the battlefield, but through her work in the Quartermaster Department's Clothing Bureau in Richmond. This department, vital to the logistical operations of the Confederacy, was responsible for producing and distributing uniforms and other essential garments to Southern troops. Mary is officially recorded as a seamstress for the bureau in February 1863. She worked alongside Lucy Cardwell—presumed to be her niece—and Tennie Cardwell, whose exact relationship to the family remains uncertain.

The women employed in the Clothing Bureau labored under difficult conditions, sewing uniforms and repairing garments for a Confederate army that was perpetually short on supplies. Though they are often overlooked in historical accounts, their efforts were critical to the daily functioning of the military. Mary's service, like that of thousands of other women, exemplified the silent but indispensable work carried out on the home front in support of the Confederate cause.

Mary's three brothers—Conrad P. Cardwell, David Adams Cardwell, and John Wesley Cardwell—also contributed to the Southern war effort. Due to their advanced age or specialized skills, they served in reserve capacities or support roles, often within Richmond's industrial or administrative infrastructure. Mary's work as a seamstress complemented their efforts, reinforcing the Cardwell family's collective contribution to the Confederacy.

After the war, Mary continued to live with her brother John and his family, as documented in the 1880 census of Richmond, Henrico County, Virginia.[20] She never married and remained a devoted member of the household throughout her life. Mary passed away from dysentery on 18 October 1897 in Richmond. She was buried in an unmarked grave at Shockoe Hill Cemetery, one of the city's most historic burial grounds.[21]

Though she left behind no children or personal legacy in the conventional sense, Mary F. Cardwell's quiet, consistent service during the war and steadfast familial devotion in peacetime are lasting reminders of the many women whose roles were vital, if often unrecorded, in shaping the course of Southern life during and after the Civil War.

Note: Careful examination of genealogical records, census data, and Confederate service files strongly supports the conclusion that Mary F. Cardwell, daughter of Richard Lee Cardwell, is the individual referenced in Confederate documents as serving as a seamstress for the Clothing Bureau. No other Mary F. Cardwell living in the Richmond area during that period has been found whose age, residence, and family connections align as closely with the historical record. Cardwell Line I - Predicted. Photo Credit[22]

* * *

Photo 12.3: *Richard Henry Cardwell (1846-1931) - circa 1880 -*
Source: Wikipedia

Photo 12.4: *Judge Richard Henry Cardwell (1846-1931) - Hanover*
County, Virginia - circa 1925

Photo 12.5: *Richard Henry Cardwell (1846-1931) Headstone -
Woodland Cemetery, Ashland, Hanover County, Virginia.*

Richard Henry Cardwell (1846-1931) - *Private - 1st Regiment, Confederate Engineer Troops, CSA -* **Prisoner of War**

Richard Henry Cardwell was born on 01 August 1846 in Madison, Rockingham County, North Carolina. He was the youngest child of Richard Perrin Cardwell and Elizabeth Martin (Dalton) Cardwell. His father died just two months after his birth, leaving Richard to be raised by his widowed mother, whose strength and guidance he credited for shaping both his character and intellect. Richard appears in her household in the 1850 and 1860 Rockingham County census records.[23],[24] Despite the hardships of losing a parent in infancy and growing up in modest circumstances, he received an early education from his mother and later attended the Beulah Male Institute and the Madison Male Academy.

At the age of sixteen, Richard enlisted as a Private in Company F of the 1st Confederate Engineer Troops, CSA, on 09 May 1864 at Wentworth, Rockingham County. This specialized unit was responsible for constructing fortifications, roads, bridges, and other military infrastructure essential to the Confederate war effort. On 02 June 1864, he was sent to a military hospital in Richmond, though the nature of his illness is not specified. He was furloughed through 10 September 1864 and eventually returned to duty. On 24 May 1865, near the war's conclusion, he was surrendered as a Prisoner of War and paroled the next day at Greensboro, North Carolina.

His mother's burden during the war must have been immense—Richard was her last surviving son after losing two others, Joseph Nathaniel Cardwell and Pleasant Dalton Cardwell, in earlier Confederate service with North Carolina units. Richard's survival marked a turning point in his life and the beginning of a distinguished postwar legacy.

On 07 February 1865, shortly before the end of the war, Richard married Katherine "Kate" Howard in Rockingham County.[25] The couple had seven children: Howard Cardwell (1866–1870), William Duval Cardwell (1868–1954), Lucy Crump Cardwell (1870–1956), Elizabeth Dalton "Lizzie" Cardwell (1872–1936), Charles Patterson Cardwell (1873–1941), Katherine "Kate" Cardwell (1875–), and Julia Cardwell (1877–). In 1869, the family relocated to Hanover County, Virginia, to be closer to Kate's relatives. He is listed in the 1870, 1880, 1900, 1910, 1920, and 1930 Hanover County, Virginia census.[26,27,28,29,30,31]

While supporting his family as a farm laborer, Richard continued his education by studying law during evenings and later apprenticing under attorney Samuel C. Redd. He was admitted to the bar in 1874 and began practicing law in Richmond. His reputation grew quickly, and by 1881 he was elected to the Virginia House of Delegates, representing Hanover County. From 1887 to 1895, he served as Speaker of the House and gained further prominence as a persuasive Democratic campaign orator. In 1884, he was appointed as a presidential elector, and in 1892 he served on the Virginia State Debt Commission.

Richard was instrumental in resolving the long-standing boundary dispute between Virginia and Maryland, drafting the agreement that was ratified by both state legislatures. In 1894, he was elected to the Virginia Supreme Court of Appeals for a twelve-year term and was re-elected in 1906. He became president of the court on 12 June 1916, serving briefly in that role before resigning on 6 November of the same year.

Known for his clarity, integrity, and legal acumen, Justice Cardwell was widely respected across Virginia. His son, William D. Cardwell, followed in his father's footsteps, serving as Speaker of the House of Delegates from 1906 to 1908. Richard Henry Cardwell died at his home, *Prospect Hill*, on 19 March 1931. He was laid to rest at Woodlawn Cemetery in Ashland, Hanover County, Virginia.[32] From humble beginnings and the crucible of war, he rose to become one of the most esteemed jurists in the Common-wealth of Virginia's history. Cardwell Line I - Predicted. Photo Credits[33,34,35]

* * *

The following are incorrectly indexed in the Confederate Service Records, that have extensive service records under units of a specific state, or are of undetermined ancestry.

J. Cardwell - *8th Regiment, Confederate Cavalry (Wade's)* - likely a Caldwell. He is listed in the same unit as M.S. Caldwell. No definitive clues in the records to assist in determining a birth year or other information that might allow proper placement in the family.

James Cardwell - *Major* - *General and Staff Officers, Non-Regimental Enlisted Men, CSA* - **Prisoner of War** - records show that James served the Confederacy as a Major of the Post Commissary at Harrisburg, Kentucky. He is recorded on a List of Prisoners of war sent to Vicksburg, Mississippi, or Louisville, Kentucky, by Provost Marshal of Lexington County. The document shows he was sent on 21 October 1862. Unfortunately, there is no descriptive details with his POW record that could provide any clues. There is a strong possibility that he surname is recorded incorrectly. Having researched this family for more than three decades, the closest fit is James M. Cardwell (b. 1810) in Mercer County, Kentucky, son to John B. "Jack" Cardwell and Mary Jane (McCoun) Cardwell. He appears to have been a lifelong bachelor and given his age of 52 in 1862, fits the profile of a senior man that would be put in charge of such an operation. He lived in the Harrisburg area during that time and is the best candidate for this man. More research is needed.

John T. Cardwell - *Hospital Stewart* - his biography is under the Tennessee Confederate Veterans chapter.

Leroy (Lee Roy) Cardwell - *Company G, 1st Confederate Cavalry* - his biography is under the Tennessee Confederate Veterans chapter.

M.S. Cardwell - *8th Regiment, Confederate Cavalry (Wade's)* - appears in more complete records for that unit as M.S. Caldwell. There are no Cardwell men from that region that have the initials of M.S. and exhaustive research finally determined the surname indexing confusion.

Samuel Cardwell - *1st Battalion, Confederate Infantry (Forney's), CSA* - appears to have been Caldwell in other records. No apparent matches in known Cardwell family in the region. The unit was formed in 1862 at Port Hudson, Louisiana. No known Cardwell family is in that area.

Tennie Cardwell - *Seamstress - Clothing Bureau - Quartermaster Department, CSA* - extensive research to determine this individual has been unsuccessful. Her connection to the Cardwell family is undetermined.

Notes

Alabama

1. United States Census - Year: 1850; Census Place: , Pike, Alabama; Roll: M432_13; Page: 186; Image: 372.
2. United States Census - Year: 1860; Census Place: Precinct 6, Coffee, Alabama; Roll: M653_6; Page: 835; Image: 284.
3. Ancestry.com. *Alabama, Texas and Virginia, U.S., Confederate Pensions, 1884-1958* [database on-line]. Provo, UT, USA: Ancestry.com Operations, Inc., 2010.
4. United States Census - Year: 1900; Census Place: Victoria, Coffee, Alabama; Roll: T623 9; Page: 2A; Enumeration District: 50.
5. United States Census - Year: 1910; Census Place: Victoria, Coffee, Alabama; Roll: T624_7; Page: 3A; Enumeration District: 58; Image: 1047.
6. United States Census - Year: 1920; Census Place: Elba, Coffee, Alabama; Roll: T625_8; Page: 12B; Enumeration District: 52; Image: 627.
7. *Find a Grave*, database and images (https://www.findagrave.com/memorial/33759254/benjamin_jones-cardwell: accessed March 5, 2025), memorial page for Benjamin Jones Cardwell (6 Oct 1844–7 Nov 1927), Find a Grave Memorial ID 33759254, citing Victoria Community Cemetery, Coffee County, Alabama, USA; Maintained by Sons of Confederate Veterans (contributor 51152750).
8. Photo 1.1: Photograph used as originally posted on FindAGrave.com (Memorial ID: 33759254). Original added by Donell Mills on 12 Nov 2010. Photograph resized, cropped, enhanced, and/or repaired by the author.
9. Alabama Marriages, 1809-1920 (Selected Counties), Dodd, Jordan R., comp., Ancestry.com Operations Inc., 1999.
10. United States Census - Year: 1860; Census Place: , Shelby, Alabama; Roll: M653_23; Page: 322; Image: 323.
11. United States Census - Year: 1870; Census Place: Precinct 1, Baker, Alabama; Roll: M593_1; Page: 154; Image: 309.
12. United States Census - Year: 1900; Census Place: Spring Creek, Shelby, Alabama; Roll: T623_39; Page: 4B; Enumeration District: 121.
13. United States Census - Year: 1910; Census Place: Spring Creek, Shelby, Alabama; Roll: ; Page: ; Enumeration District: ; Image: .
14. *Find a Grave*, database and images (https://www.findagrave.com/memorial/15318373/benjiman-cardwell: accessed March 5, 2025), memorial page for Benjiman Cardwell (22 Nov 1820–16 Aug 1910), Find a Grave Memorial ID 15318373, citing Bay Springs Baptist Church Cemetery, Shelby County, Alabama, USA; Maintained by Perry Edwards (contributor 46847006).
15. Photo 1.2: Photograph used as originally posted on FindAGrave.com (Memorial ID: 15318373). Original added by Perry Edwards on 13 Aug 2006. Photograph resized, cropped, enhanced, and/or repaired by the author.
16. United States Census - Year: 1850; Census Place: Talladega, Talladega, Alabama; Roll: M432_15; Page: 433; Image: 349.

17. United States Census - Year: 1860; Census Place: , Shelby, Alabama; Roll: ; Page: ; Image:

18. Ancestry.com. *Alabama, U.S., Marriage Index, 1800-1969* [database on-line]. Provo, UT, USA: Ancestry.com Operations Inc, 2006.

19. United States Census - Year: 1870; Census Place: Six Mile, Bibb, Alabama; Roll: M593_2; Page: 280; Image: 929.

20. United States Census - Year: 1880; Census Place: Spring Creek, Shelby, Alabama; Roll: 31; Page: 192B; Enumeration District: 167

21. United States Census - Year: 1900; Census Place: Spring Creek, Shelby, Alabama; Roll: T623_39; Page: 7B; Enumeration District: 121.

22. United States Census - Year: 1920; Census Place: Spring Creek, Shelby, Alabama; Roll: T625_40; Page: 5A; Enumeration District: 111; Image: 673.

23. United States Census - Year: 1930; Census Place: Marble Valley, Coosa, Alabama; Roll: 10; Page: 6A; Enumeration District: 18; Image: 231.0.

24. *Find a Grave*, database and images (https://www.findagrave.com/memorial/155133841/henry_c-cardwell: accessed March 6, 2025), memorial page for Henry C Cardwell (8 Jan 1846–23 Mar 1933), Find a Grave Memorial ID 155133841, citing Blue Springs Cemetery, Coosa County, Alabama, USA; Maintained by Debbie Bein (contributor 48890057). NOTE: A photo request of his headstone has been made on Find-A-Grave, but as of March 2025 it is unfulfilled.

25. Mobile Advertiser and Register, Mobile, Alabama; Friday, April 18, 1862 ·Page 2.

26. Ancestry.com. *Alabama, U.S., County Marriage Records, 1805-1967* [database on-line]. Lehi, UT, USA: Ancestry.com Operations, Inc., 2016. Original data: *Marriage Records. Alabama Marriages.* County courthouses, Alabama.

27. United States Census - Year: 1870; Census Place: Mobile Ward 5, Mobile, Alabama; Roll: M593_; Page: ; Image: .

28. United States Census - Year: 1880; Census Place: Mobile, Mobile, Alabama; Roll: 25; Family History Film: 1254025; Page: 341B; Enumeration District: 139; Image: 0406.

29. United States Census - Year: 1850; Census Place: District 2, Tuscaloosa, Alabama; Roll: M432_16; Page: 262; Image: 250.

30. United States Census - The National Archives in Washington D.C.; Record Group: Records of the Bureau of the Census; Record Group Number: 29; Series Number: M653; Residence Date: 1860; Home in 1860: Western Division, Tuscaloosa, Alabama; Roll: M653_25; Page: 715; Family History L

31. United States Census - Year: 1900; Census Place: Township 6, Chickasaw Nation, Indian Territory; Roll: ; Page: ; Enumeration District: .

32. United States Census - Year: 1910; Census Place: Justice Precinct 8, Hood, Texas; Roll: T624_1563; Page: 4B; Enumeration District: 40; Image: 542.

33. *Find a Grave*, database and images (https://www.findagrave.com/memorial/19754632/henry_clay-cardwell: accessed March 6, 2025), memorial page for Henry Clay Cardwell (14 Feb 1843–25 Apr 1910), Find a Grave Memorial ID 19754632, citing Cresson Cemetery, Cresson, Johnson County, Texas, USA; Maintained by chris easley (contributor 47918260).

34. Photo 1.3: Photograph used as originally posted on FindAGrave.com (Memorial ID: 19754632). Original added by Phil Harris on 04 Jan 2009. Photograph resized, cropped, enhanced, and/or repaired by the author.

35. United States Census - Year: 1850; Census Place: Jonesboro, Jefferson, Alabama; Roll: M432_7; Page: 149A; Image: .

36. United States Census - Year: 1850; Census Place: Talladega, Talladega, Alabama; Roll: M432_15; Page: 433B; Image: 353

Notes

37. Ancestry.com. *Alabama, U.S., Select Marriage Indexes, 1816-1942* [database on-line]. Provo, UT, USA: Ancestry.com Operations, Inc, 2014. - Original data: *Alabama, Marriages, 1816-1957*. Salt Lake City, Utah: FamilySearch, 2013

38. United States Census - Year: 1860; Census Place: Southern Division, Coosa, Alabama; Roll: M653_7; Page: 141; Image: 142.

39. United States Census - Year: 1870; Census Place: Concord, Coosa, Alabama; Roll: M593_11; Page: 379; Image: 188.

40. United States Census - Year: 1880; Census Place: Beat 10, Marion, Alabama; Roll: T9_23; Family History Film: 1254023; Page: 34.1000; Enumeration District: 238; Image: 0500.

41. United States Census - Year: 1900; Census Place: Precinct 20, Jefferson, Alabama; Roll: T623_21; Page: 16B; Enumeration District: 106.

42. *Find a Grave*, database and images (https://www.findagrave.com/memorial/96638502/james_mathew-cardwell: accessed March 3, 2025), memorial page for James Mathew Cardwell (5 May 1838–29 Mar 1904), Find a Grave Memorial ID 96638502, citing Bass Cemetery, Irondale, Jefferson County, Alabama, USA; Maintained by Anonymous (contributor 46605034).

43. Photo 1.4: Photograph used as originally posted on FindAGrave.com (Memorial ID: 96638502). Original added by Cheryel and Larry on 26 Feb 2013. Photograph resized, cropped, enhanced, and/or repaired by the author.

44. United States Census - Year: 1850; Census Place: District 2, Tuscaloosa, Alabama; Roll: M432_16; Page: 262; Image: 250.

45. United States Census - The National Archives in Washington D.C.; Record Group: Records of the Bureau of the Census; Record Group Number: 29; Series Number: M653; Residence Date: 1860; Home in 1860: Western Division, Tuscaloosa, Alabama; Roll: M653_25; Page: 715; Family History L

46. https://sites.rootsweb.com/~alcwroot/artillery_files/2nd_ala_lt_art_bn.htm

47. United States Census - Year: 1870; Census Place: District 4, Panola, Mississippi; Roll: M593

48. United States Census - Year: 1880; Census Place: Eureka & Williamson, Panola, Mississippi; Roll: T9_661; Family History Film: 1254661; Page: 176.4000; Enumeration District: 157; Image: 0355.

49. *Find a Grave*, database and images (https://www.findagrave.com/memorial/8319530/james_r-cardwell: accessed March 7, 2025), memorial page for James R. Cardwell (14 Feb 1828–18 Feb 1885), Find a Grave Memorial ID 8319530, citing Long Creek Cemetery, Shuford, Panola County, Mississippi, USA; Maintained by KenR Jr/ C Waltz Cryptic Thanatology (contributor 50427027).

50. Photo 1.5: Photograph used as originally posted on FindAGrave.com (Memorial ID: 8319530). Original added by Panola County Gal on 13 Feb 2007. Photograph resized, cropped, enhanced, and/or repaired by the author.

51. United States Census - Year: 1850; Census Place: , Pike, Alabama; Roll: M432_13; Page: 186; Image: 372.

52. United States Census - Year: 1860; Census Place: Precinct 6, Coffee, Alabama; Roll: M653_6; Page: 835; Image: 284.

53. United States Census - Year: 1850; Census Place: District 22, Marshall, Alabama; Roll: M432_10; Page: 200; Image: 400.

54. United States Census - Year: 1860; Census Place: Eastern Division, Marshall, Alabama; Roll: M653_16; Page: 838; Image: 366.

55. Ancestry.com. *Alabama, U.S., County Marriage Records, 1805-1967* [database on-line].

Lehi, UT, USA: Ancestry.com Operations, Inc., 2016. Original data: *Marriage Records. Alabama Marriages.* County courthouses, Alabama.

56. https://www.nps.gov/gett/learn/historyculture/official-report-of-colonel-james-l-sheffield .htm

57. *Find a Grave*, database and images (https://www.findagrave.com/memorial/73334258/ james-cardwell: accessed March 4, 2025), memorial page for Pvt James Cardwell (unknown–2 Jul 1863), Find a Grave Memorial ID 73334258; Burial Details Unknown; Maintained by Hutch (contributor 47312109).

58. Ancestry.com. *Alabama, U.S., County Marriage Records, 1805-1967* [database on-line]. Lehi, UT, USA: Ancestry.com Operations, Inc., 2016. Original data: *Marriage Records. Alabama Marriages.* County courthouses, Alabama.

59. United States Census - Year: 1850; Census Place: District 19 and A Half, Chambers, Alabama; Roll: M432_2; Page: 415; Image: 826.

60. Ancestry.com. *Alabama, U.S., Select Marriage Indexes, 1816-1942* [database on-line]. Provo, UT, USA: Ancestry.com Operations, Inc, 2014. Original data: *Alabama, Marriages, 1816-1957.* Salt Lake City, Utah: FamilySearch, 2013.

61. United States Census - Year: 1860; Census Place: Northern Division, Chambers, Alabama; Roll: M653_4; Page: 777; Image: 500.

62. Research correspondence from the files of the author.

63. United States Census - Year: 1870; Census Place: Beat 1, Chambers, Alabama; Roll: M593_6; Page: 2; Image: 5.

64. United States Census - Year: 1850; Census Place: Talladega, Talladega, Alabama; Roll: M432_15; Page: 433B; Image: 353

65. Ancestry.com. *Alabama, U.S., Select Marriage Indexes, 1816-1942* [database on-line]. Provo, UT, USA: Ancestry.com Operations, Inc, 2014. - Original data: *Alabama, Marriages, 1816-1957.* Salt Lake City, Utah: FamilySearch, 2013

66. United States Census - Year: 1860; Census Place: Southern Division, Coosa, Alabama; Roll: M653_7; Page: 142; Image: 143.

67. United States Census - Year: 1850; Census Place: District 22, Marshall, Alabama; Roll: M432_10; Page: 200; Image: 400.

68. United States Census - Year: 1860; Census Place: Eastern Division, Marshall, Alabama; Roll: M653_16; Page: 838; Image: 366.

69. https://www.nps.gov/gett/learn/historyculture/official-report-of-colonel-james-l-sheffield .htm

70. *The Guntersville Democrat*, 8 Jun 1899, newspaper article. Guntersville, Marshall County, Alabama.

71. United States Census - Year: 1850; Census Place: Talladega, Talladega, Alabama; Roll: M432_15; Page: 433; Image: 349.

72. United States Census - Year: 1850; Census Place: Talladega, Talladega, Alabama; Roll: M432_15; Page: 433; Image: 349.

73. Alabama Marriages, 1809-1920 (Selected Counties), Dodd, Jordan R., comp., Ancestry.com Operations Inc., 1999

74. United States Census - Year: 1880; Census Place: Uniontown, Perry, Alabama; Roll: T9_28; Family History Film: 1254028; Page: 302.4000; Enumeration District: 80; Image: 0086.

75. United States Census - Year: 1900; Census Place: Montgomery Ward 1, Montgomery, Alabama; Roll: T623_33; Page: 7A; Enumeration District: 94.

76. United States Census - Year: 1850; Census Place: Pike, Alabama; Roll: M432_13; Page: 187A; Image: 378

Notes

77. United States Census - Year: 1860; Census Place: Precinct 8, Coffee, Alabama; Roll: M653_6; Page: 873; Image: 322.

78. Escambia County, Florida Clerk Records for Marriages from 1821 to 1900. http://www.escambiaclerk.com/clerk/forms/marriage/wfgs_marriage_record s_from_1821_through_1900.pdf

79. United States Census - Year: 1870; Census Place: Escambia, Florida; Roll: M593

80. United States Census - Year: 1900; Census Place: Bluff Springs, Escambia, Florida; Roll: T623 168; Page: 11B; Enumeration District: 18.

81. United States Census - Year: 1910; Census Place: Precinct 9, Escambia, Florida; Roll: T624_160; Page: 18A; Enumeration District: 11; Image: 268.

82. *Find a Grave*, database and images (https://www.findagrave.com/memorial/39065651/wade_hampton-cardwell: accessed March 5, 2025), memorial page for Wade Hampton Cardwell (6 Oct 1840–26 Apr 1917), Find a Grave Memorial ID 39065651, citing Crary Memorial Cemetery, Century, Escambia County, Florida, USA; Maintained by The Wanderer (contributor 26488191).

83. Photo 1.6: Photograph used as originally posted on FindAGrave.com (Memorial ID: 39065651). Original added by Chronicler on 21 Apr 2013. Photograph resized, cropped, enhanced, and/or repaired by the author.

84. Unites States Census - Year: 1850; Census Place: District 19 and A Half, Chambers, Alabama; Roll: M432_2; Page: 412; Image: 820.

85. United States Census - Year: 1860; Census Place: Western Division, Tallapoosa, Alabama; Roll: M653_25; Page: 242; Image: 245.

86. United States Census - Year: 1850; Census Place: District 22, Marshall, Alabama; Roll: M432_10; Page: 200; Image: 400.

87. United States Census - Year: 1860; Census Place: Eastern Division, Marshall, Alabama; Roll: M653_16; Page: 838; Image: 366.

88. Confederate Pension File, Alabama Pension No. 16154, Marshall County.

89. Ancestry.com. *Alabama, U.S., County Marriage Records, 1805-1967* [database on-line]. Lehi, UT, USA: Ancestry.com Operations, Inc., 2016. Original data: *Marriage Records. Alabama Marriages.* County courthouses, Alabama.

90. United States Census - Year: 1880; Census Place: , Marshall, Alabama; Roll: T9_24; Family History Film: 1254024; Page: 209.3000; Enumeration District: ; Image: .

91. Ancestry.com. *Alabama, U.S., County Marriage Records, 1805-1967* [database on-line]. Lehi, UT, USA: Ancestry.com Operations, Inc., 2016. Original data: *Marriage Records. Alabama Marriages.* County courthouses, Alabama.

92. *Find a Grave*, database and images (https://www.findagrave.com/memorial/31940271/william_j-cardwell: accessed March 8, 2025), memorial page for William J. Cardwell (20 Nov 1844–30 Apr 1919), Find a Grave Memorial ID 31940271, citing Nixon Chapel Cemetery, Nixon Chapel, Marshall County, Alabama, USA; Maintained by Renee Yates (contributor 46989146).

93. Photo 1.7: Photograph used as originally posted on FindAGrave.com (Memorial ID: 31940271). Original added by Renee Yates on 07 Jun 2013. Photograph resized, cropped, enhanced, and/or repaired by the author.

94. United States Census - Year: 1850; Census Place: Pike, Alabama; Roll: M432_13; Page: 187A; Image: 378

95. United States Census - Year: 1860; Census Place: Precinct 8, Coffee, Alabama; Roll: M653_6; Page: 886; Image: 335.

96. *Find a Grave*, database and images (https://www.findagrave.com/memorial/125082961/william_mckenzie-cardwell: accessed March 2, 2025), memorial page for William

McKenzie Cardwell (30 Nov 1833–31 May 1862), Find a Grave Memorial ID 125082961, citing Seven Pines National Cemetery, Henrico County, Virginia, USA; Maintained by Carole Conrad (contributor 46532185).

97. United States Census - Year: 1850; Census Place: Talladega, Talladega, Alabama; Roll: M432_15; Page: 433B; Image: 353

98. United States Census - Year: 1860; Census Place: Southern Division, Coosa, Alabama; Roll: M653_7; Page: 142; Image: 143.

99. Alabama, County Marriages, 1805-1967. Ancestry.com. 2016.

100. United States Census - Year: 1870; Census Place: Mccords, Coosa, Alabama; Roll: M593_11; Page: 391A; Family History Library Film: 545510

101. United States Census - Year: 1880; Census Place: Concord, Coosa, Alabama; Roll: T9_9; Family History Film: 1254009; Page: 159.4000; Enumeration District: 48; Image: 0324.

102. United States Census - Year: 1900; Census Place: McCords, Coosa, Alabama; Roll: T623_11; Page: 10A; Enumeration District: 25.

103. United States Census - Year: 1910; Census Place: Mccords, Coosa, Alabama; Roll: ; Page: ; Enumeration District: ; Image: .

104. United States Census - Year: 1920; Census Place: McCords, Coosa, Alabama; Roll: T625_10; Page: 1B; Enumeration District: 63; Image: 198.

105. *Find a Grave*, database and images (https://www.findagrave.com/memorial/62515533/william_morris-cardwell: accessed March 2, 2025), memorial page for William Morris Cardwell (3 Jan 1849–30 Aug 1926), Find a Grave Memorial ID 62515533, citing Providence Methodist Church Cemetery, Elmore County, Alabama, USA; Maintained by J Lowery (contributor 47089151).

106. Photo 1.8: Photograph used as originally posted on FindAGrave.com (Memorial ID: 62515533). Original added by Marshall Britton on 08 Mar 2016. Photograph resized, cropped, enhanced, and/or repaired by the author.

107. Photo 1.9: Photo 1.8: Photograph used as originally posted on FindAGrave.com (Memorial ID: 62515533). Original added by Larry Hall on 08 Jan 2013. Photograph resized, cropped, enhanced, and/or repaired by the author.

Arkansas

1. United States Census - Year: 1850; Census Place: District 10, McNairy, Tennessee; Roll: M432_888; Page: 119; Image: 240.

2. United States Census - Year: 1860; Census Place: Alabama, Columbia, Arkansas; Roll: M653_39; Page: 383; Image: 388.

3. Ancestry.com. *Arkansas, U.S., Compiled Marriages from Select Counties, 1779-1992* [database on-line]. Provo, UT, USA: Ancestry.com Operations Inc, 2004. Original data: Hunting For Bears, comp.. *Arkansas Marriages, 1779-1992*.

4. United States Census - Year: 1880; Census Place: Precinct 3, Cass, Texas; Roll: T9_1295; Family History Film: 1255295; Page: 135.3000; Enumeration District: 12; Image: .

5. United States Census - Year: 1900; Census Place: Justice Precinct 1, Hunt, Texas; Roll: T623 1647; Page: 28A; Enumeration District: 120.

6. United States Census - Year: 1910; Census Place: Justice Precinct 5, Parker, Texas; Roll: T624_1584; Page: 8A; Enumeration District: 80; Image: 457.

7. United States Census - Year: 1920; Census Place: Justice Precinct 5, Parker, Texas; Roll: T625_1838; Page: 6A; Enumeration District: 75; Image: 963.

Notes

8. *Find a Grave*, database and images (https://www.findagrave.com/memorial/65448221/aaron_day-cardwell: accessed March 8, 2025), memorial page for Rev Aaron Day Cardwell (11 Apr 1844–21 Apr 1935), Find a Grave Memorial ID 65448221, citing Willow Pond Cemetery, Mineral Wells, Palo Pinto County, Texas, USA; Maintained by May Ashby Royer (contributor 46886807).

9. NOTE: The majority of the information concerning Hiram Clark Cardwell and his descendants (Aaron Day Cardwell, William Thomas Dobson Cardwell, and Admural Franklin Cardwell) is provided from old research letters from Doris Anderson Cardwell of Edmond, Oklahoma. This includes the exact date of birth, death, and marriage, which were in an old family Bible.

10. Photo 2.1: Photograph used as originally posted on Ancestry.com. Original added by wrcardwell_1 on 17 Aug 2012. Photograph resized, cropped, enhanced, and/or repaired by the author.

11. Photo 2.2: Photograph used as originally posted on FindAGrave.com (Memorial ID: 65448221). Original added by totsie on 17 Aug 2012. Photograph resized, cropped, enhanced, and/or repaired by the author.

12. United States Census - Year: 1850; Census Place: District 10, McNairy, Tennessee; Roll: M432_888; Page: 119; Image: 240.

13. United States Census - Year: 1860; Census Place: Alabama, Columbia, Arkansas; Roll: M653_39; Page: 383; Image: 388.

14. Ancestry.com. *Arkansas, U.S., County Marriages Index, 1837-1957* [database on-line]. Provo, UT, USA: Ancestry.com Operations, Inc., 2011. Original data: "Arkansas County Marriages, 1838–1957." Index. FamilySearch, Salt Lake City, Utah, 2009, 2011. "Arkansas County Marriages, 1838–1957," database, FamilySearch; from Arkansas Courts of Common Pleas and County Clerks. Digital images of originals housed at various county courthouses in the State of Arkansas. Marriage records.

15. United States Census - Year: 1870; Census Place: Caney, Ouachita, Arkansas; Roll: M593

16. United States Census - Year: 1880; Census Place: Caney, Nevada, Arkansas; Roll: T9_52; Family History Film: 1254052; Page: 536.4000; Enumeration District: 216; Image: 0377.

17. United States Census - Year: 1900; Census Place: Justice Precinct 7, Hunt, Texas; Roll: T623 1648; Page: 4B; Enumeration District: 138.

18. United States Census - Year: 1910; Census Place: Justice Precinct 3, Motley, Texas; Roll: T624_1580; Page: 14A; Enumeration District: 185; Image: 53.

19. *Find a Grave*, database and images (https://www.findagrave.com/memorial/38817359/admurl_franklin-cardwell: accessed April 3, 2025), memorial page for Admurl Franklin Cardwell (24 Apr 1848–17 Jun 1922), Find a Grave Memorial ID 38817359, citing Tell Baptist Cemetery, Tell, Childress County, Texas, USA; Maintained by William Green (contributor 46780427).

20. Photo 2.3: Photograph used as originally posted on FindAGrave.com (Memorial ID: 38817359). Original added by William Green on 05 Aug 2024. Photograph resized, cropped, enhanced, and/or repaired by the author.

21. Photo 2.4: Photograph used as originally posted on FindAGrave.com (Memorial ID: 38817359). Original added by rhondajo on 27 Jun 2009. Photograph resized, cropped, enhanced, and/or repaired by the author.

22. United States Census - Year: 1850; Census Place: Powell, Greene, Arkansas; Roll: M432_26; Page: 197; Image: 391.

23. United States Census - Year: 1840; Census Place: , Greene, Arkansas; Roll: 17; Page: 138.

24. United States Census - Year: 1860; Census Place: Jackson, Carroll, Arkansas; Roll: M653_38; Page: 857; Image: 408.

25. United States Census - Year: 1840; Census Place: , Mcnairy, Tennessee; Roll: ; Page: .

26. United States Census - Year: 1850; Census Place: District 10, McNairy, Tennessee; Roll: M432_888; Page: 119; Image: 240.

27. Tennessee Marriage Records

28. United States Census - Year: 1860; Census Place: Alabama, Columbia, Arkansas; Roll: M653_39; Page: 383; Image: 388.

29. Note: There is no positive documentation for Hiram being the son of William and Celia Cardwell. Family tradition in this line states that Hiram had brothers named Pryor and Aaron. This is validated in the known children of William and Celia Harper Cardwell. Finding someone in the line for the Cardwell DNA Project would be very helpful.

30. United States Census - Year: 1850; Census Place: Richland, Jefferson, Arkansas; Roll: M432_27; Page: 81A; Image: .

31. Ancestry.com. *Arkansas, U.S., Compiled Marriages, 1779-1850* [database on-line]. Provo, UT, USA: Ancestry.com Operations Inc, 1997. Original data: Dodd, Jordan R, et. al.. *Early American Marriages: Arkansas to 1850*. Bountiful, UT, USA: Precision Indexing Publishers, 19xx.

32. United States Census - Year: 1860; Census Place: Bogy, Jefferson, Arkansas; Roll: ; Page: 917; Image: 423.

33. Ancestry.com. *Arkansas, U.S., Wills and Probate Records, 1818-1998* [database on-line]. Lehi, UT, USA: Ancestry.com Operations, Inc., 2015. Original data: Arkansas County, District and Probate Courts.

34. United States Census - Year: 1850; Census Place: Powell, Greene, Arkansas; Roll: M432_26; Page: 197; Image: 391.

35. Ancestry.com. *Arkansas, U.S., County Marriages Index, 1837-1957* [database on-line]. Provo, UT, USA: Ancestry.com Operations, Inc., 2011.

36. United States Census - Year: 1860; Census Place: Salem, Greene, Arkansas; Roll: M653_42; Page: 544; Image: 33.

37. Families of Confederate Soldiers from Lawrence County, Arkansas - Friday, 27 February 1863 -- Book F page 30 - https://nlmatthews.com/confeder.htm - The records are all in Book F in the Circuit Court Records maintained at the Lawrence County Courthouse in Walnut Ridge, Lawrence County, Arkansas.

38. United States Census - Year: 1850; Census Place: Prairie, Washington, Arkansas; Roll: M432_31; Page: 399; Image: 202.

39. United States Census - Year: 1860; Census Place: Prairie, Washington, Arkansas; Roll: M653_52; Page: 662; Image: 189.

40. https://uark.as.atlas-sys.com/repositories/2/archival_objects/630311

41. *Find a Grave*, database and images (https://www.findagrave.com/memorial/33636312/thomas_addison-cardwell: accessed March 9, 2025), memorial page for Thomas Addison Cardwell (1843–unknown), Find a Grave Memorial ID 33636312, citing Stearns Cemetery, Fayetteville, Washington County, Arkansas, USA; Maintained by Melinda Roberts Lambaren (contributor 21755323).

42. United States Census - Year: 1850; Census Place: Prairie, Washington, Arkansas; Roll: M432_31; Page: 400; Image: 205.

43.

44. United States Census - Year: 1870; Census Place: Prairie, Washington, Arkansas; Roll: M593

45. United States Census - Year: 1880; Census Place: Prairie, Washington, Arkansas; Roll: T9_59; Family History Film: 1254059; Page: 705.1000; Enumeration District: 276; Image: 0091.

Notes

46. United States Census - *Find a Grave*, database and images (https://www.findagrave.com/memorial/181367384/william_john-cardwell: accessed March 9, 2025), memorial page for William John Cardwell (1842–18 Nov 1882), Find a Grave Memorial ID 181367384, citing Combs Cemetery, Fayetteville, Washington County, Arkansas, USA; Maintained by J Tack (contributor 48510818).

47. Photo 2.5: Photograph used as originally posted on FindAGrave.com (Memorial ID: 181367384). Original added by J Tack on 12 Dec 2017. Photograph resized, cropped, enhanced, and/or repaired by the author.

48. United States Census - Year: 1850; Census Place: District 10, McNairy, Tennessee; Roll: M432_888; Page: 119; Image: 240.

49. United States Census - Year: 1860; Census Place: Alabama, Columbia, Arkansas; Roll: M653-39; Page: 383; Image: 388.

50. Ancestry.com. *Arkansas, U.S., Compiled Marriages from Select Counties, 1820-1949* [database on-line]. Provo, UT, USA: Ancestry.com Operations Inc, 2004. Original data: Hunting For Bears, comp.. *Arkansas Marriages, 1820-1949*.

51. *Find a Grave*, database and images (https://www.findagrave.com/memorial/55553227/william_thomas_dobson-cardwell: accessed March 8, 2025), memorial page for William Thomas Dobson Cardwell (9 Jun 1842–30 Aug 1863), Find a Grave Memorial ID 55553227, citing Confederate Cemetery, Alton, Madison County, Illinois, USA; Maintained by Cousins by the Dozens (contributor 46904925).

52. Photo 2.6: Photograph used as originally posted on FindAGrave.com (Memorial ID: 55553227). Original added by Brian D. McKinney on 13 May 2011. Photograph resized, cropped, enhanced, and/or repaired by the author.

53. Photo 2.7: Photograph used as originally posted on FindAGrave.com (Memorial ID: 55553227). Original added by Brian D. McKinney on 13 May 2011. Photograph resized, cropped, enhanced, and/or repaired by the author.

Georgia

1. United States Census - Year: 1840; Census Place: , Chambers, Alabama; Roll: 2; Page: 221.

2. Ancestry.com. *Alabama, U.S., County Marriage Records, 1805-1967* [database on-line]. Lehi, UT, USA: Ancestry.com Operations, Inc., 2016. Original data: *Marriage Records. Alabama Marriages*. County courthouses, Alabama.

3. United States Census - Year: 1860; Census Place: Georgia Militia District 717, Harris, Georgia; Roll: M653_126; Page: 575; Image: 576.

4. United States Census - Year: 1870; Census Place: , Harris, Georgia; Roll: M593_156; Page: 58; Image: 118.

5. United States Census - Year: 1880; Census Place: Lower 19th, Harris, Georgia; Roll: T9_151; Family History Film: 1254151; Page: 546.2000; Enumeration District: 61; Image: 0557.

6. United States Census - Year: 1900; Census Place: Militia District 707, Harris, Georgia; Page: 5; Enumeration District: 0032; FHL microfilm: 1240203

7. The Macon Telegraph - Macon, Georgia · Thursday, November 23, 1905 - Death of Patriarch; page 4

Kentucky

1. United States Census - Year: 1850; Census Place: District 2, Hopkins, Kentucky; Roll: M432_205; Page: 153; Image: 307.

2. United States Census - Year: 1860; Census Place: , Hopkins, Kentucky; Roll: M653_374; Page: 0; Image: 171.

3. Ancestry.com. *Kentucky, U.S., Wills and Probate Records, 1774-1989* [database on-line]. Lehi, UT, USA: Ancestry.com Operations, Inc., 2015. Original data: Kentucky County, District and Probate Courts.

4. United States Census - Year: 1850; Census Place: District 2, Hopkins, Kentucky; Roll: M432_205; Page: 164; Image: 329.

5. United States Census - Year: 1860; Census Place: , Hopkins, Kentucky; Roll: M653_374; Page: 0; Image: 370.

6. Bibliographic details for Kentucky, Civil War Service Records of Confederate Soldiers - FamilySearch Historical Records. FamilySearch Historical Records - Author: Family-Search Wiki contributors, Publisher: *FamilySearch Wiki,* Date of last revision: 12 December 2024 17:40 UTC, Permanent URL: https://www.familysearch.org/en/wiki/index.php?title=Kentucky,_Civil_War_Service_Records_of_Confederate_Soldiers_-_Fam ilySearch_Historical_Records&oldid=6024139 - Page Version ID: 6024139

7. United States Census - Year: 1870; Census Place: Nebo, Hopkins, Kentucky; Roll: M593

8. United States Census - Year: 1880; Census Place: Earlington, Hopkins, Kentucky; Roll: T9_420; Family History Film: 1254420; Page: 434.3000; Enumeration District: 198; Image: 0872.

9. United States Census - Year: 1900; Census Place: Hopkinsville, Christian, Kentucky; Roll: T623 515; Page: 1A; Enumeration District: 5.

10. United States Census - Year: 1910; Census Place: Clarksville Ward 3, Montgomery, Tennessee; Roll: T624_1513; Page: 4B; Enumeration District: 130; Image: 979.

11. United States Census - Year: 1850; Census Place: District 2, Hopkins, Kentucky; Roll: M432_205; Page: 153; Image: 307.

12. United States Census - Year: 1860; Census Place: , Hopkins, Kentucky; Roll: M653_374; Page: 0; Image: 171.

13. Ancestry.com. *Kentucky, U.S., County Marriage Records, 1783-1965* [database on-line]. Lehi, UT, USA: Ancestry.com Operations, Inc., 2016. Original data: *Marriage Records. Kentucky Marriages.* Madison County Courthouse, Richmond, Kentucky.

14. United States Census - Year: 1880; Census Place: Dixon, Webster, Kentucky; Roll: 446; Page: 57A; Enumeration District: 025

15. United States Census - Year: 1910; Census Place: Louisville Ward 7, Jefferson, Kentucky; Roll: T624_485; Page: 11B; Enumeration District: 129; Image: 1126.

16. United States Census - Year: 1920; Census Place: Louisville Ward 7, Jefferson, Kentucky; Roll: T625_580; Page: 12A; Enumeration District: 133; Image: 873.

17. *Find a Grave*, database and images (https://www.findagrave.com/memorial/80867867/george_stuart-cardwell: accessed March 11, 2025), memorial page for George Stuart Card-well (22 Sep 1845–9 Dec 1929), Find a Grave Memorial ID 80867867, citing Cave Hill Cemetery, Louisville, Jefferson County, Kentucky, USA; Maintained by Deb Redmon (contributor 47383009).

18. Photo 4.1: Photograph used as originally posted on FindAGrave.com (Memorial ID: 80867867). Original added by Rob M on 11 Jan 2017. Photograph resized, cropped, enhanced, and/or repaired by the author.

Notes

19. United States Census - Year: 1850; Census Place: District 2, Shelby, Kentucky; Roll: M432_218; Page: 376; Image: 214.

20. United States Census - Year: 1860; Census Place: District 2, Shelby, Kentucky; Roll: M653_395; Page: 0; Image: 26.

21. United States Census - Year: 1870; Census Place: St Joesph Ward 3, Buchanan, Missouri Roll: M593

22. United States Census - Year: 1880; Census Place: Wetmore, Nemaha, Kansas; Roll: T9_390; Family History Film: 1254390; Page: 120.3000; Enumeration District: 195; Image: 0683.

23. *Find a Grave*, database and images (https://www.findagrave.com/memorial/79118113/james_j-cardwell: accessed March 11, 2025), memorial page for James J. Cardwell (unknown–7 Oct 1892), Find a Grave Memorial ID 79118113, citing Grove Hill Cemetery, Shelbyville, Shelby County, Kentucky, USA; Maintained by Deb Redmon (contributor 47383009).

24. Photo 4.2: Photograph used as originally posted on FindAGrave.com (Memorial ID: 79118113). Original added by Charlie O on 29 May 2015. Photograph resized, cropped, enhanced, and/or repaired by the author.

25. United States Census - Year: 1850; Census Place: District 1, Mercer, Kentucky; Roll: M432_213; Page: 271; Image: 205.

26. United States Census - Year: 1860; Census Place: Harrodsburg, Mercer, Kentucky; Roll: ; Page: 685; Image: 141.

27. http://www.dixieweb.com/Camp1513/9th.htm

28. United States Census - Year: 1850; Census Place: District 2, Hopkins, Kentucky; Roll: M432_205; Page: 164; Image: 329.

29. Dodd, Jordan, comp. *Kentucky, U.S., Compiled Marriages, 1851-1900* [database on-line]. Provo, UT, USA: Ancestry.com Operations Inc, 2001. Original data: Dodd, Jordan, comp. *Kentucky Marriages, 1851-1900*. See extended description for original data sources listed by county.

30. United States Census - Year: 1870; Census Place: Precinct 2, Hopkins, Kentucky; Roll: M593

31. United States Census - Year: 1880; Census Place: Court House, Hopkins, Kentucky; Roll: T9_420; Family History Film: 1254420; Page: 296.4000; Enumeration District: 191; Image: 0597.

32. United States Census - Year: 1900; Census Place: Madisonville, Hopkins, Kentucky; Roll: T623 528; Page: 15B; Enumeration District: 65.

33. *Find a Grave*, database and images (https://www.findagrave.com/memorial/68390708/john_ray-cardwell: accessed March 12, 2025), memorial page for John Ray Cardwell (24 Aug 1834–23 Apr 1904), Find a Grave Memorial ID 68390708, citing Browder's Church Cemetery, Hopkins County, Kentucky, USA; Maintained by Carl Lansden (contributor 46968416).

34. Photo 4.3: Photograph used as originally posted on FindAGrave.com (Memorial ID: 68390708). Original added by Trey Thompson on 11 Jul 2012. Photograph resized, cropped, enhanced, and/or repaired by the author.

35. United States Census - Year: 1850; Census Place: District 2, Franklin, Kentucky; Roll: M432_200; Page: 57; Image: 250.

36. United States Census - Year: 1860; Census Place: District 2, Franklin, Kentucky; Roll: M653_367; Page: 0; Image: 298.

37. United States Census - Year: 1870; Census Place: Forks of Elkhorn, Franklin, Kentucky; Roll: M593_462; Page: 76; Image: 152.

38. United States Census - Year: 1880; Census Place: Benson, Franklin, Kentucky; Roll: T9_414; Family History Film: 1254414; Page: 296.2000; Enumeration District: 77; Image: 0457.

39. United States Census - Year: 1900; Census Place: Louisville Ward 12, Jefferson, Kentucky; Roll: ; Page: ; Enumeration District: .

40. United States Census - Year: 1910; Census Place: Louisville Ward 12, Jefferson, Kentucky; Roll: T624_487; Page: 4A; Enumeration District: 226; Image: 1146.

41. *Find a Grave*, database and images (https://www.findagrave.com/memorial/67737392/john_thomas-cardwell: accessed March 13, 2025), memorial page for John Thomas Cardwell (22 Feb 1845–20 Mar 1913), Find a Grave Memorial ID 67737392, citing Cedar Grove Cemetery, Cedar Grove, Bullitt County, Kentucky, USA; Maintained by Deb Redmon (contributor 47383009).

42. Photo 4.4: Photograph used as originally posted on FindAGrave.com (Memorial ID: 67737392). Original added by Patty Shreve on 13 Nov 2016. Photograph resized, cropped, enhanced, and/or repaired by the author.

43. United States Census - Year: 1850; Census Place: District 2, Shelby, Kentucky; Roll: M432_218; Page: 376; Image: 214.

44. United States Census - Year: 1860; Census Place: District 2, Shelby, Kentucky; Roll: M653_395; Page: 0; Image: 26.

45. United States Census - Year: 1870; Census Place: District 1, Shelby, Kentucky; Roll: M593

46. United States Census - Year: 1880; Census Place: Clayville, Shelby, Kentucky; Roll: T9_441; Family History Film: 1254441; Page: 195.1000; Enumeration District: 183; Image: 0699.

47. United States Census - Year: 1900; Census Place: North Shelbyville, Shelby, Kentucky; Page: 6; Enumeration District: 0077; FHL microfilm: 1240551

48. Untied States Census - Name: Thos C Cardwell Birth Date: abt 1843 Birth Place: Kentucky Residence Date: 1910 Residence Place: Jeffersontown, Jefferson, Kentucky

49. United States Census - Year: 1920; Census Place: Jeffesontown, Jefferson, Kentucky; Roll: T625_577; Page: 9A; Enumeration District: 15

50. *Find a Grave*, database and images (https://www.findagrave.com/memorial/78470857/thomas_logan-cardwell: accessed March 11, 2025), memorial page for Thomas Logan Cardwell (22 Jan 1843–30 Nov 1920), Find a Grave Memorial ID 78470857, citing Grove Hill Cemetery, Shelbyville, Shelby County, Kentucky, USA; Maintained by Deb Redmon (contributor 47383009).

51. Photo 4.5: Photograph used with permission from Rutherford B. Hayes Presidential Library and Museums. 8th Kentucky Confederate Cavalry Photograph Album - LH-410. Photograph resized, cropped, enhanced, and/or repaired by the author.

From https://www.rbhayes.org/collection-items/local-history-collections/8th-kentucky-confederate-cavalry-photograph-album/: This photograph album, containing 25 carte de visites, of which 22 are identified Confederate soldiers of the 8th Kentucky Cavalry, who were part of General John Hunt Morgan's troops. Nearly all are believed to have been captured in Ohio on April 19 and April 26, 1863. These same men were imprisoned at Camp Douglas,, Illinois.

The album is believed to have been owned by Caleb Doyle of Shelbyville, Shelby County, Kentucky, who was a private in Company C, 8th Kentucky Cavalry. Each picture is identified in the same handwriting. Most of the images are back marked D. F. Brandon, Camp Douglas, Illinois. A single loose cdv of a Confederate soldier and one of General James Longstreet and John Wilkes Booth were unidentified. Fold3.com was used to research rank, company, date and place of capture, as well as additional information on transfers, notification of signed amnesty and/or notifications of death while imprisoned.

This collection was acquired by the Hayes Presidential Library and Museums in 2016.

Rutherford B. Hayes Presidential Library & Museums - Spiegel Grove, Fremont, OH 43420

52. Photo 4.6: Photograph used as originally posted on FindAGrave.com (Memorial ID: 78470857). Original added by Charlie O on 14 Mar 2014. Photograph resized, cropped, enhanced, and/or repaired by the author.

53. United States Census - Year: 1850; Census Place: District 1, Mercer, Kentucky; Roll: M432_213; Page: 271; Image: 205.

54. United States Census - Year: 1860; Census Place: Harrodsburg, Mercer, Kentucky; Roll: ; Page: 685; Image: 141.

55. Dodd, Jordan, comp. *Kentucky, U.S., Compiled Marriages, 1851-1900* [database on-line]. Provo, UT, USA: Ancestry.com Operations Inc, 2001. Original data: Dodd, Jordan, comp. *Kentucky Marriages, 1851-1900*. See extended description for original data sources listed by county.

56. United States Census - Year: 1870; Census Place: Harrodsburg, Mercer, Kentucky; Roll: M593_488; Page: 581; Image: 342.

57. United States Census - Year: 1880; Census Place: Harrodsburg, Mercer, Kentucky; Roll: T9_434; Family History Film: 1254434; Page: 146.1000; Enumeration District: 138; Image: 0293.

58. United States Census - Year: 1900; Census Place: Harrodsburg, Mercer, Kentucky; Roll: T623 544; Page: 4B; Enumeration District: 63.

59. United States Census - Year: 1910; Census Place: Harrodsburg, Mercer, Kentucky; Roll: T624_495; Page: 13A; Enumeration District: 96; Image: 911.

60. Ancestry.com. *Kentucky, U.S., Marriage Records, 1852-1914* [database on-line]. Lehi, UT, USA: Ancestry.com Operations Inc, 2007. Original data: Kentucky. *Kentucky Birth, Marriage and Death Records – Microfilm (1852-1910)*. Microfilm rolls #994027-994058. Kentucky Department for Libraries and Archives, Frankfort, Kentucky.

61. Harrodsburg Herald, Harrodsburg, Mercer County, Kentucky - Friday, August 27, 1915.

62. *Find a Grave*, database and images (https://www.findagrave.com/memorial/80555196/thomas_mumford-cardwell: accessed March 13, 2025), memorial page for Thomas Mumford Cardwell (22 Mar 1846–26 Aug 1915), Find a Grave Memorial ID 80555196, citing Spring Hill Cemetery, Harrodsburg, Mercer County, Kentucky, USA; Maintained by Deb Redmon (contributor 47383009).

63. Photo 4.7: Photograph used as originally posted on FindAGrave.com (Memorial ID: 80555196). Original added by Family Finder on 04 Jan 2014. Photograph resized, cropped, enhanced, and/or repaired by the author.

Louisiana

1. United States Census - Year: 1850; Census Place: Charlotte, Charlotte, Virginia; Roll: M432_940; Page: 28B; Image: .

2. United States Census - The National Archives in Washington D.C.; Record Group: Records of the Bureau of the Census; Record Group Number: 29; Series Number: M653; Residence Date: 1860; Home in 1860: Ward 7, Concordia, Louisiana; Roll: M653_410; Page: 795; Family History Library F

3. Unite States Census - Year: 1850; Census Place: District 10, McNairy, Tennessee; Roll: M432_888; Page: 125A; Image: .

4. United States Census - Year: 1850; Census Place: District 10, McNairy, Tennessee; Roll: M432_888; Page: 124; Image: 250.

5. United States Census - Year: 1860; Census Place: Ward 3, Claiborne, Louisiana; Roll: M653_410; Page: 0; Image: 265.

6. United States Census - Year: 1870; Census Place: Precinct 1, Grayson, Texas; Roll: M593

7. United States Census - Year: 1880; Census Place: Precinct 4, Denton, Texas; Roll: T9_1300; Family History Film: 1255300; Page: 138.1000; Enumeration District: 106; Image: .

8. United States Census - Year: 1900; Census Place: Justice Precinct 4, Denton, Texas; Roll: T623 1627; Page: 11A; Enumeration District: 52.

9. *Find a Grave*, database and images (https://www.findagrave.com/memorial/23903873/ pryor_lewis-cardwell: accessed March 14, 2025), memorial page for Pryor Lewis Cardwell (31 Jan 1831–25 Jun 1903), Find a Grave Memorial ID 23903873, citing Elizabeth Cemetery, Roanoke, Denton County, Texas, USA; Maintained by: Find a Grave.

10. Photo 5.1: Photograph used as originally posted on FindAGrave.com (Memorial ID: 23903873). Original added by LezleeO on 10 Oct 2014. Photograph resized, cropped, enhanced, and/or repaired by the author.

Mississippi

1. Mississippi, U.S., Compiled Marriages, 1826-1900. Dodd, Jordan, Liahona Research, comp., Ancestry.com

2. United States Census - Year: 1860; Census Place: , Lafayette, Mississippi; Roll: M653_585; Page: 0; Image: 212.

3. United States Census - Year: 1870; Census Place: Oxford, Lafayette, Mississippi; Roll: M593

4. United States Census - Year: 1850; Census Place: District 2, Tuscaloosa, Alabama; Roll: M432_16; Page: 262; Image: 250.

5. Ancestry.com. *Alabama, U.S., Marriage Index, 1800-1969* [database on-line]. Provo, UT, USA: Ancestry.com Operations Inc, 2006. Original data: Alabama Center for Health Statistics. *Alabama Marriage Index, 1936-1969.* Alabama Center for Health Statistics, Montgomery, Alabama.

6. United States Census - Year: 1860; Census Place: , Panola, Mississippi; Roll: M653_589; Page: 0; Image: 218.

7. United States Census - Year: 1870; Census Place: Township 23 Range 9, Calhoun, Mississippi; Roll: M593

8. United States Census - Year: 1880; Census Place: Beat 5, Calhoun, Mississippi; Roll: T9_642; Family History Film: 1254642; Page: 646.2000; Enumeration District: 17; Image: 0454.

9. United States Census - Year: 1900; Census Place: Beat 4, Calhoun, Mississippi; Roll: ; Page: ; Enumeration District: .

10. *Find a Grave*, database and images (https://www.findagrave.com/memorial/109970166/ john_foster-cardwell: accessed March 15, 2025), memorial page for John Foster Cardwell (21 Feb 1829–2 Oct 1900), Find a Grave Memorial ID 109970166, citing Benela Cemetery, Derma, Calhoun County, Mississippi, USA; Maintained by GMG (contributor 47391530).

11. Photo 6.1: Photograph used as originally posted on FindAGrave.com (Memorial ID: 109970166). Original added by mary dossmary on 04 May 2013. Photograph resized, cropped, enhanced, and/or repaired by the author.

Missouri

1. United States Census - Year: 1850; Census Place: Piney Fork, Lawrence, Arkansas; Roll: M432_27; Page: 192; Image: 384.
2. United States Census - Year: 1870; Census Place: Carrollton, Carroll, Arkansas; Roll: M593
3. Ancestry.com. *Arkansas, U.S., Compiled Marriages, 1851-1900* [database on-line]. Provo, UT, USA: Ancestry.com Operations Inc, 2001. Original data: Dodd, Jordan, Liahona Research, comp.. *Arkansas Marriages, 1851-1900.*
4. United States Census - Year: 1880; Census Place: Carrollton, Boone, Arkansas; Roll: T9_39; Family History Film: 1254039; Page: 494.3000; Enumeration District: 16; Image: 0064.
5. United States Census - Year: 1900; Census Place: East Pomeroy, Garfield, Washington; Roll: 1743; Page: 2B; Enumeration District: 0020; FHL microfilm: 1241743
6. United States Census - Year: 1910; Census Place: East Pomeroy, Garfield, Washington; Roll: T624_1654; Page: 5A; Enumeration District: 68; Image: 1177.
7. United States Census - Year: 1920; Census Place: Pomeroy, Garfield, Washington; Roll: T625_1920; Page: 7B; Enumeration District: 51; Image: 546.
8. *Find a Grave*, database and images (https://www.findagrave.com/memorial/5334486/jasper_newton-cardwell: accessed April 20, 2025), memorial page for Jasper Newton Cardwell (7 Aug 1847–Sep 1929), Find a Grave Memorial ID 5334486, citing Mount Pleasant Cemetery, Seattle, King County, Washington, USA; Maintained by Carolyn Farnum (contributor 10411580).
9. Photo 7.1: Photograph used as originally posted on FindAGrave.com (Memorial ID: 5334486). Original added by John Speer on 22 Aug 2012. Photograph resized, cropped, enhanced, and/or repaired by the author.

North Carolina

1. United States Census - Year: 1850; Census Place: Subdivision 33, Gilmer, Georgia; Roll: M432_70; Page: 358; Image: 242.
2. Ancestry.com. *North Carolina, U.S., Index to Marriage Bonds, 1741-1868* [database on-line]. Provo, UT, USA: Ancestry.com Operations Inc, 2000. Original data: State of North Carolina. *An Index to Marriage Bonds Filed in the North Carolina State Archives.* Raleigh, NC, USA: North Carolina Division of Archives and History, 1977.
3. United States Census - Year: 1860; Census Place: Upper Division, Wilkes, North Carolina; Roll: M653_918; Page: 139; Image: 279.
4. United States Census - Year: 1870; Census Place: Jobs Cabin, Wilkes, North Carolina; Roll: M593
5. United States Census - Year: 1880; Census Place: Lewis Fork, Wilkes, North Carolina; Roll: T9_987; Family History Film: 1254987; Page: 93.2000; Enumeration District: 210; Image: 0191.
6. United States Census - Year: 1900; Census Place: Lewis Fork, Wilkes, North Carolina; Roll: T623 1224; Page: 3A; Enumeration District: 149.

7. *Find a Grave*, database and images (https://www.findagrave.com/memorial/123748578/daniel_franklin-cardwell: accessed April 14, 2025), memorial page for Daniel Franklin "Frank" Cardwell (7 Oct 1819–unknown), Find a Grave Memorial ID 123748578, citing Mount Pleasant Baptist Church Cemetery, Wilkesboro, Wilkes County, North Carolina, USA; Burial Details Unknown; Maintained by Barbara Spears Pipek (contributor 46800452).

8. United States Census - Year: 1850; Census Place: Western District, Rockingham, North Carolina; Roll: M432_643; Page: 88; Image: 178.

9. Ancestry.com. *North Carolina, U.S., Marriage Index, 1741-2004* [database on-line]. Provo, UT, USA: Ancestry.com Operations Inc, 2007. Original data: Dodd, Jordan, Liahona Research, comp. (P.O. Box 740, Orem, Utah 84059) from county marriage records on microfilm located at the Family History Library in Salt Lake City, Utah, in published books cataloged by the Library of Congress, or county records in possession of the individual county clerks or courthouses. North Carolina State Archives. *North Carolina County Marriage Indexes.* North Carolina State Archives, Raleigh, North Carolina. North Carolina State Center for Health Statistics. *North Carolina Marriage Index, 1962-2004.* North Carolina State Center for Health Statistics, Raleigh, North Carolina.

10. United States Census - Year: 1870; Census Place: Mayo, Rockingham, North Carolina; Roll: M593

11. United States Census - Year: 1880; Census Place: Madison, Rockingham, North Carolina; Roll: T9_980; Family History Film: 1254980; Page: 59.4000; Enumeration District: 229; Image: 0121.

12. *Find a Grave*, database and images (https://www.findagrave.com/memorial/67017024/hiram_henry-cardwell: accessed March 16, 2025), memorial page for PVT Hiram Henry Cardwell (1827–6 May 1900), Find a Grave Memorial ID 67017024, citing Hartman Cemetery, Hartman, Stokes County, North Carolina, USA; Maintained by isabel (contributor 46810993).

13. Photo 8.1: Photograph used as originally posted on FindAGrave.com (Memorial ID: 67017024). Original added by bncheek on 07 Oct 2011. Photograph resized, cropped, enhanced, and/or repaired by the author.

14. United States Census - The National Archives in Washington, DC; Record Group: Records of the Bureau of the Census; Record Group Number: 29; Series Number: M432; Residence Date: 1850; Home in 1850: Wilkes, North Carolina; Roll: 649; Page: 295a - NOTE: The family is incorrectly listed under the surname of Carter, but the given names all match with the 1860 census records.

15. United States Census - Year: 1860; Census Place: Upper Division, Wilkes, North Carolina; Roll: M653_918; Page: 113; Image: 228.

16. United States Census - Year: 1850; Census Place: , Wilkes, North Carolina; Roll: M432_649; Page: 374; Image: 251.

17. United States Census - Year: 1850; Census Place: Western District, Rockingham, North Carolina; Roll: M432_643; Page: 71; Image: 144.

18. United States Census - Year: 1860; Census Place: Northern Division, Rockingham, North Carolina; Roll: M653_912; Page: 93; Image: 186.

19. Ancestry.com. *North Carolina, U.S., Marriage Index, 1741-2004* [database on-line]. Provo, UT, USA: Ancestry.com Operations Inc, 2007. Original data: Dodd, Jordan, Liahona Research, comp. (P.O. Box 740, Orem, Utah 84059) from county marriage records on microfilm located at the Family History Library in Salt Lake City, Utah, in published books cataloged by the Library of Congress, or county records in possession of the individual county clerks or courthouses. North Carolina State Archives. *North Carolina*

Notes

County Marriage Indexes. North Carolina State Archives, Raleigh, North Carolina. North Carolina State Center for Health Statistics. *North Carolina Marriage Index, 1962-2004.* North Carolina State Center for Health Statistics, Raleigh, North Carolina.

20. *Find a Grave*, database and images (https://www.findagrave.com/memorial/39643849/joel_richard-cardwell: accessed March 17, 2025), memorial page for 2LT Joel Richard Cardwell (1843–1867), Find a Grave Memorial ID 39643849, citing Madison Presbyterian Church Cemetery, Madison, Rockingham County, North Carolina, USA; Maintained by Donna P. (contributor 47124677).

21. Photo 8.2: Photograph used as originally posted on FindAGrave.com (Memorial ID: 39643849). Original added by Sharon Sloan on 10 May 2013. Photograph resized, cropped, enhanced, and/or repaired by the author.

22. United States Census - Year: 1850; Census Place: Subdivision 33, Gilmer, Georgia; Roll: M432_70; Page: 358; Image: 242.

23. United States Census - Year: 1860; Census Place: Upper Division, Wilkes, North Carolina; Roll: M653_918; Page: 139; Image: 279.

24. Ancestry.com. *North Carolina, U.S., Index to Marriage Bonds, 1741-1868* [database online]. Provo, UT, USA: Ancestry.com Operations Inc, 2000. Original data: State of North Carolina. *An Index to Marriage Bonds Filed in the North Carolina State Archives.* Raleigh, NC, USA: North Carolina Division of Archives and History, 1977.

25. United States Census - Year: 1870; Census Place: Lewis Fork, Wilkes, North Carolina; Roll: M593

26. United States Census - Year: 1880; Census Place: Lewis Fork, Wilkes, North Carolina; Roll: T9_987; Family History Film: 1254987; Page: 90.3000; Enumeration District: 210; Image: 0184.

27. United States Census - Year: 1850; Census Place: Western District, Rockingham, North Carolina; Roll: M432_643; Page: 105; Image: 212.

28. United States Census - Year: 1860; Census Place: Northern Division, Rockingham, North Carolina; Roll: M653_912; Page: 93; Image: 185.

29. *Find a Grave*, database and images (https://www.findagrave.com/memorial/39645005/joseph_nathaniel-cardwell: accessed March 16, 2025), memorial page for Pvt Joseph Nathaniel Cardwell (1841–1862), Find a Grave Memorial ID 39645005, citing Madison Presbyterian Church Cemetery, Madison, Rockingham County, North Carolina, USA; Maintained by George Seitz (contributor 40539541).

30. Photo 8.3: Photograph used as originally posted on FindAGrave.com (Memorial ID: 39645005). Original added by George Seitz on 19 Jul 2009. Photograph resized, cropped, enhanced, and/or repaired by the author.

31. Ancestry.com. *North Carolina, U.S., Index to Marriage Bonds, 1741-1868* [database online]. Provo, UT, USA: Ancestry.com Operations Inc, 2000. Original data: State of North Carolina. *An Index to Marriage Bonds Filed in the North Carolina State Archives.* Raleigh, NC, USA: North Carolina Division of Archives and History, 1977.

32. United States Census - The National Archives in Washington, DC; Record Group: Records of the Bureau of the Census; Record Group Number: 29; Series Number: M432; Residence Date: 1850; Home in 1850: Wilkes, North Carolina; Roll: 649; Page: 295a

33. United States Census - Year: 1860; Census Place: Upper Division, Wilkes, North Carolina; Roll: M653_918; Page: 113; Image: 228.

34. United States Census - Year: 1870; Census Place: Lewis Fork, Wilkes, North Carolina; Roll: M593

35. United States Census - Year: 1880; Census Place: Lewis Fork, Wilkes, North Carolina;

Roll: T9_987; Family History Film: 1254987; Page: 95.2000; Enumeration District: 210; Image: 0195.

36. *Find a Grave*, database and images (https://www.findagrave.com/memorial/43894771/ nathan_parker-cardwell: accessed March 18, 2025), memorial page for Nathan Parker Cardwell (6 Feb 1811–1 Feb 1892), Find a Grave Memorial ID 43894771, citing Mount Pleasant Baptist Church Cemetery, Wilkesboro, Wilkes County, North Carolina, USA; Maintained by Barbara Spears Pipek (contributor 46800452).

37. Photo 8.4: Photograph used as originally posted on FindAGrave.com (Memorial ID: 43894771). Original added by C. Fairchild on 03 Nov 2009. Photograph resized, cropped, enhanced, and/or repaired by the author.

38. Ancestry.com. *North Carolina, U.S., Marriage Records, 1741-2011* [database on-line]. Provo, UT, USA: Ancestry.com Operations, Inc., 2015. Original data: North Carolina County Registers of Deeds. Microfilm. Record Group 048. North Carolina State Archives, Raleigh, NC.

39. United States Census - Year: 1850; Census Place: Western District, Rockingham, North Carolina; Roll: M432_643; Page: 90; Image: 182.

40. United States Census - Year: 1860; Census Place: Northern Division, Rockingham, North Carolina; Roll: M653_912; Page: 98; Image: 196.

41. *Find a Grave*, database and images (https://www.findagrave.com/memorial/58280819/ parker-cardwell: accessed March 16, 2025), memorial page for Parker Cardwell (1825–12 Jul 1864), Find a Grave Memorial ID 58280819, citing Old City Cemetery, Lynchburg, Lynchburg City, Virginia, USA; Maintained by Mander (contributor 47110820).

42. Photo 8.5: Photograph used as originally posted on FindAGrave.com (Memorial ID: 58280819). Original added by Darrell Landrum on 26 Apr 2015. Photograph resized, cropped, enhanced, and/or repaired by the author.

43. United States Census - Year: 1850; Census Place: Western District, Rockingham, North Carolina; Roll: M432_643; Page: 105; Image: 212.

44. United States Census - Year: 1860; Census Place: Northern Division, Rockingham, North Carolina; Roll: M653_912; Page: 93; Image: 185.

45. https://pmc.ncbi.nlm.nih.gov/articles/PMC5914396/

46. *Find a Grave*, database and images (https://www.findagrave.com/memorial/39651990/ pleasant_d-cardwell: accessed March 16, 2025), memorial page for Sgt Pleasant D. Cardwell (1843–1 Jun 1864), Find a Grave Memorial ID 39651990, citing Madison Presbyterian Church Cemetery, Madison, Rockingham County, North Carolina, USA; Maintained by George Seitz (contributor 40539541).

47. Photo 8.6: Photograph used as originally posted on FindAGrave.com (Memorial ID: 39651990). Original added by Sharon Shown on 10 May 2013. Photograph resized, cropped, enhanced, and/or repaired by the author.

48. United States Census - Year: 1850; Census Place: Snow Creek, Stokes, North Carolina; Roll: M432_645; Page: 137; Image: 276.

49. Ancestry.com. *North Carolina, U.S., Marriage Records, 1741-2011* [database on-line]. Provo, UT, USA: Ancestry.com Operations, Inc., 2015. Original data: North Carolina County Registers of Deeds. Microfilm. Record Group 048. North Carolina State Archives, Raleigh, NC.

50. United States Census - Year: 1860; Census Place: Northern Division, Rockingham, North Carolina; Roll: M653_912; Page: 98; Image: 195.

51. *Find a Grave*, database and images (https://www.findagrave.com/memorial/144571693/ thomas-cardwell: accessed March 16, 2025), memorial page for Pvt Thomas Cardwell (1832–Sep 1863), Find a Grave Memorial ID 144571693, citing Vernon Cemetery,

Notes

Ayersville, Rockingham County, North Carolina, USA; Maintained by RIcky Clark (contributor 47828749).

52. Photo 8.7: Photograph used as originally posted on FindAGrave.com (Memorial ID: 144571693). Original added by Rick Calvert on 28 Jan 2012. Photograph resized, cropped, enhanced, and/or repaired by the author.

53. Photo 8.8: Photograph used as originally posted on FindAGrave.com (Memorial ID: 144571693). Original added by Ricky Clark on 04 Apr 2015. Photograph resized, cropped, enhanced, and/or repaired by the author.

54. United States Census - Year: 1840; Census Place: Rockingham, North Carolina; Roll: 369; Page: 171; Image: 348; Family History Library Film: 0018097

55. United States Census - Year: 1850; Census Place: Snow Creek, Stokes, North Carolina; Roll: M432_645; Page: 137; Image: 276.

56. United States Census - Year: 1860; Census Place: District 2, Polk, Tennessee; Roll: M653_1268; Page: 428; Image: 279.

57. Ancestry.com. *North Carolina, U.S., Marriage Records, 1741-2011* [database on-line]. Provo, UT, USA: Ancestry.com Operations, Inc., 2015.
    Original data: North Carolina County Registers of Deeds. Microfilm. Record Group 048. North Carolina State Archives, Raleigh, NC.

58. United States Census - Year: 1870; Census Place: Mayo, Rockingham, North Carolina; Roll: M593

59. United States Census - Year: 1880; Census Place: Madison, Rockingham, North Carolina; Roll: T9_980; Family History Film: 1254980; Page: 64.1000; Enumeration District: 229; Image: 0130.

60. United States Census - Year: 1900; Census Place: Madison, Rockingham, North Carolina; Roll: T623 1215; Page: 19A; Enumeration District: 74.

61. *Find a Grave*, database and images (https://www.findagrave.com/memorial/54855880/walker_c-cardwell: accessed February 24, 2025), memorial page for Walker C. "Dock" Cardwell (Mar 1833–14 Feb 1905), Find a Grave Memorial ID 54855880, citing Cardwell Family Cemetery, Ayersville, Rockingham County, North Carolina, USA; Maintained by Barbara Spears Pipek (contributor 46800452).

62. Photo 8.9: Photograph used as originally posted on FindAGrave.com (Memorial ID: 54855880). Original added by Jan Bellard on 17 Mar 2011. Photograph resized, cropped, enhanced, and/or repaired by the author.

63. United States Census - Year: 1850; Census Place: Western District, Rockingham, North Carolina; Roll: M432_643; Page: 71; Image: 144.

64. United States Census - Year: 1860; Census Place: Northern Division, Rockingham, North Carolina; Roll: M653_912; Page: 93; Image: 186.

65. United States Census - Year: 1870; Census Place: Madison Mayo, Rockingham, North Carolina; Roll: M593_1157; Page: 308A; Family History Library Film: 552656

66. United States Census - Year: 1850; Census Place: Snow Creek, Stokes, North Carolina; Roll: M432_645; Page: 137; Image: 276.

67. United States Census - Ancestry.com. *North Carolina, U.S., Marriage Records, 1741-2011* [database on-line]. Provo, UT, USA: Ancestry.com Operations, Inc., 2015. Original data: North Carolina County Registers of Deeds. Microfilm. Record Group 048. North Carolina State Archives, Raleigh, NC.

68. United States Census - Year: 1860; Census Place: , Stokes, North Carolina; Roll: M653_914; Page: 153; Image: 306.

69. United States Census - Year: 1870; Census Place: Snow Creek, Stokes, North Carolina; Roll: M593

70. United States Census - Year: 1880; Census Place: Peters Creek, Stokes, North Carolina; Roll: T9_982; Family History Film: 1254982; Page: 372.4000; Enumeration District: 247; Image: 0421.

71. *Find a Grave*, database and images (https://www.findagrave.com/memorial/47419212/wyatt-cardwell: accessed March 16, 2025), memorial page for Pvt Wyatt Cardwell (1824–1894), Find a Grave Memorial ID 47419212, citing Wyatt Cardwell Cemetery, Sandy Ridge, Stokes County, North Carolina, USA; Maintained by isabel (contributor 46810993).

72. Photo 8.10: Photograph used as originally posted on FindAGrave.com (Memorial ID: 54855880). Original added by Jan Bellard on 17 Mar 2011. Photograph resized, cropped, enhanced, and/or repaired by the author.

Tennessee

1. United States Census - Year: 1850; Census Place: Campbellsville, Giles, Tennessee; Roll: M432_879; Page: 356; Image: 98.

2. United States Census - Year: 1860; Census Place: Northern Subdivision, Giles, Tennessee; Roll: M653_1251; Page: 57; Image: 117.

3. *Find a Grave*, database and images (https://www.findagrave.com/memorial/7093666/a_e-cardwell: accessed March 19, 2025), memorial page for Sgt A. E. Cardwell (unknown–4 Sep 1862), Find a Grave Memorial ID 7093666, citing Oak Woods Cemetery, Chicago, Cook County, Illinois, USA; Maintained by Cousins by the Dozens (contributor 46904925).

4. Photo 9.1: Photograph used as originally posted on FindAGrave.com (Memorial ID: 7093666). Original added by HallowedGround on 11 Sep 2012. Photograph resized, cropped, enhanced, and/or repaired by the author.

5. Photo 9.2: Photograph used as originally posted on FindAGrave.com (Memorial ID: 7093666). Original added by HallowedGround on 11 Sep 2012. Photograph resized, cropped, enhanced, and/or repaired by the author.

6. United States Census - Year: 1830; Census Place: , Warren, Tennessee; Roll: 181; Page: 371.

7. United States Census - Year: 1840; Census Place: , Warren, Tennessee; Roll: 537; Page: 351.

8. https://gw.geneanet.org/rustyc772?n=cardwell&oc=&p=henry+jefferson

9. United States Census - Year: 1850; Census Place: District 15, Warren, Tennessee; Roll: M432_898; Page: 17; Image: 35.

10. United States Census - Year: 1860; Census Place: , Warren, Tennessee; Roll: M653_1274; Page: 458; Image: 104.

11. United States Census - Year: 1870; Census Place: District 2, Warren, Tennessee; Roll: M593

12. United States Census - Year: 1880; Census Place: District 2, Warren, Tennessee; Roll: T9_1283; Family History Film: 1255283; Page: 325.4000; Enumeration District: 131; Image: .

13. *Find a Grave*, database and images (https://www.findagrave.com/memorial/85642545/henry_jefferson-cardwell: accessed March 21, 2025), memorial page for MAJ Henry Jefferson Cardwell (1823–13 Jul 1895), Find a Grave Memorial ID 85642545, citing New Union Cemetery, Rock Island, Warren County, Tennessee, USA; Maintained by Barbara (contributor 47867334).

Notes

14. Photo 9.3: Photograph used as originally posted on FindAGrave.com (Memorial ID: 85642545). Original added by Barbara on 12 Nov 2012. Photograph resized, cropped, enhanced, and/or repaired by the author.

15. United States Census - Year: 1850; Census Place: North of Cumberland and East of Caney Fork Rivers, Smith, Tennessee; Roll: M432_896; Page: 214; Image: 12.

16. Tennessee, U.S., Compiled Marriages, 1851-1900 - Dodd, Jordan R comp.. Tennessee, Marriages, 1851-1900. Ancestry.com

17. United States Census - Year: 1860; Census Place: District 1, Smith, Tennessee; Roll: M653_1272; Page: 271; Image: 15.

18. United States Census - Year: 1870; Census Place: District 1, Smith, Tennessee; Roll: M593

19. United States Census - Year: 1880; Census Place: District 2, Smith, Tennessee; Roll: T9_1280; Family History Film: 1255280; Page: 12.3000; Enumeration District: 114; Image: .

20. United States Census - Year: 1900; Census Place: Civil District 20, Smith, Tennessee; Roll: ; Page: ; Enumeration District: .

21. Photo 9.4: Photograph used as originally posted on FindAGrave.com (Memorial ID: 33273008). Original added by utkamb on 25 Jan 2009. Photograph resized, cropped, enhanced, and/or repaired by the author.

22. United States Census - Year: 1850; Census Place: District 15, Warren, Tennessee; Roll: M432_898; Page: 18; Image: 37.

23. United States Census - Year: 1860; Census Place: , Warren, Tennessee; Roll: M653_1274; Page: 458; Image: 105.

24. Ancestry.com. *Tennessee, U.S., Compiled Marriages, 1851-1900* [database on-line]. Provo, UT, USA: Ancestry.com Operations Inc, 2000. Original data: Dodd, Jordan R comp.. *Tennessee, Marriages, 1851-1900*. See extended description for original data sources listed by county.

25. Ancestry.com. *Tennessee, U.S., Marriage Records, 1780-2002* [database on-line]. Lehi, UT, USA: Ancestry.com Operations Inc, 2008. Original data: *Tennessee State Marriages, 1780-2002*. Nashville, TN, USA: Tennessee State Library and Archives. Microfilm.

26. United States Census - Year: 1870; Census Place: District 2, Warren, Tennessee; Roll: M593_; Page: ; Image:

27. United States Census - Year: 1880; Census Place: District 2, Warren, Tennessee; Roll: T9_1283; Family History Film: 1255283; Page: 326.2000; Enumeration District: 131; Image: .

28. United States Census - Year: 1900; Census Place: Civil District 1, Warren, Tennessee; Roll: T623 1603; Page: 14B; Enumeration District: 136.

29. United States Census - Year: 1910; Census Place: Civil District 1, Warren, Tennessee; Roll: T624_1524; Page: 12B; Enumeration District: 173; Image: 96.

30. United States Census - Year: 1920; Census Place: Civil District 1, Warren, Tennessee; Roll: T625_1769; Page: 10B; Enumeration District: 123; Image: 594.

31. *Find a Grave*, database and images (https://www.findagrave.com/memorial/9338107/james-cardwell: accessed April 10, 2025), memorial page for James Cardwell (9 May 1845–28 Mar 1920), Find a Grave Memorial ID 9338107, citing Shellsford Cemetery, McMinnville, Warren County, Tennessee, USA; Maintained by Michael Neal (contributor 50532883).

32. Photo 9.5: Photograph used as originally posted on Ancestry.com. wrcardwell_1 originally shared this on 16 Nov 2007. Photograph resized, cropped, enhanced, and/or repaired by the author.

33. Photo 9.6: Photograph used as originally posted on FindAGrave.com (Memorial ID: 9338107). Original added by James on 19 Aug 2004. Photograph resized, cropped, enhanced, and/or repaired by the author.

34. United States Census - Year: 1850; Census Place: Western District, Rockingham, North Carolina; Roll: M432_643; Page: 108A; Image: 222

35. United States Census - Year: 1860; Census Place: District 3, Union, Tennessee; Roll: M653_1276; Page: 438; Image: 196.

36. Ancestry.com. *Tennessee, U.S., Marriage Records, 1780-2002* [database on-line]. Lehi, UT, USA: Ancestry.com Operations Inc, 2008. Original data: *Tennessee State Marriages, 1780-2002.* Nashville, TN, USA: Tennessee State Library and Archives. Microfilm.

37. United States Census - Year: 1870; Census Place: District 15, Grainger, Tennessee; Roll: M593_1530; Page: 161A; Image: 326; Family History Library Film: 553029

38. United States Census - Year: 1880; Census Place: District 11, Grainger, Tennessee; Roll: T9_1257; Family History Film: 1255257; Page: 514.3000; Enumeration District: 102; Image: .

39. United States Census - Year: 1900; Census Place: Civil District 11, Grainger, Tennessee; Roll: T623 1572; Page: 5A; Enumeration District: 26.

40. *Find a Grave*, database and images (https://www.findagrave.com/memorial/5285981/james_r-cardwell: accessed March 19, 2025), memorial page for PVT James R. Cardwell (23 Sep 1837–29 Oct 1911), Find a Grave Memorial ID 5285981, citing Cardwell Cemetery, Grainger County, Tennessee, USA; Maintained by b.r.green (contributor 46903236).

41. Photo 9.7: Photograph used as originally posted on FindAGrave.com (Memorial ID: 5285981). Original added by Rick Miller on 14 Feb 2017. Photograph resized, cropped, enhanced, and/or repaired by the author.

42. United States Census - Year: 1850; Census Place: South Division, Smith, Tennessee; Roll: M432_896; Page: 374; Image: 331.

43. United States Census - Year: 1860; Census Place: District 7, Obion, Tennessee; Roll: M653_1267; Page: 86; Image: 172.

44. United States Census - Year: 1870; Census Place: Nashville Ward 2, Davidson, Tennessee; Roll: M593

45. United States Census - The National Archives in Washington, DC; Record Group: Records of the Bureau of the Census; Record Group Number: 29; Series Number: M432; Residence Date: 1850; Home in 1850: District 19, Sumner, Tennessee; Roll: 897; Page: 226a

46. United States Census - Year: 1860; Census Place: , Simpson, Kentucky; Roll: M653_395; Page: 0; Image: 316.

47. United States Census - Year: 1870; Census Place: Subdistrict 150, Simpson, Kentucky; Roll: M593

48. United States Census - Year: 1880; Census Place: South Carrollton, Muhlenberg, Kentucky; Roll: T9_435; Family History Film: 1254435; Page: 9.1000; Enumeration District: 132; Image: 0224.

49. United States Census - Year: 1850; Census Place: North of Cumberland and East of Caney Fork Rivers, Smith, Tennessee; Roll: M432_896; Page: 253; Image: 90.

50. United States Census - Year: 1860; Census Place: District 2, Smith, Tennessee; Roll: M653_1272; Page: 280; Image: 32.

51. Ancestry.com. *Tennessee, U.S., Marriage Records, 1780-2002* [database on-line]. Lehi, UT, USA: Ancestry.com Operations Inc, 2008. Original data: *Tennessee State Marriages, 1780-2002.* Nashville, TN, USA: Tennessee State Library and Archives. Microfilm.

Notes

52. United States Census - Year: 1870; Census Place: District 2, Smith, Tennessee; Roll: M593

53. United States Census - Year: 1880; Census Place: District 2, Smith, Tennessee; Roll: T9_1280; Family History Film: 1255280; Page: 20.3000; Enumeration District: 114; Image: .

54. United States Census - Year: 1900; Census Place: Civil District 2, Smith, Tennessee; Roll: ; Page: ; Enumeration District: .

55. United States Census - Year: 1910; Census Place: Civil District 2, Smith, Tennessee; Roll: T624_1521; Page: 8A; Enumeration District: 114; Image: 1147.

56. United States Census - Year: 1920; Census Place: Civil District 2, Smith, Tennessee; Roll: T625_1766; Page: 5A; Enumeration District: 105; Image: 687.

57. *Find a Grave*, database and images (https://www.findagrave.com/memorial/63317229/john_bransford-cardwell: accessed April 10, 2025), memorial page for John Bransford Cardwell (24 Aug 1839–23 Jan 1924), Find a Grave Memorial ID 63317229, citing Cardwell Cemetery, Smith County, Tennessee, USA; Maintained by Fay C. Leonard (contributor 47190206).

58. Photo 9.8: Photograph used as originally posted on FindAGrave.com (Memorial ID: 63317229). Original added by JWaggoner on 13 Sep 2012. Photograph resized, cropped, enhanced, and/or repaired by the author.

59. Unites States Census - Year: 1850; Census Place: District 14, Shelby, Tennessee; Roll: M432_895; Page: 95; Image: 395.

60. Unites States Census - Year: 1860; Census Place: Dresden, Weakley, Tennessee; Roll: M653_1278; Page: 391; Image: 161.

61. https://en.wikipedia.org/wiki/First_Battle_of_Bull_Run

62. United States Census - Year: 1850; Census Place: Campbellsville, Giles, Tennessee; Roll: M432_879; Page: 356; Image: 98.

63. United States Census - Year: 1860; Census Place: Northern Subdivision, Giles, Tennessee; Roll: M653_1251; Page: 57; Image: 117.

64. Ancestry.com. *U.S., Appointments of U. S. Postmasters, 1832-1971* [database on-line]. Lehi, UT, USA: Ancestry.com Operations, Inc., 2010. This collection was indexed by Ancestry World Archives Project contributors. Original data: *Record of Appointment of Postmasters, 1832-1971*; Microfilm publication M841, 145 rolls; NAID: 596306 and 17027522; Records of the Post Office Department, 1773 - 1971, Record Group 28; The National Archives in Washington, D.C.

65. United States Census - Year: 1850; Census Place: District 9, Blount, Tennessee; Roll: M432_871; Page: 72B; Image: .

66. United States Census - The National Archives in Washington D.C.; Record Group: Records of the Bureau of the Census; Record Group Number: 29; Series Number: M653; Residence Date: 1860; Home in 1860: District 9, Blount, Tennessee; Roll: M653_1241; Page: 75; Family History Library

67. United States Census - Year: 1860; Census Place: District 1, Knox, Tennessee; Roll: M653_1259; Page: 102; Image: 207.

68. United States Census - Year: 1850; Census Place: District 1, Calloway, Kentucky; Roll: M432_194; Page: 473B; Image: .

69. United States Census - Year: 1860; Census Place: District 1, Weakley, Tennessee; Roll: M653_1278; Page: 317; Image: 11.

70. Tennessee, U.S., Civil War Confederate Pension Applications Index. Tennessee State Library and Archives, comp.. <i>Index to Tennessee Confederate Pension Applications</i>. Nashville, TN, USA: 1964 (revised 1994).

71. United States Census - Year: 1870; Census Place: District 1, Weakley, Tennessee; Roll: M593

72. United States Census - Year: 1880; Census Place: Abernatheys, Weakley, Tennessee; Roll: T9_1284; Family History Film: 1255284; Page: 138.1000; Enumeration District: 165; Image: .

73. *Find a Grave*, database and images (https://www.findagrave.com/memorial/186597892/ john_wesley-cardwell: accessed April 13, 2025), memorial page for John Wesley Cardwell (1841–1890), Find a Grave Memorial ID 186597892, citing Cardwell Cemetery, Palmersville, Weakley County, Tennessee, USA; Maintained by Greg Roach (contributor 48815881).

74. United States Census - Year: 1850; Census Place: North of Cumberland and East of Caney Fork Rivers, Smith, Tennessee; Roll: M432_896; Page: 266; Image: 116.

75. United States Census - Year: 1860; Census Place: , Macon, Tennessee; Roll: M653_1263; Page: 54; Image: 108.

76. United States Census - Year: 1870; Census Place: District 16, Smith, Tennessee; Roll: M593

77. United States Census - Year: 1880; Census Place: District 16, Smith, Tennessee; Roll: T9_1280; Family History Film: 1255280; Page: 178.1000; Enumeration District: 125; Image: .

78. United States Census - Year: 1900; Census Place: Civil District 16, Smith, Tennessee; Roll: ; Page: ; Enumeration District: .

79. United States Census - Year: 1910; Census Place: Civil District 16, Smith, Tennessee; Roll: T624_1521; Page: 5B; Enumeration District: 113; Image: 1124.

80. United States Census - Year: 1920; Census Place: Civil District 10, Wilson, Tennessee; Roll: T625_1771; Page: 19A; Enumeration District: 145; Image: 880.

81. *Find a Grave*, database and images (https://www.findagrave.com/memorial/98867456/ joseph_leonard-cardwell: accessed March 21, 2025), memorial page for Joseph Leonard Cardwell (30 Sep 1835–15 Nov 1925), Find a Grave Memorial ID 98867456, citing Cedar Grove Cemetery, Lebanon, Wilson County, Tennessee, USA; Maintained by Stone Branches (contributor 47411175).

82. Photo 9.9: Photograph used as originally posted on Ancestry.com. elt37 originally shared this on 7 Jul 2017. Photograph resized, cropped, enhanced, and/or repaired by the author.

83. Photo 9.10: Photograph used as originally posted on Ancestry.com. wrcardwell_1 originally shared this on 21 Jul 2018Photograph resized, cropped, enhanced, and/or repaired by the author.

84. Photo 9.11: Photograph used as originally posted on FindAGrave.com (Memorial ID: 98867456). Original added by Cindy on 17 Apr 2014. Photograph resized, cropped, enhanced, and/or repaired by the author.

85. United States Census - Year: 1850; Census Place: Prairie, Washington, Arkansas; Roll: M432_31; Page: 400; Image: 205.

86. United States Census - The National Archives in Washington D.C.; Record Group: Records of the Bureau of the Census; Record Group Number: 29; Series Number: M653; Residence Date: 1860; Home in 1860: Hopkins, Kentucky; Roll: M653_374; Page: 746; Family History Library Film: 803374

87. Ancestry.com. *Tennessee, U.S., Marriage Records, 1780-2002* [database on-line]. Lehi, UT, USA: Ancestry.com Operations Inc, 2008. Original data: *Tennessee State Marriages, 1780-2002*. Nashville, TN, USA: Tennessee State Library and Archives. Microfilm.

88. United States Census - Year: 1870; Census Place: District 4, Bedford, Tennessee; Roll: M593_; Page: ; Image: .

Notes

89. United States Census - Year: 1880; Census Place: District 17, Coffee, Tennessee; Roll: T9_1248; Family History Film: 1255248; Page: 43.4000; Enumeration District: 17; Image: .

90. United States Census - Year: 1900; Census Place: Civil District 16, Coffee, Tennessee; Roll: T623_1562; Page: 3A; Enumeration District: 33.

91. United States Census - Year: 1910; Census Place: Civil District 16, Coffee, Tennessee; Roll: T624_1494; Page: 5B; Enumeration District: 51; Image: 756.

92. Ancestry.com. *Tennessee, U.S., Civil War Confederate Pension Applications Index* [database on-line]. Provo, UT, USA: Ancestry.com Operations Inc, 2005. Original data: Tennessee State Library and Archives, comp.. *Index to Tennessee Confederate Pension Applications.* Nashville, TN, USA: 1964 (revised 1994).

93. United States Census - Year: 1850; Census Place: District 10, McNairy, Tennessee; Roll: M432_888; Page: 124; Image: 250.

94. United States Census - Year: 1860; Census Place: District 5, McNairy, Tennessee; Roll: M653_1262; Page: 405; Image: 404.

95. Ancestry.com. *Tennessee, U.S., Marriage Records, 1780-2002* [database on-line]. Lehi, UT, USA: Ancestry.com Operations Inc, 2008. Original data: *Tennessee State Marriages, 1780-2002.* Nashville, TN, USA: Tennessee State Library and Archives. Microfilm. Lee Roy's name is incorrectly listed as "L.P. Cardoolle", but examination of the original record photo confirms it is Lee Roy Cardwell.

96. United States Census - Year: 1870; Census Place: District 5, McNairy, Tennessee; Roll: M593

97. United States Census - Year: 1880; Census Place: District 5, Dyer, Tennessee; Roll: T9_1253; Family History Film: 1255253; Page: 136.4000; Enumeration District: 15; Image:

98. United States Census - Year: 1900; Census Place: Civil District 4, Dyer, Tennessee; Roll: T623 1568; Page: 7A; Enumeration District: 14.

99. United States Census - Year: 1910; Census Place: Civil District 8, Gibson, Tennessee; Roll: T624_1499; Page: 5B; Enumeration District: 47; Image: 936.

100. *Find a Grave*, database and images (https://www.findagrave.com/memorial/57272247/lee_roy-cardwell: accessed March 3, 2025), memorial page for Lee Roy Cardwell (1843–1917), Find a Grave Memorial ID 57272247, citing Bells Chapel Cemetery, Dyer, Gibson County, Tennessee, USA; Maintained by Gibson County (contributor 51664679).

101. Photo 9.12: Photograph used as originally posted on FindAGrave.com (Memorial ID: 57272247). Original added by Mark O on 02 Oct 2010. Photograph resized, cropped, enhanced, and/or repaired by the author.

102. Ancestry.com. *Tennessee, U.S., Marriage Records, 1780-2002* [database on-line]. Lehi, UT, USA: Ancestry.com Operations Inc, 2008. Original data: *Tennessee State Marriages, 1780-2002.* Nashville, TN, USA: Tennessee State Library and Archives. Microfilm.

103. United States Census - Year: 1850; Census Place: Kingston, Roane, Tennessee; Roll: M432_893; Page: 448; Image: 354.

104. United States Census - Year: 1860; Census Place: District 3, Knox, Tennessee; Roll: M653_1259; Page: 128; Image: 262.

105. United States Census - Year: 1870; Census Place: Kingston, Roane, Tennessee; Roll: M593

106. United States Census - Year: 1880; Census Place: District 18, Knox, Tennessee; Roll: T9_1265; Family History Film: 1255265; Page: 255.2000; Enumeration District: 153; Image: .

107. Ancestry.com. *Tennessee, U.S., City Death Records, 1872-1923* [database on-line]. Provo, UT, USA: Ancestry.com Operations, Inc., 2012.

Original data: *Tennessee City Death Records, Nashville, Knoxville, Chattanooga, Memphis, 1848-1907*. Nashville, Tennessee: Tennessee State Library and Archives. *Tennessee City Death Records Nashville, Knoxville, Chattanooga, Memphis 1848-1907*. Nashville, Tennessee: Tennessee State Library and Archives. Knox County, Death Register, 1892-1897.

108. United States Census - The National Archives in Washington, DC; Record Group: Records of the Bureau of the Census; Record Group Number: 29; Series Number: M432; Residence Date: 1850; Home in 1850: District 4, Macon, Tennessee; Roll: 888; Page: 185b

109. United States Census - Year: 1860; Census Place: , Simpson, Kentucky; Roll: M653_395; Page: 0; Image: 316.

110. United States Census - Year: 1880; Census Place: Hardison, Logan, Kentucky; Roll: T9_429; Family History Film: 1254429; Page: 551.3000; Enumeration District: 171; Image: 0545.

111. United States Census - Year: 1900; Census Place: Louisville Ward 11, Jefferson, Kentucky; Roll: ; Page: ; Enumeration District: .

112. United States Census - Year: 1910; Census Place: Louisville Ward 11, Jefferson, Kentucky; Roll: T624_486; Page: 11B; Enumeration District: 173; Image: 947.

113. United States Census - Year: 1920; Census Place: Chicago Ward 13, Cook (Chicago), Illinois; Roll: T625_322; Page: 4A; Enumeration District: 757; Image: 243.

114. Ancestry.com. *Cook County, Illinois Death Index, 1908-1988* [database on-line]. Lehi, UT, USA: Ancestry.com Operations Inc, 2008. Original data: Cook County Clerk. *Cook County Clerk Genealogy Records*. Cook County Clerk's Office, Chicago, IL: Cook County Clerk, 2008.

115. *Find a Grave*, database and images (https://www.findagrave.com/memorial/78365816/samyell-cardwell: accessed March 20, 2025), memorial page for Samyell Cardwell (unknown–unknown), Find a Grave Memorial ID 78365816, citing Oakland Cemetery, Trenton, Gibson County, Tennessee, USA; Maintained by Mark O (contributor 47363755).

116. Photo 9.13: Photograph used as originally posted on Ancestry.com. Marjorie_FowlerRunning originally shared this on 13 Nov 2008. Photograph resized, cropped, enhanced, and/or repaired by the author.

117. Photo 9.14: Photograph used as originally posted on FindAGrave.com (Memorial ID: 78365816). Original added by   joyce Osborne on 14 Oct 2011. Photograph resized, cropped, enhanced, and/or repaired by the author.

118. United States Census - Year: 1850; Census Place: North of Cumberland and East of Caney Fork Rivers, Smith, Tennessee; Roll: M432_896; Page: 214; Image: 11.

119. United States Census - Year: 1860; Census Place: District 2, Smith, Tennessee; Roll: M653_1272; Page: 276; Image: 25.

120. Ancestry.com. *Tennessee, U.S., Marriage Records, 1780-2002* [database on-line]. Lehi, UT, USA: Ancestry.com Operations Inc, 2008. Original data: *Tennessee State Marriages, 1780-2002*. Nashville, TN, USA: Tennessee State Library and Archives. Microfilm.

121. United States Census - Year: 1880; Census Place: District 8, Smith, Tennessee; Roll: 1280; Family History Film: 1255280; Page: 95D; Enumeration District: 119; Image: .

122. United States Census - Year: 1900; Census Place: Civil District 8, Smith, Tennessee; Roll: T623 1600; Page: 5A; Enumeration District: 97.

Notes

123. *Find a Grave*, database and images (https://www.findagrave.com/memorial/122988530/samuel_s-cardwell: accessed February 26, 2025), memorial page for Samuel S Cardwell (18 Dec 1841–27 Sep 1906), Find a Grave Memorial ID 122988530, citing Cardwell Family Cemetery, Chestnut Mound, Smith County, Tennessee, USA; Maintained by: Find a Grave.

124. Photo 9.15: Photograph used as originally posted on Ancestry.com. RoyGSpurlock originally shared this on 3 Nov 2010. Photograph resized, cropped, enhanced, and/or repaired by the author.

125. Photo 9.16: Photograph used as originally posted on FindAGrave.com (Memorial ID: 122988530). Original added by   Roy G Spurlock on 27 Feb 2016. Photograph resized, cropped, enhanced, and/or repaired by the author.

126. United States Census - Year: 1850; Census Place: North of Cumberland and East of Caney Fork Rivers, Smith, Tennessee; Roll: M432_896; Page: 214; Image: 11.

127. United States Census - Year: 1860; Census Place: District 2, Smith, Tennessee; Roll: M653_1272; Page: 276; Image: 25.

128. United States Census - Year: 1870; Census Place: District 1, Jackson, Tennessee; Roll: M593_1539; Page: 130B; Family History Library Film: 553038

129. United States Census - Year: 1880; Census Place: District 15, Smith, Tennessee; Roll: T9_1280; Family History Film: 1255280; Page: 156.4000; Enumeration District: 124; Image: .

130. United States Census - Year: 1910; Census Place: Hot Springs Ward 6, Garland, Arkansas; Roll: T624_50; Page: 7A; Enumeration District: 0068; FHL microfilm: 1374063

131. *Directory of Deceased American Physicians, 1804-1929* [database on-line]. Ancestry.com.

132. United State Census - Year: 1850; Census Place: District 10, McNairy, Tennessee; Roll: M432_888; Page: 124; Image: 250.

133. United States Census - Year: 1870; Census Place: District 5, McNairy, Tennessee; Roll: M593

134. United States Census - Year: 1880; Census Place: District 5, Mc Nairy, Tennessee; Roll: T9_1268; Family History Film: 1255268; Page: 71.2000; Enumeration District: 120; Image: .

135. United States Census - Year: 1900; Census Place: Civil District 4, Dyer, Tennessee; Roll: T623 1568; Page: 9B; Enumeration District: 14.

136. United States Census - Year: 1910; Census Place: Civil District 4, Dyer, Tennessee; Roll: T624_1497; Page: 20A; Enumeration District: 17; Image: 965.

137. *Find a Grave*, database and images (https://www.findagrave.com/memorial/37091938/thomas_d-cardwell: accessed March 3, 2025), memorial page for Thomas D. Cardwell (May 1833–29 Jan 1915), Find a Grave Memorial ID 37091938, citing Mount Hope Church Cemetery, Jenkinsville, Dyer County, Tennessee, USA; Maintained by D & J Cloninger (contributor 47020801).

NOTE: A Photo Request has been placed for a photo of his headstone on Find-A-Grave, but as of March 2025 it is unfulfilled.

138. United States Census - Year: 1850; Census Place: District 3, Warren, Tennessee; Roll: M432_898; Page: 24; Image: 48.

139. United States Census - Year: 1860; Census Place: , Warren, Tennessee; Roll: M653_1274; Page: 473; Image: 134.

140. United States Census - Year: 1870; Census Place: District 2, Warren, Tennessee; Roll: M593

141. United States Census - Year: 1880; Census Place: District 2, Warren, Tennessee; Roll: T9_1283; Family History Film: 1255283; Page: 325.3000; Enumeration District: 131; Image: .

142. United States Census - Year: 1900; Census Place: Justice Precinct 3, McLennan, Texas; Roll: T623 1658; Page: 7A; Enumeration District: 84.

143. United States Census - Year: 1910; Census Place: Justice Precinct 2, Nolan, Texas; Roll: T624_1581; Page: 2A; Enumeration District: 176; Image: 946.

144. *Find a Grave*, database and images (https://www.findagrave.com/memorial/7752327/thomas_w-cardwell: accessed March 22, 2025), memorial page for Thomas W. Cardwell (1835–26 Dec 1922), Find a Grave Memorial ID 7752327, citing Roby Cemetery, Roby, Fisher County, Texas, USA; Maintained by Janie Healer Davis (contributor 46586213).

145. Photo 9.17: Photograph used as originally posted on FindAGrave.com (Memorial ID: 7752327). Original added by Janie Healer Davis on 10 Aug 2003. Photograph resized, cropped, enhanced, and/or repaired by the author.

146. Photo 9.18: Photograph used as originally posted on FindAGrave.com (Memorial ID: 7752327). Original added by Janie Healer Davis on 10 Aug 2003. Photograph resized, cropped, enhanced, and/or repaired by the author.

147. United States Census - Year: 1850; Census Place: North of Cumberland and East of Caney Fork Rivers, Smith, Tennessee; Roll: M432_896; Page: 257; Image: 99.

148. United States Census - Year: 1860; Census Place: District 2, Smith, Tennessee; Roll: M653_1272; Page: 276; Image: 25.

149. United States Census - Year: 1870; Census Place: District 1, Smith, Tennessee; Roll: M593_; Page: ; Image: .

150. United States Census - Year: 1850; Census Place: , Simpson, Kentucky; Roll: M432_218; Page: 12; Image: 493.

151. United States Census - Year: 1860; Census Place: District 19, Sumner, Tennessee; Roll: M653_1275; Page: 340; Image: 689.

152. United States Census - Year: 1870; Census Place: District 19, Sumner, Tennessee; Roll: M593

153. United States Census - Year: 1880; Census Place: Wea, Miami, Kansas; Roll: T9_389; Family History Film: 1254389; Page: 496.1000; Enumeration District: 146; Image: 0247.

154. United States Census - Year: 1900; Census Place: Ottumwa, Coffey, Kansas; Roll: ; Page: ; Enumeration District: .

155. United States Census - Year: 1910; Census Place: Ottumwa, Coffey, Kansas; Roll: T624_435; Page: 4B; Enumeration District: 18; Image: 684.

156. United States Census - Year: 1920; Census Place: Reno, Reno, Kansas; Roll: T625_546; Page: 4A; Enumeration District: 192; Image: 390.

157. *Find a Grave*, database and images (https://www.findagrave.com/memorial/85050616/william_dudley-cardwell: accessed March 20, 2025), memorial page for William Dudley Cardwell (16 Dec 1842–5 Feb 1926), Find a Grave Memorial ID 85050616, citing Fairview Cemetery, Elmer, Reno County, Kansas, USA; Maintained by 46495383 (contributor 46495383).

158. Photo 9.19: Photograph used as originally posted on Ancestry.com. Marjorie_FowlerRunning originally shared this on 13 Nov 2008. Photograph resized, cropped, enhanced, and/or repaired by the author.

159. Photo 9.20: Photograph used as originally posted on FindAGrave.com (Memorial ID: 85050616). Original added by 46495383 on 05 Jun 2012. Photograph resized, cropped, enhanced, and/or repaired by the author.

Notes

160. United States Census - Year: 1840; Census Place: , Hardeman, Tennessee; Roll: 522; Page: 298.

161. United States Census - Year: 1850; Census Place: District 4, Madison, Tennessee; Roll: M432_889; Page: 254; Image: 80.

162. United States Census - Year: 1860; Census Place: District 4, Madison, Tennessee; Roll: M653_1263; Page: 116; Image: 233.

163. United States Census - Year: 1850; Census Place: South Division, Smith, Tennessee; Roll: M432_896; Page: 374; Image: 331.

164. United States Census - Year: 1860; Census Place: District 7, Obion, Tennessee; Roll: M653_1267; Page: 86; Image: 172.

165. *Find a Grave*, database and images (https://www.findagrave.com/memorial/6598399/william_h-cardwell: accessed March 19, 2025), memorial page for Pvt William H. Cardwell (unknown–4 Nov 1864), Find a Grave Memorial ID 6598399, citing Oak Woods Cemetery, Chicago, Cook County, Illinois, USA; Maintained by Cousins by the Dozens (contributor 46904925).

166. Photo 9.21: Photograph used as originally posted on FindAGrave.com (Memorial ID: 7093666). Original added by HallowedGround on 11 Sep 2012. Photograph resized, cropped, enhanced, and/or repaired by the author.

167. Photo 9.22: Photograph used as originally posted on FindAGrave.com (Memorial ID: 6598399). Original added by Jane Clary Bermijo on 26 Jul 2022. Photograph resized, cropped, enhanced, and/or repaired by the author.

168. United States Census - Year: 1850; Census Place: North of Cumberland and East of Caney Fork Rivers, Smith, Tennessee; Roll: M432_896; Page: 214; Image: 11.

169. United States Census - Year: 1860; Census Place: District 2, Smith, Tennessee; Roll: M653_1272; Page: 276; Image: 25.

170. Ancestry.com. *Tennessee, U.S., Marriage Records, 1780-2002* [database on-line]. Lehi, UT, USA: Ancestry.com Operations Inc, 2008. Original data: *Tennessee State Marriages, 1780-2002.* Nashville, TN, USA: Tennessee State Library and Archives. Microfilm.

171. United States Census - Year: 1870; Census Place: District 21, Smith, Tennessee; Roll: M593_1564; Page: 209A; Family History Library Film: 553063

172. United States Census - Year: 1850; Census Place: North of Cumberland and East of Caney Fork Rivers, Smith, Tennessee; Roll: M432_896; Page: 253; Image: 90.

173. United States Census - Year: 1860; Census Place: District 2, Smith, Tennessee; Roll: M653_1272; Page: 280; Image: 33.

174. United States Census - Year: 1870; Census Place: District 2, Smith, Tennessee; Roll: M593

175. United States Census - Year: 1880; Census Place: District 5, Smith, Tennessee; Roll: T9_1280; Family History Film: 1255280; Page: 57.2000; Enumeration District: 117; Image: .

176. United States Census - Year: 1900; Census Place: Justice Precinct 6, McLennan, Texas; Roll: ; Page: ; Enumeration District: .

177. United States Census - Year: 1910; Census Place: Justice Precinct 6, McLennan, Texas; Roll: T624_1576; Page: 7A; Enumeration District: 106; Image: 284.

178. United States Census - Year: 1920; Census Place: Bruceville, McLennan, Texas; Roll: T625_1831; Page: 1A; Enumeration District: 144; Image: 1008.

179. *Find a Grave*, database and images (https://www.findagrave.com/memorial/227526473/william_m-cardwell: accessed April 14, 2025), memorial page for William M. Cardwell (8 Dec 1842–5 Nov 1922), Find a Grave Memorial ID 227526473, citing Confederate

Cemetery, Alvin, Brazoria County, Texas, USA; Maintained by LJCL16 (contributor 47878768).

180. United States Census - Year: 1850; Census Place: Western District, Rockingham, North Carolina; Roll: M432_643; Page: 108A; Image: 222

181. United States Census - Year: 1860; Census Place: District 3, Union, Tennessee; Roll: M653_1276; Page: 438; Image: 196.

182. Photo 9.23: Photograph used as originally posted on FindAGrave.com (Memorial ID: 7093666). Original added by HallowedGround on 11 Sep 2012. Photograph resized, cropped, enhanced, and/or repaired by the author.

183. Photo 9.24: Photograph used as originally posted on FindAGrave.com (Memorial ID: 7093674). Original added by Time Traveler on 21 Sep 2014. Photograph resized, cropped, enhanced, and/or repaired by the author.

184. United State Census - Year: 1850; Census Place: District 10, McNairy, Tennessee; Roll: M432_888; Page: 124; Image: 250.

185. United States Census - Year: 1860; Census Place: District 9, McNairy, Tennessee; Roll: M653_1262; Page: 465; Image: 526.

186. Tennessee State Marriages, 1780-2002. http://search.ancestry.com/cgi-bin/sse.dll?db=tnstatemarriages&h=2376026&ti=0&indiv=try&gss=pt

187. Fold3, *US, Compiled Service Records of Confederate Soldiers Who Served in Organizations from the State of Alabama, 1861-1865* (https://www.fold3.com/publication/26/us-civil-war-service-records-cmsr-confederate-alabama-1861-1865

188. Photo 9.25: Photograph used as originally posted on FindAGrave.com (Memorial ID: 15857367). Original added by Brian D. McKinney on 13 May 2011. Photograph resized, cropped, enhanced, and/or repaired by the author.

189. Photo 9.26: Photograph used as originally posted on FindAGrave.com (Memorial ID: 15857367). Original added by peanuts on 23 Sep 2006. Photograph resized, cropped, enhanced, and/or repaired by the author.

Texas

1. United States Census - Year: 1850; Census Place: District 13, Jefferson, Tennessee; Roll: M432_885; Page: 378; Image: 439.

2. United States Census - The National Archives in Washington D.C.; Record Group: Records of the Bureau of the Census; Record Group Number: 29; Series Number: M653; Residence Date: 1860; Home in 1860: Caldwell, Texas; Roll: M653_1289; Page: 190; Family History Library Film: 805289

3. United States Census - Year: 1870; Census Place: Caldwell, Texas; Roll: M593

4. United States Census - Year: 1880; Census Place: Precinct 5, Caldwell, Texas; Roll: T9_1294; Family History Film: 1255294; Page: 286.2000; Enumeration District: 30; Image: .

5. United States Census - Year: 1900; Census Place: Justice Precinct 5, Caldwell, Texas; Roll: T623 1616; Page: 14B; Enumeration District: 124.

6. Photo 10.1: Photograph used as originally posted on FindAGrave.com (Memorial ID: 25828629). Original added by Bobby J. Chamberlain on 18 Dec 2011. Photograph resized, cropped, enhanced, and/or repaired by the author.

7. Photo 10.2: Photograph used as originally posted on FindAGrave.com (Memorial ID: 25828629). Original added by Lynn Moore on 13 Apr 2008. Photograph resized, cropped, enhanced, and/or repaired by the author.

Notes

8. United States Census - Year: 1850; Census Place: District 13, Jefferson, Tennessee; Roll: M432_885; Page: 381; Image: 445.

9. United States Census - Year: 1860; Census Place: , Caldwell, Texas; Roll: M653_1289; Page: 218; Image: 440.

10. Ancestry.com. *Texas, U.S., Select County Marriage Index, 1837-1965* [database on-line]. Provo, UT, USA: Ancestry.com Operations, Inc., 2014. Original data: *Texas, County Marriage Index, 1837-1977*. Salt Lake City, Utah: FamilySearch, 2013.

11. United States Census - Year: 1870; Census Place: Caldwell, Texas; Roll: M593

12. United States Census - Year: 1880; Census Place: , Caldwell, Texas; Roll: T9_1293; Family History Film: 1255293; Page: 212.3000; Enumeration District: 27; Image: .

13. United States Census - Year: 1900; Census Place: Justice Precinct 1, Caldwell, Texas; Roll: T623 1616; Page: 7A; Enumeration District: 116.

14. United States Census - Year: 1910; Census Place: Justice Precinct 1, Caldwell, Texas; Roll: T624_1536; Page: 37A; Enumeration District: 26; Image: 196.

15. *Find a Grave*, database and images (https://www.findagrave.com/memorial/40090790/john_madison-cardwell: accessed April 1, 2025), memorial page for John Madison Cardwell (18 Jun 1836–22 Dec 1917), Find a Grave Memorial ID 40090790, citing Lockhart Municipal Burial Park, Lockhart, Caldwell County, Texas, USA; Maintained by Judy Rodgers (contributor 46828494).

16. Photo 10.3: Photograph used as originally posted on FindAGrave.com (Memorial ID: 40090790). Original added by Rand Cardwell on 01 Apr 2025. Photograph resized, cropped, enhanced, and/or repaired by the author.

17. Photo 10.4: Photograph used as originally posted on FindAGrave.com (Memorial ID: 40090790). Original added by Mick Williams on 13 Aug 2014. Photograph resized, cropped, enhanced, and/or repaired by the author.

18. United States Census - Year: 1850; Census Place: District 13, Jefferson, Tennessee; Roll: M432_885; Page: 381; Image: 445.

19. United States Census - Year: 1860; Census Place: , Caldwell, Texas; Roll: M653_1289; Page: 189; Image: 383.

20. *Find a Grave*, database and images (https://www.findagrave.com/memorial/25828557/robert_w-cardwell: accessed April 1, 2025), memorial page for Robert W Cardwell (14 Jul 1829–3 Feb 1914), Find a Grave Memorial ID 25828557, citing Lytton Springs Cemetery, Lytton Springs, Caldwell County, Texas, USA; Maintained by Judy Rodgers (contributor 46828494).

21. Photo 10.5: Photograph used as originally posted on FindAGrave.com (Memorial ID: 25828557). Original added by Lynn Moore on 17 Apr 2008. Photograph resized, cropped, enhanced, and/or repaired by the author.

22. United States Census - Year: 1850; Census Place: District 13, Jefferson, Tennessee; Roll: M432_885; Page: 381; Image: 445.

23. Ancestry.com. *Texas, U.S., County Marriage Records, 1817-1965* [database on-line]. Lehi, UT, USA: Ancestry.com Operations, Inc., 2016. Original data: *Marriage Records. Texas Marriages*. Texas State Library and Archives Commission and various county clerk offices, Texas.

24. United States Census - The National Archives in Washington D.C.; Record Group: Records of the Bureau of the Census; Record Group Number: 29; Series Number: M653; Residence Date: 1860; Home in 1860: Caldwell, Texas; Roll: M653_1289; Page: 194; Family History Library Film: 805289

25. United States Census - Year: 1870; Census Place: Caldwell, Texas; Roll: M593

26. United States Census - Year: 1880; Census Place: , Caldwell, Texas; Roll: T9_1293; Family History Film: 1255293; Page: 196.4000; Enumeration District: 27; Image: .

27. United States Census - Year: 1900; Census Place: Lockhart, Caldwell, Texas; Roll: T623_1616; Page: 19A; Enumeration District: 118.

28. *Find a Grave*, database and images (https://www.findagrave.com/memorial/39805230/ thomas_sterling-cardwell: accessed April 1, 2025), memorial page for Thomas Sterling Cardwell (4 Aug 1833–16 Dec 1899), Find a Grave Memorial ID 39805230, citing Lockhart Municipal Burial Park, Lockhart, Caldwell County, Texas, USA; Maintained by Judy Rodgers (contributor 46828494).

29. Photo 10.6: Photograph used as originally posted on FindAGrave.com (Memorial ID: 39805230). Original added by Rand Cardwell on 01 Apr 2025. Photograph resized, cropped, enhanced, and/or repaired by the author.

30. Photo 10.7: Photograph used as originally posted on FindAGrave.com (Memorial ID: 39805230). Original added by Donna McClary on 06 Mar 2012. Photograph resized, cropped, enhanced, and/or repaired by the author.

Virginia

1.

2. United States Census - Year: 1870; Census Place: Bruton, York, Virginia; Roll: M593_; Page: ; Image: .

3. United States Census - Year: 1850; Census Place: , Appomattox, Virginia; Roll: M432_933; Page: 179A; Image: .

4. United States Census - Year: 1860; Census Place: Eastern District, Campbell, Virginia; Roll: ; Page: 254; Image: 261.

5. A Place Called Appomattox, by William Marvel; Southern Illinois University Press, Feb 12, 2008 - History - 416 pages -

6. United States Census - Year: 1880; Census Place: Stonewall, Appomattox, Virginia; Roll: 1354; Family History Film: 1255354; Page: 420A; Enumeration District: 11; Image: .

7. United States Census - Year: 1900; Census Place: Stonewall, Appomattox, Virginia; Roll: _; Page: 13B; Enumeration District: 20.

8. United States Census - Year: 1910; Census Place: Stonewall, Appomattox, Virginia; Roll: ; Page: ; Enumeration District: ; Image: .

9. United States Census - Year: 1930; Census Place: Stonewall, Appomattox, Virginia; Roll: 2435; Page: 3B; Enumeration District: 7; Image: 123.0.

10. United States Census - Year: 1940; Census Place: Stonewall, Appomattox, Virginia; Roll: m-t0627-04244; Page: 10B; Enumeration District: 6-9

11. *Find a Grave*, database and images (https://www.findagrave.com/memorial/61086989/ charles_wesley-cardwell: accessed March 25, 2025), memorial page for Charles Wesley Cardwell (28 Jan 1848–4 Nov 1947), Find a Grave Memorial ID 61086989, citing Concord Cemetery, Concord, Appomattox County, Virginia, USA; Maintained by J. M. Palm Robertson (contributor 47185380).

12. Photo 11.1: Photograph used as originally posted on Ancestry.com. marktooley2003 originally shared this on 6 Jul 2018. Photograph resized, cropped, enhanced, and/or repaired by the author.

13. Photo 11.2: Photograph used as originally posted on Ancestry.com. marktooley2003 originally shared this on 6 Jul 2018. Photograph resized, cropped, enhanced, and/or repaired by the author.

Notes

14. Photo 11.3: Photograph used as originally posted on FindAGrave.com (Memorial ID: 61086989). Original added by Darrell Landrum on 31 Dec 2011. Photograph resized, cropped, enhanced, and/or repaired by the author.

15. United States Census - Year: 1850; Census Place: , Campbell, Virginia; Roll: M432_938; Page: 210; Image: 420.

16. United States Census - Year: 1860; Census Place: Eastern District, Campbell, Virginia; Roll: M653_1338; Page: 246; Image: 250.

17. United States Census - Year: 1870; Census Place: Eastern Division, Campbell, Virginia; Roll: M593

18. United States Census - Year: 1880; Census Place: Rustburgh, Campbell, Virginia; Roll: T9_1358; Family History Film: 1255358; Page: 135.2000; Enumeration District: 45; Image: .

19. United States Census - Year: 1900; Census Place: Southside, Appomattox, Virginia; Roll: T623 1699; Page: 11A; Enumeration District: 17.

20. United States Census - Year: 1910; Census Place: Southside, Appomattox, Virginia; Roll: T624_1620; Page: 1B; Enumeration District: 22; Image: 306.

21. *Find a Grave*, database and images (https://www.findagrave.com/memorial/127103887/christopher-cardwell: accessed March 23, 2025), memorial page for Christopher Cardwell (unknown–26 Apr 1926), Find a Grave Memorial ID 127103887, citing Cardwell Cemetery, Concord, Campbell County, Virginia, USA; Maintained by VAGenealogist (contributor 47216247).

22. *Find a Grave*, database and images (https://www.findagrave.com/memorial/127103887/christopher-cardwell: accessed March 23, 2025), memorial page for Christopher Cardwell (unknown–26 Apr 1926), Find a Grave Memorial ID 127103887, citing Cardwell Cemetery, Concord, Campbell County, Virginia, USA; Maintained by VAGenealogist (contributor 47216247).

23. Photo 11.4: Photograph used as originally posted on FindAGrave.com (Memorial ID: 61086990). Original added by Darrell Landrum on 01 Jan 2012. Photograph resized, cropped, enhanced, and/or repaired by the author.

24. United States Census - Year: 1850; Census Place: Washington Ward 5, Washington, District of Columbia; Roll: M432_57; Page: 6; Image: 14.

25. United States Census - Year: 1860; Census Place: Washington Ward 4, Washington, District of Columbia; Roll: M653_103; Page: 420; Image: 423.

26. United States Census - Year: 1880; Census Place: Columbia, Richland, South Carolina; Roll: T9_1238; Family History Film: 1255238; Page: 285.4000; Enumeration District: 164; Image: .

27. United States Census - Year: 1900; Census Place: Columbia Ward 1, Richland, South Carolina; Roll: ; Page: ; Enumeration District: .

28. United States Census - Year: 1910; Census Place: Columbia Ward 1, Richland, South Carolina; Roll: T624_1471; Page: 8A; Enumeration District: 79; Image: 88.

29. United States Census - Year: 1920; Census Place: Columbia Ward 1, Richland, South Carolina; Roll: T625_1707; Page: 29B; Enumeration District: 80; Image: 128.

30. These specifics are paraphrased from newspaper articles and a biography for David Adams Cardwell, Jr., in the authors possession.

31. *Find a Grave*, database and images (https://www.findagrave.com/memorial/65639528/david_adams-cardwell: accessed March 26, 2025), memorial page for David Adams Cardwell II (22 Feb 1846–19 Feb 1921), Find a Grave Memorial ID 65639528, citing First Presbyterian Churchyard, Columbia, Richland County, South Carolina, USA; Maintained by Anna (contributor 47329432).

32. Photo 11.5: Photograph used as originally posted on FindAGrave.com (Memorial ID: 65639528). Original added by Rand Cardwell on 27 April 2025. Photograph resized, cropped, enhanced, and/or repaired by the author.

33. Photo 11.6: Photograph used as originally posted on FindAGrave.com (Memorial ID: 65639528). Original added by Anna on 25 Sep 2013. Photograph resized, cropped, enhanced, and/or repaired by the author.

34. Photo 11.7: Photograph used as originally posted on FindAGrave.com (Memorial ID: 65639528). Original added by Jordan on 14 Oct 2024. Photograph resized, cropped, enhanced, and/or repaired by the author.

35. United States Census - Year: 1850; Census Place: Washington Ward 5, Washington, District of Columbia; Roll: M432_57; Page: 6; Image: 14.

36. United States Census - Year: 1860; Census Place: Washington Ward 4, Washington, District of Columbia; Roll: M653_103; Page: 420; Image: 423.

37. United States Census - Year: 1870; Census Place: Richmond Monroe Ward, Richmond (Independent City), Virginia; Roll: M593_1654; Page: 326; Image: 650.

38. United States Census - Year: 1880; Census Place: Richmond, Henrico, Virginia; Roll: T9_1371; Family History Film: 1255371; Page: 473.2000; Enumeration District: 78; Image: .

39. *Find a Grave*, database and images (https://www.findagrave.com/memorial/158463976/david_adams-cardwell: accessed March 26, 2025), memorial page for David Adams Cardwell (1808–31 Mar 1898), Find a Grave Memorial ID 158463976, citing Shockoe Hill Cemetery, Richmond, Richmond City, Virginia, USA; Maintained by Jeffry Burden (contributor 46873454).

40. Ancestry.com. *Virginia, U.S., Compiled Marriages, 1740-1850* [database on-line]. Lehi, UT, USA: Ancestry.com Operations Inc, 1999. Original data: Dodd, Jordan R., et al.. *Early American Marriages: Virginia to 1850*. Bountiful, UT, USA: Precision Indexing Publishers.

41. Oregon State Census - Online publication - Provo, UT, USA: The Generations Network, Inc., 1999.Original data - Compiled and digitized by Mr. Jackson and AIS from microfilmed schedules of the U.S. Federal Decennial Census, territorial/state censuses, and/or census substitutes. Residence date: 1854 Residence place: Jackson County, OR

42. United States Census - Year: 1850; Census Place: Charlotte, Charlotte, Virginia; Roll: M432_940; Page: 28A; Image: .

43. United States Census - Year: 1860; Census Place: , Charlotte, Virginia; Roll: ; Page: ; Image: .

44. *Find a Grave*, database and images (https://www.findagrave.com/memorial/187357651/f_f-cardwell: accessed March 25, 2025), memorial page for F. F. Cardwell (unknown–16 Oct 1891), Find a Grave Memorial ID 187357651, citing Bethel Methodist Church Cemetery, Mountain Hill, Pittsylvania County, Virginia, USA; Maintained by Ann (contributor 46964942).

45. United States Census - Year: 1850; Census Place: Washington Ward 5, Washington, District of Columbia; Roll: M432_57; Page: 6; Image: 14.

46. United States Census - Roll: M653_103; Page: 420; Image: 423.

47. United States Census - Year: 1870; Census Place: Richmond Monroe Ward, Richmond (Independent City), Virginia; Roll: M593_1654; Page: 326; Image: 650.

48. United States Census - Year: 1880; Census Place: Richmond, Henrico, Virginia; Roll: T9_1371; Family History Film: 1255371; Page: 473.2000; Enumeration District: 78; Image: .

Notes

49. *Find a Grave*, database and images (https://www.findagrave.com/memorial/42346452/george_drinker-cardwell: accessed March 26, 2025), memorial page for George Drinker Cardwell (1844–1883), Find a Grave Memorial ID 42346452, citing Hollywood Cemetery, Richmond, Richmond City, Virginia, USA; Maintained by George Seitz (contributor 40539541).

50. Photo 11.8: Photograph used as originally posted on FindAGrave.com (Memorial ID: 42346452). Original added by George Seitz on 25 Sep 2009. Photograph resized, cropped, enhanced, and/or repaired by the author.

51. United States Census - Year: 1850; Census Place: Stratton Major Parish, King and Queen, Virginia; Roll: M432_954; Page: 167B; Image: .

52. United States Census - Year: 1860; Census Place: , King and Queen, Virginia; Roll: ; Page: ; Image: .

53. United States Census - Year: 1860; Census Place: , King and Queen, Virginia; Roll: ; Page: ; Image: .

54. United States Census - Year: 1870; Census Place: Buena Vista, King and Queen, Virginia; Roll: M593_; Page: ; Image: .

55. Untied States Census - Year: 1880; Census Place: Buena Vista, King and Queen, Virginia; Roll: T9_1374; Family History Film: 1255374; Page: 416.4000; Enumeration District: 36; Image: .

56. United States Census - Year: 1900; Census Place: Buena Vista, King and Queen, Virginia; Roll: T623_1714; Page: 10A; Enumeration District: 37.

57. United States Census - Year: 1910; Census Place: Baltimore Ward 1, Baltimore (Independent City), Maryland; Roll: T624_552; Page: 6B; Enumeration District: 0007; FHL microfilm: 1374565

58. United States Census - Year: 1850; Census Place: Southern District, Pittsylvania, Virginia; Roll: M432_968; Page: 126B; Image: .

59. United States Census - Year: 1860; Census Place: Southern District, Pittsylvania, Virginia; Roll: ; Page: ; Image: .

60. Based on the 1900 Pittsylvania County, Virginia census.

61. United States Census - Year: 1870; Census Place: Subdivision North of Dan River, Pittsylvania, Virginia; Roll: M593_; Page: ; Image: .

62. United States Census - Year: 1880; Census Place: Tunstall, Pittsylvania, Virginia; Roll: T9_1385; Family History Film: 1255385; Page: 351.3000; Enumeration District: 175; Image: .

63. United States Census - Year: 1900; Census Place: Tunstall, Pittsylvania, Virginia; Roll: T623_1723; Page: 10B; Enumeration District: 91.

64. United States Census - Year: 1860; Census Place: , Greensville, Virginia; Roll: ; Page: ; Image: .

65. Ancestry.com. *Virginia, U.S., Select Marriages, 1785-1940* [database on-line]. Provo, UT, USA: Ancestry.com Operations, Inc, 2014. Original data: *Virginia, Marriages, 1785-1940.* Salt Lake City, Utah: FamilySearch, 2013.

66. United States Census - Year: 1870; Census Place: Petersburg Ward 4, Petersburg (Independent City), Virginia; Roll: M593_; Page: ; Image: .

67. United States Census - Year: 1880; Census Place: Petersburg, Dinwiddie, Virginia; Roll: T9_1363; Family History Film: 1255363; Page: 291.3000; Enumeration District: 90; Image: .

68. United States Census - Year: 1900; Census Place: Petersburg Ward 1, Petersburg City, Virginia; Roll: T623_1736; Page: 15B; Enumeration District: 92.

69. United States Census - Year: 1910; Census Place: Petersburg Ward 1, Petersburg (Independent City), Virginia; Roll: T624_1641; Page: 14A; Enumeration District: 76; Image: 70.

70. *Find a Grave*, database and images (https://www.findagrave.com/memorial/12678490/george_washington-cardwell: accessed March 22, 2025), memorial page for George Washington Cardwell (13 Feb 1840–5 May 1916), Find a Grave Memorial ID 12678490, citing Blandford Cemetery, Petersburg, Petersburg City, Virginia, USA; Maintained by CG (contributor 48429368).

71. Photo 11.9: Photograph used as originally posted on FindAGrave.com (Memorial ID: 12678490). Original added by Mandy W. on 07 Aug 2009. Photograph resized, cropped, enhanced, and/or repaired by the author.

72. United States Census - Year: 1860; Census Place: Upper Revenue District, Hanover, Virginia; Roll: ; Page: ; Image: .

73. United States Census - Year: 1870; Census Place: Upper Revenue District, Hanover, Virginia; Roll: M593_; Page: ; Image: .

74. United States Census - Year: 1870; Census Place: Upper Revenue District, Hanover, Virginia; Roll: M593_; Page: ; Image: .

75. United States Census - The National Archives in Washington, DC; Record Group: Records of the Bureau of the Census; Record Group Number: 29; Series Number: M432; Residence Date: 1850; Home in 1850: Campbell, Virginia; Roll: 938; Page: 211a

76. United States Census - The National Archives in Washington D.C.; Record Group: Records of the Bureau of the Census; Record Group Number: 29; Series Number: M653; Residence Date: 1860; Home in 1860: Eastern District, Campbell, Virginia; Roll: M653_1338; Page: 244; Family History

77. United States Census - Year: 1870; Census Place:Eastern Division, Campbell, Virginia; Roll: M593

78. United States Census - Year: 1880; Census Place: Rustburgh, Campbell, Virginia; Roll: T9_1358; Family History Film: 1255358; Page: 131.1000; Enumeration District: 45; Image: .

79. United States Census - Year: 1900; Census Place: Rustburg, Campbell, Virginia; Roll: T623 1703; Page: 16A; Enumeration District: 26.

80. United States Census - Year: 1850; Census Place: St Stephens Parish, King and Queen, Virginia; Roll: M432_954; Page: 152A; Image: .

81. *Find a Grave*, database and images (https://www.findagrave.com/memorial/463202/james-cardwell: accessed March 27, 2025), memorial page for PVT James Cardwell (unknown–5 Sep 1864), Find a Grave Memorial ID 463202, citing Woodlawn National Cemetery, Elmira, Chemung County, New York, USA; Maintained by Hope (contributor 46790939).

82. Photo 11.10: Photograph used as originally posted on FindAGrave.com (Memorial ID: 463202). Original added by Jim Hackett on 19 Jun 2012. Photograph resized, cropped, enhanced, and/or repaired by the author.

83. United States Census - Year: 1850; Census Place: , Campbell, Virginia; Roll: M432_938; Page: 210; Image: 420.

84. Ancestry.com. *Virginia, U.S., Select Marriages, 1785-1940* [database on-line]. Provo, UT, USA: Ancestry.com Operations, Inc, 2014. Original data: *Virginia, Marriages, 1785-1940*. Salt Lake City, Utah: FamilySearch, 2013.

85. United States Census - Year: 1860; Census Place: Eastern District, Campbell, Virginia; Roll: M653_1338; Page: 318; Image: 322.

Notes

86. United States Census - Year: 1870; Census Place: Eastern Division, Campbell, Virginia; Roll: M593_; Page: ; Image: .

87. United States Census - Year: 1880; Census Place: Rustburgh, Campbell, Virginia; Roll: T9_1358; Family History Film: 1255358; Page: 125.1000; Enumeration District: 45; Image: .

88. *Find a Grave*, database and images (https://www.findagrave.com/memorial/131775512/john_alexander-cardwell: accessed April 20, 2025), memorial page for John Alexander Cardwell (13 Aug 1833–23 Mar 1883), Find a Grave Memorial ID 131775512, citing Dixon Cemetery, Concord, Campbell County, Virginia, USA; Maintained by Brett Martin (contributor 48000196).

89. Photo 11.11: Photograph used as originally posted on FindAGrave.com (Memorial ID: 131775512). Original added by Lisa Blanchard Osmulski on 20 Apr 2025. Photograph resized, cropped, enhanced, and/or repaired by the author.

90. United States Census - Year: 1850; Census Place: , King William, Virginia; Roll: M432_955; Page: 252B; Image: .

91. United States Census - Year: 1860; Census Place: , King William, Virginia; Roll: ; Page: ; Image: .

92. *Find a Grave*, database and images (https://www.findagrave.com/memorial/8245090/john_lewis-cardwell: accessed March 29, 2025), memorial page for John Lewis Cardwell (1832–17 Jan 1899), Find a Grave Memorial ID 8245090, citing Hollywood Cemetery, Richmond, Richmond City, Virginia, USA; Maintained by BigFrench (contributor 46554304).

93. Photo 11.12: Photograph used as originally posted on FindAGrave.com (Memorial ID: 8245090). Original added by Bob Olsen on 09 Apr 2023. Photograph resized, cropped, enhanced, and/or repaired by the author.

94. United States Census -

95. United States Census - Year: 1860; Census Place: , Charlotte, Virginia; Roll: M653_1340; Page: 274; Image: 279.

96. United States Census - Year: 1850; Census Place: Abingdon, Washington, Virginia; Roll: M432_980; Page: 212; Image: 424.

97. United States Census - Year: 1860; Census Place: Western District, Washington, Virginia; Roll: M653_1383; Page: 565; Image: 204.

98. United States Census - Year: 1870; Census Place: Abingdon, Washington, Virginia; Roll: M593

99. United States Census - Year: 1880; Census Place: Abingdon, Washington, Virginia; Roll: T9_1394; Family History Film: 1255394; Page: 47.1000; Enumeration District: 93; Image: .

100. United States Census - Year: 1860; Census Place: , Greensville, Virginia; Roll: ; Page: ; Image: .

101. United States Census - Year: 1850; Census Place: Lower, Chesterfield, Virginia; Roll: M432_940; Page: 160B; Image: .

102. Ancestry.com. *Virginia, U.S., Select Marriages, 1785-1940* [database on-line]. Provo, UT, USA: Ancestry.com Operations, Inc, 2014. Original data: *Virginia, Marriages, 1785-1940*. Salt Lake City, Utah: FamilySearch, 2013.

103. United States Census - Year: 1870; Census Place: Petersburg Ward 4, Petersburg (Independent City), Virginia; Roll: M593_; Page: ; Image: .

104. United States Census - Year: 1880; Census Place: Petersburg, Dinwiddie, Virginia; Roll: T9_1363; Family History Film: 1255363; Page: 371.3000; Enumeration District: 94; Image: .

105. United States Census - Year: 1900; Census Place: Petersburg Ward 4, Petersburg City, Virginia; Roll: T623_1736; Page: 8A; Enumeration District: 98.

106. The Richmond Times-Dispatch, Tuesday, February 12, 1907.

107. *Find a Grave*, database and images (https://www.findagrave.com/memorial/57017433/john_t-cardwell: accessed March 22, 2025), memorial page for John T. Cardwell (22 Feb 1840–10 Feb 1907), Find a Grave Memorial ID 57017433, citing Blandford Cemetery, Petersburg, Petersburg City, Virginia, USA; Maintained by Dee Burris Blakley (contributor 47047047).

108. Photo 11.13: Photograph used as originally posted on FindAGrave.com (Memorial ID: 57017433). Original added by CG on 13 Aug 2014. Photograph resized, cropped, enhanced, and/or repaired by the author.

109. United States Census - Year: 1850; Census Place: Richmond, Richmond (Independent City), Virginia; Roll: M432_951; Page: 319; Image: 167.

110. United States Census - Year: 1860; Census Place: Richmond Ward 3, Henrico, Virginia; Roll: M653_1353; Page: 459; Image: 16.

111. United States Census - Year: 1880; Census Place: Richmond, Henrico, Virginia; Roll: T9_1371; Family History Film: 1255371; Page: 172.2000; Enumeration District: 84; Image: .

112. *Find a Grave*, database and images (https://www.findagrave.com/memorial/158464218/john_wesley-cardwell: accessed March 30, 2025), memorial page for John Wesley Cardwell (25 Feb 1821–10 Jan 1887), Find a Grave Memorial ID 158464218, citing Shockoe Hill Cemetery, Richmond, Richmond City, Virginia, USA; Maintained by Jeffry Burden (contributor 46873454).

113. Photo 11.14: Photograph used as originally posted on Ancestry.com. wrcardwell_1 originally shared this on 28 Jul 2009. Photo contributed to the author by Nancy Harding. Photograph resized, cropped, enhanced, and/or repaired by the author.

114. United States Census - Year: 1850; Census Place: Campbell, Virginia; Roll: M432_938; Page: 216B; Image: 436

115. United States Census - Year: 1860; Census Place: Eastern District, Campbell, Virginia; Roll: M653_1338; Page: 284; Image: 288.

116. Texas State Library and Archives Commission and Alabama Department of Archives and History. Ancestry.com. *Alabama, Texas and Virginia, U.S., Confederate Pensions, 1884-1958* [database on-line]. Provo, UT, USA: Ancestry.com Operations, Inc., 2010.

117. United States Census - Year: 1870; Census Place: Eastern Division, Campbell, Virginia; Roll: M593

118. United States Census - Year: 1880; Census Place: Rustburgh, Campbell, Virginia; Roll: T9_1358; Family History Film: 1255358; Page: 138.4000; Enumeration District: ; Image: .

119. United States Census - Year: 1900; Census Place: Rustburg, Campbell, Virginia; Roll: T623 1703; Page: 12A; Enumeration District: 27.

120. United States Census - Year: 1910; Census Place: Rustburg, Campbell, Virginia; Roll: T624_1624; Page: 8A; Enumeration District: 0028; Image: 440; FHL microfilm: 1375637.

121. *Find a Grave*, database and images (https://www.findagrave.com/memorial/91949302/john_william-cardwell: accessed March 23, 2025), memorial page for John William Cardwell (15 Feb 1847–1 Dec 1919), Find a Grave Memorial ID 91949302, citing Earlys Chapel UMC Cemetery, Concord, Campbell County, Virginia, USA; Maintained by Gerald Deckard (contributor 47609545).

Notes

122. Photo 11.15: Photograph used as originally posted on FindAGrave.com (Memorial ID: 91949302). Original added by LJH on 15 Jun 2012. Photograph resized, cropped, enhanced, and/or repaired by the author.

123. United States Census - Year: 1850; Census Place: St Stephens Parish, King and Queen, Virginia; Roll: M432_954; Page: 151B; Image: .

124. United States Census - Year: 1860; Census Place: King and Queen, Virginia; Page: 486

125. *Find a Grave*, database and images (https://www.findagrave.com/memorial/463207/joseph_b-cardwell: accessed March 27, 2025), memorial page for PVT Joseph B. Cardwell (1823–20 Oct 1864), Find a Grave Memorial ID 463207, citing Woodlawn National Cemetery, Elmira, Chemung County, New York, USA; Maintained by Hope (contributor 46790939).

126. Photo 11.16: Photograph used as originally posted on FindAGrave.com (Memorial ID: 463207). Original added by Jim Hackett on 15 Jul 2012. Photograph resized, cropped, enhanced, and/or repaired by the author.

127. United States Census - Year: 1850; Census Place: , Campbell, Virginia; Roll: M432_938; Page: 210; Image: 420.

128. Ancestry.com. *Virginia, U.S., Select Marriages, 1785-1940* [database on-line]. Provo, UT, USA: Ancestry.com Operations, Inc, 2014. Original data: *Virginia, Marriages, 1785-1940*. Salt Lake City, Utah: FamilySearch, 2013.

129. United States Census - Year: Year: 1870; Census Place: Eastern Division, Campbell, Virginia; Roll: M593

130. United States Census - Year: 1880; Census Place: Rustburgh, Campbell, Virginia; Roll: T9_1358; Family History Film: 1255358; Page: 132.3000; Enumeration District: 45; Image: .

131. United States Census - Year: 1900; Census Place: Rustburg, Campbell, Virginia; Roll: T623_1703; Page: 16B; Enumeration District: 26.

132. United States Census - Year: 1910; Census Place: Rustburg, Campbell, Virginia; Roll: T624_1624; Page: 2A; Enumeration District: 27; Image: 377.

133. United States Census - Year: 1920; Census Place: Rustburg, Campbell, Virginia; Roll: T625_1884; Page: 13B; Enumeration District: 80; Image: 432.

134. *Find a Grave*, database and images (https://www.findagrave.com/memorial/103413967/josephus-cardwell: accessed March 23, 2025), memorial page for Josephus Cardwell (4 Aug 1843–11 Aug 1924), Find a Grave Memorial ID 103413967, citing New Concord Presbyterian Church Cemetery, Concord, Campbell County, Virginia, USA; Maintained by Joan Mays (contributor 47005914).

135. Photo 11.17: Photograph used as originally posted on FindAGrave.com (Memorial ID: 103413967). Original added by KathyR on 20 Jun 2018. Photograph resized, cropped, enhanced, and/or repaired by the author.

136. United States Census - Year: 1850; Census Place: , James City, Virginia; Roll: M432_953; Page: 280A; Image: .

137. United States Census - Year: 1860; Census Place: Eastern Division, Henrico, Virginia; Page: 706

138. United States Census - Year: 1870; Census Place: Bruton, York, Virginia; Roll: M593_1682; Page: 526B

139. United States Census - Year: 1880; Census Place: Stone House, James City, Virginia; Roll: 1374; Page: 369B; Enumeration District: 035

140. *Find a Grave*, database and images (https://www.findagrave.com/memorial/14135057/patrick_h-cardwell: accessed March 1, 2025), memorial page for Patrick H. Cardwell (unknown–19 Apr 1908), Find a Grave Memorial ID 14135057, citing Greenlawn

Memorial Park, Newport News, Newport News City, Virginia, USA; Maintained by Dawn Bilik (contributor 46839075).

141. Photo 11.18: Photograph used as originally posted on FindAGrave.com (Memorial ID: 14135057). Original added by Dawn Bilik on 01 May 2006. Photograph resized, cropped, enhanced, and/or repaired by the author.

142. United States Census - Year: 1850; Census Place: Northern District, Halifax, Virginia; Roll: M432_948; Page: 36; Image: 74.

143. Ancestry.com. *Virginia, U.S., Select Marriages, 1785-1940* [database on-line]. Provo, UT, USA: Ancestry.com Operations, Inc, 2014. Original data: *Virginia, Marriages, 1785-1940*. Salt Lake City, Utah: FamilySearch, 2013.

144. United States Census - Year: 1860; Census Place: Northern District, Halifax, Virginia; Roll: M653_1349; Page: 655; Image: 180.

145. United States Census - Year: 1870; Census Place: Roanoke, Halifax, Virginia; Roll: M593

146. United States Census - Year: 1880; Census Place: Roanoke, Halifax, Virginia; Roll: T9_1369; Family History Film: 1255369; Page: 364.2000; Enumeration District: 123; Image: .

147. *Find a Grave*, database and images (https://www.findagrave.com/memorial/76720533/ peter_s-cardwell: accessed March 20, 2025), memorial page for Peter S Cardwell (20 Nov 1820–17 Apr 1889), Find a Grave Memorial ID 76720533, citing Cardwell-McCormick Family Cemetery, Clays Mill, Halifax County, Virginia, USA; Maintained by Brad Campbell (contributor 47381815).

148. Photo 11.19: Photograph used as originally posted on FindAGrave.com (Memorial ID: 76720533). Original added by C Boetsch on 17 May 2017. Photograph resized, cropped, enhanced, and/or repaired by the author.

149. United States Census - Year: 1850; Census Place: Lower, Chesterfield, Virginia; Roll: M432_940; Page: 160B; Image: .

150. United States Census - Year: 1860; Census Place: Petersburg West Ward, Petersburg (Independent City), Virginia; Roll: ; Page: ; Image: .

151. *Find a Grave*, database and images (https://www.findagrave.com/memorial/6406981/ richard_h-cardwell: accessed March 23, 2025), memorial page for Richard H. Cardwell (1834–1 Jul 1862), Find a Grave Memorial ID 6406981, citing Ettrick Cemetery, Chesterfield, Chesterfield County, Virginia, USA; Maintained by Virginian (contributor 47189242).

152. Photo 11.20: Photograph used as originally posted on FindAGrave.com (Memorial ID: 76720533). Original added by C Boetsch on 17 May 2017. Photograph resized, cropped, enhanced, and/or repaired by the author.

153. United States Census - Name: Robert D Cordwell Birth Date: abt 1846 Birth Place: Virginia Residence Date: 1850 Residence Place: Appomattox, Virginia

154. United States Census - Year: 1860; Census Place: Eastern District, Campbell, Virginia; Roll: M653_1338; Page: 284; Family History Library Film: 805338

155. United States Census - Year: 1870; Census Place: Eastern Division, Campbell, Virginia; Roll: M593

156. Ancestry.com. *Virginia, U.S., Select Marriages, 1785-1940* [database on-line]. Provo, UT, USA: Ancestry.com Operations, Inc, 2014. Original data: *Virginia, Marriages, 1785-1940*. Salt Lake City, Utah: FamilySearch, 2013.

157. United States Census - Year: 1880; Census Place: Big Lick, Roanoke, Virginia; Roll: T9_1386; Family History Film: 1255386; Page: 478.3000; Enumeration District: 60; Image: .

Notes

158. United States Census - Year: 1900; Census Place: Roanoke Ward 1, Roanoke City, Virginia; Roll: T623_1739; Page: 24A; Enumeration District: 91.

159. United States Census - Year: 1910; Census Place: Roanoke Highland Ward, Roanoke (Independent City), Virginia; Roll: T624_1646; Page: 12A; Enumeration District: 110; Image: 502.

160. *Find a Grave*, database and images (https://www.findagrave.com/memorial/77370606/robert_d-cardwell: accessed March 26, 2025), memorial page for PVT Robert D Cardwell (20 Mar 1846–12 Sep 1918), Find a Grave Memorial ID 77370606, citing City Cemetery, Roanoke, Roanoke City, Virginia, USA; Maintained by Laurie (contributor 2811407).

161. Photo 11.21: Photograph used as originally posted on FindAGrave.com (Memorial ID: 77370606). Original added by George Seitz on 15 Jul 2016. Photograph resized, cropped, enhanced, and/or repaired by the author.

162. Photo 11.22: Photograph used as originally posted on Ancestry.com. marktooley2003 originally shared this on 7 Jul 2018. Photograph resized, cropped, enhanced, and/or repaired by the author.

163. Photo 11.23: Photograph used as originally posted on FindAGrave.com (Memorial ID: 77370606). Original added by George W. Anderson on 04 Feb 2012. Photograph resized, cropped, enhanced, and/or repaired by the author.

164. United States Census - Year: 1850; Census Place: Middletown, Delaware, Pennsylvania; Roll: M432_776; Page: 197A; Image: .

165. United States Census - Year: 1860; Census Place: Chester, Delaware, Pennsylvania; Roll: ; Page: ; Image: .

166. *Find a Grave*, database and images (https://www.findagrave.com/memorial/192347448/robert_e-cardwell: accessed March 27, 2025), memorial page for Robert E. Cardwell (unknown–unknown), Find a Grave Memorial ID 192347448, citing Chester Rural Cemetery, Chester, Delaware County, Pennsylvania, USA; Maintained by Crypt Tonight (contributor 48494116).

167. United States Census - Year: 1850; Census Place: Campbell, Virginia; Roll: M432_938; Page: 216B; Image: 436

168. United States Census - Year: 1860; Census Place: Eastern District, Campbell, Virginia; Roll: M653_1338; Page: 284; Image: 288.

169. Texas State Library and Archives Commission and Alabama Department of Archives and History. Ancestry.com. *Alabama, Texas and Virginia, U.S., Confederate Pensions, 1884-1958* [database on-line]. Provo, UT, USA: Ancestry.com Operations, Inc., 2010.

170. United States Census - Year: 1870; Census Place: Eastern Division, Campbell, Virginia; Roll: M593_1638; Page: 52A; Family History Library Film: 553137

171. United States Census - Year: 1880; Census Place: Rustburgh, Campbell, Virginia; Roll: T9_1358; Family History Film: 1255358; Page: 140.3000; Enumeration District: 45; Image: .

172. United States Census - Year: 1900; Census Place: Rustburg, Campbell, Virginia; Roll: T623_1703; Page: 5B; Enumeration District: 27.

173. United States Census - Year: 1910; Census Place: Rustburg, Campbell, Virginia; Roll: T624_1624; Page: 16B; Enumeration District: 27; Image: 406.

174. United States Census - Year: 1920; Census Place: Rustburg, Campbell, Virginia; Roll: T625_1884; Page: 6A; Enumeration District: 80; Image: 417.

175. *Find a Grave*, database and images (https://www.findagrave.com/memorial/93946750/robert_richardson-cardwell: accessed March 23, 2025), memorial page for PVT Robert Richardson Cardwell (8 Jul 1844–20 Dec 1922), Find a Grave Memorial ID 93946750,

citing Bethany United Methodist Church Cemetery, Rustburg, Campbell County, Virginia, USA; Maintained by Gerald Deckard (contributor 47609545).

176. Photo 11.24: Photograph used as originally posted on FindAGrave.com (Memorial ID: 93946750). Original added by Laurie Goodman Lenz on 20 Jul 2012. Photograph resized, cropped, enhanced, and/or repaired by the author.

177. United States Census - Year: 1850; Census Place: , Campbell, Virginia; Roll: M432_938; Page: 210; Image: 420.

178. United States Census - Year: 1860; Census Place: Eastern District, Campbell, Virginia; Roll: M653_1338; Page: 246; Image: 250.

179. United States Census - Year: 1870; Census Place: Eastern Division, Campbell, Virginia; Roll: M593

180. United States Census - Year: 1880; Census Place: Rustburgh, Campbell, Virginia; Roll: T9_1358; Family History Film: 1255358; Page: 132.4000; Enumeration District: 45; Image: .

181. United States Census - Year: 1900; Census Place: Rustburg, Campbell, Virginia; Roll: T623 1703; Page: 7B; Enumeration District: 27.

182. United States Census - Year: 1910; Census Place: Rustburg, Campbell, Virginia; Roll: T624_1624; Page: 6A; Enumeration District: 0027; FHL microfilm: 1375637

183. *Find a Grave*, database and images (https://www.findagrave.com/memorial/131777817/ thomas_henry-cardwell: accessed March 23, 2025), memorial page for Thomas Henry Cardwell (20 Apr 1838–12 Feb 1915), Find a Grave Memorial ID 131777817, citing Dixon Cemetery, Concord, Campbell County, Virginia, USA; Maintained by Brett Martin (contributor 48000196).

184. Ancestry.com. *Virginia, U.S., Select Marriages, 1785-1940* [database on-line]. Provo, UT, USA: Ancestry.com Operations, Inc, 2014. Original data: *Virginia, Marriages, 1785-1940*. Salt Lake City, Utah: FamilySearch, 2013.

185. United States Census - Year: 1850; Census Place: , Campbell, Virginia; Roll: M432_938; Page: 210; Image: 419.

186. United States Census - Year: 1860; Census Place: Eastern District, Campbell, Virginia; Roll: M653_1338; Page: 250; Image: 254.

187. United States Census - Year: 1880; Census Place: Saltville, Washington, Virginia; Roll: T9_1394; Family History Film: 1255394; Page: 211.1000; Enumeration District: 99; Image: .

188. Posted by Deb Frye at http://www.genforum.genealogy.com/cardwell/mes-sages/1635.html

189. Virginia, U.S., Death Registers, 1853-1911. Library of Virginia; Richmond, VA, USA; Virginia Deaths and Burials, 1853-1912. Ancestry.com

190. United States Census - Year: 1850; Census Place: Stratton Major Parish, King and Queen, Virginia; Roll: M432_954; Page: 157A; Image: .

191. United States Census - Year: 1880; Census Place: King and Queen, Virginia; Roll: 1374; Page: 502b; Enumeration District: 039

192. United States Census - Year: 1900; Census Place: Richmond, Jefferson Ward, Richmond City, Virginia; Roll: 1738; Page: 9; Enumeration District: 0091

193. Yates Publishing. *U.S. and International Marriage Records, 1560-1900* [database on-line]. Provo, UT, USA: Ancestry.com Operations Inc, 2004. Original data: This unique collection of records was extracted from a variety of sources including family group sheets and electronic databases.

194. United States Census - Year: 1850; Census Place: Southern District, Halifax, Virginia; Roll: M432_948; Page: 87A; Image: .

Notes

195. United States Census - Year: 1860; Census Place: Southern District, Pittsylvania, Virginia; Roll: ; Page: ; Image: .

196. United States Census - Year: 1870; Census Place: Subdivision North of Dan River, Pittsylvania, Virginia; Roll: M593_; Page: ; Image: .

197. United States Census - Year: 1880; Census Place: Tunstall, Pittsylvania, Virginia; Roll: T9_1385; Family History Film: 1255385; Page: 355.1000; Enumeration District: 175; Image: .

198. United States Census - Year: 1900; Census Place: Tunstall, Pittsylvania, Virginia; Roll: T623_1723; Page: 20B; Enumeration District: 90.

199. *Find a Grave*, database and images (https://www.findagrave.com/memorial/132075495/william_thomas-cardwell: accessed March 24, 2025), memorial page for William Thomas Cardwell (15 Oct 1815–12 Feb 1907), Find a Grave Memorial ID 132075495, citing Highland Burial Park, Danville, Danville City, Virginia, USA; Maintained by FRW (contributor 47453387).

200. Photo 11.25: Photograph used as originally posted on FindAGrave.com (Memorial ID: 132075495). Original added by D. Townsend on 27 Sep 2014. Photograph resized, cropped, enhanced, and/or repaired by the author.

201. United States Census - Year: 1850; Census Place: Charlotte, Charlotte, Virginia; Roll: M432_940; Page: 13B; Image: .

202. United States Census - Year: 1860; Census Place: , Charlotte, Virginia; Roll: ; Page: ; Image: .

203. Ancestry.com. *North Carolina, U.S., Marriage Records, 1741-2011* [database on-line]. Provo, UT, USA: Ancestry.com Operations, Inc., 2015. Original data: North Carolina County Registers of Deeds. Microfilm. Record Group 048. North Carolina State Archives, Raleigh, NC.

204. United States Census - Year: 1870; Census Place: Locust Hill, Caswell, North Carolina; Roll: M593_; Page: ; Image: .

205. United States Census - Year: 1880; Census Place: Locust Hill, Caswell, North Carolina; Roll: T9_956; Family History Film: 1254956; Page: 184.4000; Enumeration District: 12; Image: 0370.

206. *Find a Grave*, database and images (https://www.findagrave.com/memorial/56974478/william_w-cardwell: accessed March 26, 2025), memorial page for William W. Cardwell (unknown–unknown), Find a Grave Memorial ID 56974478, citing Hatchett - Womack Family Cemetery, West Yanceyville, Caswell County, North Carolina, USA; Maintained by Carolina Caswell (contributor 47164136).

207. Photo 11.26: Photograph used as originally posted on Ancestry.com. Joseph Harper originally shared this on 14 Jul 2020. Portrait of "Grampa Cardwell" in possession Joseph Harper. Passed down from Judge Allen Gwyn and Janie Johnston Gwyn. Photograph resized, cropped, enhanced, and/or repaired by the author.

208. United States Census - Year: 1850; Census Place: Charlotte, Charlotte, Virginia; Roll: M432_940; Page: 45A; Image: .

209. United States Census - The National Archives in Washington D.C.; Record Group: Records of the Bureau of the Census; Record Group Number: 29; Series Number: M653; Residence Date: 1860; Home in 1860: Charlotte, Virginia; Roll: M653_1340; Page: 211; Family History Library Film: 805

210. United States Census - The National Archives in Washington, DC; Record Group: Records of the Bureau of the Census; Record Group Number: 29; Series Number: M432; Residence Date: 1850; Home in 1850: Charlotte, Charlotte, Virginia; Roll: 940; Page: 28b

211. United States Census - Year: 1870; Census Place: Subdivision North of Dan River, Pittsylvania, Virginia; Roll: M593

212. United States Census - Year: 1880; Census Place: Dan River, Pittsylvania, Virginia; Roll: T9_1384; Family History Film: 1255384; Page: 190.4000; Enumeration District: 169; Image: .

213. United States Census - Year: 1900; Census Place: Dan River, Pittsylvania, Virginia; Roll: T623 1722; Page: 5B; Enumeration District: 77.

214. United States Census - Year: 1910; Census Place: Dan River, Pittsylvania, Virginia; Roll: T624_1642; Page: 19B; Enumeration District: 94; Image: 41.Year: 1910; Census Place: Dan River, Pittsylvania, Virginia; Roll: T624_1642; Page: 19B; Enumeration District: 94; Image: 41.

215. United States Census - Year: 1920; Census Place: Dan River, Pittsylvania, Virginia; Roll: T625_1904; Page: 2B; Enumeration District: 151; Image: 473.

216. Ancestry.com. *Virginia, U.S., Death Records, 1912-2014* [database on-line]. Lehi, UT, USA: Ancestry.com Operations, Inc., 2015. Original data: Virginia, Deaths, 1912–2014. Virginia Department of Health, Richmond, Virginia.

217. United States Census - Year: 1850; Census Place: Regiment 22, Mecklenburg, Virginia; Roll: M432_960; Page: 113; Image: 224.

218. Freeport Daily Bulletin, Friday, 28 October 1881, page 2; "The Prince of Tramps."

219. *Find a Grave*, database and images (https://www.findagrave.com/memorial/114836877/w_h-cardwell: accessed April 4, 2025), memorial page for W H Cardwell (1845–27 May 1895), Find a Grave Memorial ID 114836877, citing Oakwood Cemetery, Waco, McLennan County, Texas, USA; Maintained by Waco Graver (contributor 48000669).

Miscellaneous

1. United States Census - Year: 1850; Census Place: District 19 and A Half, Chambers, Alabama; Roll: M432_2; Page: 415; Image: 826.

2. United States Census - Year: 1860; Census Place: Northern Division, Chambers, Alabama; Roll: M653_4; Page: 777; Image: 500.

3. United States Census - Year: 1870; Census Place: Beat 8, Shelby, Alabama; Roll: M593_39; Page: 471B; Family History Library Film: 545538

4. United States Census - Year: 1870; Census Place: Beat 8, Shelby, Alabama; Roll: M593_39; Page: 471B; Family History Library Film: 545538

5. United States Census - Year: 1900; Census Place: Jonesboro, Jefferson, Alabama; Roll: T623_20; Page: 16B; Enumeration District: 85.

6. United States Census - Year: 1910; Census Place: Precinct 3, Jefferson, Alabama; Roll: T624_17; Page: 7B; Enumeration District: 33; Image: 131.

7. United States Census - Year: 1930; Census Place: Precinct 41, Jefferson, Alabama; Page: 12B; Enumeration District: 0190; FHL microfilm: 2339767

8. Alabama, County Marriages, 1805-1967 - Ancestry.com Operations, Inc., Lehi, UT, USA, 2016

9. Alabama, Deaths and Burials Index, 1881-1974: Online publication - Provo, UT, USA: Ancestry.com Operations, Inc., 2011.Original data - "Alabama Deaths and Burials, 1881–1952." Index. FamilySearch, Salt Lake City, Utah, 2009, 2010.

10. United States Census - Year: 1850; Census Place: Richmond, Richmond (Independent City), Virginia; Roll: M432_951; Page: 319; Image: 167.

Notes

11. United States Census - Year: 1860; Census Place: Richmond Ward 3, Henrico, Virginia; Roll: M653_1353; Page: 459; Image: 16.

12. *Find a Grave*, database and images (https://www.findagrave.com/memorial/157940764/conrad_p-cardwell: accessed April 22, 2025), memorial page for Conrad P. Cardwell (1806–28 Sep 1879), Find a Grave Memorial ID 157940764, citing Shockoe Hill Cemetery, Richmond, Richmond City, Virginia, USA; Maintained by Jeffry Burden (contributor 46873454).

13. Photo 12.1: Photograph used as originally posted on Ancestry.com. wrcardwell_1 originally shared this on 28 Jul 2009. Photograph resized, cropped, enhanced, and/or repaired by the author. Original courtesy of Nancy Harding.

14. United States Census - The National Archives in Washington, DC; Record Group: Records of the Bureau of the Census; Record Group Number: 29; Series Number: M432; Residence Date: 1850; Home in 1850: Washington Ward 5, Washington, District of Columbia; Roll: 57; Page: 6a

15. United States Census - The National Archives in Washington D.C.; Record Group: Records of the Bureau of the Census; Record Group Number: 29; Series Number: M653; Residence Date: 1860; Home in 1860: Washington Ward 4, Washington, District of Columbia; Roll: M653_103; Page: 420; F

16. Unites States Census - Year: 1870; Census Place: Richmond Monroe Ward, Henrico, Virginia; Roll: M593_1654; Page: 326A

17. *Find a Grave*, database and images (https://www.findagrave.com/memorial/37432046/lucy_adams-fisher: accessed April 23, 2025), memorial page for Lucy Adams *Cardwell* Fisher (unknown–14 Apr 1873), Find a Grave Memorial ID 37432046, citing Hollywood Cemetery, Richmond, Richmond City, Virginia, USA; Maintained by Barbara Haddon Blankenship (contributor 46872971).

18. United States Census - Year: 1850; Census Place: Richmond, Richmond (Independent City), Virginia; Roll: M432_951; Page: 319; Image: 167.

19. United States Census - Year: 1860; Census Place: Richmond Ward 3, Henrico, Virginia; Roll: M653_1353; Page: 459; Image: 16.

20. United States Census - Year: 1880; Census Place: Richmond, Henrico, Virginia; Roll: T9_1371; Family History Film: 1255371; Page: 172.2000; Enumeration District: 84; Image: .

21. *Find a Grave*, database and images (https://www.findagrave.com/memorial/158464357/mary_f-cardwell: accessed April 23, 2025), memorial page for Mary F. Cardwell (1828–18 Oct 1897), Find a Grave Memorial ID 158464357, citing Shockoe Hill Cemetery, Richmond, Richmond City, Virginia, USA; Maintained by Jeffry Burden (contributor 46873454).

22. Photo 12.2: Photograph used as originally posted on Ancestry.com. wrcardwell_1 originally shared this on 28 Jul 2009. Photograph resized, cropped, enhanced, and/or repaired by the author. Original photo courtesy of Nancy Harding.

23. United States Census - Year: 1850; Census Place: Western District, Rockingham, North Carolina; Roll: M432_643; Page: 105; Image: 212.

24. United States Census - Year: 1860; Census Place: Northern Division, Rockingham, North Carolina; Roll: M653_912; Page: 93; Image: 185.

25. Ancestry.com. *North Carolina, U.S., Marriage Index, 1741-2004* [database on-line]. Provo, UT, USA: Ancestry.com Operations Inc, 2007. Original data: Dodd, Jordan, Liahona Research, comp. (P.O. Box 740, Orem, Utah 84059)

26. United States Census - Year: 1870; Census Place: Lower Revenue District, Hanover, Virginia; Roll: M593

27. United States Census - Year: 1880; Census Place: Ashland, Hanover, Virginia; Roll: T9_1370; Family History Film: 1255370; Page: 26.1000; Enumeration District: 62; Image: .

28. United States Census - Year: 1900; Census Place: Ashland, Hanover, Virginia; Roll: T623 1712; Page: 1A; Enumeration District: 19.

29. United States Census - Year: 1910; Census Place: Ashland, Hanover, Virginia; Roll: T624_1631; Page: 24A; Enumeration District: 21; Image: 568.

30. United States Census - Year: 1920; Census Place: Ashland, Hanover, Virginia; Roll: T625_1889; Page: 11B; Enumeration District: 28; Image: 306.

31. United States Census - Year: 1930; Census Place: Ashland, Hanover, Virginia; Roll: 2445; Page: 3A; Enumeration District: 4; Image: 812.0.

32. *Find a Grave*, database and images (https://www.findagrave.com/memorial/5639626/richard_henry-cardwell: accessed April 22, 2025), memorial page for Judge Richard Henry Cardwell (1 Aug 1846–19 Mar 1931), Find a Grave Memorial ID 5639626, citing Woodland Cemetery, Ashland, Hanover County, Virginia, USA; Maintained by George Seitz (contributor 40539541).

33. Photo 12.3: Photograph used as originally posted on FindAGrave.com (Memorial ID: 5639626). Original added by Added by Jessica Bennett on 20 Dec 2022. Original photo from: The City on the James by Andrew Morrison ed; Richmond Chamber of Commerce, 1893. Photograph resized, cropped, enhanced, and/or repaired by the author.

34. Photo 12.4: Photograph used as originally posted on FindAGrave.com (Memorial ID: 5639626). Original added by Added by George Seitz on 14 Nov 2007. Portrait of Judge Cardwell: Original portrait hangs in the Virginia Supreme Court painted by S. Feildman, donated by the Cardwell Family in the 1930's. Photograph resized, cropped, enhanced, and/or repaired by the author.

35. Photo 12.5: Photograph used as originally posted on FindAGrave.com (Memorial ID: 5639626). Original added by Added by George Seitz on 09 Jan 2007. Photograph resized, cropped, enhanced, and/or repaired by the author.

INDEX

A

ALABAMA CONFEDERATE VETERANS

BATTLES, CAMPAIGNS, RAIDS, SIEGES, & SKIRMISHES
APPOMATTOX CAMPAIGN

ATLANTA CAMPAIGN

CAROLINAS CAMPAIGN

. . .

Battle of Antietam, Maryland, 2, 25, 31, 35, 90, 101, 116, 187, 201, 218, 223, 232, 241, 244

Battle of Sharpsburg, Maryland, 31, 101. See also Battle of Antietam, Maryland

MOBILE CAMPAIGN

Battle of Fort Blakely, Alabama, 12

Battle of Mobile, Alabama, 12–14, 16–17, 21–23, 33–34, 36, 41–42, 64, 132, 154, 190, 195, 205, 216, 241, 244–245, 248, 252, 254, 260, 274

Battle of Spanish Fort, Alabama, 12, 22, 83

MORGAN'S RAID

Battle of Buffington Island, Ohio, 75, 161

Battle of Corydon, Indiana, 70, 79

Battle of Salineville, Ohio, 71, 75, 79

OVERLAND CAMPAIGN

Battle of Cold Harbor, Virginia, 35, 105, 113, 182, 187, 190, 197, 212, 237, 245

Battle of Spotsylvania, Virginia, 35, 105, 111, 113, 182, 236

Battle of the Wilderness, Virginia, 35, 90, 104–105, 111, 113, 120, 190, 236

Battle of Trevilian Station, Virginia, 182, 246

Battle of Yellow Tavern, Virginia, 190

PENINSULA CAMPAIGN

Battle of Drewry's Bluff, Virginia, 197

Battle of Hanover Court House, Virginia, 102

Battle of Lee's Mill, Virginia, 102

Battle of Seven Pines, Virginia, 36, 39–40, 120, 190, 278

Battles of Mechanicsville, Virginia (Beaver Dam Creek), 234

Siege of Yorktown, Virginia, 102

· · ·

. . .

C

D

E

F

G

GEORGIA CONFEDERATE UNITS

GEORGIA CONFEDERATE VETERANS

H

I

J

K

KENTUCKY CONFEDERATE UNITS

Orphan Brigade, 65. See also 4th Kentucky Mounted Infantry

Kentucky Confederate Veteran Rolls, 66

KENTUCKY CONFEDERATE VETERANS
Charles T. Cardwell (1843-1865), 65, 69
George H. Cardwell (1828->1910), 66–67, 73, 75
George Stuart Cardwell (1845-1929), 66, 68–69, 283
James Jesse Cardwell (1840-1892), 70–71, 73, 80
James Madison Cardwell (1841-1864), 71–73, 81
John Ray Cardwell (1834-1904), 73–75, 283
John Thomas Cardwell (1845-1913), 76–77
Thomas Logan Cardwell (1843-1920), 70–71, 73, 78–80, 284
Thomas Mumford Cardwell (1846-1915), 72, 80–81, 285

Killed in Action, 24–25, 31, 36, 39, 54, 56, 71, 73, 81, 84, 102, 109, 131, 137, 159, 233–234
King and Queen County, Virginia, 197, 207, 225, 245–246
King County, Washington, 95, 97, 287
King William County, Virginia, 202, 211
Kirk, Ellen, 77
Kirkpatrick, J. D., 73
Kitrell, Mary Jane, 135
Knoxville, Tennessee, 79, 131, 136, 138, 165
Kyle, Addalid, 132, 160

L

Lafayette County, Mississippi, 90–91
Lambaren, Melinda Roberts, 280
Lambert, Lucy Ann Adams, 202
Land, Ann "Annie" Maria, 206
Lauderdale County, Mississippi, 12, 33
Lawrence County, Arkansas, 53–54, 95, 280
Lebow, Judah, 125, 154

LOUISIANA CONFEDERATE UNITS

LOUISIANA CONFEDERATE VETERANS

M

MISCELLANEOUS CONFEDERATE UNITS

MISCELLANEOUS CONFEDERATE VETERANS

MISSISSIPPI CONFEDERATE UNITS

MISSISSIPPI CONFEDERATE VETERANS

NORTH CAROLINA CONFEDERATE UNITS

NORTH CAROLINA CONFEDERATE VETERANS

INDEX

SOUTH CAROLINA CONFEDERATE UNITS

T

. . .

TENNESSEE CONFEDERATE VETERANS

TEXAS CONFEDERATE UNITS

· · ·

· · ·

INDEX

VIRGINIA CONFEDERATE VETERANS

INDEX

About the Author

Rand Cardwell has dedicated more than forty years to the meticulous research of his family's American roots, with a particular focus on those bearing the Cardwell surname. He is the former publisher of the *Cardwell Family* website and served as the original administrator of the *Cardwell Family DNA Project*, a role through which he helped uncover vital connections between family branches and deepened the understanding of Cardwell lineage across generations.

Known for his generous spirit, Cardwell has long assisted fellow researchers and distant relatives with their own family history efforts, always eager to share records, insight, and guidance. His reputation in genealogical circles is grounded not only in his extensive knowledge but in his collaborative approach to the often solitary pursuit of ancestry.

This book is the culmination of decades of work—painstaking documentation, archival digging, and personal correspondence—all united by a single purpose: to preserve the stories of Cardwell men who served in the American Civil War and to honor their legacy for future generations.

Though genealogy has long been his central passion, Cardwell is also a writer and thinker of diverse interests. He is the author of the *Becoming Stoic* series, a multi-volume exploration of Stoic philosophy drawn from his own lived experience and more than twenty-five years of study. His published works also include titles on martial arts history and poetic reflection, most notably *Unhurried: and other poems*.

He resides in East Tennessee, where he balances his time between historical research, writing, trout fishing, and enjoying life's simple pleasures.

f

Also by Rand Cardwell

The Western Bubishi

The 36 Deadly Bubishi Points

Unhurried: and other poems

Becoming Stoic: Lessons on Perception

Becoming Stoic: Lessons on Action

Becoming Stoic: Lessons on Will

* * *

New titles will be announced at:

www.randcardwell.com